OTHER BOOKS BY LAURO MARTINES:

The Social World of the Florentine Humanists (1963)

Lawyers and Statecraft in Renaissance Florence (1968)

Violence and Civil Disorder in Italian Cities, 1200–1500 (1972)

*Not in God's Image: Women in History from the Greeks
to the Victorians* (1973), with Julia O'Faolain

POWER AND IMAGINATION

POWER AND IMAGINATION

CITY-STATES IN RENAISSANCE ITALY

BY

LAURO MARTINES

ALFRED A. KNOPF

NEW YORK   1979

THIS IS A BORZOI BOOK,
PUBLISHED BY ALFRED A. KNOPF, INC.

Copyright © 1979 by Lauro Martines
All rights reserved under International and Pan-American Copyright
Conventions. Published in the United States by Alfred A. Knopf, Inc.,
New York, and simultaneously in Canada by Random House of Canada
Limited, Toronto. Distributed by Random House, Inc., New York.

Library of Congress Cataloging in Publication Data
Martines, Lauro. (Date)
Power and imagination, city-states in Renaissance Italy.
Bibliography: p.
Includes index.
1. Italy—Politics and government—476-1268.
2. Italy—Politics and government—1268-1559.
3. Cities and towns—Italy—History. 4. Italy—
Civilization—476-1268. 5. Italy—Civilization—1268-
1559. I. Title.
DG494.M37 1979   945   78-11666
ISBN 0-394-50112-8

Manufactured in the United States of America

First Edition

CONTENTS

Contents

Contents

Illustrations follow page 242

PREFACE

The story to be told here begins in the eleventh century, with the rise of warlike citics and their rush, under the leadership of communes, to seize local political power. The years around 1300 betray a break in development: urban Italy passes from one stage to another. The first stage is, however, an organic part of the period as a whole, for the Italian Renaissance issued forth in two "grand" stages. The first, lasting to about 1300, saw the laying of a basic groundwork: the physical building of cities and the rise of a new economy, a new society, new states, and a new set of vivid, shaping values. In the second stage, extending from about 1300 to the late sixteenth century, "high" culture—literature, art, and ideas—pushed forward and became more prominent, more important. But the achievement of the second stage was vitally rooted in the resources and values of the first. No other validation is needed, it seems to me, for giving the eleventh and twelfth centuries a place in this history.

The title *Power and Imagination* is my way of referring to, and altering, the more conventional distinction between "society" and "culture." In telling a story which courses across five centuries, I was driven to pursue a central theme, a thread more easily visible than "society." I chose to center attention on the fortunes of "power" because, in tracing the movement of political authority, I was also compelled, all the way along, to track the direction of social and economic change. And I chose "imagination" over "culture" because my supreme concern is with relations between dominant social groups (power) and the articulated, formal, refined, or idealizing consciousness of those who speak for the powerful. In this interplay, the workings of imagination tend to be foremost.

Lauro Martines
Florence, Los Angeles, London
1966–1978

ix

POWER AND IMAGINATION

CITIES: THE LEADING COMMUNES ABOUT 1200

ITALY: POLITICAL BOUNDARIES ABOUT 1000

Territories under theoretical Byzantine rule

Territories directly under Byzantine rule

Lombard Principalities of Capua, Benevento, Salerno

MILES 0 100

KM 0 100

Trent

Novara Milan Bergamo
Turin Vercelli Crema Brescia
Pavia Lodi Cremona Verona Vicenza Treviso
Asti Tortona Mantua Padua Venice
PO R.

THE ITALIC KINGDOM

Savona Genoa Parma Ferrara PO R.
Modena Ravenna
Bologna
Lucca Pistoia Rimini
Pisa Florence
Livorno ARNO R. Pesaro
Volterra Ancona
Siena Arezzo
Perugia Fermo
Orvieto
Viterbo
TIBER R.
Rome
PAPAL STATE
Gaeta
Naples

ADRIATIC SEA

SARDINIA

TYRRHENIAN SEA

ARAB SICILY

MEDITERRANEAN SEA

N
W E
S

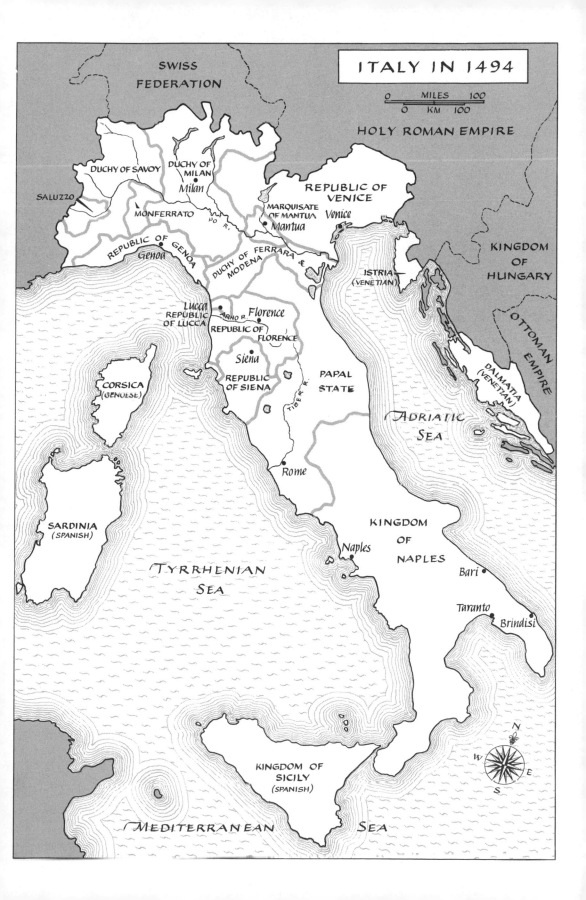

CHAPTER I

THE ASCENT
OF COMMUNES

BACKGROUND

It is hard to summarize chaos, yet the narrative history of Italy in the eleventh and early twelfth centuries is a story of political wreckage and confused authority. An image for the age is from the spring of 1121, when the antipope Gregory VIII was led into Rome sitting backward on a camel—a gesture of disgrace and howling derision; fitting too, in view of the preeminence of violence. For eleventh-century kings and popes were deposed, physically assaulted, or driven into flight as if no better than small game. Bishops and feudal lords were scattered like leaves; some were murdered, maimed, or merely brushed aside, while others, such as Alrico, bishop of Asti, were cut down in full battle gear (1035). Authority had been laid low.

Power in upper Italy was received or seized from the hands of weak kings in the tenth century, with the result that government passed increasingly to the control of feudal magnates. In the eleventh century the fragmentation of authority went further: real power ended by being local power in the hands of local magnates, usually bishops, though it was soon enough claimed or grabbed by cities.

With the end of the Carolingian kings and of others drawn mostly from among the peninsula's Frankish and Lombard feudatories, Italy north of Rome turned to a line of German kings, beginning with the Ottonians (962), who managed dangerously to wear three crowns—the crown of Germany, the iron crown of the Italic kingdom (upper Italy), and the crown of the Holy Roman Empire. They would wage a bitter and vain struggle, centuries long, to impose some kind of central rule on their Italian territories. Their invincible opponents were Roman popes, feudal and episcopal potentates, and a teeming expanse of self-willed cities.

Italy was nothing more than a geographic expression—the Italian peninsula. Nearly all the upper part belonged to the German kings. In 961, traveling south across the Alps, the king-elect, Otto I, made for the royal capital of Pavia, where he donned the iron crown of Lombardy and then went on to Rome to be crowned Holy Roman Emperor. The Italic kingdom (Map 1) stretched from the southern Alps, taking in the whole northern plain but excluding Venice, down to central Italy along both coasts. Papal territory was the entire region around Rome, from Perugia to Terracino, but reaching only halfway across the narrow width of the peninsula. Next south, on the western side, were the independent principalities of Benevento and Salerno; and farther south still, travelers entered Byzantine territory, which included Naples and the entire foot of the peninsula. Sicily was under Arab rule until the Norman conquest in the 1070s.

The geographic focus of this history will be the Italic kingdom, where dozens of cities were to make an armed bid for independence and the strongest converted themselves into petty empires and city-states.

Apart from their wars in Germany, the emperors of the eleventh century were plagued by four problems in Italy: (1) the rebelliousness of cities and mighty vassals, (2) a blazing reform movement directed against a simonist clergy, (3) the resolute violence of papal factions and a riotous baronage in Rome, and (4) the menacing pressure in southern Italy of Byzantine and especially Norman armies. Each of the century's triple sovereigns was harried by two or more of these. Henry II (1002–1024) spent his expeditions to Italy mainly in a struggle against the supporters of his rival for the Lombard crown, the Marquis Arduin, a Piedmontese magnate. The news of Henry's death was greeted with an uprising in Pavia, capital of the kingdom, and the populace set fire to the government palace. Feeling against the royal establishment was rife. Conrad II (1024–1039) took the field against Pavia and had also to wage wars against stubborn feudatories, Roman noblemen, Milan, and the proud and powerful archbishop of Milan, Ariberto, whom he deposed. He also seized the bishops of Cremona, Vercelli, and Piacenza and packed them off to prison in Germany, thereby making formidable enemies in those cities. Henry III (1039–1056) enjoyed more peaceful relations with the Church. He inherited, however, the struggle against Ariberto and the big Milanese nobility, and he had formidable opponents in his own vassals, the lords of Canossa, in the antipopes Silvester III and Benedict IX, in their prepotent Roman backers, and then, in 1052–1053, in the reformer Pope Leo IX. The reign of Henry IV (1056–1106), which included the years of a regency, was a tumult of criticism against the immoral life and economic practices of the cathedral clergy. Concubinage, simony, and the lay investiture of bishops came under violent attack. The consecrated bread of simonists was called manure and their churches were called stables. The wars of investiture peaked, and every one of Henry IV's trips to Italy must have aged him as he found himself in mortal combat with a reformist papacy, with rebellious cities, and with the prestigious house of Canossa, while also scurrying around to hold on to the allegiance of other cities and of his imperial bishops. Henry fought, in effect, to maintain imperial control over the feudal Church, whose economic and social relations with the entire class of vassals formed a tough membrane which could not be broken save by damage to the landed wealth of the great feudal nobility.

Behind the audacity and power of those who fought kings and emperors —feudal chieftains, bishops, popes, and cities—stretched a world alive with economic energies, a swarming population, and social change without precedent. The fact that two Jews turned Christian, Pietro di Leone and Leone di Benedetto, were leaders in the rival papal factions at Rome in the 1060s is a mark of the latitude and swiftly changing fortunes of the age. We must look to the course of change so as to track the rise of cities and understand the struggle for power.

The basic changes and new directions of the eleventh century had to do with a rising birth rate, agricultural productivity, and the swelling tide of trade. From the later tenth century, and for about 300 years, the rate of growth in the population was such that agricultural production scarcely seemed able to keep up with demand. Great tracts of land were opened up for cultivation: estate managers and humble folk cut down forests, drained fen and marshland, built canals and dikes, and irrigated the drier lands. Land values soared. The peninsula's valleys and northern plain filled with men driven by a hunger for land. Their hunger fixed on the vast estates of Church, crown, and feudal magnates. Much ecclesiastical land and land held in fief—for which military and other services were due—was imperceptibly alienated, to be turned eventually into private property. The means used to effect this wholesale transfer involved grants, exchanges, long-term leases, and sly usurpation. Subvassals, knights, and petty proprietors were the prime beneficiaries. Among these, and beyond their number, historians have seen a middle class of aggressive and canny concessionaires—men who responded to the demand for more cereal grain and other produce by angling to enlarge their landholdings and by their readiness to sacrifice manorial tradition to arrangements that freed the land for a more mobile, exploitative, profitable mode of farming. In certain parts of Italy, in the space of a few decades, the value of land rose by four or five times. Agricultural strains in the countryside around Genoa and Lucca wore away the manorial system, all but eliminating it in the course of the eleventh century. Many serfs and other servile tenants shed their bonds.

The increase and movement of rural folk took many of them into the budding towns and older urban agglomerations. Such movement was well under way by the beginning of the eleventh century and would continue, on a massive scale, down to nearly 1300. The immigrants were the landless and poor who worked with their hands, but also, and more visibly, the propertied: vassals and subvassals, knights, small landowners, and random or itinerant country merchants.

Rude little settlements like Prato and Macerata burst into thriving towns; and ancient cities like Milan, Pavia, Cremona, and Mantua were borne up once again in a rising flood of people, property transactions, commerce, and feverish activity in the building trades. The river towns and obscure ports—Florence, Pisa, Genoa—exhibited spectacular dynamism; and the tiny cities of the northern plain—Piacenza, Verona, Crema, Padua—eagerly received foreign merchants or as eagerly dispatched their own. Records offer up the names of individuals, often in the act of making property or commercial transactions, and at times we can even make out fragmentary genealogies and the doings of particular families: thus the Ingonidi family from near Milan (ca. 940–1010), who counted landed proprietors, traders, and at least one judge; or a family married into the Ingonidi, the Arduinidi (960–1000), also to be found in trade, land, and minting.[1]

Italy's resurgence was momentarily complicated by ethnic differences. When the north was invaded by Germanic peoples in the sixth and eighth centuries, public offices and dignities, like much of the land, went to the victors. The true feudal nobility, groomed for a life of war, came mainly of Langobard, Frankish, Saxon, and Swabian stock. Even after the Germanic tongues disappeared, say by 950, certain localities remained under two laws, Langobard and Roman. The Saxon emperors frequently appointed Germans to leading church posts in Italy. In the first quarter of the eleventh century, under Henry II, something like a fourth of all bishoprics in the kingdom were held by Germans. The German element was felt down to the middle of the eleventh century. Then, in the next hundred years or less, in the cities first, persisting distinctions vanished. The velocity of change in land transfer, in trade, in urbanization, and in immigration wiped out the differences of blood and outlook, even where the tenacity of Langobard law, especially in feudal relations, long endured.

The process of swift change was ground into the whole of Italian life. From bishop to serf, from soap to landscape, what Italy had known was changing fast. Italian society had not been simple before, with its variety of tenancies and servitudes, slaves and serfs, freeholders and gradations of vassals, merchants and free or bonded artisans, its feudal magnates, and its medley of imperial and episcopal officials. But henceforth the complexity deepened and a surge of political instabilities altered the composition of the ruling class. A single illustration must suffice.

In the late tenth century the archbishop of Milan, Landulf, was plunged into an obscure struggle for power. Driven from the city, despite the support of the Emperor Otto II, he was forced to enfeoff the lands of the Milanese church, a vast corporate patrimony. He handed out lands and churches as fiefs to the leading knights and noblemen of the city, in return for their homage and fidelity. A new powerful group thus was born, the captains (*capitanei*). These men, in turn, seeking to consolidate their own authority in the countryside, sub-infeudated their holdings to a host of petty rural knights. Another new group was born, the *valvassori* or vavasors. The aim of the captains was to create loyal bands of armed men in the country-side, while at the same time leaving them, the captains, free to pursue their own interests in the city. But the country knightlings, lifted to a higher status and vitality by the new lands, gravitated toward the city, settled there, and in the 1030s entered into conflict with the captains. Thus were born two powerful blocs which in time would check all higher authority.

A similar redistribution of land took place over much of upper Italy, also in the wake of challenges to authority, and vavasors everywhere were able to make good their insistence upon the irrevocable and inheritable nature of their feudal holdings, as guaranteed by a royal decree of 1037.

Nearly all the Italian cities of any importance had Roman and even pre-Roman foundations. In central and upper Italy this meant about forty differ-ent sites. The peninsula's urban-civic traditions had survived even in the north, despite the devastating invasions of the sixth and early tenth centuries —which is not to deny breaks in those traditions. The organization of trades largely collapsed; twelfth-century guilds were new forms mainly; those of the thirteenth century were radically new.

Venice in 1000—an agglomeration of fishermen, sailors, and traders—was already a thriving small port. Its islands were not yet connected by massive wooden bridges but soon would be. On Italy's northwestern coast were the little ports of Pisa and Genoa—pugnacious, venturesome, and explosively vital, even if walled in against Muslim attack. Like Venice, they already had tiny fleets that stabbed out beyond the Tyrrhenian Sea into the Mediter-ranean to repel the Muslims. In 1005, hard by Reggio Calabria in the far south, Pisa fought and won a naval battle against Muslim forces, only a year after having come under their direct attack. If the gathering force of the two cities, Pisa and Genoa, was the product of geography, the connections must forever evade us. Genoa, one face to the sea, was closely hemmed in by rocky hills, whereas Pisa lay at the mouth of a river estuary.

The chain of Italy's populous cities lay under the arch of the Alps, on the rich northern plain with its inviting rivers and tributaries, and in the north-central regions, along the principal roads and valleys that cut or skirted the Apennines, in Emilia, Tuscany, and Umbria. Travelers moving from the plain of Piedmont eastward across Lombardy might visit Torino, Pavia, Milan, Piacenza, Cremona, Brescia, and Mantua. Along the way were more than another dozen urban clusters—cathedral towns and centers of local trade: Asti, Vercelli, Novara, Tortona, Lodi, Crema, and others. Nearer Venice, cities were to have aggressive communes and an intense autonomous development: Verona, Vicenza, Treviso, and Padua. South of these, in Emilia and the edges of the Romagna, lay Parma, Modena, Bologna, and Ferrara, also strongholds of local autonomy.

Down to the twelfth century, Lucca was the old capital of Tuscany, but this city of coming usurers and silk merchants was soon surpassed in spirit, riches, and ruthlessness by neighboring Florence and Pisa. Some sixty miles away, another city of knights and usurers, Siena, came very close to matching Lucca's economic and demographic achievements. Farther south we shall be hearing of Perugia, perched in papal territory, the largest city in Umbria. To the far south, finally, were the Italo-Byzantine cities of Naples, Amalfi, and Gaeta, and mentioning them must suffice, for these cities had a different tradition and history.

COMMUNES EMERGE

We have seen that the peninsula had several sovereignties—royal, papal, Byzantine, and independent. Only one, however, offered the environment for city-states, the feudal kingdom of upper Italy: land of bellicose cities, communes, and astonishing urban energies. Royal authority here, in accord with the nature of feudal kingship, was divided among a number of parts, specifically seven marquisates at the beginning of the eleventh century. But the marquisates were themselves subdivided into counties, and it was at the county level, or at the level of even lesser feuds (e.g., the *pieve* and castle), that power was effectively exercised. The countryside around Pisa, for example, was under the immediate rule of a hereditary viscount, supposedly the representative of an overlord based in Lucca, the marquis of Tuscany. This dignitary was, in his turn, a royal-imperial official, holding the marquisate as a fief from the crown of the Italic kingdom. In fact, keeping with feudal realities, the authority of the marquis was far from complete, for after 1052 the bishops of Arezzo and Volterra held the preponderance of temporal authority in these Tuscan cities. And the viscount of Pisa independently managed his own affairs, while also claiming (as *gastaldo*) some authority directly from the crown and having to share still other jurisdictions with the powerful archbishop of Pisa.

There was no necessary coordination, no shaping policy, and only a phantom central administration linking together the different parts of the kingdom. Real authority was local authority, wielded by one or several lords: marquis, bishop, count, viscount, abbot, *gastaldo*, or captain. Once these had been weakened or elbowed aside, the political history of the Italy of the German kings became the history of cities driving aggressively out beyond their horizons.

The starting point in the city's territorial expansion was the diocese, the major unit of church administration, headed by a bishop. The realistic unit of royal administration was the county. For all practical purposes diocese and county tended to be viewed as one geographically, and where a county boundary fell short, the attempt was inevitably made to extend it. When the diocese of Genoa was enlarged in the eleventh century and the bishop raised to the dignity of archbishop, the Genoese assumed that their political authority was thereby extended and they set out to enforce the claim.

All the main urban centers were cathedral sites. The cathedral church was the heart of the diocese, the moral and civic center. Many cities survived the early Middle Ages, came through as fortified urban clusters, precisely because they held the seats of local church government and could provide the leadership for defense and the restoration of order when local lay authority fell apart. In the middle of the eleventh century, at Milan as in other cities, the metropolitan clergy and their families were already so numerous as to seem, in the words of one chronicler, "like the sand of the sea." The city was a magnet, exercising strong powers of economic attraction throughout the countryside, and urban land often came to be valued at twenty or thirty times more than that in the country.

During the tenth and eleventh centuries, in response to local pressures, the German emperors increasingly transferred the jurisdictions of counts over to bishops. By 1050 most leading bishops in northern Italy had comitial powers. Even in Umbria, the province least familiar with the temporalities of bishops, the holders of the episcopal dignity inevitably had rights *de facto* in temporal affairs. This marriage of authorities, spiritual and temporal, went especially far in the eleventh century, for in the collision between papacy and empire, each side struggled for diocesan support, often by elevating local authority. Henry IV's great strength was in the fact that at critical moments, and really for long intervals, he commanded the allegiance of most Lombard, Emilian, and Tuscan bishops; but he did not have the populace. At Piacenza, in 1089, a reform-minded throng rebelled against the bishop, Winrico, a German supporter of the imperial cause, and drove him out of the city. Bonizone da Sutri, an ardent backer of the reformist papacy, was then appointed bishop. In the ensuing battle, a band of feudal noblemen, acting in the name of imperial legitimacy, captured Bonizone and blinded and barbarously killed him. At Cremona, in 1093, in similar circumstances, the "popular party" cast out one bishop and brought in another. Excommunications and counter-excommunications went out like crossfire. Bishops used their swelling comitial powers to gain still others, thereby inflating the prestige of cities and further increasing their moral and social dominance over the surrounding regions.

Legal historians make much of the fact that the German kings almost never granted cities out as feuds. Here the so-called "regalian rights"—the inalienable public rights of the crown—were meant to remain undiminished, especially the power to appoint magistrates and to collect the full range of taxes and tolls. These rights could not be given, bought, sold, inherited, or exchanged, despite alleged practice and elapsed time. At least this was the claim of the crown and public-law theory. In fact, as we shall see, the crown lost all its regalian rights.

The encircling flood of feudal practices brimmed over into the cities. In the rural part of each diocese, much of the public authority was held by the bishop-count, who, however, came continually upon immunities to his authority. The like also took place in the city, where he might have the right to collect taxes but not to appoint magistrates (or the converse), to collect some taxes but not others, or to compel military service but not other kinds of obligations. In these cases the unaccounted-for jurisdictions belonged to other local authorities: agents of the crown (*missi domni regis*) or descendants of marquises, counts, viscounts, and *gastaldi*. This fragmentation of public authority, so characteristic of feudalism, was to be the main challenge to the forthcoming commune. Apart from its poisonous social divisions, nothing would agonize the commune more than the problem of drawing together, under one government, the variety of public rights and powers. At Arezzo in the late eleventh century the commune already claimed about one-third the sum of jurisdictions.

What were the social and emotional elements that gave birth to communes and ripped up all the existing political arrangements?

The nobility stood at the social forefront of the eleventh-century cities: bishop, resident feudal magnates, episcopal clergy, the principal knights, and the array of their surrounding kinsmen. Deacons and cathedral canons headed the metropolitan clergy. The principal knights—captains and vavasors—composed the larger part of the nobility. Since the episcopal clergy were recruited largely from among the nobility, social relations between the two orders were close. As a rule, the captains were the great vassals of the bishop, count, or marquis. They held their lands as fiefs and in return gave fidelity, military service, and counsel. The vavasors, vassals of the captains, were really subvassals. Although captains and vavasors had successfully turned their feuds and tenures into hereditary holdings by 1040, they remained a military class bred to arms, fighting on horseback, and stubbornly preoccupied with jockeying for civic authority.

Next in urban dignity, according to the testimony of eleventh-century chroniclers, were the *cives*, the thriving popular or plebeian element. They were propertied, city-based, sometimes engaged in trade, and free, in contrast to the multitudes of serfs and servile tenants beyond the city walls, though there was servitude within the city too. The *cives* were a broadly comprehensive lot: notaries, moneylenders, coin makers, merchants, landed proprietors, and in certain cities (e.g., Como) even a handful of small tradesmen and artisans. They included inhabitants not long established in the city, as well as families long associated with civic traditions. In time the richest and most eminent *cives* intermarried and mixed with the old nobility, some even taking to the haughty carriage of mounted noblemen; certain of the latter, in turn, took up international trade and banking. At Pisa and Genoa the descendants of counts and viscounts turned to shipbuilding, maritime trade, banking, and marine insurance, while yet clinging to more than the vestigial exercise of arms. Florence and Siena also had some social mobility of this sort. But in parts of the north, as at Bergamo and Padua, the old noble families remained more closely attached to arms, to income from land, and to the pursuit of urban dignities.

It remains to touch on the numerical majority: poor artisans and petty tradesmen free or semi-free; workers skilled and unskilled, as in the building trades; and the many laborers in various degrees of servitude, who moved in and out of the city according to the seasonal demands of agriculture and the urban call for hauling, carting, and lifting. Some laborers came into the city by day and left before nightfall; others, in warm weather, quite likely slept in the open air. Among the "little people" (the *popolino*) were the host of servants and domestics who served the metropolitan clergy, the nobility, and the *cives*. In the chronicled crowd scenes, the *popolino* sometimes appear as a force for public violence. Their vitality and sheer numbers constituted a powerful element in the city's expansion and economic health, and in re-cruitment for the middle classes. The *popolino* had no individual voices, like those of petty noblemen or rich young burghers turned saint, such as St. Arialdo and St. Francis.

In the eleventh century, the psychological stresses of the volatile urban cluster were best seen among the episcopal clergy, the nobility, and the *cives*. An uncontrolled greed for land, occasioned by a booming economy, had rendered the estates of the Church endlessly attractive. Bishops and regional synods cried out against the sly alienation of church property. Nobles and the kinsmen of episcopal clergymen, including the sons of priests, profited above all; no measure seemed strict enough, no device fine enough, to expose or terminate the abuse. The itch to seize land, by fair means or foul, must have been no less strong than the urge, in modern Western societies, to defraud government by padding income-tax statements or withholding information. In addition, the eleventh-century city imposed the strains of a sharply rising birth rate. The fields spilled forth their men and women. There was a surge in the building of private churches. Noble-men and *cives* built more and more houses in the city. Clerics often lived at home, scarcely distinguishable from laymen. The incidence of married and concubinary priests was so common down to the 1060s as to seem a fixed way of life. At Milan, Cremona, Piacenza, Florence, and Lucca, as in other leading cities, the cardinal clergy—as the deacons and canons proudly called themselves—were bold enough to resist the violent cry for reform by hav-ing recourse to violence. Simony too—the purchase of profitable church dignities and benefices—was venerable practice.

The condition of the feudal church points up the economic and social strains of the age, with what dramatic results we shall soon glimpse. The economic and reproductive exuberance of the upper classes led to the mul-tiplication and splintering of families. In the absence of primogeniture, there was an urgent, continuing need for additional sources of income. At Pisa and Genoa the strain was greatly relieved by what the Church provided in the way of incomes, but even more so by the allurements of the sea: naval warfare, piracy, ransom payments, shipping, and long-distance trade. In less than a century, Pisans, Genoese, and Venetians made themselves masters of most of the Mediterranean.

The multiplying upper-class families responded to the economic challenge by striking out in a variety of lucrative directions, among which, in the inland cities, were land reclamation and the altering of land tenures. The determining atmosphere was one of change, complicated by a concurrent crisis—the calling into question of the foundations of public authority. Not much more than a shadowy sovereignty anyway, the state vanished altogether in the third quarter of the eleventh century, when, with the death of the Emperor Henry III (1056) and Henry IV's minority, the cities of Italy were left rather to their own devices. They lay under the uncertain rule of feudal lords spiritual and temporal, men whose authority was very often incomplete or under dispute. The urban space generated unsettling questions. Had the bishop of Como been invested with comital powers?[2] Why exactly were the bishops of Arezzo and Volterra now stronger in those cities and the power of the marquis weaker? Why was the powerful marquis of Canossa, Boniface, assassinated by two of his vassals in 1052? What psychological barriers fell away at Genoa and Lucca in the 1070s and 1080s, enabling the *cives* to rise up briefly against their bishops and nobility? What was the effect on civil morality of having two archbishops in violent rivalry for the same archdiocese, each claiming the support of other bishops and of either pope or emperor? Or the effect in Florence and Lucca of having the marquis of Tuscany, a prince of the empire, siding with the pope against the emperor in the great Investiture Controversy? Whom could people look up to, where was civil stability, who was really entitled to local authority and how far did it go?

The profundity of the crisis was no greater at Milan than in five or six other cities, but we can more readily find a focus there. The feudal church was the first victim of Milanese urban tensions. Rich, soft, and self-assured, it became, in its decorous visibility, the target of raging criticism, despite its economic and social ties with the nobility. Milan had no eleventh-century archbishop to match a Florentine counterpart, Hildebrand (d. 1025), who used to hold episcopal court and council with his mistress, Alberga, at his side. But there, too, concubinage and marriage were widespread among the richer priests, nor was any benefice of the Milanese church obtainable without a price. In 1045 the emperor's appointment of Guido da Velate as new archbishop of Milan infuriated the nobles and episcopal clergy because Guido was not one of them. They labeled him a simonist, gossiped about his alleged corruption, and called him "that ignoramus from the country." He came from a village not far from Milan, but his family were big landowners.

Then, in the early 1050s, Guido's enemies had to close ranks with him, in face of the mounting force and voices of the Pataria, a movement mainly of laymen determined to reform the worldly conduct of the clergy. Rapidity of social change awakened intensity of feeling. Reforming influences sifted in from the countryside, where parishes were alive with religious agitation. Bitter resentment swelled over the abyss which divided the beggarly and serflike country clerics from the rich metropolitan clergy. Finding a startlingly receptive setting in Milan, the call for reform burst into a crusading movement. The Milanese Pataria came under the captaincy of two fiery clerics, Arialdo, who hailed from the country, and Landolfo Cotta, a minor Milanese nobleman. They began to preach in the spring of 1057, provoking, on May 10, a tumultuous demonstration against married and concubinary clerics, many of whom were expelled from their churches and houses. The Patarini then hit out at simony. But the most menacing note was sounded in the emerging view regarding the dubious value of sacraments when these were administered by simonists and keepers of concubines.

Stunned by the force of the attack, the clergy fumbled. Archbishop and nobility, losing the initiative, withdrew from the city. For the next dozen years the Patarini held the upper hand, owing largely to the support of the reformist popes Alexander II and Gregory VII. In the 1060s they even flew the papal banner. But leading Patarini were eliminated. After two assassination attempts, Landolfo Cotta died in 1059, in part perhaps from wounds suffered in an ambush in the neighboring city of Piacenza. Seven years later Arialdo was cut down, also outside Milan. Blamed for this murder, Guido da Velate was violently assaulted, and he then abdicated (1067). The reform movement had long since passed (1062) to the leadership of Landolfo's immensely capable brother, Erlembaldo Cotta—fearless soldier, charismatic zealot, trampler of holy oil consecrated by unworthy priests, described by a contemporary as having "the eyes of an eagle and the chest of a lion." In 1071 two men were locked in a ruthless contest for the archepiscopal dignity: Goffredo, supported by the nobility and future emperor, Henry IV, but unable to enter Milan; and Azzone, Erlembaldo's man, supported by the papacy but not allowed by parts of the Milanese clergy and other groups to be consecrated. Having drifted back into Milan in the 1060s, the nobility fought back and divided the less fervent of the reformers. Tensions rose in the early 1070s—the city had been without an archbishop since 1067—and came to a head in June 1075, when Erlembaldo was trapped and slain in a battle with the nobility. This ended the predominance, not yet the influence, of the Patarini.

Casting around the high points of these events, we perceive a city fraught with passion. Episcopal authority was kicked around. The rich, influential clergy were not brought down, but the intervention of the laity in church and political affairs was massive and decisive. In these events was born a municipal spirit which pointed directly to the commune. Princes were spurned, and in Rome, Gregory VII, the greatest of popes, was assaulted bodily. No man was above stinging criticism. The Patarini took their leaders and got some backing from the nobility and clergy. Indeed, in its heyday the reform movement managed to divide the nobility, for a bloc of vavasors sided with the reformers. Unsteady and even old loyalties crumbled under the siege of conflicting, choleric views. The movement of loyalties across group lines marked the depth of the crisis.

During its years of triumph, the Pataria got its noise and explosive vigor from crowds—tradesmen, artisans, laborers, rustics, and women, lots of women; but its guidance, respectability, and persistence came from learned clerics and men of the upper classes. When the captains and vavasors reconsolidated their forces in the early 1070s, some of the *cives* began to draw away from the Pataria's intransigence. Compromise was in the air. Erlembaldo's oligarchical dictatorship—he relied upon a supporting advisory council of thirty men—provoked strong resistance among the nobility, at the same time alienating his remaining upper-class support. The lines were soon drawn. Captains and vavasors used armed force to overwhelm Erlembaldo and the Patarini. A new archbishop was able finally to enter the city. The victory really belonged to the nobility, which would convert its renewed dominance into a commune.

If a commune be defined, in its opening phase, as a sworn association of free men collectively holding some public authority, then Milan certainly had the makings of a commune in the 1060s. There was no formal evidence of its existence, however, until 1081, when a collectivity of laymen, represented by consuls, shared certain civic powers with the archbishop. This was the age of the birth of communes:

Pisa	1080s	Arezzo	1098
Lucca	1080s	Genoa	1099
Milan	1081	Como	ca.1100
Parma	1081	Pistoia	1105
Rome	1083	Verona	1107
Pavia	1084	Bologna	1123
Piacenza	1090	Siena	1125
Asti	1095	Florence	1138

The dates refer to the earliest documentary traces of formal communal activity in these cities, but the commune had in some cases bounded into being some years before. We cannot take the details of the Milanese experience as typical, for communes came out of a rich variety of local circumstances. But the dramatic rise of communes after about 1070, along a space extending from central Italy to the northern plain, speaks for a common ground.

In the 1050s and 1060s Milan exhibits all the conditions that attended the birth of urban communes: the frailty of imperial-royal power, the subtle and then blunt enfeeblement of episcopal authority, religious and moral malaise, a readiness for violence, and the pressing forward of a laity prepared to seize public authority.

The first urban communes were aristocratic (*signorile*) in their composition. Even their counterparts in the country, rural communes, were associations of knights, small landed proprietors, and freeholders: men of substance bound together by oaths in order to defend existing rights or to seize new jurisdictions in the neighboring hills and valleys; they razed castles, exacted vows of fidelity (made usually to the bishop), and forced their potent rural enemies to reside in Siena for a certain part of the year.

The triumph of the commune at Pisa and Genoa was the crowning political effect of maritime wealth—of piracy, naval organization, trade, shipbuilding, and vast profits. Pisan public authority had been in the hands mainly of a hereditary viscount, who acted in part for the marquis of Tuscany. In the eleventh century the influence of the marquis was eliminated and the viscount himself was slowly drawn into the dynamic association of shipowners, captains, and merchants, most of whom were of noble lineage or from families of big landowners. With its naval wars and nascent colonizing, the life of the city was so much dominated by the association's enterprises that the direction of urban affairs slipped from the viscount's hands. At the end of the century he was no more than the first-listed among the chief officials (consuls) of the commune. Pisa's government had been gradually stolen by the rich and eminent.

Genoa was witness to a similar transfer, or stealing, of power. There public authority belonged to an agent of the Obertenghi marquises, the viscount Ido (fl. 950s). In the eleventh century his descendants broke up into three different branches and all took the viscountal title. They clashed with the bishop of Genoa over fiscal and judicial rights, until a bishop was chosen from among them. Then the fertile viscounts fought for the lucrative rights and properties of the Genoese church, until they were turned into the vassals of their kinsman, the bishop. In 1056 they put an end to the authority of the Obertengho marquis, in part by buying it up. The city was already under the rule of a quasi-commune with the bishop (afterwards archbishop) as head. He was flanked by lay advisers and relatives who were also the underwriters of extraordinary naval and commercial exploits. The arrogance and power of the viscounts, and the connivance and softness of the Genoese church, gave rise to a reform movement akin to the Milanese Pataria. Popular insurrections broke out in 1080, and the years following would have been among the more troubled and bloody in the history of Genoa had there not been, in those very years, the alluring profits and adventures offered by the high seas and Near East, now open for trade and conquest. The flow of new wealth into Genoa went to buoy many a man and family up from obscurity. In 1099 the city's seven entrepreneurial associations (*compagne*) drew together into a *compagna* of the whole community. Although the different *compagne* long retained their separate identities and neighborhood spheres of influence, henceforth all men in the city were to be considered members of the larger communal or umbrella *compagna*; they were also to be under its government. Overnight, Genoa's great commercial associations were turned into a commune, but the commune was governed strictly by the nobility and rich: the descendants of viscounts and vassals, the archbishop ones. Founded at about the same time as the equivalent urban associations, the early rural commune had little truck with nonsense about emancipating serfs. Its objectives were those of propertied or privileged men, responding to local needs and perils and taking collective (*viz.* communal) action in order to be more effective. So also the conscious formation of the urban commune was the work of men privileged and wellborn, enlisted mainly from among the large class of resident urban knights: the lesser captains and vavasors, the sons and grandsons of episcopal and royal officials, and even the more modest descendants of marquises and counts. The latter, although so called, no longer had true jurisdiction, owing to the proliferation of families and the ensuing fragmentation of their original feudal holdings. Ceva, for example, had fifty families which claimed and used the title of marquis. The emerging commune also included a scatter of *cives*—rich merchants and moneylenders, the few local men trained in law, and a handful of small landed proprietors of some antiquity in the city.

What took place late in the eleventh century, in city after city, propelling noblemen and rich *cives* to draw together into sworn associations? The men of rank and property were the very ones most subject to the stresses imposed by the faltering of authority. Bishops and archbishops had made a practice of having prominent laymen (captains, vavasors, and titled men) among their advisers. The giving of counsel figured among the duties of vassals, and episcopal vassals owed such service to their bishops. When, therefore, the moment came to push forward and seize the usurpable public power, the leading knights instantly took the positions of command within the commune of nobles and preeminent *cives*.

But the moment itself of communal formation eludes us, the moment of condensation, for it lasted too long. It was a process of gradual encroachment, and chroniclers did not identify a moment but rather a long-term series of civil disorders.[3] Noblemen and prominent citizens formed a voluntary sworn association and then reached out for political power *or* they successfully turned a pre-existing association into a citizen body with public jurisdictions. Both happened: the creation of communes *ex novo* and the turning of pre-existing associations into communes. At Milan the aristocratic commune sprang from the wreckage of royal-imperial authority and from the struggle against the Patarini and wrathful popes. At Mantua, in the 1050s, the commune was born of a union of noble families driven by fear of the area's chief lord, the Canossa marquis of Tuscany. Obtaining support and major concessions of jurisdiction from their bishop (Eliseo), the Mantuan nobility united to end the role of the viscount, representative of the marquis, in the public life of the city. Here bishop and commune worked together, evolving a tradition of mutual cooperation. The like occurred at Siena, where bishop and commune, in the first half of the twelfth century, cooperated in their struggle against the feudatories of the surrouding countryside. Sienese nobles fought to enlarge their own lands and the city's and big landowners, and a few of the commoners who had made large fortunes at sea.

The emergence of communes was an act of political and social assertion. Leading local men were resolved to have self-government. They had been pushed to it and prepared for it by the instability of authority and by decades of conflicting violent claims. They were also pushed toward the seizure of power by the inflating self-assurance that went with the tremendous expansion of rights over property, as the city spilled beyond its walls and new wealth flowed in, along with waves of immigrants. There was more at stake in 1080 than in 980, in the availability of riches as well as in matters of personal identity, and therefore involvement in public affairs was more urgent and attractive. Nearly everywhere bishops, viscounts, and marquises had been made to surrender authority, and the prime benefactors were the local nobles and respected *cives*.

In the first century of their existence, communes coexisted with an older authority, usually that of the bishop or viscounts. At Mantua and Siena the commune cooperated with the bishop but carefully excluded the biggest of the surrounding feudatories from its membership. At Genoa and Pisa the commune was rich and powerful enough to absorb the viscounts. At Mantua, until 1233, the bishop occasionally figured as an important communal official. But most communes terminated such dual or interlocking authority in the course of the twelfth century. Once the commune won recognition, it pressed inexorably for more and more power, until it held the bulk of local authority *de facto*, whatever the claims of ceremony and legal theory. But, however bellicose or able, no commune was strong enough to seize at the outset the full range of public powers.

CHAPTER II

THE EARLY
COMMUNE AND
ITS NOBILITY

COMMUNES AND EMPIRE

Communes were fairly synonymous with self-government, but around the year 1100 self-government was realized by seizing it. The early commune bristled with weapons. Its members looked to the defense of the city and its walls; they engaged in mounted combat or naval warfare; and while they were committed to keeping the peace, they were also sworn to help in the repelling of all threats to the existence or powers of the commune. Born in a climate of revolutionary change, whether with the aid of the bishop or against him, the commune straightway made enemies: the bishop or archbishop, counts or viscounts, the Pataria, feudal magnates in the outlying districts, neighboring cities or rival naval powers, marquis, pope, or emperor.

From the earliest times, the intensity of local patriotism was amazingly strong. Pavia, the old capital of the Italic kingdom, never forgave Milan, some twenty or twenty-five miles away, for its dramatic rise and importance on the Lombard Plain. As early as 1058 the two went to war over the question of Pavia's claims to jurisdictions in Milan. No sooner were communes established than they looked out suspiciously and jealously on their strongest or nearest urban neighbors. Suddenly they were implacable rivals, and open warfare soon broke out. They battled for the control of roads and riverways, tolls and customs, seaways and traffic, and for the right to monopolize commerce in certain goods.

Pisa and Genoa quarreled bitterly not long after 1016, and war raged between them almost continuously between 1067 and 1085; the hostilities would persist down to the fourteenth century. Siena and Florence went to war in 1082, drawing deep satisfaction from devastating each other's lands and crops. Florence conquered Fiesole in 1125 and afterward went to war with Lucca. In 1107 Milan and Tortona were allies in wars against Pavia,

Cremona, and Lodi. Milan ravaged Lodi in 1111 and Como in 1127; their conflicts involved traffic rights on the Po and Lambro rivers. Similar rivalries pitted Mantua against Como. Although bankers and merchants from Florence, Siena, Lucca, Asti, and Piacenza were to be found all over the peninsula and parts of Northern Europe, the most dynamic of the inland cities in industrial terms was Milan, which in the late twelfth century may already have had some 80,000 or 90,000 inhabitants, of whom some 20,000 were workers and artisans in textiles, metalworking, the building trades, and other crafts. At the start of the twelfth century Pisa's explosive energies made it seem many times its size: it had a population then, probably, of not more than 15,000 souls, a tiny figure in view of its spectacular naval achievements.

The major cities and even the little towns that started out as hardly more than castles (e.g., Prato) were social whirlpools, drawing in large numbers of immigrants from the rural sea around. Conversely, too, the economic interests and vitalities of the urban cluster spilled out into the deep countryside: *cittadini* (city folk) acquired more and more land, bought up feudal rights, and toiled to evade feudal claims. Propertied rustics and country knights, while holding on to their rural properties, often moved into the city and joined their interests with those of *cittadini*. The authority of the urban commune thus spread out through the expanding property interests and commercial ties of its citizens, flowing ever more deeply into the countryside and overwhelming resistance there, whether from rural communes or feudal magnates.

The "consular commune" was the commune in its first stage of development, so called because it was governed by officials known as "consuls." And if consular leadership was often unsure of its political authority, such uncertainty was also felt in the rural parishes, all the more so as the power of the empire evaporated, as feudal magnates were challenged, and as cities increased their intimidating pressures. In these circumstances the strong carried the day; might was right. The clash between giants, Henry IV and Gregory VII, or between Henrician and Gregorian bishops, burst through matters of abstract law and spread tumult in the country parishes as in the cities. When in February of 1111, in a fit of fury, Henry V suddenly had Pope Pascual II seized in the Church of St. Peter, news of this snaked immediately through the nervous northern dioceses.

During the twelfth century, at Genoa, Siena, Pisa, Florence, Milan, and other cities, the consular commune made continual war on feudal lords for miles around, defeating them in the field, razing castles, turning vassals against overlords, and eventually compelling the latter to establish residence in the city for some part of the year. Lucca tried this and failed with the lords of Riprafata, who turned to Pisa for help. But Pisa successfully brought the Caproni, Cattani, Porcari, Corvaia, and others under her domination. Once in the city, this baronage built houses, entered the commune, married into the municipal nobility, and found a place in the commune's expanding ambitions—in its armies, offices, and commercial ventures. Such at Florence, for example, was the fortune of the Adimari, Uberti, Ricasoli, and Buondelmonti families; and this pattern was repeated all over upper Italy.

In the later twelfth century, as we shall see, in commune after commune, the nobility was to be torn by homicidal rivalries. But before this happened the commune benefited from two or three generations of relative internal concord. External threat made for internal communal unity. The threat might come from the local bishop or count, but more often the source lay outside the city, in the form of armed claims advanced by marquises, by leading *capitanei*, or by other hereditary officials of the weakened imperial-royal power. The communes of Ferrara and Padua were long menaced by the Estensi; Florence waged war against the counts Guidi, Ubaldini, and Alberti; Asti and Tortona had to contend with the Aleramici; Siena was plagued by the Aldobrandeschi, Lucca by the Cattani of Garfagnana, and Modena and Parma by the Malaspina lords. The challenge of the emperor himself also encouraged the harmony of the consular nobility.

Since the story of twelfth-century relations between Italian communes and German emperors has often been told, we shall note only the main lines of policy and development, the better to understand the behavior of urban communes not only in their conquest of the world beyond the city walls, but also in their pretensions to command within the city.

Late in the eleventh century, amidst his violent controversy with the papacy and with Countess Matilda of Tuscany, the Emperor Henry IV found it advantageous to grant concessions to certain communes, chiefly Lucca and Pisa. Succeeding emperors also made additional concessions. It was an era of civil war in Germany, of profound division among German princes and contenders for the imperial crown. The authority of the empire was badly rent. Yet no emperor went so far as to recognize the autonomy of communes—specific grants of privileges, yes, as in imperial commitments not to build royal fortresses inside Lucca or Pisa, or not to deploy foreign judges there, and other particular concessions as well; but there was nothing broad in such grants, no surrender of principle. All the same, urban communes were often able to realize their political claims by means of barefaced usurpation.

Suddenly a remarkable figure appeared on the scene—he made six expeditions to Italy—and the direction of events shifted. Frederick I Barbarossa, a prince of the Hohenstaufen line and duke of Swabia, entered Italy in 1154, to be crowned emperor in 1155. The honor and dignity of the imperial office swelled in the mind of this golden-haired prince. Putting himself in line with the emperors of ancient Rome, he resolved to rebuild the substance of the imperial power in Italy, and he started by demanding that Milan give up its claims to Como and Lodi. Refusing to do so, Milan was put under a ban of empire in 1155.

In 1158, Barbarossa returned to Italy, this time at the head of a mighty German army, and overwhelmed rich and prestigious Milan. The other cities trembled and toed the line. He called a general diet on the plain of Roncaglia (1158), which was attended by German and Italian dignitaries lay and ecclesiastical, by consuls from the different Lombard cities, and by four outstanding jurists from the capital of European legal studies, Bologna. Twenty-eight other jurists—two from each of fourteen North Italian cities —also attended the diet and fully endorsed Barbarossa's claims. Relying upon the Bolognese professors, who invoked Roman law and conceived of him as an absolute ruler and heir to the imperial laws of Justinian, Barbarossa reclaimed his "regalian rights," which had been usurped by the communes. Foremost among the "regalia" were fiscal rights over waterways and city gates, tolls and customs duties, rights of minting, taxes on fish and salt, and the rather full authority to appoint court magistrates. Far from being arbitrary, Barbarossa sought to be scrupulously correct legally; and so doing, he proposed to bring the cities back under some imperial rule. He planned to lodge imperial agents in each, where they would perform political and judicial functions. But there was absolutely no question of his eliminating communes; he merely sought to shear them of some of the powers that they had been grabbing for a half-century and more.

Against tenacious local resistance in city after city, neither manifest law nor the emperor prevailed. Milan spurned the imperial podestà in 1159 and openly rebelled against the emperor. Piacenza and Brescia supported Milan, but Barbarossa had the help of Milan's enemies—Lodi, Pavia, Cremona, and Como. Destroying Crema first, he then turned on Milan and razed it in 1162. He granted imperial diplomas to Pisa, Genoa, Cremona, and—in 1164—Pavia, conceding them the privilege of freely electing their chief executives (consuls) and of governing their own counties. The consuls were endowed with the powers of high justice, which barred in effect the possibility of judicial appeal to the empire. These, however, were exceptional grants. On the Lombard plain and especially in Tuscany (Pisa and Lucca excepted), the emperor resolved to keep public affairs under closer imperial control, and urban communes were not allowed to rule their counties and countryside.

Barbarossa aroused the deepest suspicions and fears, not by acting outside the law but by working within it. He became the most alarming obstacle to the ambitions of the leading communes. In 1163–1164, Venice and three neighboring cities—Verona, Vicenza, and Padua—entered a league against him; his interests in Sicily and concessions to Pisa and Genoa struck the Venetians as dangerous to Venice's commerce and naval deployments. In 1167, apparently under Venetian inspiration, the major cities of Lombardy and Emilia formed an alliance and then concluded a league with the allied cities near Venice. This was the famous First Lombard League against Frederick Barbarossa. At its height in 1168 the league numbered sixteen cities, including even Cremona and Lodi (much favored by Barbarossa), and stretched from Piedmont and Lombardy to Emilia and the Venice region, thus taking in the whole of northern Italy.

Called back to Germany by urgent matters in 1168, the emperor did not reappear in Italy until 1174, when he entered Lombardy at the head of an army mainly of mercenaries and too weak to win any stunning victories. He was joined by additional German contingents early in 1176 and then marched on Milan. The army of the league—Pavia and Como defected to Barbarossa—intercepted him at Legnano and there dealt him a humiliating defeat (May 29, 1176). A peace—the Peace of Constance—was finally agreed upon and ratified in 1183. And for all the verbal tribute paid in it to the emperor, it marked a historic victory for the communes. The articles of the Peace of Constance became the formal foundation of communal autonomy, and ever after the freedom of the cities was to be taken back to the imperial recognition allegedly contained there. Privileges previously granted to two or three cities were enlarged upon and extended to nearly a score of other cities. Barbarossa affected to grant the privileges out of his good grace, now that the Lombard and other communes were supposedly returning to a position of obedience to the empire. Constance established the following major rights: the cities of northern Italy were authorized (1) to elect freely their own consuls, (2) to govern their own counties, and (3) to make their own local laws. In return, citizens were to swear an oath of loyalty to the emperor; communal consuls were to receive imperial investiture before taking office; citizens were granted the right of appeal to the empire in cases exceeding twenty-five pounds in gold; and the cities were to pay an imperial levy (*fodro*) when the emperor-elect made his way through Italy to be crowned.

The rights of the empire, as guaranteed at Constance, were soon ignored, and cities which had never belonged to the Lombard League began successfully to claim the benefits accorded at Constance. Emperors pursued a tougher imperial line in Tuscany, where the communal movement was less volatile at first. But with the death of Henry VI (1197), which occasioned another double imperial election, and the new outbreak of civil war in Germany, Tuscan communes formed a league to ensure that each would govern its own rural territory. They had strong papal support.

CONSULAR INSTITUTIONS

The consular commune's battle for public rights went hand in hand with the rise within the city of increasingly complex institutions. Here, much more than in the struggle with the empire, we can begin to make out the intensity and richness of the spreading urban experience, the variety of social groups, the political wizardry of emerging elites and transient pressure groups, and the imagination of ambitious men driven by worldly hopes, yet checked and divided, sometimes more and sometimes less, by some regard for the law. They wanted to respect the law, but their engulfing needs and desires often carried them outside it. One result was the emergence of a new body of public and private law.

Information on institutions in the consular age is scanty and comes largely from sources of the late twelfth and early thirteenth centuries, the very period when consular government was breaking up. But if we allow for some variation from city to city, a working profile is possible.

The commune was an association of men bound together by an oath and common interests. They swore to aid and defend one another; they pooled their prestige and minute jurisdictions, if they had any; and they invested their consuls, the official heads of the association, with executive and judicial powers. The associates—that is, the members of the commune—swore to obey and follow the consuls, who in turn swore to defend and uphold the association in all its rights and interests.

The oldest communal institution was the general assembly of all the members of the commune. These were the founding members and their descendants, in addition to all those who were taken into the commune from time to time. The consuls were always drawn from among this corps. During the first generation or so of the commune's existence, the general assembly was quite likely convened with some regularity, and in times of trouble even more often. Here the views of leading men were heard and important decisions taken, usually by acclamation. Later, as the commune expanded and assembly meetings became more difficult to manage, the "parliament of the whole" was called less often—on Sundays, say, or even once a year—and it carried less weight, save in emergency sessions.

Voting in the general assembly was done by fiat: men shouted yes or no. All real communal authority issued from this body and could return to it. A parliament was the supreme authority, the final decision-making body. But the legislative initiative, the power to move change, lay with the consuls; and historians suspect that no true discussion was permitted in the general assembly. The consuls introduced all proposals. One of the leading consuls defended the motion before the assembled commune; then, possibly, two or three of the more experienced notables were invited to speak and the assembly moved directly to a vote by acclamation.

The consulate, the assembled body of consuls, was the commune's highest executive and judicial magistracy. All important daily matters were discussed and decided here. Having sounded out the general assembly, the consuls made war and peace, led the communal armies, were responsible for the defense of the city, levied taxes, sired legislation, and served as the final appellate court. The consulate was the focus of power in the early commune: it was always coveted, always prized by the ambitious. The number of consuls varied according to time and place. A range of from four to twenty consuls was not uncommon; more often they numbered from four to twelve. Generally speaking, a term of office was for one year—initially at Genoa for three years—and an incumbent could not return to the consulate until after the elapse of one or two additional terms. In the early years of the commune's existence, consuls were probably elected by vote in the general assembly. But this practice was abolished. The commune sheltered groups in favor of a tighter hold over elections and over the sorting out of power. Triumphing, these groups evolved the practice whereby consuls elected their own successors directly or indirectly. To be most effective, consulates doubtless sought to have amicable relations with the commune's collective manifestation, the general assembly. But it is clear, too, that some limiting principle, attaching most likely to *quality* as a function of property and status, served to restrict effective power to a select number of men and families.

By the 1160s the major communes had seen the surfacing of clusters of families which outranked the rest by their political honors and preeminence. Members of these families were constantly in the public eye—as consuls, ambassadors, or advisers. Genoa had the Embriaci, Della Volta, Avvocati, Doria, De Mari, and Spinola at the head of her lists. Florence produced the Giandonati, Fifanti, Abbati, and Iudi. At Milan the political names to reckon with were those of the Pusterla, Soresina, Mandello, Vimercati, Marcellino, and Della Torre. In the 1150s Verona already had two powerful merchant families with lordly pretensions, the Monticoli and Crescenzi. And Pisa was the city of the Visconti, Gaetani, Gualandi, Gherardesca, and Da Caprona.

Communal society was marked by strong ties of cooperation, but it was also competitive, intensely so. It condoned and complimented the accumulation of riches and worldly honors, despite the contrary tug in medieval Christian doctrine. Most men who rose to prominence in the commune enjoyed the all-important backing of their large and busy families, often powerful families which disposed of riches, contacts, prestige—all the initial material advantages. Moreover, growing directly out of feudal society but long coexisting with it, communal society had a profound respect for social hierarchy, for the trappings of worldly as well as spiritual dignity.

Turning from general description to particular procedures, we find communal groups tending their political interests with the help of clever devices. In twelfth-century Bergamo, for instance, as in some other cities, the outgoing consuls held elections which might even take place in the general assembly. They elected a group, which elected a second group, which elected the new consuls. Electing a new set of consuls thus required three separate elections, and though these might take place in the general assembly, only certain members seem to have had the right to nominate candidates. Indeed some communes—e.g., Siena and Genoa—distinguished between major and minor associates or greater and lesser members, so that invidious social distinctions might be a very part of the commune's corporate legal structure.

After 1160, when a hardening ruling elite came into view, members of the commune began to criticize election procedures. Efforts were made to keep consuls and other officials from fixing elections. Communal regulations at Genoa in 1157 and 1161 laid it down that no elector should or could take counsel with another elector so as to gain the consulate for himself or another. In its statutes of 1173, the commune of Pistoia bound each of "the electors of the consulate's electors" to swear, "I am party to no agreement to give or to take any public office."

These dry enactments reflect the strains and gathering complexities of the developing commune. In time the burden of public affairs became too heavy and delicate for the consulate and general assembly. In the late twelfth century a large legislative council came into being, brought out of the old *concione* or general assembly. It was large enough to seem representative and to provide the needed voice of consensus, yet compact enough to allow for swifter consultations. The commune also altered the scope and functions of the consulate. Being a more sensitive charge, the administration of high justice—when it was finally taken from the empire's agents—required more technical skills. Certain consuls were specifically assigned, or devoted themselves to, the handling of civil and criminal proceedings, until a separate magistracy split off from the consulate. The specialization of functions went even farther: the traditional consulate came to be joined by a formal body of advisers—known as *sapientes* or *credentiari*—who held regular consultations with the consuls. They also were recruited from among the city's more influential families. The other agencies of the consular period, such as the police and fisc, had no clear profile until the thirteenth century, and by then the institutions of the early commune had been revolutionized.

The nobility dominated the consulate, manipulated the general assembly, and ruled the city, except where the emperor successfully intervened, as at Vicenza, Siena, and Volterra, or where the political power of the bishop persisted. From about 1130 the commune of Milan regularly gave a few places in its consulate to men from old merchant and notarial families, but they soon passed over and disappeared into the nobility. Verona had some rich and eminent businessmen who "made it" into the consulate, but they also took up the ways and political pretensions of men descended from marquises, counts, and leading vassals. In the 1180s, Genoa occasionally carried obscurely born men on her consular rosters, and although they were rich, they were no match, in public office or in the streets, for the consuls sprung from families of viscountal origins, such as the Doria, De Mari, Della Volta, and Embriaci, around all of whom there orbited lesser families.

THE NOBILITY

Historians are not in agreement about the nature and identity of the urban nobility. Was it a closed or an open caste? A class in decline or one which reformed and revitalized itself by means of shrewd marriages and commercial enterprise? Was it a nobility of birth, claiming past or present feudal jurisdictions on the basis of an imperial act or an act of enfoeffment by an imperial agent? Or was it a nobility based merely upon old wealth and public service? To what extent did noblemen go into commerce or refrain from it altogether? Was there a distinction inside the city between a municipal aristocracy and an urban warrior nobility, or between an older urban nobility and one more recently arrived from the country? Was knighthood a social or a military order? Did mounted combat in itself confer noble status? Or was nobility a state of mind: wealth and prowess combined with lordly ways and the qualities of leadership? The *stilnovisti*, the idealist poets of Dante's generation (ca. 1280–1310), held that nobility resided in virtue, in "a gentle heart," but theirs was a moral posture and a social subtlety. No one believed them.

Emilio Cristiani's book on Pisa emphasizes, as much as any study, the changing, fluid character of the urban nobility in the twelfth and thirteenth centuries.[1] The class was not as formless as he suggests.

The nobility of the eleventh-century city was made up first of all of the direct vassals (the captains) of the bishop or the resident marquis, count, or viscount, as at Genoa, Milan, Lucca, Mantua, and Florence. The vassals of the captains constituted, in turn, a lesser but still honored and influential nobility. The great feudatories—the really big nobility and the leading men around them—often kept to the deep country. Of this sort were the Guidi counts around Florence, the Biandrate counts from near Novara and Vercelli, and the counts of Panico around Bologna. They had nothing to do with the formation of communes; in fact, they often went to war with these.

To fight, to help govern, to provide counsel: these sum up the distinctive activities of the eleventh-century urban nobility. In the course of the next century, this nobility changed, owing to other key changes that have already been discussed: (1) the fragmentation of vast feudal estates, putting property into many more hands; (2) the explosive birth rate, which both attracted rural noblemen into the city and multiplied the urban nobility, so that in some instances thirty or forty counts sprang up where once there had been one; (3) the rise and cyclonic force of urban communes, at first manned and captained mainly by noblemen; (4) intermarriage of the urbanized vassalry with rich municipal families of old standing; (5) the ascent of a scatter of new men to positions of command in the commune, where they faded into the nobility, thus helping to reconstitute the elite groups; (6) the crescendo of economic opportunities for the nobility, made possible by long-distance commerce, maritime trade, the boom in real property values, and by the wars between cities; and finally (7) the increasing honors and incomes made available by the commune's expanding range of public offices.

The Early Commune and Its Nobility

New blood, additional functions, new outlets for a driving energy, and new aggregates of property: these transformed the urban nobility, making it, in the late twelfth century, different from what it had been 150 years before. But a nobility thrived. About the year 1190, noblemen in the cities answered to the following description. In general, they were well off economically but worried and at times harassed by the effects of inflation and large families. They possessed land and had vital social contacts in the neighboring and more distant countryside. Not rarely their hereditary patrimonies included effective feudal claims over specific tolls, customs fees, certain episcopal incomes, and other pecuniary rights. They might have investments in trade and maritime ventures, or even on occasion be directly engaged in these, as at Genoa, Pisa, Florence, Asti, Piacenza, and Siena. They were traditionally associated with important posts in the Church or commune. They were well connected, and they used marriage vows to extend those connections, so that there was apt to be some link with old blood, whether by marriage or by long association with the groups at the top. Unless forbidden by a religious vow, they were likely to be practiced in the use of arms and mounted combat. And finally they tended to be sworn members of family associations that disposed of fortified houses or turreted fortresses inside the city.

The sum of the preceding features defines the urban nobility around the year 1190 in terms of property, public and private functions, social contacts, and family traditions. Descent from old stock, or an affiliation therewith by marriage, was also a feature, but it was not absolutely essential. Although in 1190 the nobility had a stranglehold on the commune, or very nearly so, there was evidence of some loosening. Noblemen took the lion's share of communal dignities, but they were being compelled by the direction of social change to alter the communal constitution and to establish new councils in which their control would be less certain. Their own quarrels, however, made for the greatest danger to their authority in the city. By 1180 or 1190 they were hopelessly divided in all the great communes—Milan, Florence, Genoa, Pisa, Bologna, and so on.

The best twentieth-century scholarship reduces the civil wars of the communal nobility to the appealing mysteries of an ethico-social psychology: noblemen were ambitious, arrogant, jealous, self-willed, unruly, and belligerent—a view already held by twelfth- and thirteenth-century chroniclers. Not unnaturally, therefore, in competing for public office they clashed. This view is valid but simplistic. To complete the analysis we must move out of the realm of moral psychology to the world around. Any man's psychology is part of the external world for all other men, but the sum of all individual psychologies is not the sum of social realities.

The twelfth-century nobility was not a congeries of individualists overruled by their passions. They had a keen and abiding sense of cooperation, a strong feeling for family and group. They flourished in collectivities.

In many cases their forebears had served in a *curia vassalorum*, an informal advisory group which had aided the local marquis, count, or governing bishop. Such men drew together into communes. They closed ranks to fight emperors, local magnates, or schismatic popes. They founded associations to keep the peace. Later they founded family associations (*consorterie*), in which the deviant or unique interests of the individual had no validity save in relation to the interests of the group. The identity of the individual nobleman was obtained and retained through the multiple family.

What caused the outbreak of internecine conflict among the nobility in the later twelfth century? Chroniclers pointed to the unrestrained competition for civil honors: wildly ambitious noblemen struggled for the principal offices. The Peace of Constance (1183) served to release pent-up passions and rivalries. But deeper stresses lay behind the competitive psychology: the effects of inflation, large families, abounding economic opportunities, diverging urban commitments to the network of surrounding agrarian and feudal interests, and the inviting effects of the empire's failing authority—a vacuum tugging away irresistibly at those who already enjoyed local prominence. The urban ruling class had tended locally to present a united front to the imperial challenge, but already in the 1170s and 1180s, as the commune was triumphing over the empire, the nobility began to suffer sharp divisions in city after city. The stresses noted above and the velocity of social change proved to be too much for harmonious development. Moreover, the ruling class itself was in process of transformation and included powerful crosscurrents. Authority at all levels had been under persistent assault for more than a century. The passionate rivalry between ecclesiastical and temporal heads, in addition to the droning presence of heresy, had disseminated religious malaise. And the practice of vendetta, of blood feud in perpetuity, borne into the cities by the immigrant nobility, further exacerbated the array of urban tensions.

To protect and reorient themselves, noblemen began to jell into smaller and more defined corporate units—family blocs. Two or three such blocs eventually dominated in most cities. To their rivalries was added, at the end of the twelfth century, the pressure of a multiplying and prosperous middle class, toiling under the disadvantage of political impotence but pressing forward to claim a voice in the commune's political councils. A constituency within the nobility was ready to compromise, ready to give way and enlarge the ranks of the officeholders. Where the wounds of civil war were deep, as at Milan, Genoa, and Siena, the readiness to compromise seems to have been motivated at times by the desire of one bloc to gain additional support in the streets and councils against an enemy bloc of families. But there were also those resolved to hold out intransigently against the granting of political citizenship to new men.

As visual drama—strikingly so in the inland cities—the deadly competition among hostile blocs was best expressed by the soaring fortresses belonging to noble families. Some towers had been erected in the eleventh century. The armed habit of the feudal countryside was carried into the city. But the period from about 1160 to 1260—the intensity peaking around 1200—was the age *par excellence* for the construction of towers. They were given a base and ground level of large blocks of stone. The great walls of the ascending shaft were built of cobbles and lime, sandwiched between two or more rows of bricks, and rose in many cases to a height of between fifty and sixty meters. In Florence the highest structures stood at an altitude of about seventy-five meters. Bologna had one, the tower of the Asinella, at a height of ninety-seven meters. The Bolognese towers, mostly rectangular in shape, varied at the base from about four and one-half to nearly eleven meters in width, narrowing as they rose. Whatever the obscure circumstances attending the construction of the earliest towers, the many towers built in the later twelfth century, like the civil wars that enveloped them, were the work of the consular nobility, the work of associations (*consorterie*) of the very families that had captured the consulate.

CHAPTER III

THE COMMUNE
AROUND 1200

In 1187, the Genoese consul Angelerio de Mari was killed in office. At Florence in 1193, Tedaldo Tedaldi was a counselor to the podestà, who hailed from the Caponsacchi family. Tedaldo descended from a married ecclesiastic and had a brother, Giannibello, who was a prominent figure among Florence's international cloth merchants.

The names roll out richly. Records of the period teem with them but seldom provide a view of personalities. And we may be wrong to look for personalities in our sense, for marked individualities with layered psychologies. The age was not fashioned by these.

The early-thirteenth-century statutes of the hill town of Bergamo, just a few miles northeast of Milan, required citizens to pledge loyalty to the commune's highest official and to swear to refrain from crimes of violence. More specifically, there were vows not to get into street fights, not to hurl missiles from high places with the intention of inflicting injury, not to carry knives, swords or other weapons, and not to wound or kill others. Pledges of this sort, imposed as a legal obligation upon citizens, were also exacted by the statutes of many other communes.

What had driven citizens into blocs and miscellaneous groupings before the year 1200, arraying them with knives to one another's throats? The course of deterioration is obscure in its details but not in its outlines.

The cities had seen astounding gains in population in the course of the twelfth century. From Vicenza and Padua to Siena and Perugia, the billowing suburbs engulfed the ancient city center and rendered the old circle of walls ineffective. New walls were erected in the twelfth century, but these also were bypassed later on in the continuing population spill. An inflationary boom in real-property values surpassed the like of anything seen before. At Venice around 1200 the ducal Ziani family alone possessed hundreds of houses and shop sites on the Rialto and in other parts of the city, including all the houses around the great square and cathedral of St. Mark. But the speed of land transfer, along with the tug of encircling energies, unleashed anxieties that were calmed neither by the crumbling of civil authority nor by the confining purviews of the city's narrow streets and great walls. A crowded layout, abrupt demarcations, winding streets, and small public squares exacerbated the rush of social energies. Soaring to heights of seventy-five meters and more, the bristling towers of the nobility were not just fortresses and surveillance posts, they were also affirmations of power, expressions of competitive arrogance, of a bounding vitality that was not being satisfied on the ground. And they were a testament of rank and privilege, for only noblemen were allowed legally to build such towers in the twelfth and early thirteenth centuries.

The seductive and yet menacing atmosphere of the city, produced by a frenzy of economic expansion in a context in which public authority had been battered, led to a regrouping of human resources at the heart of the commune. Drawing upon a strong sense of clan and consanguinity, noblemen clustered into tight-knit associations and built fortified towers so as to defend themselves or to expand their rights and privileges. Each such *consorteria* was a sworn corporate grouping, consisting of males descended from a common male ancestor. It was therefore a male lineage, although, when extinction threatened, the line might be transferred via a woman. In time the *consorteria* entered into sworn association with other like neighborhood groups. Any particular *consorteria*, or later on one of the enlarged confederations or tower societies, might include anywhere from ten to thirty or forty sworn associates. Their founding agreements often included revealing articles. When, for example, the sons of the founding members came of age (by fifteen), they were made to take the group oath. Agreements included prohibitions of marriage into specified families, evidently on the principle that if you and I were cohorts, your enemies were also mine. Girls were debarred from the right to inherit towers or to receive them as dowries. The towers, in any case, were not necessarily habitable. They were intended for military operations.

All cohorts had keys or access to the group tower or towers. Occasionally their houses were connected to the group tower by means of underground passages. More often, connecting spans were built leading from the upper parts of their houses to one of the tower's entrance windows. At Florence, in 1209, a tower facing squarely onto the Piazza of Orsanmichele had three such flyovers: one in back leading to the Truscio house, and one on each side connected to the houses of the Manni and Arcimbaldi families. When two, three, or more *consorterie* joined forces, their towers were thereupon linked, if possible, or at any rate made commonly accessible. In this fashion at Florence the Giandonati and Fifanti "clans" united their *consorterie* in 1180. When a union of this sort brought peace to a neighbor hood, that part of the city became nearly impregnable, because the linking of towers and the easy blocking up of the narrow streets made for an effective domination over the adjoining area. Verona, Milan, Pavia, Parma, Florence, Siena, Pisa, and other cities—all had numerous towers. Whether ascending to the hill city of Perugia or looking from the banks of the Arno toward Florence, the traveler came on a similar view—a nervous skyline of towers. Lucca reportedly was "a forest" of towers. Florence in 1180 had probably a hundred towers. Bologna, also studded with towers, produced copious legislation on the subject in the thirteenth century.

It is easy to see why the leading families were the first to take to corporate action. Standing at the head of a commune whose authority was shaky, they faced the gravest dangers. At the same time their wealth, their armed servitors, and their sheltering ties of kinship afforded protection to group interests and individuals. Their principal family houses and certain other immovables were often held in common, chiefly to keep the patrimony from breaking up in the absence of primogeniture. The effects of such coherence or clotting were readily visible in the urban context. As a given family multiplied, the generations built or bought houses on the same street, the same square, the same sea front, the same crossway, until all the main houses of the clan were more or less adjacent or front to front. This pattern was already apparent in eleventh-century Milan, Pavia, Lucca, Genoa, Pisa, and elsewhere.

The eleventh-century Milanese chronicler Landolfo (Seniore) speaks of living in a house surrounded by the houses of relatives. In the late twelfth century, Siena had "a Tolomei neighborhood" (*contrada Ptolomeorum*), and a document of 1246 mentions "the neighborhood of the sons of the Tolomei." Guinigi Street in Lucca was the street of the Guinigi clan. In Florence the Peruzzi were in social command of the Piazza de' Peruzzi; the Uberti, until wiped out, dominated a zone in the ancient heart of the city; and on the far side of the Arno, about 1300, a family of rich bankers and merchants, the Bardi, engrossed much space along two streets running roughly parallel to the river. At Genoa, in the late twelfth century, the houses of the Doria—descendants of viscounts—circumscribed and dominated the Piazza San Matteo. Here, as in other twelfth-century cities, houses were made of great beams of timber, although the ground floor was usually in stone. Each Genoese neighborhood (*vicinanza* or *contrada*) tended to have a nucleus of towers, loggias, and vaulted structures belonging to the leading local clan or consorterial grouping. Such a cluster invariably had outlets to the sea, where the neighborhood galley was outfitted and armed. Often, too, the neighborhood had its own *piazza* and church for the nobility, open only to members and servitors of the consorterial group.

With their concentration of houses and men, and their unquestioned predominance in their own neighborhoods, the chief clans became the first foci of corporate action. They jelled into bellicose sworn associations and tower societies when danger and the promise of rich new prizes loomed up, especially in the second half of the twelfth century, as the North Italian cities edged toward victory over the empire and released a scramble for power within the commune. The same setting—an urban scatter of physical concentrations of kinsmen—was also decisive for the growth of powerful neighborhood loyalties, a passion which in one form or another survived down to the fifteenth century.

Propertied urban inhabitants were attached tenaciously not merely to a city but to a street, a parish, an ambience—to a radius of perhaps 150 meters. And though a citizen might frequent an estate in the country, he lived in the city and there, if fortunate, he died. More likely than not, he married someone from that vicinage, and all his main blood ties, as well as his closest friendships, were there. The character of a neighborhood could be so distinctive, could leave so deep an imprint on its inhabitants, as to make for different linguistic expressions and even for different intonations or accents. Dante detected neighborhood differences in speech at Bologna.[1]

The regulations and practices of the *consorteria*—the sworn and armed family association—gave it a remarkable hold over individual members. For one thing, the corporate ownership of property meant that the group could impose harsh economic penalties on any member who broke the rules or acted against the interests of the association. It happened that in some cities *consorterie* and tower societies had significant powers of justice, including even capital punishment, over their members. That there was nothing quirky about this is clear when we recall that armed family associations might include the descendants of counts and viscounts, who long claimed effective powers of jurisdiction, as at Pisa and Genoa. Moreover, the incidence of civil war easily made for mortal dangers, and discipline was therefore essential. Just as fathers had immense authority within their family groups, so also the officers—rectors, consuls, or whatnot—of the armed family society were endowed with very considerable authority. Members swore to obey their rectors, to support them against disobedient associates, and to put the interests of the association foremost. Great emphasis was laid on the metaphor of fraternal bonds. A man's ties of loyalty and affection were strongest within the *consorteria*. If for any reason an associate lost his house or was put out of it (unless of course he was at loggerheads with the association), the others had to take him and his family in. The formal compacts governing family associations normally ran without limit of time. Periodically a new set of rectors took office. Having a ready eye for group gain, associations sometimes leased out one of their towers and shared the profits among members. In the thirteenth century, membership in one *consorteria* was no necessary bar to joining another. A nobleman might enter a friendly, neutral, or neighboring family association and thereby help to forge a union between two or more consorterial groups. As family clusters began to look beyond the neighborhood confines, individuals were encouraged to look for affiliations beyond the radius of their home ground.

The mushrooming of armed family societies intensified the struggle for power outside the city and in the commune. They turned neighborhoods into armed zones and delivered the streets to civil war. As one contemporary chronicler said of the Genoese nobility, every nobleman—or rich and aristocratized merchant—wanted to be a consul and have his family at the forefront of communal government. The same was true of noblemen at Milan and Florence, Bologna and Siena, Verona and Pisa.

If around 1180 or 1200 the sentimental and protective world of the nobility lay in the *consorteria*, what of the middle classes and more humble groups in the city? To whom and to what did they look for support and protection? They paid taxes, performed military and guard duties, and in some cases owed other services and labor. Their destinies were tied to the autonomy and policies of the commune, yet they rarely qualified for communal office and its rewards. What happened to them in the different neighborhoods? What was their relation to the sworn associations of noblemen? What part had they in the developing crisis? What impression was made on them by the skyline of formidable towers? These questions touch points of the deepest obscurity in the history of Italian communes. They are broached neither by chroniclers nor by stray records, and they are touched, if at all, only glancingly. But there are the makings of a factual framework.

From the 1150s and 1160s, in city after city, we begin to find a guild of merchants—for example, at Piacenza in 1154, at Milan in 1159, and at Florence before 1182. The élan and exigencies of international trade, as well as the manifest importance for city life of the big moneylenders and merchants, particularly drapers and spicers, enabled these men to build an organization and to become a pressure group within the commune. By about 1180 most of the larger inland cities had one or two merchant guilds, and the elected heads of these, occasionally ex-consuls of the commune, now also began to turn up as governmental advisers and diplomatic agents, representing the city's big commercial interests. They aimed to influence communal policy in the field of large-scale trade and sought to fix the norms that governed commercial practices. We are still, however, dealing with an elite, with traveled men of property and money, skilled in the use of new credit mechanisms. They constituted—the category of jurists apart—the richest, most experienced, and most "reputable" part of the middle classes.

Very little is known about the structure of the earliest merchant guilds, say from 1150 to 1180, except that in the inland cities they took in a large variety of crafts and trades whose practitioners seem to have looked to the big entrepreneurs for leadership. But around 1180 or 1190 the multiplying strains of the urban space began to disturb the parent corporation, with the result that between about 1190 and 1220 the big merchant guilds in each city broke into a medley of guilds, each now much more specialized in its occupational scope. Bankers, merchants engaged in long-distance trade, cloth finishers, jurists and notaries, furriers, physicians and apothecaries, butchers, bakers, and smiths—all went their different organizational ways and collected into separate guilds. Historians have sometimes suggested that guilds grew out of preexisting religious confraternities; the evidence for this is flimsy. Padua and Bologna had certain artisanal guilds which emphasized religious aims and seem on occasion to have opened their ranks to unfree men. But guild membership and servile status were, in general, irreconcilable. This is underlined by thirteenth-century guild statutes, and there is no reason to look for the origins of guilds outside occupational and social necessities or the political pressures of a teeming and threatening urban context. The fierce struggle for power in the late-twelfth-century commune offered cause enough for men to seek each other out in the name of common interest and self-interest. Not that religious feeling was unimportant; on the contrary, the statutes of guildsmen, like the written constitutions of communes or the compacts of *consorterie*, are richly laced with religious expressions and with metaphors that point up the religious vitality of the age. But merchants and craftsmen were pulled together into organized groups less by religious impulse than by the fact of living in cities where skies were darkened by the looming shafts of battlemented towers, where councils rang out in furious division, where tax levies were deeply preoccupying, and where political chieftains made civil war on streets and rooftops. Men created guilds not only to defend themselves but also to find and to define their true spheres of interest.

In 1171 at Verona two rich merchant families, the Monticoli and Crescenzi, got the commune to hold an inquest on the collection and rates of customs imposed at the city gates. Such income was controlled and pocketed by Veronese families descended from counts and onetime powerful attorneys (the Avvocati) of the bishop of Verona. The inquest was meant to put an end to abuses. Hence wealthy merchants could help to further the interests of small tradesmen. But we have noted a divergence of interests in the course of the 1180s and 1190s.

The new direction is seen most strikingly at Milan in 1198, in the startling emergence of the Credenza of St. Ambrose: a militant association of artisans and small retailers, consisting mainly of butchers, bakers, and other food staplers, tanners and leather makers, tailors, smiths, apothecaries, and master craftsmen in the wool industry. They broke decisively with the big merchants and money men, who were now identified with an entrenched oligarchical order. For some years, apparently, artisans and tradesmen at Milan had been drawing secretly together. Then, sometime before 1198, they coalesced into an imposing, determined, and at first clandestine federation, the Credenza of St. Ambrose (Milan's patron saint), for when this society surfaced it was fully organized. Representing a sizable number of small tradesmen, the Credenza successfully claimed a share of the commune's monies and by 1201 had been empowered to elect one of the city's three principal officials.

Milan was precocious. The biggest of the inland cities, it had the largest number of artisans and small manufacturers, and these men found a way, sooner than their equivalents in other cities, to stand up to the big landed and money interests by means of resolute organization. In 1200 none of the busy coastal cities—Venice, Genoa, or Pisa—saw such a convergence of social groups in political opposition. In other cities the serious rupture between small tradesmen and rich, powerful businessmen did not occur until the middle and later thirteenth century, but events at Milan offer us insights into affairs at the level of the neighborhood.

The menacing towers, the armed consorterial groups, and the bloody disputes of the consular nobility introduced terror and lawlessness to the streets of cities, to Genoa no less than to Siena and Florence, Lucca and Bologna, Milan, Cremona, Bergamo, Brescia, Piacenza, and so on. Bands of noblemen lorded it over the neighborhoods. Faction was rampant: nobles— including rich, "ennobled" entrepreneurs and bankers who took to the ways of the armed nobility—fought for control of the supreme political offices. They threw their weight around in streets and public places, their arrogance a function of inherited ways and of their political leadership in the commune. On occasion, to enlarge their ranks, they even brought men into the city from the rural parishes—rustics whose loyalties they commanded. The viscountal families of Genoa, like the Visconti of Milan and Pisa, always retained large estates and myriad contacts in the hinterland. In the city, they often bought or won the services of the poor, the immigrant, or the men with nothing but bluster and fighting skills. When, therefore, the long and venomous struggle broke out between the *popolo* (the "people") and the nobility, the popular movement drew its force and numbers from the middle classes, not from the poor, the day laborers, or the unskilled.

Tradesmen and merchants pressed into guilds in search of ways to stand up to the powerful men of the neighborhoods. When newly born, between about 1190 and 1220, these organizations played down or disguised their strength and aims; thus the total obscurity surrounding their origins. Evidently members sought to avoid arousing suspicions, the danger to life and property being too great. No local *consorteria* of noblemen would permit its control of the neighborhood to be challenged. Mounted knights might be stopped by the running of heavy chains across the city's narrow streets, but they had the fighting skills, the swagger, the devotion to arms, and the instrumental dignity of political leadership. By posting catapults, archers, and crossbowmen on rooftops and towers, they dominated the vicinage.

Guilds, then, were the first form of popular organization. Men in the same crafts and trades had obvious basic interests in common, and they tended, in pursuit of their trades, to gather along a given street or in a particular parish. Accordingly, they looked intuitively to one another, and easily fell into occupational groupings, when danger came and the need for defensive action arose. Guilds were not just casual and friendly occupational organizations, harmless fraternities with religious and recreational aims. They burst upon the scene to satisfy urgent needs. Many turned themselves into armed groups. They sought the control of their craft and product, but the route often lay through politics and some form of violence.

This analysis tells us why the decade which opened the struggle between the nobility and *popolo*, the decade of the 1190s, coincides with the moment when the different craft and trade guilds were springing into existence. The middle classes were headed for a frontal clash with all the dominant groups of the old commune: with the consular nobility, the urbanized feudal magnates, the petty knights turned big by war booty and land speculation, and the big entrepreneurs of shipping and international commerce who had climbed to high places in the commune. At Brescia, in 1196, there was a confrontation between the guilds and the order of knights. A similar clash took place at Piacenza in 1198, and another at Milan during the years 1198 to 1201. Assisi saw violent class and factional disturbances between 1198 and 1202. Padua also experienced the like in 1200, Cremona in 1201, Lucca in 1203, and Siena in 1212. Even little towns, such as Montepulciano in 1229 and Pistoia in 1234, rang with the clangor of the bloody altercations between the middle and upper classes.

The strife which convulsed the neighborhoods was most spectacularly seen in the streets. And although guilds were wrenched into being for economic and political purposes, they failed at first in their aims. They were not sufficiently militant, not tightly enough organized, even when, as in some cases, they were converted into paramilitary units. They could not deal effectively with emergencies, with large-scale calls to violence in the streets. When the alarm was given, members had to assemble and strike quickly, but this could not be smartly done by guilds if some members lived beyond the area of the guild's stronghold or if the stronghold was not near the fracas.

Armed popular societies suddenly bounded into existence in the neighborhoods, designed specifically to deal with street warfare. About 1220 "the association of the people" at Piacenza (the *societas populi*) depended upon armed neighborhood companies, not upon guilds. The armed federation of guilds at Milan, the Credenza of St. Ambrose, was most probably organized by neighborhoods. Cremona gave birth to an armed party of the *popolo* at the end of the twelfth century. At Lucca the *popolo* expelled the nobility from the city in 1203. In 1206 Bergamo's *popolo* had recourse to local armed groupings. Siena's neighborhoods had "people's" armed companies by 1208. At Bologna the popular movement broke through the guild framework and before 1219 had a series of armed neighborhood societies. This pattern, with local variations, was repeated at Perugia, Florence, Siena, and other cities, but it was not seen at Venice, Genoa, and Pisa, the three great seaports.

PODESTARAL GOVERNMENT

The generation between roughly 1190 and 1225 saw the constitutional shake-up of the old consular commune and the emergence of a new executive, the podestà, who held office for short terms. Collegiate government under a group of consuls gave way to a regime with more focused and potent executive functions. The swing from consular to podestaral government was connected, in most of the principal cities, with the advent of the *popolo*. So long as the consular nobility maintained its political monopoly in the city, even when convulsed by internal divisions, it had no reason to seek change or to tamper with the substance of the chief magistracies. But when the city was paralyzed by hopeless division, certain members and families of the consular ruling class were willing to experiment with new forms, all the more so on finding that they could count on the support of the new men in government and on the popular feeling then billowing up in the neighborhoods. Some no doubt believed that they would be able to turn the rising force of the *popolo* to their own factional or oligarchic ends; but others certainly hoped that the podestà would stand above faction and administer impartial government. A large part of the nobility resisted the shift to podestaral government, until the new course of events seemed inescapable. Then all resistance collapsed and the podestà carried the day.

The podestà eventually betrayed the expectation that he would stand above rival family blocs, above other social rivalries, and administer government impartially. For a few years, however, he seemed to incarnate the promise of detached and fairer government. If the consular nobility had inflicted deeply divisive wounds on the commune, then he, it was thought, would heal them. In fact, the emergence of the podestà represented a new stage in the commune's growth: he signaled the crucial need for a united authority, a need imposed by the richer and more contradictory social forces inside the city and by the escalating dangers outside, where wars with other communes and with encircling feudatories cried out for more stability and unity at home.

The authority of the podestà varied from city to city, but a general profile will serve best here. During the first decades of podestaral government, the podestà was usually elected for a term of one or two years, later more often for one year, then for six months. Some of the first podestàs were leading local men, but this passed. The chief qualifications required that he be a nobleman from another province, practiced in arms or in law, and experienced in public life. Chosen by an *ad hoc* electoral commission or by a selection of the leading communal officials, he might be subject to the approval of the commune's legislative council.

At Mantua, around 1200, the powers of the podestà were largely judicial. Two bishops of Mantua served as podestàs, but this was unusual, especially as the podestà would finally put an end to the bishop's continuing and disproportionate political authority. Almost everywhere the podestà wielded more extensive administrative and executive powers than at Mantua. He represented the commune in its foreign relations; he presided in the communal councils; he often had the power to issue short-term ordinances; he handled many of the important daily affairs of government; he was likely to have to lead the communal army in times of war; he was responsible for keeping civil disorder in check; and he had a voice in all or most of the commune's major decisions. But one of his most distinctive functions was to dole justice out; his office and corps of assistants were charged with adjudication of the major share of criminal and civil proceedings.

About 1205 the office was so authoritative at Milan, as in some other cities, that when the conflicting blocs were unable to agree on one podestà, they sometimes appointed three or even five, thus giving individual representation to the forces in conflict.

It was rare for the podestà to hold office concurrently with a team of consuls. For twenty or thirty years after his first appearance (ca. 1190) podestà and consuls alternated, as groups inside the city did battle. A generation was to pass before the podestà finally triumphed. Genoa provides a pattern.

There the first podestà (1191), Manegoldo di Tettocio, came from the Guelf city of Brescia. The consulate returned to office in 1192–1193, and for some years the two magistracies alternated. At the end of a given term the outgoing officials—consulate or podestà and his advisers—would decide on the executive form for the following year. The Genoese podestà was closely surrounded and assisted by the college of men who administered justice in the city, the *consoli dei placiti*. He did not yet dispose of the commune's judicial authority. In 1201 the office was held by a nobleman from Lucca and he died in office, whereupon government passed to a consulate made up entirely of old consular nobility. One of their number, Guglielmo Embriaco, was made the presiding head or "prior." In 1205 the podestà was a native Genoese, the only one in the city's history: Folco di Castello, a great leader and adventurer, seaman, pirate, and of course a nobleman. He was chosen by the oligarchy, it seems, so as to get the commune to legitimize the activities of Genoese merchants and pirates in and around Sicily and the Levant. Consular and podestaral regimes succeeded each other until 1212. For the next four years, government was put entirely in the hands of consuls, all noblemen born into consular families: the Spinola, Doria, Embriaci, Della Volta, Castello, De Mari, Avvocati, Guercio, Pevere, and others. In 1217, however, the commune returned definitively to podestaral government.

If the podestà was a relatively weak figure at Mantua, this was not so in most other cities. But his authority was never absolute; between about 1220 and 1270, the classical age of the podestà, he was not a dictator, or not normally so. Jealous of its prerogatives and rightly suspicious, the commune put checks on him. He came in from outside the city with his own staff—knights, judges, notaries, clerks, and police; but he was attended in all political matters by a formal body or two of indigenous advisers, all eminent members of the commune with considerable experience in public life. In some cities, the podestà's "council of wise men" was elected; in others, it was simply one of the standing councils of government. The podestà could make no important political decision without the approval of, or at least some consultation with, his advisers. He was supposed to unseal foreign correspondence only in their presence. Without their support he could not normally introduce proposals to the communal legislative assembly. He and his foreign staff swore fidelity to the commune and its constitution; they swore to abide by its laws; and on leaving office they were subjected to a formal inquiry, conducted by a communal commission specifically appointed for that purpose.

The organization of the podestaral commune was far from simple. Owing to the twelfth-century boom in population and the economy, the consular commune was faced with so many new problems and interests that it was forced to establish new offices and to extend its public functions. These were fully taken over by the podestaral commune in its prime. The major constitutional addition was, as we have seen, a legislative council which in effect replaced the old assembly (*arengo*) of the whole commune. It numbered between 150 and 400 men, depending upon the city. They served in office for terms of a year. But as this council tended to double in size during the thirteenth century, it came to be called "the great council." Henceforth, too, it became the commune's most important forum for the expression of broad communal feeling, especially because it included "new men" in small but increasing numbers—the voices of the vigorous merchant community whose crucial importance could no longer be played with or played down.

The commune had an elaborate array of other offices and functions: there was a citizen militia, treasury officials, notarial and secretarial offices, officials in charge of communal properties and profitable rights, special nocturnal police, heralds and messengers, customs supervisors at city gates, commissions on the compilation of statutes, *ad hoc* commissions of inquiry, guilds formally connected with the commune, and a variety of magistrates ranged partly under the podestà and partly not.

Italian historians have often called the communal age "an age of crisis." The description is loose but suggestive. In every major commune the magnitude and persistence of social discord had all the appearance of a grave crisis. Born in conflict, the podestaral regime was challenged from the day of its birth. First an important sector of the consular oligarchy lined up against it. Later, the nobility made an "instinctive" effort to take it over. How could the illustrious and prepotent families keep from trying to turn the podestà into their own creature? The result was, as at Vicenza and Cremona, that to one podestà another was added, or even another two or three, as happened at Milan, thus dramatizing the commune's violent schisms. Then parts of the community swung over to the view that the podestà had become the captive of one class or faction and profound resentment swelled up against communal leaders, frequently issuing in rebellion and civil war.

CHAPTER IV

POPOLO AND
POPULAR COMMUNE

THE DIVISIVE ISSUES

Historians sum up the blistering controversies of the thirteenth-century commune by referring to the conflict between "the people" and "the nobility" (*popolo* and *nobiltà*) or between "knights" and "foot soldiers" (*milites* and *pedites*). Nobility and knights tend to be seen as one and the same class, so also *popolo* and foot soldiers. The age itself donated the terminology: the words *populus, populares, pedites, minores, milites, nobiles,* and *maiores* were widely used by contemporaries. For centuries these suggested the conflict of social classes in the thirteenth-century setting. Since the 1920s, however, the dominant tendency has been to de-emphasize class and class interpretations in Italian communal history; and this fashion, in the period after World War II, was reinforced by the ideological effects of the Cold War.

Academic historians have rested their case against class interpretations on two arguments. First, in all communes troubled by the extremes of civil discord, there were noblemen who joined the *popolo* and often captained the popular movement. At the same time, the ranks of the knights and noblemen usually included *populares*, men who had neither the possessions nor the ways, neither the heritage nor the blood, of noblemen. Second, the nobility was an "open" and changing class, stubbornly difficult to define. Hence, how can an interpretation be run along class lines, when any such lines were exceedingly vague?

The supposed materialists—e.g., R. Davidsohn, R. Caggese, G. Salvemini—were perfectly aware of the well-known fact that individuals and family groups crossed class lines in their political behavior, and their accounts bring out the role of noblemen in the movement of the *popolo*. The rigidity of the supposed materialists is an invention of their detractors. But if it is true, then, that the nobility was not a closed caste, it is also true that contemporaries did take it to be a distinct social order. After about 1260 or 1270,

45

increasing numbers of rich *populares* associated themselves with the nobility and came to be seen as noblemen in their own right because of their wealth, public distinctions, connections, and bearing. Many even took to mounted combat and attained the dignity of knighthood. Evidently, therefore, a "noble" class *was* discernible: a class associated with a way of life, a cluster of interests, and a broad set of policies.

The effect of the revisionist efforts to eliminate considerations of class has been to slur over the existence of fundamental divisions in the commune, to dissolve hard issues into mere "politics" and "politicking," or to reduce grievous political stresses to psychological ones by emphasizing ambitions, jealousies, and family feuds.

Italian communal society fostered a reverence for status, bloodlines, and public honors. This persisted even at the height of the *popolo*'s political movement. Guildsmen fought and bloodied noblemen but were much impressed by their towers, experience, family connections, horses, style, and imposing properties. Understandably, then, the *popolo*—a completely new force in European history, with no political traditions of its own—accepted the leadership and military service of men born to illustrious families. There is every reason to believe that whatever noblemen hoped to gain from this association, the *popolo* also expected to advance its claims along a wide political front.

The question of how it happened that individual noblemen entered the ranks of the *popolo* is both political and psychological, but in these matters psychology obscures the historical problem and clouds sociopolitical analysis. We shall never know, and we need not know, precisely what impelled a scatter of noblemen, whether at Verona, Milan, or Siena, to array themselves with the *popolo*—although if we cannot *precisely* know in individual cases, the historical applicability of individual psychology loses its point. Bitter resentment against those at the head of the nobility, feuds between families, failure to obtain an honor here or a sinecure there, grinding ambition, or other motives fished up from the murk of individual psychology: all these moved men to abandon one side for another, but they are matters to indulge clinicians and to flummox historians. For once a nobleman joined the *popolo*, he had to take up its political claims and perhaps betray the aims of those who once had held his loyalties. Yet by serving or leading the *popolo* he reaped a host of private satisfactions: a new prominence, pride of leadership, public office won, new sources of income, new excitements, obscure revenges, and the power to dole out patronage. The reverse phenomenon, the presence of *populares* and plebeians on the side of the nobility, is no more difficult to explain. Rich merchants sometimes cultivated mounted combat, hobnobbed with knights from the consular nobility, married noblewomen, and thus found fulfillment. Poorer men, from rustics and tradesmen to servants and adventurers, could also find contentment in devoting or selling their services to noblemen.

While noting the mysteries of individual psychology, we dare not lose sight of the great issues that divided the commune. The nobility enjoyed remarkable privileges and a near-monopoly of political power. Now it was challenged by an order of resolute men. Politics became violent beyond faction: street brawls were turned into civil war.

First among the *popolo*'s demands was the call for direct representation in the commune's political councils. Before the emergence of the *popolo* a trickle of new men had entered into the legislative council and occasionally into the consulate or the podestà's body of advisers. But there was no necessary cooperation among them; they were not expected to speak for a middle class. New men and *popolo* spoke with one voice after 1200, when the popular movements got under way.

Until the *popolo* arrived on the scene, full-fledged membership in the commune was exceedingly restricted. In any given city all resident adults—the clergy and their "familiars" excluded—were subject to the commune: they paid taxes, the men served it militarily, they were under its laws and law courts. But this did not signify active citizenship. Fullness of citizenship depended on property qualifications, years of residence, and social connections. These gave the fundamental right to hold public office and to enter the commune's political councils. Only a tiny fraction of the male population enjoyed this right just before the year 1200. In the smaller cities—e.g., Crema, Arezzo, Pistoia—this meant an active citizenship of perhaps several hundred men. In the largest cities, such as Milan, Genoa, and Florence, the numbers rose to probably 800 or 1,000 men.

In the 1190s the "simple citizens" of Milan were the main source of communal revenues, yet they were entitled to only one-fifth of the places in the consulate. In 1198 the fully organized *popolo* suddenly broke in upon the Milanese scene, as the commune passed fitfully over to podestaral rule, and for the next fourteen years Milan had alternating periods of civil war and deeply divided government. With the intervention of the Emperor Otto IV, a major settlement was agreed upon in 1212; and from this time on, half of all the offices of the commune were to go to the *popolo*, the other half to the nobility. The corresponding change at Mantua in 1204 was less dramatic, but henceforth the different guilds and the association of merchants had an allotment of places in the legislative council. At Cremona in 1210 the *popolo* won one-third of the commune's sum of political offices. Here the papal legate, Sicardo, who had acted as the intermediary between the hostile camps, called "a public assembly by trumpet and bells" and announced: "I declare and direct that the *popolo* of the entire city of Cremona have . . . one-third of all the offices and honors." Similar events took place at Vicenza in 1215 and 1222: the *popolo* demanded and got one-third of the seats in the different offices and councils. The following list confirms the striking pattern of the *popolo*'s advance nearly everywhere.

1. Lucca, 1197–1203. The priors of the popular neighborhood societies

—and there were twelve before *1211*—made their formal appearance as consultants to the podestà. Suppressed in about 1217, the *popolo* suddenly returned to government in 1229.

2. Piacenza, 1222. The *popolo* and its supporters among the order of knights got one-half the number of places in government.

3. Lodi, 1224. The heads of the guilds and popular societies gained entry to the large legislative council.

4. Verona, 1227. Previously restricted to knights, communal offices were now made available to rich bourgeois: men with assets of 1,000 pounds (*lire*) or more and with a horse and arms.

5. Bologna, 1228–1231. A takeover by the *popolo*. The collectivity of guilds and armed societies of the *popolo* elected the body of "elders" (*anziani*), the commune's supreme executive magistracy.

6. Modena, 1229. The consuls of the *popolo* and rectors of the guilds secured seats in the communal legislative council, but they were still excluded from the executive magistracies and the oligarchical Council of One Hundred. The "elders" of the unified popular organization were not taken into the top level of government until 1250.

7. Bergamo, 1230. The *popolo* won representation in the councils.

8. Siena, 1233. The *popolo* got representatives from its own magistracy, the "Twenty-four," into government and from 1257 controlled half the seats in the councils and other offices.

9. Pistoia, 1237. The *popolo*, coordinating guild and neighborhood organization, effected a temporary seizure of power.

10. Parma, 1244. The *Annales Parmenses maiores* say: "And whatever the *popolo* wanted it fully got." Having used force, guild heads and the chiefs of the *popolo* obtained the right for the first time to vote in elections for communal office.

11. Florence, 1244. Thoroughly organized by this year, the *popolo* bounded into power in 1250.

12. Genoa, 1257. Under the captaincy of Guglielmo Boccanegra, the *popolo*—here meaning the lower middle class of artisans and petty tradesmen—finally won a voice in government through the presence of its guild representatives in the communal councils.

Class lines were readily obscured by the spectacle and ardor of faction. The document recording the *popolo*'s advance at Piacenza (item 2 above) makes clear that half the offices were to go to "the *popolo* of Piacenza and to the knights who serve it," while the other half were for "the knights of Piacenza and those from the *popolo* who serve the knights."[1] There could be no crisper statement of faction: nobility and *popolo* at Piacenza were each divided. In fact, however, the *popolo* was much more fully arrayed on one side, the nobility on the other. *Populares* now obtained a large bloc of places in the councils, and many new men entered public life for the first time. Moreover, a divided *popolo* was capable of healing its schisms. Something like this happened at Perugia. Here, in 1223, the *popolo* was so badly split that even the craft guilds were at loggerheads, a few having made common cause with the nobility for reasons unknown to us. But they had closed ranks by 1250, when they took the leadership of the *popolo* in hand and imposed a popular constitution with a strong guild base.

The *popolo*'s breakthrough into politics was the result of revolutionary organization. Whenever possible, therefore, the nobility sought to overwhelm the *popolo* and outlaw its neighborhood associations, on occasion outlawing even guilds.

Next to the demand for political office, fiscal grievances headed the list of the *popolo*'s complaints. Though every city had its special problems and issues were often obfuscated by the tactics of faction and the hokum of rival families, the incidence of fiscal privileges persistently engaged and divided the nobility and *popolo*. As early as the 1150s, Genoa had groups of rich consular families which lent large sums of money to the commune at high rates of interest. Becoming habit, this provoked explosive resentment in the thirteenth century. In the 1190s Milan was gripped by controversy over the high interest rates paid out to wealthy communal creditors; but a much angrier furor surrounded the *fodro*, a communal tax on real property which the nobility, adducing imperial privileges, staunchly refused to pay. Led by the tradesmen of the Credenza of St. Ambrose, the *popolo* took up the cry for payment and the city verged on civil war between about 1215 and 1225.

The upsurge of the *popolo* at Siena was especially linked to the question of equity in taxation. Arguing in 1257 that "the rich and powerful men" had "never" been justly taxed, the *popolo* demanded a voice in the distribution of the *libra*, a direct Sienese tax based upon an estimate of both real and movable property.

At Florence in 1218 the budding *popolo*, working through the guilds, was already pressing for tax reforms, first by striving to catch the country nobility and rural knights in the commune's tax nets. Such men often escaped the payment of taxes by flashing privileges obtained from the old consular commune, sometimes granted to hold their loyalty. But the popular voice could not be stilled, and in 1224, in a remarkable stroke, a twelve-man commission was appointed to inquire into the fiscal administration of the previous twenty-two years. Malfeasance in office and rural tax evasion were to be the particular targets of the commission. All officials who had administered public monies were to be reviewed, including castellans and auditors. Approval for the commission had been obtained only after an *ad hoc* group of 120 voting members, selected in blocs of twenty from among the *popolo* in each sixth (*sestiere*) of the city, had been seated in the communal legislative council. The mandate of the commission included an order to ferret out the variety of communal rights and properties—e.g., the use of city squares and the valuable remains of the old and bypassed city walls—that had strangely ended in private hands. Members of the nobility and knighthood were excluded from the commission—not by chance, for hitherto the levying of direct taxes (*dazi*) had been done by a body of knights, "who even took a certain cut of the intake!"[2]

The popular outcry against class taxation and the malversation of public funds was heard in many communes. Abuses were corrected, but some of the major problems were never solved. In the later thirteenth century, the leaders of the *popolo* continually backtracked on the old gains and demands. And yet the emergence of the *popolo* was connected partly with profound discontent over the collection and administration of public monies. In a few cities, preeminently so at Milan, the popular program urged the freer right of access to richly endowed church dignities. First among these were the cathedral canonries, which tradition earmarked for the nobility. The Milanese *popolo* turned this matter into a burning issue, in part because the archbishop and upper clergy, recruited from among the noble families, passionately supported the nobility in its struggle against the *popolo*.

Another major issue concerned the crimes of noblemen, notably physical violence and murder. A murder in 1257 provoked a popular uprising at Milan and led to the expulsion of the nobility from the city. Too often, when the victim was a commoner (*popolano*), the accused nobleman got away scot-free or with a light fine. The consular and podestaral communes were partisan: there was indulgence for noblemen in the application of the law. But this changed in the second half of the thirteenth century, when the *popolo* brought in severe penalties against the crimes of noblemen, especially when committed against *popolani*.

The condition of the communal courts, their bias and maladministration, also made for strong dissatisfactions. Conflicting jurisdictions abounded, and there were irregularities in court proceeds from fines, with the result that guilds staked out their own spheres of judicial competence, whenever they were able, in affairs that directly concerned their members and trade interests.

In sum, the *popolo* sought a place in the political councils in order to influence policies and work change. A feudal commune in many ways, the consular commune had sanctioned and defended the concrete rights of exalted privilege. And the podestaral commune, without the *popolo*, did little to alter these arrangements. At Genoa, Lucca, Milan, and other cities, leading families retained fiscal claims over particular trades and minor guilds down to the later thirteenth century: they collected certain yearly fees. Here and there a percentage of maritime customs or of duties at city gates went into the purses of archbishops, viscountal families, or particular *consorterie*. Only in the late twelfth century did guild representatives begin to have some voice in the kinds of duties to be levied upon imports of food staples, precious goods, and textiles. Then the *popolo*'s triumphant advance reshuffled priorities and put such assessments more in line with the interests of the collectivity of guilds.

The furor over public monies and over lucrative communal rights is better understood in the context of an economic inflation which threatened noblemen, or at least those among them who saw their estates being whittled away. Piracy, profitable public office, exploitative investment in the public debt, and war loot saved and maintained many a nobleman. These were the knight's reply, so to speak, to the sources of dramatic profit (long-distance trade and usury) tapped by the order of rich merchants and merchant bankers. The frantic quest for additional income toughened the armed resistance of the nobility when its ancient privileges were made the target of revolutionary attack in the early thirteenth century. Appropriately enough, this century brought the rather spectacular rise of mercenary armies, a sanctuary for hungry noblemen and scheming political exiles cut off from their sources of income. When the archbishop of Milan, Ottone Visconti, reentered the city in 1277, at the head of a victorious army of noblemen and auxiliaries, having overwhelmed the popular faction, two of his first actions underlined the nobility's needs and fears: he returned cathedral canonries to the exclusive right of noblemen, and he took all the best-paid dignities in the lands under Milanese rule, such as governorships and castellanies, and turned these also over to them.

POPULAR ORGANIZATION

By 1190, craftsmen and small retailers were discontented with the one or two big comprehensive associations of tradesmen, whose aims best served the rich and respected merchants. Yet the uncertainties and physical dangers of the urban space imposed, as we have seen, a search for protection in the resources of organized groups. This search broke forth into a welter of group interests, issuing in eight, ten, twelve, or a score and more of different guilds. Guild organization, however, was not fit to stand up to the emerging armed struggle with the nobility, even when guilds were turned into paramilitary organizations. Their discipline and training fell short; and their militancy could be misdirected because they lacked, with exceptions in a few cities, a supra-guild organization: a collective leadership that could rise above the different neighborhoods and craft interests to convert the needs of the whole trade community into a focused political force. Between 1200 and 1260, this is exactly what the *popolo* achieved in its armed neighborhood companies. Bologna, for example, was to boast of twenty-four such companies; Modena also had twenty-four, and Florence twenty.

At Milan, exceptionally, with its Credenza of St. Ambrose, the *popolo* achieved organizational unity at once. Bologna was also exceptional; there too the neighborhood companies were swiftly linked. This ordinarily took some time, for certain neighborhoods (*vicinanze* or *contrade*) were much more advanced politically than others.

The organization of the armed societies or companies varied from city to city. Their membership was drawn mainly from the ranks of guildsmen. Some companies modeled themselves partly upon guilds. Now and then a guild was permitted—e.g., the butchers at Bologna—to constitute itself into an armed society inside the *popolo*. More often, the old neighborhood militias, originally intended to serve the commune, were the matrix for the organization of the popular societies or companies. At Bologna the societies overlapped topographically, some taking in several parishes, others being more strictly confined to certain streets. They were voluntary associations, based upon personal ties, friendships, and local needs. At first, indeed, their ranks at Bologna included a sprinkling of disaffected noblemen. This was also seen in other cities. But apart from the captaincy, they were not allowed to hold offices within the formal leadership of the unified *popolo*. Later, as the social struggles climaxed, the popular ranks eliminated many of their noble members, and all were purged, even at Bologna, when the *popolo* introduced its fierce laws against the nobility in the 1280s.

The organization of the armed societies at Florence more or less paralleled arrangements in other cities with a militant *popolo*, such as Bologna, Cremona, Piacenza, Siena, Modena, Lucca, Perugia, and perhaps Milan. In the 1250s the topographical distribution of the Florentine companies followed that of the commune's quondam citizen militia, although the new companies often included men from more than one parish, as at Bologna. With the liquidation of the old association of Florentine knights, the twenty new companies absorbed the remnants of the moribund militia. Florence had six administrative districts, but the two where the *popolo* was weakest—the ancient heart of the city (Piazza della Signoria to the cathedral) and the far side of the River Arno—were each assigned four companies, while the remaining four districts had three each. Every company had its distinctive banner and every house in the city was administratively under the sign of a company. A dragon, a whip, a serpent, a bull, a bounding horse, a lion, a ladder: these, in different colors and on contrasting fields, were some of the leitmotifs of the twenty different banners. They were emblazoned on individual shields and helmets. Rigorous regulations required guildsmen to keep their arms near at hand, above all in troubled times. The call to arms for the twenty companies was the ringing of a special bell, posted near the main public square. A standard-bearer, flanked by four lieutenants, was in command of each company. These men were elected by a council of twenty-four members of the company and served one year. The Captain of the People was the commander of the twenty companies. Being an outsider, he was expected to stand above the temptations of local partisanship. His oath of office obligated him to call the companies to action whenever there was a threat to the *popolo*.

In the 1290s, recruitment for the rural militia around Siena was highly selective. Prospective members were carefully screened; only proven supporters of the regime were recruited, and even greater solicitude went into the selection of squad and company commanders. No lesser care went into recruitment for the armed companies of the *popolo* in the cities, particularly between 1240 and 1290, when the struggle against the nobility reached its most emotional levels. To maintain control over the inhabitants, the administrative districts of the different cities—thirds, quarters, sixths—were divided according to parishes, and these, in turn, were subdivided into neighborhoods (*contrade* or *vicinanze*) and finally houses. When specifying an individual's address, court orders stipulated the house (by family name or patronymic), the neighborhood, the parish church, and the larger district. In addition, the organized *popolo* had a districting by armed company. But formal information regarding individuals and families was customarily obtainable from small local bodies made up of neighborhood "heads" or "elders."

There was one other way of pinpointing people, and this was by trade: wool merchant, furrier, pork butcher, saddler, notary, construction worker, etc. Guilds were in the best position to provide character references. When a craft was barred by law from having an organized membership (e.g., weaving or dyeing), the *popolo* could turn for information to the allied governing guild (e.g., of wool merchants), which subsumed and controlled a variety of manual trades. The merchants of the controlling guild were likely to be well acquainted with the craftsmen or workers in the trade. The system fostered paternalism; it gave a constitutional advantage to the guild masters in their surveillance of a lower class, and the guild oligarchy afterward utilized this resource to retain its political supremacy and to keep the mass of hired journeymen and workers in place. Individuals and families were inevitably known in the close streets and neighborhoods. Their political inclinations, like the rancors and prides of their private lives, could not escape the knowledge of neighbors. The *popolo* had no trouble finding only the most committed and reliable men for its armed companies. The success of this was seen in moments of crisis, when the ardor of the companies won many a victory for the *popolo*.

In a famous scene from the *Paradiso* (XV, 97–135), Dante introduces a celebrated Florentine nobleman who recalls with melancholy the old heart of the city of Florence, girded by a now-demolished first circle of walls, within which most of the ancient and "gentle" families had resided. The scene is built upon the perception of a bygone reality. For the oldest parts of cities had included the houses of the illustrious lineages, family seats that went back to the period between about 1040 and 1180. And even when destroyed by fire, they were rebuilt, passing gradually from timber to stone. Then, as the city spilled beyond its original site, the "new men" and poor immigrants took lodgings or built houses in the suburbs that were soon to engulf the old city. Churches and religious houses put blocs of building lots out for lease, then for sale. Speculation was rife. And it was often there, in the so-called "new city"—as at Cremona, Brescia, and Lucca—that the *popolo* had its most militant constituencies. In 1250, when the Florentine *popolo* snatched power from the nobility, the popular leaders quickly removed their headquarters from the church of San Firenze—located in the old city and too near the towers of the fierce Uberti clan—to the church of Santa Croce, the Franciscan stronghold. There, just outside the new walls, the *popolo*'s vanguard could count upon the military and emotional support of the suburbs and of the neighborhoods lying just inside the city walls. At Brescia the upper part of the city was a later addition inhabited by newcomers; the lower part was the stronghold of the knights. Upper and lower city fought in 1220. Cremona had civil war between the "new" and the "old" city in 1211. Here, one of the organized neighborhoods of the old city (the *vicinia* of San Pantaleon) had so many resident *populares* that it joined forces with the new city and was later sacked by the nobility. At Lucca the earliest popular stronghold (1197–1203) also lay just outside the old city walls, in the parish of San Pier Maggiore.

From the moment of its taking power the *popolo* enjoyed a sophisticated organization. Its finished constitution was often modeled along the line of the podestaral commune itself. With their functions and literary-legal preparation, notaries were key figures in the drafting of constitutions and in the written work connected with all major organizations in the city. Knightly associations, guilds, confraternities, and of course the commune— all relied upon notaries. The commune had a team of them, drawing up statutes, guild constitutions, treaties, contracts, letters, copies of documents, circulars, and memoranda. Trained in Latin, in contract formularies, and in the rudiments of public law, the notary easily provided formulas and schemes for corporate bodies. But he was also a passive instrument: a perfect voice for the articulation of the dominant legal and organizational norms. The *popolo* did not have to be told how to constitute itself along communal lines. Years of struggling against the commune and against the nobility had taught it how to appoint and reappoint its internal organization. The armed companies were the *popolo*'s military embodiment, but policy came out of its deliberative councils and large legislative assembly, the Council of the People, which counterbalanced the communal legislative assembly. At the head of the *popolo* was a strong executive council, usually consisting of eight, nine, or twelve men, known in some cities as *anziani* (elders). This magistracy was charged with the daily direction of affairs until the crises of the mid-thirteenth century, when a new dignity was tempestuously created, the office of Captain of the People. A foil for the podestà, he was meant to focus the will and energies of the *popolo*. Henceforth the *anziani* gathered around him and became his formal body of advisers.

The *popolo* also had a court, which was presided over by the captain, staffed with judges and notaries, and competent in all matters touching the rights of the *popolo*. This court came instantly into conflict with the court of the podestà or with other communal courts, and the experience was frequently calamitous for the podestà.

A treasury, fiscal officials, varieties of notaries, heralds, and even arrangements for the dispatch of diplomatic envoys: these completed the organization of the *popolo*. Historians thus speak of "the commune of the *popolo*" even when it suffered defeat or was barely discernible as a body in opposition. In some respects it had seceded from the podestaral or major commune: new loyalties and new organization had made for two separate communities within the one urban space. At Siena in the 1250s the *popolo*'s imitation of the commune went so far as to include detailed electoral procedures.

The appearance of the captain in the history of the *popolo* marks its high point and culmination. And whatever the demagogic dangers posed by the captain, as alleged by modern historians of both conservative and liberal stripe, he enabled the *popolo* to strike with overpowering speed. As its unique head in moments of grave danger, the captain was more likely than a collegiate body to have quickness, ardor, flash, color, and an emotional following, especially as pageantry and symbolism were exceedingly important. This was more a visual than a literate society.

DISCIPLINE AND TAKEOVER

Violence was the *popolo*'s prime means of taking power. In 1200 the families at the fore of the commune could not or would not respond to the popular call for change, and above all to the request that political office be opened to men who had not previously appeared in the councils of government. No precedent gave warrant for awarding a political voice to a more representative portion of the urban community. Deeply ingrained notions of hierarchy, rank, and privilege provided the emotional and intellectual scaffolding for the then dominant view of the world. Those who thought about these matters assumed that authority and law issued down from the top of the social hierarchy, while obedience was due from below, in replica of the "natural" order of things, according to presuppositions regarding natural and divine law. But realities could flash forth and overturn the natural order.

And so they did. Just as in 1100, municipal noblemen, working through their commune, pushed forward to take power away from bishops or empire, so also in the decades after 1200 the *popolo*, becoming ever more able and numerous, confronted the aristocratic commune, grasped piecemeal for its authority, or took it over altogether by throwing armed men into the fray.

The *popolo*'s breakthrough into government pivoted on discipline in organization. Exceptions to this were rare. At Vicenza the *popolo*'s arrival on the scene seems almost haphazard. In 1206 two great rivals, leaders of Vicenza's principal families (counts on one side and former episcopal attorneys on the other), used arms to bully the legislative council into making them podestàs of the city. The two then fell into violent disagreement and precipitously abandoned the government palace, whereupon a force of *populares* rushed in, occupied the building, bypassed the legislature, and elected a new podestà, an outsider from Milan. These events, producing the first trace of an identifiable *popolo* in Vicenza, served to draw the *populares* together. They organized a "fictitious commune" (so called by the chronicler Maurisio) and in 1215 forced the government to allot one-third of all communal offices to them. For more than ten years thereafter, they maintained continual pressure on the commune and drew keen support from energetic foreign podestàs, who relied on the *popolo* to help keep the turbulent nobility at bay. But in the late 1220s violent discord erupted with such force among the rival noble blocs that the commune of the *popolo*, caught somehow in the middle, was swept away, not to be heard from again. Vicenza's commercial and industrial community was not populous enough to withstand the cyclonic force and ambitions of the mighty consorterial associations in and around Vicenza. That whole region—but especially the counties of Treviso, Vicenza, and even Padua—was a thick network of feudal enclaves. Milan aside, popular movements had more likelihood of success in the economic and social conditions farther south, particularly in Tuscany.

The *popolo* at Siena reorganized its armed companies between 1208 and 1226, but the first critical clash with the nobility was probably that recorded in 1233. Thereafter the council of the twenty-four heads of the *popolo* often participated in important governmental consultations. The capital act of violence came twenty years later, with the revolutionary establishment of a captain of the *popolo*. Resorting to intimidation and sly encroachment, the *popolo* hammered insistently at the old commune, chipping away the powers of the podestà. In 1257 it claimed and took half of all the communal offices in a flurry of aggressive self-assertion that carried the movement to its peak in the 1260s. Much of the Sienese *popolo*'s success must be credited to a flair for compact and disciplined organization. Its representatives in the communal councils were expected to vote as a bloc, on pain of heavy penalties.

The popular ranks at Bologna were also bound by a tough discipline. There the early *popolo* was captained by the big merchants and moneychangers. Bolognese guilds and armed popular companies were fully organized by 1218. An aristocratic reaction in 1219–1220 eliminated their political representation and dissolved the companies, a temporary reversal of the sort seen in a dozen other cities. But in November 1228, fast on the heels of the nobility's disastrous failure in a campaign against Modena, the guilds took up arms and stormed the government palace by night. They were led by a rich merchant and son of a judge, Gioseffo Toschi, a bold and experienced man. The armed crowd around Toschi was composed of modest guildsmen, rich bourgeois, and a smattering of knights—a union that proved too much for the oligarchical nobility. The commune passed into the hands of the *popolo* and a magistracy of "elders." Many of the illustrious old names disappeared from the political rolls. Decisive power swung over to the richest and most experienced part of the bourgeoisie, flanked by a fraction of the nobility. In the next two decades this regime provided fierce military opposition to the imperial armies of Frederick II, making Bologna one of the truly outstanding communes of the Second Lombard League.

In the course of the 1250s the Bolognese *popolo* underwent an important change. The butchers and the guilds of other substantial tradesmen gained seats in the ruling council (*anziani*). Notaries and jurists became more and more influential, no surprising trend in view of the fact that Bologna had a formidable body of jurists and professors with considerable experience in public affairs.

Foremost among the file of new leaders at Bologna was Rolandino Passageri, then a young professor of notarial science. He and others led the *popolo* in a struggle which had to be fought increasingly on two sides. On the one side—though Rolandino was not yet involved at this stage—there was an accelerating campaign against serfdom, launched in 1256–1257. This campaign aimed not only to undermine the feudal-rural base of the nobility but also to bring the unfree folk of the surrounding region under the fiscal control of the *popolo*, for serfs, as personal property, were not liable for communal taxes and labor services. On the other side, the *popolo* faced the menacing swell of a new enemy: hired labor and petty tradesmen of the sort denied the right to form guilds and barred from the *popolo*'s political councils. Deeply discontented, this populace was infiltrated by the Lambertazzi, alleged Ghibelline nobles who hoped to use the numbers and emotional force of Bologna's laboring poor to crack the *popolo*'s political bulwark. In reaction, the *popolani* leaders organized an elite company, the Society of the Cross (theirs was a sacred enterprise), to bolster the twenty armed companies of the neighborhoods. In 1274, captained by Rolandino, these units drove the Ghibelline nobility from the city. Along with the fleeing nobility went large numbers of humble folk who—unrepresented in the *popolo* and hailing from the poorer and wretched parts of the populace—had joined forces with the Ghibellines. The victorious *popolo* then turned to confront serious dissension in its own ranks, which still included a noble faction, Guelf noblemen known as the Geremei. Sharing in the *popolo*'s victory, the Geremei demanded the repeal of the anti-magnate laws, enacted against the unruly part of the nobility in 1272. Refused, the Geremei waited for a moment of critical military difficulty and then suddenly abandoned the communal army in the field. The laws against magnates were fashioned to curb the political influence of the nobility, to reduce urban violence, and to strike down noblemen who made physical assaults on *popolani* (members of the *popolo*). They were not repealed until 1280, when a papal legate succeeded in placating the *popolo*. Two years later, however, the *popolo* restored the draconian measures and laid on still more crippling penalties. Referring to magnates as "wolves" and to *popolani* as "lambs," the ordinances required all shops and law courts to be shut whenever the authorities failed to impose the due penalties on transgressors. Moreover, on pain of having their houses and towers destroyed and their goods confiscated, the heads of all magnate households were ordered to post a bond of 1,000 pounds each in guarantee of their good behavior, to tender a kind of blind obedience to the podestà and Captain of the People, and to swear to be personally responsible for political crimes—such as assaulting a *popolano*—committed by members of their families. In 1284 yet another set of measures was unleashed against the recalcitrant nobility.

Florence also was deeply riven from the 1240s onward, and there again the discipline of the *popolo* was decisive. After a first breakthrough in 1244–1246, the *popolo* pressed forward again four years later, spurred on by the military bungling of the communal nobility in September 1250. A wave of discontent, reaching socially from the poorest classes up to the rich merchant groups, flooded the city. And the armed *popolo* rose up, overthrew the imperial podestà, Ranieri da Montemurlo of Tortona, abolished offices, dissolved councils, and barred the great majority of noblemen from government. Ranieri and his officials were allowed to make an orderly exit from the city. The popular armed companies constituted the organizational base of the Florentine *popolo*, and the *popolo*'s chief magistracy, the *anziani*, became the head of communal government. But this regime went down in 1260, overturned by its terrible defeat at Montaperti, only to bound back into power in 1266. Now the influence of the richest and most "ennobled" of the *popolani*, the Guelf chieftains, prevailed until the early 1280s, when angry resentment over the street violence of the magnates, many of them Guelfs, served to regroup the business community. A bloc of the dominant men from the major guilds, drawing upon their guild organization, imposed a council of guild priors alongside the commune's ruling magistracy of fourteen. But within the year (1282–1283) the priors ended by eliminating the fourteen and taking over the government. Once again intimidation and force, applied at the strategic moment, brought a government down and shifted the social moorings of power.

THE CHANGING POPOLO

The *popolo* made for the richest movement of men and issues in all the commune's history. It transformed perceptions of reality. The art of Giotto and his followers would have been impossible without the psychological stamp of the *popolo*. Plebeian uprisings in fourteenth-century Perugia, Florence, and Siena threatened to be more revolutionary and promised a more radical cargo of reform, but they were a will-o'-the-wisp, all glow and no substance. They had neither organization nor program. The *popolo*, however, by its sustained assaults on authority, altered the political and social organization of the old urban space and changed the disposition and thrust of values. This, in turn, had a pervasive effect upon imaginative literature, political thought, and historical writing.

The *popolo* was never a fixed force. It was continually changing in its aims, composition, militancy, and appeals. Socially it could be broadly or more narrowly based, depending upon the city, the phase of popular development, or the perimeter of immediate pressures. It could strive for bedrock reforms and slash at the bonds of serfdom in the countryside, or it might demand more limited fiscal and electoral reforms; and it might break bitterly and bloodily with the rich moneymen to seek compromise with a disaffected fraction of noblemen. It could not favor rural servitude, but it was ready to tolerate serfdom for the sake of gaining political advantages inside the city. In a dynamic and troubled setting, there was no way for a vital institution, the *popolo*, to be anything but a force in process.

At Milan about 1200 the popular movement had its focus in the middle class. The old set of big merchants and bankers were grouped together with a large array of knights in an organization known as the Motta. *Popolo* and Motta cooperated nervously, as the Credenza of St. Ambrose, the popular vanguard, pressed the nobility (the *capitanei*) for important reforms. From the later 1220s, the need to face the armies and agents of the Emperor Frederick II helped to restore some concord in Milan, but when the imperial danger passed in 1250, the uneasiness came forth again in relations between Credenza and Motta, leading to a violent rupture in 1259. The knights and moneymen of the Motta feared the despotic designs of the captain of the Credenza, Martino della Torre, and turned passionately against him. This rupture was a final parting of the ways between the moderate and more radical wings of the popular movement, with results that terminated in the overwhelming triumph of the nobility in 1277.

Siena had conditions reminiscent of those at Milan. There the two guilds of bankers and international merchants ("spicers")—*campsores* and *pizicaioli*—conferred a group identity apart from that of the organized *popolo*, the core of whose constituency lay with the artisans and small tradesmen. During the early thirteenth century, *popolo* and moneymen cooperated; indeed, the latter's imposing entry into government in the years around 1200 led the way for the *popolo*. But there was a schism after 1240, as the strain of bad Sienese relations with the papacy deepened divisiveness at home. A small bloc of old noble families, those given more to land and arms than to trade, sought the help of the *petite bourgeoisie*, which in the 1250s and 1260s called for sharper reforms, while the Guelf bankers, big merchants, and richer nobility passed to the opposition. Between 1265 and 1270, maneuvering cleverly from exile, the rich businessmen and their part of the nobility gradually gained the upper political hand. The *popolo* was backed into purging the nobles from its ranks. Deprived of the more able part of its leadership, the *popolo* became easier prey for the Guelf banking and mercantile elite. Tradesmen and artisans were edged out of government and out of the *popolo*'s key offices, save for the few names required as political window dressing. If in 1210 or so the fledgling Sienese *popolo* needed and had the halfhearted endorsement of the bankers and leading merchants, in 1270 it was brought down by this group.

The effect of rural concerns upon the popular movement was sharpest at Bologna, where the *popolo* decreed (1257) the emancipation of the serfs in the feudal vicinage. In 1282 a series of ordinances struck at nobles who challenged the rural title deeds of *populares* and dissolved all contracts entailing agrarian servitude. Other cities, however, saw less of this concentrated "radicalism." The Bolognese *haute bourgeoisie* was successfully struggling for its presumptive right to much enfeoffed and church land, which had been gradually usurped since the twelfth century.

Almost nothing is known about the structure and membership of guilds in thirteenth-century Milan. Those records, like so much else, were destroyed in fire and civil disorders. We know only that artisans and small tradesmen were the backbone of the Credenza of St. Ambrose, and we suspect that they had a well-articulated guild structure. If guild organization at Milan was strong, owing to a marked industrial development, the same cannot be said of other northern cities, although Padua and Verona, for example, had militant guilds; so also Cremona and Piacenza. But Genoa, Pisa, and Venice—the big coastal cities—never developed aggressive guilds. At Venice they were too closely supervised by the ruling class. Venetian guilds, like those at Genoa and Pisa, were no match for the vigor of the shipping interests; and they were overshadowed by the élan of long-distance commerce and the opportunities of a booming maritime trade. The failure of the thirteenth-century popular movement in the coastal cities must be ascribed to the very conditions that kept the guilds puny. Seen in this light, the fervor of the *popolo* at Genoa in the 1250s probably had a more demagogic strain, would have less to do with branch and root reform, than at Bologna and Florence, which saw brilliant coordination between a strong guild system and the *popolo*'s armed companies of the neighborhoods.

In studying popular movements, we can make no bigger mistake at the level of *concrete* analysis than to associate the *popolo* with trade and manufacture, the nobility with land and feudal interests. Something like this was seen in part and in general terms, but any specific situation was bound to be more complicated. Norms can only have an abstract reality, like averages in demography. And certainly Genoese and some Pisan noblemen dedicated themselves to shipping and long-distance trade, while also holding feudal estates. Again, if Pisa had many noblemen who avoided commerce, Siena had a noble clique whose celebrity lay in their ability and wealth as merchant bankers. But this bond between noble blood and commerce was rather less characteristic of Florence, where many of the illustrious old houses—Ricasoli, Uberti, Guidi, Pazzi, Buondelmonti—long refrained from going into trade.

Among the men and families given to commerce and banking, those at the top had wealth and contacts which pulled them emotionally away from the community of artisans and small tradesmen. Up to about the middle of the thirteenth century, it was in the interest of bankers and long-distance traders to batter the entrenched communal oligarchy with an eye to loosening the political monopoly of the old consular families, mostly of noble lineage and very often divided among themselves. Then, frequently, it was a matter of getting more "commoners" such as merchants into the political councils. As long as the power of the consular nobility remained intact, rich merchants, shippers, and bankers were ready to accept the support of the emerging *popolo*, so seeming to endorse it. But after about 1250 or 1260, having fully achieved their aims and in fact now menaced by the political ambitions of the middle classes, they broke with the *popolo*, thereby dividing and undermining the popular movement. What remained of the old *popolo* in 1290 was very different indeed from what the *popolo* had been in 1200 or 1220.

CHAPTER V

THE END
OF THE POPULAR
COMMUNE

ACHIEVEMENT

The popular political movements of the thirteenth century ended in dictatorship or oligarchy. They were defeated by the organized resources—men, skills, and arms—of land and big money: by feudal magnates in upper Italy; by merchants, bankers, and entrepreneurs in north-central Italy west of the Apennines; and by alliances everywhere between big money and feudal-landed interests. But the popular movements were also defeated by the *popolo*'s own limitations.

In the north, some cities already experienced spasmodic one-man rule in the 1250s, often with the connivance of local elite groups. Ferrara, for example, was caught up in the feudal network of the Salinguerra family and the Este marquises before midcentury. The great feudal baron Ezzelino da Romano seized and held Verona, Vicenza, and Padua for just over twenty years (1236 to 1256–1259). And another magnate, Oberto Pallavicini (afterward an imperial vicar), held Cremona (1250–1266) and ruled over Piacenza, Pavia, and Vercelli during part of the 1250s. But the cities that fell under one-man rule, even those brutalized by Ezzelino, returned fitfully to their republican institutions for a generation or two and were not faced with the constant menace of despotism until the late thirteenth and early four-teenth centuries. As a matter of fact, popular initiative and energies were far from spent in Tuscany and Umbria even in the second half of the four-teenth century, when something more than the ghost of the old *popolo* remained to haunt the commune.

A trend in recent historical writing downgrades the achievement of the *popolo* and seems to prefer the paternalism of tyranny. Especially evident in England, the trend has inadvertent ideological roots. Conservative historians cannot see much to admire in the *popolo*, being repelled by its supposed inability to impose law and order and by its readiness to strike at the old commune, to bloody the nobility, and to introduce outright class legislation against swaggering magnates and noblemen. Here was a frank use of government to prop up certain groups and classes, because of which historians are prepared to give points to the *signori* (despots), who had the virtue, allegedly, of restoring peace to the cities and a modicum of law and order. Yet the *popolo* did no more than go to school to the aristocratic commune, which showed it the way to use government in the defense of ancient blood ties, political privilege, tax immunities, guaranteed income (and graft) from office, and partisan courts of law.

Historians on the political left also dislike the popular commune. With an eye to the masses of people, they note the *popolo*'s penchant for excluding workers and poor folk from its ranks; they see the sway of the big merchant class or of a few noblemen within the *popolo;* they therefore see no telling moral differences between the triumphant *popolo*, as it turns conservative, and the eventual triumph of signorial (i.e., despotic) government. In this view the advent of the signory, one-man rule, made little if any difference to the better harnessing of human resources.

We must avoid the impulse to limit the movement of the *popolo* to politics, which only catches the most obvious aspect of the *popolo*'s advance along a broad historical front. For the foundations of that advance were economic, social, and demographic, with innumerable offshoots and side effects involving social mores, education, burgeoning mercenary armies, public finance, state-building, political thought, historical writing, the arts, and vernacular literature. When the *popolo*, even as it foundered, had done its job, the city-state world had been irreversibly transformed.

The urban economy and population reached their maximum growth in the course of the thirteenth century, at a rate and in ways never to be repeated. For all the civil wars and lamentations of contemporaries, the *popolo*'s commitment to trade and industry, combined with its breakthrough into government, had incalculably beneficial effects upon the economy. Social mores changed in subtle and in obvious ways. In some cities a more informal, congenial, and familiar manner came into fashion, as Opicino de Canistris observed, speaking of Pavia.[1] Boccaccio's rich Florentine baker (*Decameron*, VI, 2) cannot bring himself to address a nobleman who often passes his shop, but when contact between the two is finally made, the baker, fully conscious of his own worth, finds the way to apprise the nobleman of it. The thirteenth century produced the first primers of conduct, written by *popolani* such as Brunetto Latini and Bonvesin de la Riva. Usually set down in verse form, they were designed to correct table manners, to polish "new men" and their daughters, and to make for more urbanity. Notaries compiled formularies of speeches for inexperienced men and sought to give a politico-administrative education to the *popolo*. Frequently they translated communal and guild statutes from Latin into the vernacular. The hugger-mugger world of politics was opened to new eyes and to *völkisch* experience. Education was affected. The *popolo*'s advance introduced a demand for the laicization of schools: for more literacy, as required in commercial affairs, and for new course material, such as arithmetic for bookkeeping and a more utilitarian Latin for contracts and business transactions. By 1300, literacy levels in Italian cities surpassed the like anywhere else in Europe.

One inevitable consequence of the *popolo*'s political ascent was the rapid expansion of government, the spread of officialdom in the creation of new offices and councils. The successors to the *popolo*, signories and oligarchies, inherited swelling administrations and turned these to their own purposes.

Since *popolani* were less given to war than their rivals on horseback, and because the victories of the *popolo* drove more and more noblemen into exile and professional armies, the numbers of mercenaries grew steadily and war became increasingly expensive. Records of disbursements from Siena, Florence, Genoa, and other cities point up this trend. The costs of government rose and the complexities of public finance multiplied, particularly as the leading cities extended their rule over neighboring lands and towns. But it was the bourgeois commune, in the second half of the thirteenth century, with its commercial elite in control of the fisc, that popularized or devised a range of new taxes and fiscal devices: notably tax farming (which now was more widely practiced), war loans, forced loans, and indirect taxes on a large variety of goods. These already denoted, however, a period when the *popolo* was hardening into an oligarchy, when only the name remained and occasionally even the name, *popolo*, was outlawed in public use; but we should not underestimate the *popolo*'s long-term impact on the fisc, without which no state-building was possible.

The *popolo*'s ranks nourished much hatred for despotic government, and the effects of this entered into the informal political thought of the time. Leading writers, from Rolandino and Brunetto Latini to Ptolemy of Lucca and Marsilius of Padua, had an acute sense of the civic community: a sense which derived from having known a corpus of active citizens and officeholders so much larger than anything seen by the aristocratic commune that the contrast touches two different realities. Consequently, enhanced community consciousness, whether in imperialist thought (Dante) or in more localized rumination (Rolandino, De Canistris, the Anonimo Genovese), owed an enormous debt to the assertiveness of the *popolo* and to the aftereffects when its heyday was over. The sense of a larger political community —one of the *popolo*'s major legacies—passed over into the feeling and thinking of the republican oligarchies: Lucca, Siena, Florence, and for a time Genoa, Perugia, Pavia, Bologna, and Padua. The effect is clearly seen at the highest level of legal-political thought, in the concept of the *populus liber* ("free people") and its attendant notions regarding local sovereignty, as developed by the most influential jurist of the fourteenth century, Bartolus of Sassoferrato (d. 1357).

Turning to municipal architecture, we find that the aristocratic commune was responsible for many new building projects. This activity continued under the *popolo*, in civil as in religious construction, peaking in many cities during the thirteenth and early fourteenth centuries, the very period of the *popolo*'s hegemony. New or larger palaces were required to house the commune's expanding courts, councils, and offices. Until the middle of the thirteenth century, Genoa's podestaral commune used the premises of the archbishop or lodged its officials in *palazzi* or quarters rented from big propertied families. But the *popolo* or collectivity of guilds, nearly everywhere, put up its own *palazzi* with the characteristic towers and battlements of their aristocratic predecessors. In some cities these buildings presently became the seat of communal government. Pavia's twenty-five guilds, reports De Canistris, had "a great palace for themselves, called the Palace of the *Popolo*, and a large bell, at the ringing of which, a rare event, all the *popolo* takes up arms."

Historical writing did not escape the *popolo*'s imprint. The vernacular chronicles of Dino Compagni and Giovanni Villani are only the best known of chronicles from Florence, Lucca, Siena, and elsewhere, showing the effects of the *popolo* on the perceptions of their authors. Generally speaking, chroniclers of this school prefer the government of merchants and prominent guildsmen drawn from the rich guilds. They emphasize the rule of law, election procedures, and costs of government; they oppose dashing political figures, fancy dress, and ostentation; they study the play of social forces and stress the economic health of the community. Taken as a cluster of interests in the fourteenth-century context, these are *bürgerlich* preoccupations first and foremost, a legacy of the *popolo*'s influence.

It is not an accident that Italy's great vernacular literature had its brilliant inception in the thirteenth century, in concatenation with the rise of the *popolo*. Major changes in language cannot be separated from demography and from great historical movements, popular or elitist. In his *De vulgari eloquentia*, Dante, a *popolano* with aristocratic velleities, reviews Italy's rich variety of dialects. His concern is the common speech of the peninsula's different regions, with the aim of finding the one best suited for use in highbrow poetry. Let us note the points of contact between the *popolo* and the "sweet new style" (*dolce stil novo*), the refined lyric verse of Dante's age.

While drawing heavily upon a courtly literary tradition, the "new stylists" rely upon a strikingly simple vocabulary, even when making learned statements. Guido Cavalcanti's verse may have bookish passages, but its diction is clear and simple. And this lucidity is related directly to the pervasive influence of the *popolo*, whose energies and exertions, demographic and political, tilted the scales of literary culture away from feudal court, from clergy, and from the domination of medieval Latin. Rightly enough, the *stilnovo* was most cultivated where popular movements were

strongest, as in Bologna and the Tuscan cities. But though the simplicity of
the *stilnovo* poets takes something from the language of the *popolo*, they
also express a strong note of reaction against the popular tide; and this brings
us to a basic element in their enterprise—their social and intellectual elitism.
They appear to stand with the *popolo* in dismissing the idea of a blood
nobility.[2] Nobility is not in a man's lineage but in his "heart," in his virtue
and loftiness of mind. A chaste and idealized woman—the woman loved—
becomes the vehicle of the poet's moral ascent. Those whom society takes to
be noble by birth may really be ignoble, but the common mass of people
cannot claim nobility either. Hence this view of nobility, with its moral
edge, was really double-edged. By reason, however, of its highly select
diction, imagery, and lofty thinking, the new style went against the overall
social manner of the *popolo*. In short, despite their commitment to the
vernacular, the *stilnovo* poets found their poetic identity in opposition to
the triumphant "vulgarity" of the *popolo*. They needed a foil, as much as
good needs bad, and so in their verse they put the recurring image of the
vilan in the sharpest contrast to nobility—*vilan* being the lowly rustic,
plebeian, or coarse-minded individual. The word had all these meanings.
Nobility and villainy were opposites, but the key word *vilan* was, lexico-
graphically, a statement about class and social lowliness. From the image of
the *vilan* the poet groped up and away, away from such lowliness and up
toward the angelic lady, in a quest which continually set him off from his
vulgar contemporaries. Reality included the occasional butcher and artisan
ensconced in public office; it circumscribed the victory of *nouveaux riches*
and the wave of draconian laws appointed to penalize noblemen. Something,
therefore, in the essential makeup of the period's "high" lyric verse was a
passionate and pointed rebuttal to the pretensions of the *popolo*. *Stilnovo*
and *popolo* are vitally linked both in a dialectic of opposition and, more
concordantly, in the vernacular tongue.

FAILURE

In its demand for a share of political power, the *popolo* both expressed
and effected a leap in consciousness beyond anything that had gone before.
But the popular commune failed because its more novel claims were buried
by the eventual triumph of oligarchy and one-man rule, and because its
political institutions, which promised to pivot on a more representative part
of the community, were wiped out or turned into facades that were then
used to defeat the *popolo*'s original purposes.

Collecting together into effective political, occupational, and kinship
organizations was a practice confined largely to the men of the middle and
upper classes. Like the associations of noblemen and like the aristocratic
commune itself, the *popolo* was an exclusive organization but its constitu-

ency was primarily middle-class. In its drive for power, the *popolo* worked for a decisive enlargement of the commune's political membership. Between about 1200 and 1260, Pavia's legislative council went from 150 to 1,000 members and Milan's from 400 to 900. But even at its most democratic the *popolo* always excluded a mass of men—the unskilled, the poor, the part-time or seasonal field workers, recent immigrants, and whole categories of artisans who were not allowed to form their own guilds. As a result, in the political crises that came after 1260, when the *popolo* needed broader community support to help ensure the survival of the popular commune, it was not to be found.

The exclusive and sectarian character of the *popolo* came sharply forth in its restrictions on political citizenship. The latter was the only true form of membership in the *universitas* or corporation of active citizens—that is, the commune. When the *popolo* took power, whether at Milan, Piacenza, Bologna, or Florence, it did not throw open all doors and offer political citizenship to every man who met the age and tax requirements. The *popolo* changed the requirements for citizenship, with an eye to breaking the control of the nobility and richest citizens, but it always insisted that certain conditions be met, although these varied with time and place. Chief among the requirements were: (1) five to thirty years of residence in the city, (2) membership in a guild, (3) property qualifications or minimum tax assessments, and (4) continuous tax disbursements for periods of up to twenty-five years. The *popolo* was more demanding in some cities than in others, but the principle of selectivity remained. Again, by 1300, membership in all the influential or well-established guilds was also hedged in by strict requirements of residence and taxation, as well as by high matriculation fees. Here, once more, the sectarianism of the *popolo* surfaced: guilds frankly preferred the close relatives of current and past members.

More remarkable still was the fact that the *popolo* excluded, or could not attract and hold, certain groups from the middle reaches of society. Pavia, for instance, had three political orders: knights, *popolo*, and notaries, each with its own podestà and council of advisers. Not until about 1260 did the notaries pass over to the support of the *popolo*, retaining, however, their separate organization. At Milan the split between the more modest and richer strata of the middle class was deep enough for each to have its own association: artisans and small shopkeepers went into the Credenza of St. Ambrose; bankers and big merchants, in alliance with the lesser knights, constituted the Motta. After 1225, Motta and Credenza cooperated in a popular front, but when civil war broke out between the two and the Motta was swept from the city, the great nobility, for long held at bay, instantly gained the advantage which it would eventually convert into a definitive victory. At Bologna the *popolo* excluded the *lanaioli* (wool merchants and manufacturers) but took in other merchants and rich professionals. Siena, in the third quarter of the century, saw her bankers and big merchant-importers turn conclusively against the *popolo* and thereby work its ruin. And at Florence, Bologna, and Siena, the butchers, traditionally associated with the *popolo*, had such a tough and independent guild organization that the *popolo* could not always rely upon them.

The *popolo*'s disabilities may be seen from another viewpoint. The corporatism of the commune—that is, the self-protective impulse to draw together into sworn associations—not only made and strengthened the *popolo* but also, paradoxically, weakened it by encouraging internal rifts. Here was a structural deficiency which touched all classes in the commune and characterized the very composition of urban government with its variety of contributing parts—guilds, neighborhood societies, political orders, and intercorporate groupings.

The *popolo* in opposition was not the same as the *popolo* in victory. In opposition to the nobility, the *popolo* collected wider support or more effectively attracted the bankers and rich international merchants. But once popular victories had weakened the nobility and once the plutocratic guilds had realized their own separatist ends, the *popolo* lost the richest parts of the middle classes. If, however, the plutocratic guildsmen remained within the popular fold in victory, then the nature and direction of the popular claims changed and the *popolo* endured in name only. This happened at Pavia, Verona, Bologna, and Perugia. At Genoa the popular movement, remaining under the direction of rich merchants, entrepreneurs, and a sector of the nobility, never attained a serious revolutionary momentum. At Siena, where the call for reform went much farther, the Guelf mercantile and banking magnates took control of the *popolo* in the 1270s and eviscerated it. Something like this also occurred at Florence, but the process was more gradual.

As we move from city to city in search of the *popolo*'s structural difficulties, we continually encounter one decisive cleavage: the social and psychological distance that divided the artisans and small shopkeepers from the bankers and wealthy long-distance merchants. At key moments artisans and rich merchants converged to form a middle class with respect to the governing nobility and to certain commercial and tax policies. But when their interests diverged, artisan and rich merchant drew apart; the commercial plutocracy gradually turned to shore up the ranks of the enfeebled nobility. The deepest and most enduring division lay between the poorer and rich bourgeoisie. This went far to undermine the early environment for republicanism. Profits from large-scale commerce, from lucrative real estate, and from big moneylending were surpassingly large in the thirteenth century; and there could be no order of comparison between such returns and the petty profits of artisans and modest tradesmen. The differences were aggravated by the urban topography: a close setting with narrow spaces, characteristic of walled-in cities, where the marks of privilege and high status had a powerful attraction, and where these were both echoed and fostered by the hierarchy and ceremonial ideology of the Church. In many cities the rich *popolano* was sometimes indistinguishable from the nobleman, save to the old families themselves, to snobs, and to observers with an eye for the subtle play of social values. The distinctions were drawn by Dino Compagni in his contemporary profile of the Cerchi, leaders in 1301 of the White faction in Florence: "There was a family named Cerchi, men of low estate but good merchants and very rich. They dressed well, kept many servants and horses, and had a handsome appearance. Some of them bought the palace of the counts [Guidi], which was near the houses of the Pazzi and the Donati, who were of more ancient blood but not so rich; whereupon seeing the Cerchi rising high, as they enlarged the palace and kept a grand style of life, the Donati began to hate them." Again, "People who did not know them [the Cerchi and other members of the White faction] thought them rich, powerful and prudent. . . . But those who knew said: 'They're only merchants and so they're naturally cowardly, whereas their enemies [the noble Donati and other Blacks] are proud, valorous men and experts in warfare.' "[3]

In the early fourteenth century Taddeo Pepoli, jurist and budding lord of Bologna, inherited great riches from his immediate forebears, who rose through the ranks of the *popolo* to figure among the richest bankers in Italy. In August 1336, Taddeo and all the men of the Pepoli clan, together with sixty of their company—and contrary to the laws of the commune—were licensed to go fully armed in and out of the government palace. Bologna was veering toward one-man rule. The figure cut by the Pepoli exaggerates but illustrates the devastating power of big merchant wealth in a divided *popolo* and a shaky political context.

Sprung from the *popolo*, the Cerchi and Pepoli were by no means typical, but there was enough about them to suggest the manner or bearing of rich and successful *popolani* in many a city. Their employees, retainers, servants, and business dependents formed a bloc of men who counted for something in the troubled streets and whose cohesiveness could not be ignored in the councils of government.

The *popolo*'s deficiencies—a restricted constituency, internal rifts, and the unreliable role of the big moneymen—reveal the ground of its failure to develop an egalitarian ideology. When first moving its attack against the nobility, the *popolo* pressed a variety of forceful complaints against the aristocratic commune and thereby attracted support. But it lost appeal once it had smashed its way into the councils of government. Even at its most radical, as at Bologna or Florence, when hounding the nobles and magnates with fierce class legislation, the *popolo* was defending its own constituency above all, not the lowly weaver or laborer who might be assaulted in the streets by well-connected bullies. Aside from its short-lived campaign against serfdom, the *popolo* offered nothing tangible inside the city to the crowds of poorer men who were not in its organized ranks. The *popolo* could produce no program to help draw behind it a more comprehensive part of the community. This failure in ideology speaks for the excessive control of the plutocratic guildsmen over the *popolo*.

The fact that the *popolo* was frequently captained by noblemen—Della Torre at Milan, Della Scala at Verona—does not itself betray a necessary constitutional weakness. Leadership and crisis often go together. The *popolo*'s readiness to be led by noblemen saved it from a string of grave dangers. Time and again the dangers were in the approach of small armies, and war was preeminently the profession of noblemen. Verona saw her army of exiled noblemen as a threat to the popular commune for nearly forty years (ca. 1260–1300). The exiled Milanese nobility menaced the commune of Milan during most of the third quarter of the thirteenth century. Florence and Siena faced similar dangers. In these circumstances, relations between the *popolo* and its leadership changed. In the Northern Plain, where a numerous feudal nobility endured, external pressures altered the internal character of the *popolo*. Popular leaders tightened their controls and their dignities were gradually converted into dictatorships, but the causes of change started outside the *popolo*.

The law-and-order view has provided the classic argument for the main cause of the *popolo*'s decline, but it is so misleading as to deserve particular care.

When summarizing the causes of the transition from republican commune, where the *popolo* was dominant or influential, to despotism and the suppression of the popular movement, historians turn and return to the theme of violence, disorder, and instability. When they consider it from the quiet of their studies, that tormented world seems fated to pass, and this appears to provide a comprehensive, satisfactory accounting. It is easy to reason that the failure of the popular commune was its inability to impose law and order and to bring internal peace to the city, whether in Lombardy or Tuscany. The entire communal age was, in the view of leading historians, an age of crisis: institutions were profoundly unsteady, violence and instabilities proliferated, and law was flagrantly spurned. The necessary outcome seemed to be the irresistible rise of a strong man, *signore* or despot, determined to overcome factions, family feuds, and class conflict. He imposed peace, for citizens were weary of conflict. Civil strife and *coups d'état* were the fruit of selfish interests. All higher principles had long since vanished. Political cynicism was complete. The poet Immanuel Romano cried out: "Hurrah for him who wins, for I am on his side."[4]

These are the accents of the law-and-order view, claiming that long-term conflict undermined the nerve and independence of citizens. Conflict made them willing to have civic peace even at the price of dictatorship. Particularly was this supposed to have been true of the *popolo*'s tradesmen and merchants, who wanted nothing more than to tend their businesses and families, although, oddly, the thirteenth-century commune was never pusillanimous.

Thirteenth- and fourteenth-century Italians frequently expressed the wish for peace. There was a fashion among fourteenth-century poets for writing verse in praise of *signori* and their harmonious, peaceful reigns. Saviozzo of Siena exclaimed: "O fair and just *signore*, mild father, illustrious and good, through whom the little widow hopes to garner peace and rest."[5] But there are difficulties about law-and-order as a guide to explain the details of any transition from commune to signory. The model does not fit the discernible realities. There is no instance of a single city in which revulsion against violence and civil disorder made for the exit into one-man rule. There was fear of violence, to be sure, and the unease of the commune breaks at times through the surface of its most serene enactments. But it is one thing to detect a longing for peace and something else to make it the ground of the *popolo*'s defeat.

The law-and-order argument works neither in specific cases nor as a general model with imprecise applications. Siena, Lucca, and Florence, which experienced intense and prolonged civil conflict, retained their republican polities for centuries after many other cities had fallen to signorial rule. From the 1290s, Genoa, whose political travails were no less grave, passed back and forth between signorial and republican government for more than two centuries and in 1528 returned definitively to a stable form of aristocratic republicanism. Ferrara never even developed a popular commune: encircled by powerful feudatories and much disturbed internally by two great rival families (the Estensi and Torelli), the city was already slipping toward signorial rule in the 1220s, yet it was very far from having suffered the magnitude of civil violence which characterized some twenty other cities. In the 1330s, violent Bologna was still struggling to hold on to communal institutions introduced by the *popolo*, while Pavia did not succumb to one-man rule until the end of the 1350s, and then the city, claimed by the lord of Milan, had to be taken by a Milanese army after an agonizing siege.

The commune's susceptibility to violence cannot be used to explain the triumph of despotism. But the law-and-order interpretation may go to help explain the success of the early-fourteenth-century communal regimes, now more oligarchically appointed, at Florence and Siena, where the wholesale civic violence of the previous century had finally given way to an era of relative tranquillity, at all events until the 1340s. Bergamo, instead, drawn under the signorial rule of the Visconti in 1332, did not find peace; nor did Bologna under her spasmodic signories. Both at Bergamo and Bologna, city and countryside were bloodied by fierce municipal faction right down to the late fifteenth century. It is not true, as is continually claimed, that the signory brought law, order, and peace. In certain cities the job of pacification took several generations, and the fourteenth century, in this regard, is transitional.

CHAPTER VI

THE COURSE
OF URBAN VALUES

URBAN SPACE AND PERSONALITY

Cities and the problems of cities have haunted the European imagination since the twelfth century. Already then cities routed imperial armies in northern Italy and were in turn reconquered or razed to the ground, only to spring forth again a few years later—larger, more combative, and more populous. Urban vitality seemed at times a function of temporary defeat: strike down a city and you were sure to call forth—at all events in Italy—a still more formidable enemy. The vigor of the inland cities was fully matched by the explosive energies of the seaports.

Citizens (*cives, cittadini*) were the full-fledged city folk. They came swiftly to see the world in terms of cities, though these were spots in a boundless expanse of hills and valleys, of wooded and rocky and arable land. Citizens were keenly aware of the countryside: of profitable rural properties, of the quantities of agricultural produce carted into the city, of rustic folk and feudal barons. But power, and hence friends or real dangers, lay chiefly in the neighboring cities, or in leagues among cities and great feudal chieftains. By the later thirteenth century, we already find writers—and the overwhelming majority come from cities—casually skipping over the importance of the vast rural spaces in order to emphasize the regional pull and clout of cities. This emphasis issued from passionate local attachments and feelings. Down to the end of the Renaissance, men counted themselves especially fortunate to have been born or brought up in a celebrated city, with its brilliant history and civil advantages, rather than in a subject town or rural hamlet. This was the feeling as much of thirteenth-century chroniclers as of fifteenth-century humanists.

In the 1260s, in his long didactic poem *Il Tesoretto*, Brunetto Latini sketched a revealing picture of the proper way for a mounted gentleman to enter a city:

When going through cities,
Go, I advise you,
In a stately manner [*cortesemente*],
Ride handsomely,
Head slightly bowed.
It's not urbane
To move without restraint.
And don't stare at the height
Of every house you pass.
Guard against moving
Like a man from the country;
Don't squirm like an eel,
Go self-assuredly
Through the streets and people.
[ll. 1805–1818]

The image of the "hick" had appeared. Latini was addressing an audience which aspired to have the designated restraint and bearing. One of the key words, *cortesemente*, hints at the world of noble courts, but the setting is actually urban and upper-class, Latini's own world. To the same setting, too, writers were already bringing detailed rules regarding table manners.

The most sophisticated political chronicle of the whole period, Dino Compagni's Florentine *Cronica* (written 1310–1312), following a terse announcement of intention, begins with a statement of Florence's place in Tuscany. Straightway the chronicler puts Florence in its geographic relation to the neighboring cities—Pisa, Lucca, Pistoia, Bologna, Arezzo, and Siena—and provides the location and distances of five other fortified towns and castles. These, he notes, and the surrounding lands "have many noblemen, counts and captains [feudal lords], who love Florence in civil disorder rather than in peace and who obey her more from fear than from love." Compagni's field of observation takes in (1) the major cities, (2) the main towns and fortresses, and (3) a muffled perception which contrasts city and country, while alluding to the anarchic psychology of feudal noblemen.

The dynamic contrast between country and city lasted beyond the Renaissance period but was first roundly articulated in the thirteenth century, when urban Italians already measured historical reality in terms of cities. The upstart custom of buying up rural estates and abandoning the city for the country was seen in western and northern Europe, and then only in part; never in central or upper Italy, whose wealthy urban families acquired or maintained large estates but rarely deserted the city for more than two or three months a year.

Dante wrote a lost poem on the sixty most beautiful women of Florence. He had seen them all and quite likely named them in the poem. We cannot imagine the like today. The contrast suggests the personal, close quality of life in the early urban space, the daily contacts and face-to-face encounters guaranteed by the confined streets, bridges, and squares of the late-medieval and Renaissance city. Women of the upper classes, like Dante's Beatrice, were chaperoned in the streets, but encounters were unavoidable, and even the most ephemeral were not necessarily void of meaning. This indeed, for social history, is the significance of Dante's fleeting encounters with Beatrice. He sees her, they exchange glances, and he turns the experience into a long-remembered vision.

Life in the Italian walled-in city of about 1300 went on in a tight world of personal relations and public settings. Gossip and rumor rippled back and forth across the warp and woof of close family ties, inherited family friendships and animosities, numerous street acquaintances, and peripheral contacts that were endlessly being renewed. These relations were especially dense for the rich citizens in politics, because such bonds were multiplied and vitalized by property and influence. Guido Cavalcanti (d. 1300), in his most intimate moments, had his poetry to think about; but he also thought about the mortal enemies of the Cavalcanti family, the Donati, and he and Corso de' Donati made attempts to assassinate each other.

Late-medieval cities outside of Italy also provided the environment for close spatial and personal relations, but there were major differences too. The preeminence of families in the Italian cities merged with the power of government almost as a matter of course. As from the late twelfth century, moreover, local power in urban Italy was well on its way to being absolute: those who disposed of local political authority disposed of the power of life and death over every citizen and subject, and that power was often harshly used in political emergencies. The merger of private interest and public authority thus raised the importance of personal relations inside the city to a new order, particularly among members of the upper classes. In this, other European cities offered little competition.

The personal-public texture of life in the Italian commune lies beyond anything in our experience, but we catch glimpses of that vanished reality in the age's lyric poetry, which teems with personal allusions, apostrophes, references to streets, direct discourse, and dedications to friends. These caught the public element in private experience: they made rhetorical demands on poetry, giving it, in its immediate accessibility and communicability, a sharper public form. As they wrote poetry, *stilnovisti* such as Dante and Cino da Pistoia, no less than the comic realists Rustico di Filippo and Cecco Angiolieri, continually looked to their friends, or to a circle just beyond, even in verses that seemed addressed directly to the loved one. They wrote with a definite audience in mind, thus answering to the public and "communal" accents in their private experiences, and they frequently entered into sonnet-dialogues with other poets.

To an allegation by Guido Cavalcanti that Cino da Pistoia was guilty of plagiarism, Cino replies with a sonnet beginning, "What are the things I take from you, / O Guido, that you make of me so base a thief?" Dante, Cino,

Guido, Gianni Alfani, and others exchanged sonnets on the nature of love. The exchanges keep to a particular vision: love of the sort which refines, ennobles, and spiritualizes. The theme is moral, public, and responsible. Alfani sings to the ladies of Venice of his lady ("De la mia donna vó cantar con voi, / madonne da Vinegia"). Others speak to their readers in direct discourse, in praise of the virtues and beauty of their beloved. Guido Cavalcanti summons up a whole street scene with two opening lines: "Who is this coming, drawing the gaze of all men, / as she makes the air one trembling clarity?" And Lapo Gianni lists all good things in one of his most moving sonnets: his lady, his love and youth and happiness, universal peace, the miraculous turning of Florence's great walls to silver and the River Arno to balsam.

Private experience is articulated by means of public evocations. The poetry of Dante's age is never private, never turned away from a context of public meanings. It carries the stamp of communal experience. There was a genre of personal invective, practiced even by the idealist poets (the *stilnovisti*), which heaped abuse on acquaintances—naming them, describing them or their close relatives, providing intimate details, and on occasion savaging them. Dante's three sonnets (ca. 1293–1296) against Forese Donati describe the underwear worn by his rheum-prone wife and make Forese out to be a bastard, a glutton, an adulterer, a thief, and possibly guilty of incest with his sisters-in-law. More than any conventional historical document— statute, letter, deed, or business ledger—such verse conveys a sense of the absence of barriers between private and public life. The most awful personal details easily become public knowledge. Dante's financial distress and his father's alleged usurious practices were loudly bruited by Forese. Antagonists instinctively drew verbal daggers that cut deeply into the personal— an area so special for us that we hedge it in with laws of libel, whereas they shared it with the commune.

No urban Italian could escape the eyes and curiosity, or almost the very need to know, of his neighbors. An adulterous wife might be known in a court of law by the opinion of her neighbors. Such was the intent of certain statutes. Moving through the Florentine rural suburbs in the early morning, Guido Cavalcanti could easily hear the cries of a peasant as he scolded his wife and children. Sounds of this sort were more effectively conducted by the habitat of the city, where narrow streets, lying between high stone constructs, amplified noises and smells, quarrels and conversations. We must strive to comprehend the public-social framework of life along those ways and in the facing rooms and apartments.

For shopkeepers and the mercantile classes generally, domestic life and the money-making trades had a unified existence. Economic and family functions were joined. The separation of the two functions came later, in the course of the fifteenth century, and then only among citizens of the richer sort. The separation, presented as a relatively novel ideal, is clearly seen in Francesco di Giorgio's architectural treatise (1470s): family rooms and workshop are separated, in part so as to keep women and children beyond the purview of customers and other merchants. In the thirteenth and fourteenth centuries, home and workshop were one; so also home and countinghouse, home and warehouse, home and the part of it facing the retail outlet. Residential quarters on the ground floor gave directly out on the streets, while the large windows of the floor above also took in the nearby spectacle. Home and public world faced each other in a relationship that made for a continuous exchange. A reciprocity not unlike this also characterized the life of poor folk. Enormously high real-estate values determined their physical environment. The really poor hired themselves out as day laborers, odd-jobbers, or pieceworkers on a daily basis. They lived in crowded quarters where an exposed public existence was part of the nature of things.

The same people walked the same streets daily. There was mutual instant recognition. Retail outlets continually put all local people shoulder to shoulder. Servants, sent on errands, reduced such frequent contact for their masters, but even the chaperoned women of the rich had their public space in the parish church and in the streets immediately outside the family residence. Every neighbor had his or her particular identity associated with a trade, a name, a reputation, a clan or family. Strangers were immediately picked out in the streets and doubtless stared at. Births, marriages, and deaths were neighborhood events—for the common knowledge and feeling of all. Wedding parties were shared with neighbors. Funerals were the affair of the neighborhood, and a ritual mourning was provided not only by the women of the bereaved family but also by a host of women from the parish, while kinsmen and other neighbors gathered in front of the house. At Bologna, when an academic procession wound its way to a doctoral ceremony in the cathedral, all shops along the way were shut and afterward the new doctor of laws entertained his neighborhood.

The eyes of the neighborhood witnessed all unusual arrivals and departures. Nocturnal visits could not be perfectly stealthy, perfectly discreet. True privacy had a high price: it belonged to the floors well above and away from the streets; it called for particular care and psychological strain; and it cost money or labor—a large town house or a place in the country, and even then privacy had no security. The strongest personalities were those which were most at home in a public or corporate space.

Thoroughfares were few and customarily ran from the city gates to the cathedral, to the government square, or, where they existed, to the city's one or two bridges. If the byways or smaller streets were neighborhood strongholds, the few thoroughfares were less parochial and more communal in that they collected neighborhood life and plugged it into the larger life of the commune by pointing it toward the city walls, the cathedral, or the courts and government palace. On the thoroughfares, the powerful kinship groupings (the *consorterie*) got away from their immediate local interests and entered into a larger arena, where the battle for the control of the commune really took place. Here also the rich and prominent—far more than the poor and obscure—occupied a public space, were on show, and were known by their colors or carriage. They were instantly identifiable by their peers and knew themselves to belong to a name, a reputation, faction, or policy—in short, to something that went far beyond the individual. At Florence in 1300, the vivacious and brilliant Corso Donati, leader of one of the two factions, was recognized, said Compagni, wherever he went in the city, and "as he passed through the streets, many used to cry 'Long live the baron!' " (*Cronica*, II, xx).

As an environment for intensifying the social-communal texture of life, the layout of walled-in streets got much support from the guilds and armed neighborhood societies. Thirteenth-century guilds demanded and got a concrete emotional commitment from their members. Guild statutes called for a spirit of strong mutual aid and solicitude. No one could matriculate in a guild without the personal recommendation and friendship of several other guild members. When a guildsman died, all other members were expected to attend his funeral. They worked together in running the guild; they frequented one another; their families intermarried; they helped other guild families in distress; and they regulated the chosen trade through their consuls and governing bodies. They had their own guildhalls, courts, and guardsmen, and even, in the case of leading guilds, their own prisons. In certain cities, depending upon the violence and frequency of political emergencies, guilds were turned into paramilitary organizations, though these collaborated with, or yielded to, the armed popular societies of the neighborhoods. Where a trade was largely concentrated in a given street or a particular quarter, relations among kindred guildsmen were closer and more constant. They lived in neighboring houses, attended the same parish church, and daily brushed one another in the streets. Guildsmen instinctively looked to their guild for protection and help, for solidarity and for goals. Bakers, wool merchants, and others were militant in their trade claims, at times notoriously so, as in the case of the butchers, whose *esprit de corps* was extraordinary. Living so much of their life in the midst of a bustling community, in an atmosphere of close and confined streets, guildsmen moved and proved themselves in a corporate space, except in cases where the attachment to guild was overcome by the more powerful bonds of family and *consorteria*.

Guilds in the coastal cities were not nearly so formidable as those of the inland cities. At Genoa and Venice especially, guilds were less protective and had a timid or no voice in government. This made family and factional loyalties all the stronger, but did not alter the preponderance of public situations and corporate influences. In the early fourteenth century, the political class in Venice cut itself decisively off from the rest of the community and turned into a ruling caste. It thus became the city's most power-ful corporation, the Venetian nobility. Members were inscribed in its ranks from birth, their names entered into the special books of the nobility. At Genoa about 1300, where the ruling class was thoroughly divided, the domi-nant factions won more of the loyalties which in other cities were absorbed by the guilds or *popolo*.

The armed companies of the *popolo* included men from most guilds. They kept pretty much to their given neighborhoods and were made up of men selected for their loyalty, fighting skills, and fervor. They introduced a more coherent militancy into the neighborhoods; they put streets and fami-lies under a closer scrutiny, and hence more of whatever had been private became public.

The acute political and social strains of the thirteenth century increased the burdens of the guilds, neighborhood companies, and family associations. Fighting ever more urgently for control of the urban space, the different corporate groupings laid a tremendous burden of loyalty upon the individ-ual. He was known, and largely knew himself, by that loyalty. Enjoying no membership in a clan or sworn association, he was friendless, weak, vulner-able, and ill-directed. Inside an association he was bolstered, protected, and surrounded by friends, and had a strong sense of direction. Government was too weak and fumbling to protect him fully, and so he looked to a corporate grouping.

Contemporaries attest to the force of Dante's personality, yet his passions were moored inescapably in community and public matters. His overriding intellectual and moral interests, even in his verse, were the message of Chris-tianity, local and imperial politics, the vernacular language and literature, and the *civilizing* effects of love. He was not the exponent of an in-turned personal and private vision. All his pronouncements had a public ring.

Personal identity in the Italian cities was best realized and delineated in communal, social, and corporate terms. Guilds and neighborhood societies, more than the parish church, furnished the practical moral setting. The intimate streets and squares of the city supplied the corresponding physical setting. But nothing worked so well, in the making of a personal identity, as the appurtenances, name, and psychological resources available to any lead-ing family. Its commanding place in the political system, a system that affected every house in the city; its cluster of imposing houses; its reputed traditions and outlook; the street, square, or neighborhood associated with its name: these all went to fill the individual family member with a sense of his identity. And what is more, his neighbors and more distant peers recog-nized and paid tribute to that identity. It is no wonder that between about 1250 and 1320 the popular forces were compelled to wage a bitter and bloody campaign against the violence in streets and *piazze* of a whole class of magnates and noblemen, who saw that their identity was gravely threat-ened and that their day, in many cities, was passing.

FLORINS: THE BEST OF KIN

Preach what you will,
Florins are the best of kin:
Blood brothers and cousins true,
Father, mother, sons, and daughters too;
Kinfolk of the sort no one regrets,
Also horses, mules and beautiful dress.
The French and the Italians bow to them,
So do noblemen, knights, and learned men.
Florins clear your eyes and give you fires,
Turn to facts all your desires
And into all the world's vast possibilities.
So no man say, I'm nobly born, if
He have not money. Let him say,
I was born like a mushroom, in obscurity and wind.

This vision of money tells us more about the psychological and moral effects of economics than a panoply of statistical tables. The poet, Cecco Angiolieri of Siena (ca. 1260–ca. 1312), has taken the most powerful emotional bonds, the bonds of family, and cast them in the imagery of money; or rather, he has taken gold coins (florins) and represented them as family in order to demonstrate their force. He is not content to tell us that money can do anything, although he does this too. He uses metaphor to show that money *is* family and better than family; for money not only procures all the world's goods but also gives the emotional and psychological sustenance which hitherto had come exclusively from the family. Opening with a statement about kinfolk and closing with one about ancestry, the verses recycle a set of ardent traditional feelings by attaching them to that new and disturbing value—money. The family is robbed of its resources.

It is impossible for the twentieth-century reader to read Cecco's lines with a sense of shock, anxiety, and instantaneous humorous release—the probable reaction in the poet's time. We take the easy flow of money for granted; we recognize that the sudden influx of wealth can overturn social systems; but we cannot summon the powerful gut feelings, engendered by family, that were a daily reality for urban Italians of Cecco's day. In the thirteenth-century urban context, where family and personal identity were ineffably fused, Cecco's verses must have come as a disturbing flash of outrageous truth. Only a laugh could drain the instant anxiety. He was saying things that were disturbingly true but couching them in exaggeration. In middle- and upper-class Siena and Florence, as at Bologna, Genoa, and Milan, nothing rode higher in the passions of people than family, especially among those who claimed a place in government and politics. But it is also true that for a hundred years and more, urban Italians had seen wild inflation, the economic ruin of numerous old families, the spectacular rise of new fortunes and families, and the rise of revolutionary new credit mechanisms. Checkered by a rampant instability, the life of cities was best represented either by the image of money and what it could do or by the image, in whatever guise, of bloody contests for political power.

Ambrogio Lorenzetti's frescos of *Good and Bad Government* (Siena, Palazzo Pubblico, 1338–1339) are utterances of hope and distress in a mercurial time. Government in Siena, as in other cities, had constantly to be on the lookout for internal plotters and the machinations of political exiles. In this gravely disturbed world, the idealist poets of the "sweet new style" (ca. 1280–1320) sought a corrective, a range of stable perceptions summed up by a lofty ideal of love. City poets all, and well placed socially, they dreamed of a chaste and knowing and unreal woman: the vehicle of their own intellectual and moral cleansing. She—Beatrice, Vanna, Laggia, or another—provided her devotee with a sense of stability and raised him above the vulgar crowd of merchants, upstarts, and money-grubbers. Through his dedication to her, he entered a new spiritual aristocracy which affected to spurn social nobility (position, blood lineage, and money). The lexicon of the *stilnovisti*, the poets of the new style, conscientiously avoided all words and references denoting any practical or gainful activity. Thus Guinizzelli, Cavalcanti, Dante, Cino da Pistoia, and others. But money was the supreme object of aversion, the one item never to be mentioned in their elevated lyric verse. And we ransack the new style in vain for marginal or passing references, whether in metaphor or simile, to the force that seems to turn their world upside down—money. The result is that its calculated omission makes for its spectral presence. The fact that the *stilnovisti* systematically avoided the imagery of money puts us on the trail of its explosive effect in their overcrowded cities, all the more in that it preoccupied their more popular contemporaries, the so-called "comic" or "bourgeois realist" poets. We are able, in the verses of the realists, to see the psychological impact of a money economy, and we can follow its track in urban consciousness by tracing the appropriate diction in poetry.

Cecco's invasion of the family precincts was a revelation. His contemporaries, he suggests, put everything on a cash basis. This was of course not true, even if they were already drafting punctilious contracts for a remarkable variety of transactions.

After Cecco, for centuries to come, poets and diarists often fused the images of money, family, and friendship. Here is an early example with a devious composition, a sonnet by a Florentine, Pieraccio Tedaldi (ca. 1285–ca. 1355).

> The little florins all of gold and silver
> Have utterly abandoned me;
> Each has gone so far away
> As is Fucecchio from Pianoro.

> And so I ache and suffer more
> Than the sick in bed, for
> Not a single florin wants a home
> In my cash box, hand, purse, or at my side.
> More do I need florins
> Than the man with scabby ringworm needs caps.
> Day and night I long for them and dream of them,
> Yet none wants lodging in my house.
> And nought it boots to say that I love florins,
> As every one of them's a rebel against me.

The poet turns "little florins" into people and puts them as far from himself as the distance between two country towns. But they are not just people: the only two verbs of the first quatrain (*abandon* and *go*) combine with the verbs of domesticity in lines seven and twelve to indicate that Tedaldi's florins are relatives and friends. Thus converted, their refusal to live with him, or even to be near him, multiplies his grief. He is more wretched than a man with ringworm and so, by implication, people (florins) also flee from that. Still dissatisfied with the effect, the poet suddenly pivots in the last line and converts florins into rebels, while he, by necessary contrast, becomes the suffering commune—the city abandoned by its rebel citizens.

Tedaldi grabs at the emotive resources of family, friendship, and high politics (his society's capital sources of pain) with an eye to reenacting the anguish of being without florins. So doing, he recycles a set of strong traditional sentiments.

Colder and more direct perceptions were not necessarily more truthful, more illuminating. An anonymous Tuscan merchant of the second half of the fourteenth century advised fellow merchants in distant lands to "remember that money is all the help you have. It is your defense, honor, profit, and adornment."[1] But the Florentine diarist Giovanni Morelli, laying down advice to his heirs at the beginning of the fifteenth century, returned to Cecco Angiolieri's vision: "Be sure to have cash on hand at all times. Guard it carefully, and use it wisely, for it is your best friend and relative." By exploiting family feeling, this metaphor attained the highest possible level of persuasion. Next to it stood only a form of sacrilegious expression, such as God is money.

From at least the time of Cecco, then, writers had to dip into the nomenclature of the closest human relationships to illustrate the power and effects of money. No matter what the message of Christianity was, and no matter how men explained their behavior, the urban economy was straining and battering all the old relations and loyalties—guilds, confederations of families, and other associations. These were bombarded, their coherence was loosened, and the individual was gradually stripped of most of his traditional protections; but the process of stripping lasted two or three centuries. So far as Renaissance Italy saw the ascent of "the individual," the causes were not, as Burckhardt thought, in signorial politics but in the course of urban economic relations, and in the expanding effects of cash and credit mechanisms.

Looking back to the consular commune, we can see that next to piracy and long-distance trade, the large interest-bearing loan was the earliest fast maker of big money. The capacity to make mammoth loans was very often, however, the result of having made innumerable small ones. The twelfth and thirteenth centuries brought the rise and triumph of the credit mechanisms —loans direct and indirect—that would come to characterize and underpin the trade and public finance of the Italian communes. In the thirteenth century, new necessities forced the communes to reappoint their tax structures and to rely increasingly upon the loans of wealthy individuals.[2] By the 1290s tax farming—auctioning certain taxes—was being turned into ordinary procedure. As moralists feared, florins were becoming the supreme value; and unless poets recoiled from this, as did the *stilnovisti*, they had to construct a new lexicon for getting at the new meanings. Everything from niggling private transactions to the fighting of major wars appeared to take place under the sign of money or the devices of credit and financing. The effect of this brimmed over into whatever there was of private fantasy worlds. Cecco Angiolieri's sonnet on his gloom begins:

> Per si gran somma ho' mpegnate le risa,
> che io non so vedere come possa
> prender modo di far la rescossa:
> per piu l' ho' n pegno che non monta Pisa.

("I've pawned my laughter for so much that I can't see how I'll ever be able to redeem the pledge: it's in hock for more than the value/height of Pisa.")

The Sienese poet has pawned his laughter for a sum of money higher than the value and/or height of Pisa, a leading rival of the Sienese. With a single metaphor he knocks Pisa, establishes his gloom, and lets flicker before us one of the age's main sources of profit, usury, and pawn-taking. His language is spare but its resonances are rich. Here poetry's mystifications reveal the age. Attuned to the rhetoric of money, Cecco affixes a pawn ticket to his laughter, thus representing his melancholy in coins. The image speaks for a whole realm of experience: borrowing and lending, profit and loss, investment, risk, and financial crisis—indeed, the world of business.

Between about 1250 and 1350, poets of the realist school are struggling to come to terms with the effects and experience of money. A straining for metaphors is evident in the enterprise, and this suggests a disturbed value system, an effort to get hold of a malady. Tedaldi puts his finger on the sore: "The world is so base nowadays that wisdom and noble stock are worth nothing unless they are mixed with money [*richezza*], which condiments and seasons every good dish." And he concludes: "So let him who has money know how to hold on to it, if he wants to avoid being told one day, 'I can't bear the sight of you.' "[3] At about the same time, Niccolò de' Rossi, a nobleman from Treviso, also devoted a sonnet to the theme. He earned a doctorate in law at Bologna (1317), became a cleric, and died sometime after 1348. The sonnet "Denari fanno l' omo comparare" spells things out:

> Money makes the man,
> Money makes the stupid pass for bright,
> Money buys the treasury of sins,
> Money shows;
> Money buys the pleasure-giving women,
> Money keeps the soul in bliss,
> Money puts the plebe in high estate,
> Money brings your en'mies down.
> And every man seems down without it,
> The world and fortune being ruled by it,
> Which even opens, if you want, the doors of paradise.
> So wise he seems to me who piles up
> What more than any other virtue
> Conquers gloom and leavens the whole spirit.[4]

Here all the stops have been pulled out—almost anything goes: God is not money and the tone is a mixture of irony and acid truth, but lines six and eleven join the pecuniary to the spiritual.

Rossi's sonnet and Tedaldi's "The world is so base" pick up a common theme of the period, to be found even in the idealist poets: the theme of the loudmouth, villainous upstart. In Cecco Angiolieri, as in Tedaldi, Rossi, and other realists, the figure of the upstart is always framed in the imagery of ill-got money, earned by usury or lowly trades and pursuits. And here again poetry provides a fresh insight to a major theme.

Over much of central and upper Italy, the chroniclers of the thirteenth and fourteenth centuries frequently speak of "new men," "new citizens," "new people"—mainly in the context of party politics. Italy had seen the rise of new men in town and country since the tenth century. Not, however, until the late twelfth and early thirteenth centuries, when they become a distinct historical force, do they figure importantly in the chronicles, and then only, as we have seen, in bloc form, in connection with the ascent of the *popolo*. In the second half of the thirteenth century, with the victory of the *popolo* and the emergence of a strong vernacular literature of didactic bent, the image of the new man is glimpsed more often and in more detail, to the point of his becoming a literary obsession. The result is a view of the upstart not to be found in the chroniclers. For the new man was not just a political force; his numbers were also having an effect on social and moral attitudes. And the poet, with his way of seeing and his preoccupation with the contours of experience, grappled with the nuances, possibly exaggerated the changes, but never forgot that money and upstarts were as one, that underlying the "bad" moral effects of the rich *vilan* or parvenu was the greasy and showy and intimidating power of money.

Two long-term trends served to elevate the rich *vilan* to a place in literature: first, in Tuscany and other parts of north-central Italy, the decline of the old nobility took a sharper fall in the second half of the thirteenth century; and second, in the north, from Genoa to Lombardy and the Trevisan March, the civil wars had knocked down many old houses and the feeling of instability was rife. Money and riches, as profiled in the vigor of the rich *vilan*, thus seemed the one fixed worldly value. No wonder Rossi, Cecco, and the others sing bitterly and longingly of money. Even Dante, not only of course in *The Divine Comedy* but also in his late lyric verse, turns to skewer the moneymen, as in the third *canzone* of the *Convivio*: "riches . . . are by nature base" and "bring only anxiety, not peace." And again in his *canzone* "Doglia mi reca ne lo core ardire":

> What have you done, tell,
> Blind, undone miser?
> Answer me, if you can, other than "nothing."
>
> . . . . .
>
> Damned your wasted bread,
> Not even on a dog wasted!
> For night and day
> You have gathered up and squeezed with two hands
> That which so soon is utterly lost.

The sort of men who throw money around are also denied "a place among the worthy." They would be wiser, Dante tells them, "to hold on to their cash."

The way men looked (and look) at money and parvenus was so much a matter of class and point of view that we had better get our perspective right. I have been quoting men who traded in exaggeration, not in fictions—poets. The point is to find and outline the reality lodged in their hyperbolic vision. Certainly we should beware of the snobbery and jealousy present in most indictments of the upstart, for these tell us something about the poet and little about the larger historical reality. It was untrue, as was snobbishly lamented, that all "courtesy," style, and the gentle virtues were disappearing with the decay of the ancient and distinguished houses. In the *canzone* "Dear Florence mine," Matteo Frescobaldi (d. 1348) grieves at the loss of the city's generous and brave qualities:

> As long as you were still adorned, O Florence,
> by good and ancient citizens and dear,
> people far and near
> admired the Lion and its sons. [Lion: symbol of Florence]
> Touted among even Muslims,
> Whore you are now the world round.
>
> [ll. 23–28]

This conservative nostalgia for a nobler world is first lyrically heard in the 1260s and will be continually repeated for more than a century.

A writer from Genoa, working in the 1290s, has three poems on the plebe (*vilan*) who "climbs from lowliness to great prosperity" and attains political office: he is a man void of "measure, grace, and kindness." He can do nothing but harm his neighbors.[5]

Although more than a trace of the alleged graces had existed and persisted, their representation was much idealized by the poets. So much for poetic license. But all idealizations have a root in reality. It is not that noblemen such as the Doria, Visconti, Este, and Tolomei were fine, valiant, and generous, while the merchants and upstarts were coarse, cowardly, and greedy. In many cases the opposite was true. The real point was elsewhere: poets were saying that there was something tougher about the moneymen, something more coldly efficient and more persistent in streets, shops, and personal dealings. The thirteenth century offers conclusive testimony to the fact that merchants were already strictly enjoined to keep careful accounts of all their transactions. Moreover, a whole series of changes touched directly upon the nostalgic ideology of the poets: (1) a powerful class of new men had pushed their way into the political and social foreground by means of money; (2) in many cities money was undermining the old claims of birth and place, so that blood without money lost esteem; (3) rich ignoramuses were now heard occasionally in council, as illiterate knights once had been; (4) the effects of money were felt ever more keenly in an inflationary time of congenital wars; and finally (5) as attested by the performance of its poets, communal society was still struggling to absorb the moral consequences of money and credit mechanisms into its religious view of the world—a view that made a point of downgrading worldly enterprise.

There was a social reality behind the metaphors of the poets, but we need the poets to help us get at it. Their images of money and upstarts can be drawn together to reveal the emerging profile of a new order of values. Snobbery and jealousy aside, the rich *vilan* represented the triumph of commerce in everyday life—of bookkeeping, contracts, credit, and sharper perimeters in personal relations. The moneyman—merchant, speculator, or moneylender—was not greedy or more heartless than men sprung from the grand old houses; he was merely more efficient and predictable. His account books spelled out the quiddities of economic experience, and from these there was no deviating, save in economic irrationalities and excesses of piety. These, indeed, endured in the powerful push and tug of religious feeling, but they came to be part of a surprisingly coherent "system," as we shall see in the following section of this chapter.

There was violence in the acid humor of Niccolò de' Rossi's sonnet "Money makes the man," with its incantatory first eight lines, each starting with the word "money" (*denari*), and the force of the feeling was linked to an economic reality that was transforming values. The fact that personal diatribes in literature could turn on the lack of money, as in Forese Donati's scurrilous exchange with Dante, reveals that poverty easily invited sneers. Only the infamy of sexual perversion or the adultery of women seemed to

equal, in urban society, the dishonor of being without money and possessions—so far had the malady gone, and it was no less present among
noblemen who had plunged into commercial enterprise, such as the Spinola,
Saraceni, and others. But at least some contemporaries thought they could
remember a time when there were fewer account books around and fewer
merchants and parvenus at the helm of state.

EXPERIENCE AND RELIGIOUS
FEELING: AN ANONYMOUS MORALIST

A consideration of urban values in early Renaissance Italy would be
strange indeed without a discussion of religious sentiment.

Residents of cities encountered the Church's presence and promise
everywhere. We may begin with the fact that cities were first districted by
parish church, and the association of person with parish persisted always.
The existential events—birth, marriage, death—were concluded under the
seal of religion. A religious oath went with matriculation in guilds and hence
underwrote the pursuit of trades. The ideal of chastity, anchored in religious sentiment, was drummed into every girl, particularly among the
middle and upper classes. City streets teemed with clerics, and many citizens
had relatives in holy orders. In cities unafflicted by the noises and rumble of
machines, the reigning and habitual sounds were those of street cries, the clat-
ter of wheels, and the pealing of church bells, but the bells were far the
loudest, marking the hours, the sacred offices, and the major breaks in the
day.

Artistic subject matter was almost wholly religious: in fresco, panel
painting, stone sculpture, and carved wood. Crucifixes and images of the
Virgin abounded. All contracts and public transactions began, "In the name
of the Lord" or "In the year of the Lord." All cities had popular religious
confraternities. Membership in neighborhood societies and associations of
noblemen (as well as guilds) was sealed with a solemn religious oath. All
serious agreements required an oath, whether in trade, politics, or engagements to marry. The statutes of cities, guilds, and other associations were
studded with appeals to God and the saints. Decrees of political exile were
frequently read out in church as a first formality. Men began diaries, chronicles, and account books with religious invocations. To live in an Italian city
around 1300 was to assess good fortune and bad, and anything unusual, in
religious terms. The impulse was automatic. Comets, bankruptcies, earthquakes, and monstrous births were seen as expressions of a divine arrangement; and the devil frolicked everywhere.

Much of what went into religious utterances was probably mechanical:
men often follow formulas. Accordingly, sentiment ranged from ecstatic
fervor at one extreme to a half-cynical allegiance at the other; but frenzies

of religious feeling and the persistence of passionate heresy were more sensational and more likely to rivet the attention of contemporaries.

Historians have noted occasionally that the thirteenth was Italy's most religious century. This observation squares with the evidence if we bear in mind that religious fervor often appears in tandem with rich social and political ferment. Originally a lynching, the burning of heretics in the thirteenth century was moved by a vision of danger to the whole society, not merely by the fear of unorthodoxy. Religious doctrine was also social doctrine, and, conversely, social thought had a solid religious underpinning. The rush of political and social energies in urban Italy, like its economic and demographic vigor, was greatest in the thirteenth century; hence this was also a century of keen religious agitation and inflamed faiths. Heresy spawned in and around all the upper Italian cities. And just as traveling or fugitive heretics, in the guise of merchants and itinerant artisans, spread their message of rebellion or reform from Asti and Como to Orvieto and Viterbo, almost to the very doors of Rome, so also did the new preaching orders of mendicants—Franciscans, Dominicans, Servites, and others—go among city folk to fight the alleged poison of the heretics. From the late twelfth century, the Cathars (dualists) first, then the Waldensians, and next the Poor Lombards, Umiliati, "Apostles" of different persuasions, and Flagellants all disseminated their heretical doctrines or their ideals of evangelical poverty, repentance, and renewal. No city escaped the taint of heresy, and some—Milan, Vicenza, Florence—were accused of openly protecting heretics. Like orthodoxy itself, heresy knew no class boundaries, though its perimeters were restricted largely to the artisanal world, to the commercial middle class, and to a smattering here and there of the nobility. Mystics and excitable men, such as Gherardo Segarelli, sprung from the poorer ranks of society, were offset by their kind higher up on the social scale—St. Francis of Assisi or the ardent Florentine mystic Umiliana de' Cerchi. Giving herself to charity and the succoring of the poor, Umiliana turned violently against her rich upstart family, secluded herself in one part of the family *palazzo*, and refused to have any contact with them.

But let us consider a less dramatic figure, one who was so much closer to representative views that he comes down to us without a name: Dante's anonymous Genoese contemporary, the Anonimo Genovese, moralist and poetaster.[6] For he exhibits, to a remarkable degree, the archetypal contradiction of the age: the conflict between the Christian preoccupation with salvation and the spontaneous commitment, in the vitalizing urban context, to the rewards of this world. The Anonimo was a practical man with a mystic turn of mind: he approved fully of commercial venture and almost certainly engaged in it, while yet railing against the attachment to worldly pleasures and the immoderate quest for profits.

Writing between about 1295 and 1311, the Anonimo was born into the upper-middle class of Genoa and possibly had noble connections. He seems to have enjoyed material comfort, but he criticized pleasure-loving, well-dressed men and their "delicate" ways; and he was equally repelled by upstarts. Since he offered much practical business advice, he was probably a merchant. He held public office in and outside Genoa and was well acquainted with certain members of the powerful Doria clan. His verse reveals a detailed grasp of maritime ways and naval equipment, and so betrays his familiarity with the sea. The Anonimo was a very active member of the religious confraternity of St. Catharine of Alexandria, which left numerous bequests. He was hardheaded, down to earth, patriotic, abreast of current events, and a tough moralist with strong religious feelings—all this, however, in ways that were sometimes contradictory, though without seeming so to him.

In poem after poem, the Anonimo highlights the variety and brevity of human life. His themes are behavior good and bad, sin and redemption, and the terrors of hell. He stresses the vanity of earthly existence but is not led into quietism. On the contrary, he underlines the importance of action for the Christian (LXXXIX):

> This wretched life,
> finite and brief,
> was lent by the Lord
> for our useful work
> and labor with honor; . . .
> But men who live leisurely,
> negligent and sleepy,
> not working or scarcely,
> reviled will be,
> cast into prison eternally,
> where there's no salvation,
> but only weeping and groaning
> and a great grinding of teeth.
>
> [ll. 21–36]

The lines may seem childlike, but the author, well versed in religious literature, was far from being so. His rejoinder to the charge of being naive would have cited the vanity of learning and the need of simple folk to be told things simply and directly.

The Anonimo's religious outlook took in a wide range of events and activities, from wars between Genoa and Venice to the payment of workers, the selecting of a wife, and the size and appointment of private houses. In his view, four of the worst sins were: (1) homicide, (2) sodomy, "which is so filthy and grave that anyone who commits it deserves death by fire," (3) hurting poor people or orphans, whom the Lord "claims to Himself," and (4) withholding or refusing to pay money due "to any of your workers." Twice at least, in 1294 and 1298, he celebrated Genoese naval victories over Venice and attributed these to God's favor. The poem on the battle of Curzola (September 1298) he wrote in order to record the event and glorify

God. "Our Lord, by His great goodness, has raised our city of Genoa to great honor and by His power caused the Genoese to be sovereign over the proud Venetians" (XLIX). On learning of the victory, "Nearly all the city paraded, praying that God would bring the fleet back safely and soundly and in prosperity." Which did not keep them from calling the Venetians "scabby bastards" (*tignosi*), who in turn referred to the Genoese as "filthy leprous pigs" (XLVII, 19).

The Anonimo tendered advice on choosing a wife. There were four things to consider (LXXXVIII): the girl's forebears, her customs and habits, her honor, and the size of her dowry. If all these were right, then he advised marriage "in God's name." In another short poem (CXXX) he listed the married woman's ideal qualities: she should honor her father-in-law, love her husband unreservedly, know how to care for the family, know how to manage the household and its material things, and take great care of her honor. Nothing is said about the religious foundations of these qualities; they are taken for granted.

As a moralist, the Anonimo saves his most biting and picturesque indictments for the lovers of money and luxuries, indeed for all people—and he often singles women out—attached to worldly goods and pleasures. His emphasis is ancient and conventional, fully in line with the contempt-for-the-world tradition: he is the clear-eyed Christian reminding his contemporaries of their pilgrimage. But in the process he regales us with images and themes of the time, many garnered from the opulent style of Genoa's leading houses —the Doria, Spinola, Embriaci, and others. He affects pity for the men who take expensive and princesslike wives, wives who insist on wearing ornate dresses, while decorating their heads with pearls and precious stones. They are guilty of symbolic sacrilege (LIII): "Their beds seem altars, decked out for Easter and for Christmas." They keep "a train of lords and knights, courtiers and musicians with whistles and drums" (ll. 62–67). But all "this glory isn't worth a fig" and, compared with death and hell, it "passes in a flash." The Anonimo goes on to draw a picture of the way in which certain men set up house. They want the house "long, wide, high and bright, made of beautiful well-cut stone, fit for soaring windows that give light and a grand brightness." Suddenly everything is reversed (LIII):

> But the house where man ends up
> Is just the opposite—
> short, cramped, low, dark,
> void of windows, even slits.
> Of earth it's made and under the ground,
> and if of stone, little it's worth,
> for gain and profit follow not
> a handsome tomb.
> Thus are gulled
> the lovers of this world.
>
> [ll. 150–159]

He almost delights in the belief that big spenders and expensive women are soon enough taken off to their true destiny. Earthly life is not a shadow but it is not the end. This is the Anonimo's most recurrent and basic theme. He is therefore puzzled by the fact that mortals can forget the state of their immortal souls (XXXV): "I marvel greatly at the men who have no knowledge of self, burning away night and day with the desire to heap up silver, gold, and pennies, knowing not for whom; and yet they advise, 'rake the money in!' " He often returned to this incomprehension, to the figure of the man who uses every trick and even violence "to acquire power, possessions, lands, and goods for the sake of his children, thereby condemning himself to eternal damnation" [LX].

This was not thirteenth-century moralistic provincialism but a view based on a Continent-wide assumption about the nature and purposes of human life. And if the age really took the assumption seriously, the Anonimo's shafts were not out of place, not even the one beginning with the lines "I like no woman / who disfigures her face" (LXII). Like many of his contemporaries, he condemned the use of cosmetics, then much favored by women of the upper classes. Genoese society obviously tolerated the use of makeup. Although the Anonimo was strict, he reminded society of its contradictions. He had no trouble seeing makeup as a labor of seduction and the work of the devil. But he was equally critical of "dainty men—precious, vain, undisciplined [desordenai], lascivious, and always taken up with oddities and ornaments" (LIV, 138–141). These strictures he balanced with others that thoroughly reflected the snobberies of his class, although they were easily justified on religious grounds. He lashed out against the upstart, the rustic or poor commoner (vilan) who made money and rose to high station. It is clear to the Anonimo that such a man is worthy of being reviled because he has risen by hurting his neighbors (LXVII). "I know nothing more callous, nor more wicked, than a lowborn plebe who rises from the depths to great prosperity: he's a man transformed beyond all bounds, full of pride and sins" (CXVII). As we have seen, the image of the parvenu obsessed and upset upper-class urban Italy around 1300.

Moralists seem extreme because they take the prevailing system of values, cast its basic assumptions into the field of practical activity, and so confront society with its contradictions. The moralist sticks out because he speaks out: society resents having to face its ideal premises. This puts the Anonimo in perspective. He was not naive or shrill; rather, his society purported to move from difficult and perhaps impossible premises. For the rest, he could dole out advice with the most hard-nosed of his contemporaries, and here, suddenly, he capsized into contradiction with his Christian tenets. One short poem, "Contra iniurias" (LV), warns: "When you have been injured by someone and you want vengeance, guard lest you give this away. Hold your tongue, all the better to be revenged." Elsewhere (LI) he urges his reader not to lend money, not to borrow, not to be a guarantor, and never to conduct affairs without keeping a written record of things. Still other poems repeat these themes.

But his pride in and love of Genoa drove him into the sharpest contradictions. He could not free himself from his society. In a long poem on "The Condition of Genoa" (CXXXVIII), supposedly written for a citizen from Brescia, he abandons himself to his patriotism. The Brescian had reported that in his parts Venice was deemed to be the supreme naval power. Whereupon the Anonimo rushed into an excited description of Genoa's splendors and accomplishments. Amid assertions that God favors and has always defended Genoa, he praises the city's beautiful harbor, palaces, houses, shops, and towers. He celebrates its merchants, seamen, craftsmen, profits, rich diversity of textile goods, wares, spices, large population, colonies, and great fleet of ships. He is a "gut" imperialist: "There are so many Genoese scattered through the world that wherever they go they create another Genoa." Forgetting the moral indignation of other poems, he even praises the dress of Genoese merchants ("each one seems a marquis") and the city's "well-adorned" women who "in truth look like queens." There was no reconciling this eulogy of the earthly city of Genoa with his vision of the heavenly city of God, but he followed with no palinode.

In his long poem on voyaging through the world, "Exposicio de mondo navigandi" (CXLV), the Anonimo takes one of the fundamental Genoese drives, the quest for profit in maritime commerce, and transforms it into the mystery of a spiritual voyage. The first third of the poem is straight advice to Genoese merchants and sailors setting out to sea, with some promptings to prayer both before the voyage and as needed thereafter. More specifically, the advice is directed to ship captains and entrepreneurs, thereby setting its social perimeters. For 140 lines the Anonimo dwells in detail on the ship, its caulking, sails and rigging, on navigation, crosswinds, and the way to conduct business abroad. Then, quite unexpectedly, he passes fully over into allegory: "Every man is a merchant, roaming through the world" (ll. 149–150); and elsewhere, "We are all navigators" (l. 186) and "the heart" is a ship, "navigating where it wishes," so it should be "good and strong" (ll. 189–195). He universalizes the enabling experience—trade—of the Genoese:

> Now every man is in the market,
> so aim accordingly to get
> such merchandise and goods
> as bring you peace.
> Of many wares both dear and cheap
> . . . the cheap are sins,
> and so I say,
> had I a thousand ships of inexpensive wares,
> I'd still not have a cent,

for honest works alone and virtues
are merchandise of quality.

[ll. 151–162]

Again and again he draws upon the language of commerce and the sea to
convey his message of the Christian life as voyage: "I hold every man to be a
mariner who never ceases to voyage . . . until his end has come" (ll.
166–169). The sea is "bitter and very deep" and therefore much "like this
world." In fact, "The world signifies the sea, which can never be still because of some wind" (ll. 170–173).

Like Cecco Angiolieri, pilfering from the verbal bank of family feelings
to convey the force of money in a completely new way, so the Genoese
poet raided the imagery of maritime trade to help him deliver his lessons.

The Anonimo's perceptions and diction indicate that he was not speaking
for the stay-at-home Genoese: for the great bloc of women, the illiterate
petty craftsmen, the neighboring peasantry, nor even the rustics and other
obscure men who were sometimes dragooned into Genoese naval service.
He was speaking to and for the entrepreneurs, the international merchants
big and small who roamed the seas, once even as part-time pirates. They
organized expeditions, transported goods, bought cheap and sold dear, risked
mortal dangers, developed marine insurance, and lent money or made heavy
investments in the enterprises of others. Theological subtleties aside, they
answered best to the domineering vision of these lines (ll. 142–147):

All men are their own masters
as long as they have life.
Theirs is the free will to do
what they will, evil or good,
and other creatures live, then,
to serve them.

The long-distance merchants were the apparent makers of Genoa and its
overseas colonies. Others served them. The Anonimo tells them to draw up
their last wills, to put their affairs in order, to confess often, and to pray
hourly, especially when in danger (ll. 267–275). But no lines are more
marvelously crude and revealing than those which enable the rich en-
trepreneur to live with his wealth: "If you want to make good use of your
money, give out a lot in charity and do works of mercy for those in need,
doing so with discretion and tender compassion." Referring to the charitable
giving of money as "merchandise" (merze), he sums up his point: "There is
good treasure in such merchandise—to give away the sweepings and take in
gold, to get an expensive gift in return for a cheap one, for a perishable gift
to receive an eternal one" (ll. 251–264).

The Anonimo Genovese poured the experience of the great merchant-
mariner into an ethico-religious mold. The result was, in verse as in life, a
nervous union of contradictions: of moral austerity and earthly wealth,

economic intrepidity and religious fear, rapacious greed and frenzies of generosity, and a tight shuttling back and forth between sin and prayer. The seventeenth-century Calvinist merchant was more of a piece; his late-thirteenth-century counterpart more of a Manichean, tormented, in the words of the Anonimo, "by our three hard enemies: the devil, the flesh, and the world, which drag the soul down into the deep" (ll. 245–247).

CHAPTER VII

DESPOTISM: SIGNORIES

THE SEIZURE OF POWER

Among the problems of Italian history, none has been more studied from the earliest times than that concerning the causes and origins of the signory: despotism or one-man rule. Despotism already preoccupied thirteenth-century citizens. In 1267, in a region that was to be infested with signories, three communes—Treviso, Vicenza, Padua—concluded a treaty, renewed in 1277 and 1279, swearing to conserve themselves in perpetuity against the rule of any particular person, even "by means of sword, fire and blood." Dante deplored the fact that "the cities of Italy are full of tyrants" (*Purgatory*, VI, 124–125); and republican circles decried the spreading stain of "tyranny," a value-charged word of the time. Before 1350 the strongholds of communal republicanism—Florence, Lucca, and Siena—had experienced signorial rule; and Venice brushed up against it in the Tiepolo-Quirini conspiracy of 1310. Their political classes knew that the signory entailed enormous differences for citizens. Even noncitizens felt changes in tax and guild policies, and all people saw changes at the focal points of power. But the old nobility and the category of bourgeois magnates were especially affected by the signory.

Much influenced by legal historians, traditional views of the signory look to three or four thirteenth-century officials: the podestà, the captain of the people, the rector of the union of guilds, and the military captain general. In times of acute tension, a general assembly or council of the commune might vote special powers to one of these dignitaries, at the same time renewing his term of office. Later, there would be additional allocations of power and another renewal, confirming the man in office for five years, ten years, or life. In the next generation, in real or alleged responses to continuing crisis, hereditary leadership advanced its claims: the office, with its dictatorial powers, passed into the man's family. His sons, brothers, or grandsons succeeded him.

At the critical moment one of the leading dignities had been turned into a springboard for despotism. But the critical moment was essential. In Milan, four members of the Della Torre family were elected to head the Credenza's executive council: Pagano, 1240–1241; Martino, 1257–1263; Filippo, 1263–1265; and Napo, 1265–1277. In effect, they were the captains of the *popolo*. Not really lords of Milan, they were yet vastly influential because they led the *popolo* against the armed might of the exiled nobility, which often menaced the city in the 1260s and 1270s. In emergency, therefore, the power of the Della Torre swelled. Save for the brief emergency lordship of Manfredo Lancia (1253–1256), Ottone Visconti, archbishop of Milan, was the first native leader to be declared lord of the city and commune (1277), and he was eventually followed by Matteo, his grandnephew.

At Verona, Ezzelino da Romano had battered the nobility, owing to which the guilds and *popolo* were able to break into government. After 1259, to help them withstand the power of the illustrious old families, the Veronese guilds turned to the leadership of a rich magnate, Mastino della Scala, and named him captain of the *popolo* in 1262. Assassinated in 1277, he was succeeded by his brother, Alberto, who was elected captain and rector of the guilds and of all the people of Verona. The election was the work of a general assembly (*concione*) of the commune. Alberto was granted very broad powers, including the authority to enact statutory law, to alienate communal properties, and indeed to rule according to his own will. Yet he had to proceed warily, eyes fixed on constitutional forms. Not for another twenty years (1298) did he feel confident enough to strike at the guilds with a reform forbidding the council of guilds to assemble without a special license from the two captains, Alberto himself and his son, Bartolommeo.

The victories of the Estensi at Ferrara (1220s, 1264), the Caminesi at Treviso (1283), and the Carraresi at Padua (1318, 1328) also provide examples of internal takeovers, but the details would add little to the pattern already noted in the slow turn, or leap, from key office to signorial rule. Moreover, the traditional analysis, by its attention to the powers of office, is more an account of how the signory was born than why. Excessive attention is given to the office, to the election of the man, to the subsequent mandates, to any changes in title—e.g., captain, captain general, *dominus, potestas perpetuus*—and to the legal formulas that summed up the man's authority. The focus is legalistic. Fledgling *signori* and their partisans were careful, it is true, to make constitutional gestures; but what we need is a picture of causes, a view of crisis and stress. The argument from office carries weight only when it is laden with the particulars of crisis.

Milan again offers an instructive setting. Here the founder of the Visconti signory, Ottone, was also the head of the Milanese church. He provided the nobility with a rudimentary program and rallying point. After nearly eight decades of fitful civil war, the hatred between *popolo* and nobility was implacable. Milan's feudal nobility numbered several thousand men and retainers. Defeated periodically and compelled to spend long periods in exile, noblemen succumbed to desperation and sought military allies abroad. They lived off lands, off paid military activity, sinecures, church posts, castellanies, and public offices. Economically and psychologically, they were more dependent than the *popolo* upon the spoils and disbursements of government. Their alliances and diplomatic movements show that they preferred to live under a *signore*, expecting to benefit from his government, rather than under the yoke of their own *popolo*. In 1259 they made a secret pact with Ezzelino da Romano, lord of Verona, Vicenza, and Brescia. They offered him Milan and he was to help them against the Milanese *popolo*. But Ezzelino died that year of wounds suffered in battle. And so, in the 1270s, economic need, rage, and despair arrayed the Milanese nobility behind Ottone Visconti. As archbishop of Milan, Ottone also brought the dignity of the Church to his ascendancy over the nobility.

In the seizure of power by *signori*, economic pressures were often decisive. The Pisan ruling group turned power over to two native *signori*, the counts and close relatives Ugolino della Gherardesca and Nino Visconti (no relation to the Milanese Visconti), following Pisa's calamitous naval loss to Genoa at Meloria (1284). The city was in a state of shock. Dependent upon overseas trade, the whole Pisan economy lay in the shadow of disaster. The regime of the *popolo* was restored in 1288, but the nervousness persisted. Twice, in 1309 and 1313, the Pisans sought unsuccessfully to put themselves under the king of Aragon in the interests of their economic hold over Sardinia, considered by them to be the "head and mainstay" of the Pisan economy. Opposed by the Guelf League of Tuscan cities, they then offered themselves to Amadeus of Savoy, and he also declined, whereupon the rich merchant families threw their support behind the military leadership of the Romagnol nobleman Uguccione della Faggiola, who promptly used his position to seize power in Pisa (1314–1316).

At Florence the signory of the French nobleman Walter of Brienne, lasting only a year (1342–1343), was brought on by a financial crisis which had so frightened the mercantile and banking patricians that, fearing a popular uprising, they invited Walter to the city and handed power to him.

The rise of signories was not rooted in specific economic crises, for in such instances the regime of the *signore* was apt to be short-lived. Uguccione lost Pisa in 1316; his son, Neri, lost Lucca at the same time and in rather similar circumstances. War and its fiscal stresses often produced the call for a *signore*, but just as often he lost his office in the aftermath.

The economic causes of the signory were a matter of long-term endemic strains. Not one but a dozen wars, one after the other, laid intolerable burdens upon the commune's political and public-finance institutions. Threats of war also clawed at its resources. No one has bothered to count Milan's wars during the third quarter of the thirteenth century, or the wars among the communes of the Trevisan March in the early fourteenth century, but the results of any such count would surprise us by the urban capacity, financial and moral, to make war for so long.

Yet we must not isolate the fiscal urgencies of a whole string of wars and the consequent disruptions for traffic and trade from other primary conditions. For a century after about 1240 the cities of Tuscany were continually engaged in serious wars. Governments fell; communes faced the menace of conspiracy; taxes soared along a wide front; temporary signories were established. But with the exception of Pisa, those cities came to be the centers of republican government. Even Genoa, continually buffeted by war and civil strife, hung on to its communal institutions during the fourteenth and fifteenth centuries, as it swung back and forth between signories and republican regimes. So we must look beyond war and fiscal emergency for the sources of the signory.

The intolerable strains on communal institutions—crisis—derived from three or four different sources: (1) war and economic need; (2) implacable party conflict and an ensuing atmosphere of disruption, instability, and fear; (3) the force of intercity party alliances; and (4) the propensities of a strong and numerous nobility. Aside from the last of these, none sufficed by itself to impose a signory; and, indeed, even the workings of two or three might fail to ensure its triumph, as the experience of Tuscany shows. However, in cities where the nobility was populous and resolute but yet stood off from the middle classes and largely refrained from active trade, it could drag the commune under signorial government and keep it there, as happened in Milan. It is true that at Verona and Mantua the emergence of the signory was associated with the *popolo* and union of guilds; but as soon as any *signore* was able, he eviscerated all popular organizations and turned to ground his regime in the local nobility, his "natural" allies. No signory could survive in tandem with a vital guild movement. One of the two had to die. At Ferrara, in 1287, the lord of the city, Obizzo d'Este, responding to Venetian economic pressures, suppressed the guilds and thereby did his share to undermine the commercial-industrial part of the Ferrarese economy.

After 1250, from Umbria to the Alps, there was a dramatic escalation in the strife between political blocs: the alignments became sharper, the sides more uncompromising, the wars bloodier and more expensive. Political passion rose to fever pitch and remained so until the 1330s. In a number of cities—Perugia, Bologna, Pisa, Genoa—the ferocity of party and sometimes class conflict persisted for long thereafter. Mass exile became commonplace; so also the wholesale confiscation of enemy properties, the razing of houses, and the formation of exile armies. In 1261, Milan's popular commune captured 900 Milanese noblemen, exiles who had made war on the city since 1254. The populace wanted them put to the sword, but the government resisted and the mob managed to catch and kill only a few, as they were being transferred from one prison to another. During the Emperor Henry VII's attack on Florence in 1312–1313, the Florentine exiles in his train were the most rabid in urging the use of violence, as Henry's forces ravaged and looted the lands surrounding the city. Around 1300, Genoese exiles did not shrink from leading flotillas into the port of Genoa to make war on the commune. From March 1318 to February 1319, the exiled Genoese Ghibellines besieged Genoa with an army of more than 20,000 men. Civil war lasted until 1331, during part of which time Robert, king of Naples and count of Provence, was lord of the city.

The foregoing particulars suggest the extremes of conflict. War and emergency encouraged the ascent of astute and talented party leaders, who, in the bloody tumult of civil war, were sometimes able to convert their leadership into dictatorships. Having overwhelmed the political opposition or entering triumphantly into the home city, leader and followers were now ready for the takeover. With troops massed in or near the main government square, they could "persuade" any assembly of the commune to do their bidding. But it also happened that the victorious might take two or three decades to build up strength within the city, meanwhile cowing the opposition, until an emergency broke forth and the leading man, flanked by adherents and troops, could suddenly get himself elected *signore*.

Exceptionally at Padua, in July 1318, Jacopo da Carrara's election to the office of captain general in perpetuity (i.e., *signore*) was not preceded by civil strife, by exile en bloc, or by mass confiscations. Facing a war of survival against Verona and its Della Scala signory, Padua's ruling Guelf party reached an agreement on Jacopo's election with the rival Ghibellines, and a bloc of Ghibelline exiles probably returned to the city. But compromise of this sort was unusual. The pattern at Genoa indicates that abrupt changes in government were normally set off by civil war, rebellion, or suddenly inflated party strength.

Treviso provides a characteristic illustration. There party struggle between the Reds (Ghibellines) and Whites (Guelfs) reached a climax in the course of the 1270s. Many Whites were driven into exile. On November 15, 1283, with the *popolo* holding back to see the outcome, the two sides took to armed conflict and all the most active Reds fled from the city or in some cases ended in jail. The Whites then called a meeting of the chief executive council and the legislative Council of Three Hundred. A judge, Pietro d'Arpo, got up and moved that Gherardo da Camino, head of the Whites, be made captain of the city and Trevisan district. The proposal passed easily, and the Whites then called for a general communal assembly (*concione*). Nearly all resident citizens (more than 2,000) with public-office rights attended. Once again Pietro d'Arpo stepped forward to recommend that Gherardo be proclaimed captain. This was immediately seconded by Alberto Ricco, who came of a rich and distinguished Trevisan family. Intimidated, the citizens fell silent. Not a single dissenting vote was voiced in the *concione*, for each member of the assembly was individually called upon to stand up and give his vote of approval. By plebiscitarian vote, accordingly, Gherardo was made captain general in perpetuity. Two other members of the *concione* then got up and successfully proposed a new law, overturning the communal constitution. They proposed that the statutes of the commune "be in the full power of the captain, Gherardo, and that these should be understood *plus et minus* according to his will." On the same day, too, Gherardo's claque secured the appointment of a commission with the authority, if need be, to exile all Reds. Many Reds submitted; others turned to friends and relatives for help; and some were pardoned. Altogether about a hundred men from the city and district were exiled; their properties and goods were impounded and in certain cases their family seats were destroyed. The worst hit were the Castelli, a powerful feudal clan and leaders of the Reds. Any citizen who offered them aid or succor was subject *ipso facto* to capital punishment and forfeiture of all his properties.

The transition from commune to signory was not nearly so swift in other cities. Orvieto, a hill town in Umbria, drifted toward signorial rule. There, in the 1290s, guilds and *popolo* edged their way toward supreme authority. In the early fourteenth century they enacted stiff class legislation against the nobility. A crisis was building up, particularly as the nobility remained strong and numerous. Later, in the early 1320s, the *popolo* began to lose the initiative and to flounder in leaderlessness, owing probably to its internal divisions. Noblemen appeared in the powerful emergency councils (*balie*) as full-fledged members; they conducted embassies, in some cases passed as *popolani*, and insinuated themselves into other public offices. The decade also recorded acute fiscal strains. The commune was heavily indebted to the nobility; taxes were increased; revolts broke out in the countryside; citizens resorted to fiscal expedients; there was conflict with Perugia over the town of Chiusi; and civil discontent gripped the commune. Although the nobility was itself split, the emergency atmosphere enabled a group of oligarchs to strip the popular councils of most of their powers (1325–1326). This plunge toward closer oligarchy ended in 1334, when Napoleone Monaldeschi—a distant cousin to Ormanno Monaldeschi, the most authoritative nobleman in the city—was murdered in the streets. Orvieto's leading family clan, the Monaldeschi, had been divided for years. The murder was carried out by Ormanno's son, Corrado, with the help of servants and followers. The government was too weak to take punitive action. A few weeks later, in the council of the *popolo*, one of Ormanno's adherents called successfully for the suspension of thirty-four constitutional clauses. He then followed with a revolutionary reform: the establishment of a special emergency council, twenty men in all, whose powers were so great that they eliminated the council and captain of the *popolo* in all but name. Three days later the emergency council transferred full powers to Ormanno and made him "Gonfalonier of the *Popolo* and of Justice" for life. The council was packed with his friends and supporters, but he also had the help of the bishop of Orvieto, Beltramo Monaldeschi, his brother. It was a tight, if not cozy, world.

In these outlines, as in the chronicle of Trevisan events, we have no trouble imagining the attendant atmosphere of open and undercover violence, of psychological duress, and of disarray on the part of the defeated groups. The stakes were the highest: the power of the state, life, property, exile for oneself and male descendants in perpetuity. It is a wonder—and the manifestation of an academic viewpoint—that historians have habitually tinkered with the legal question of signorial origins at the expense of the reign of terror which frequently accompanied the seizure of power. And here again economic interests affected events. For when the victorious party came out of months or years of exile and deprivation, the rage for economic vengeance was wild and the losers were shorn clean of their properties. Political defeat and the forfeiture of property were joined like the two sides of a coin. The new *signore* won supporters and loyalty by doling out the houses and lands of the defeated, or by selling these to adherents for derisory sums. At Ferrara and Mantua, the signorial seizure of power was followed by the large-scale transfer of rural properties to the political victors and their friends, supporters, and vassals. Much the same took place in other cities, especially east of the Apennines.

In sorting out the origins of the signory, recent study has emphasized the regional bonds among political parties of neighboring cities. Proximity and shared or similar problems were such as to foster parallel party alignments, whether in relation to the papacy, the empire, the *popolo*, or the region's most powerful city. Moreover, mass exile, which sometimes drove thousands of men far from their city walls, naturally brought together the kindred groups of scheming exiles from different cities: Guelfs or Ghibellines, magnates or *popolani*, or factions known by other names. In the early fourteenth century, a miserable band of Pisan Guelfs, working together with the Upezzinghi feudatories from around Pisa, looked for assistance from the Guelf League of Tuscan cities, chiefly Florence and Lucca. In 1312, more than a thousand Florentine exiles (Ghibellines) joined the small imperial army which ravaged the Florentine countryside, sacked and burned villas, and terrorized the rural populace. But the dense network of alliances among parties of different cities was thickest in the Northern Plain, from Piedmont across Lombardy to the Trevisan March. There feudal jurisdictions were larger, stronger, and more enduring; there conflicts or alliances among the principal feudal clans could reduce a region to chaos or bring it under a tighter control; there, on the whole, feudatories had larger estates, more tenants and *fideles*, and larger private armies; and there, as Machiavelli and Guicciardini shrewdly observed, the habits of deference—they said "servitude"—were more deeply ingrained. Finally, there also the initiatives of commerce and industry were unable to prevail over the residual values of feudalism—over its habits of homage, deference, paternalism, and the ritual fuss associated with rank and status. In this context even Milan, for all its bustling industry, could not escape the coils of feudalism: after 1260 the bulk of the Milanese nobility desired an overlord to whom loyalty and obedience were due.

The significance of an alliance among the kindred parties of different cities is that it often enabled a *signore* to seize power over a whole region. This he did with the help of local groups and leaders within the alliance, as happened in the cities that fell under the domination of the Visconti of Milan. As an action prepared by local groups, the seizure of signorial power by outsiders was first seen in the 1250s, with the takeovers by Ezzelino da Romano, Oberto Pallavicini, and others. We have seen that in 1259 the Milanese nobility plotted to procure the lordship of Milan for Ezzelino. A successful maneuver of this sort was carried out at Modena in 1288–1289. There the Grasolfi (Ghibellines) had long been in exile and the party in power, the Aigoni, had split. In the autumn of 1288 the weaker faction of the Aigoni, having withdrawn from the city, seemed about to make a deal with the Grasolfi exiles. Popular agitation was swelling and threatened to exclude noblemen from public office. Whereupon the Aigoni nobility, feeling gravely endangered, dispatched an embassy to Obizzo d'Este, lord of Ferrara, to offer Modena to him. Immediately accepting the offer (December 1288), Obizzo sent out a vicar to take charge of the city, and he himself finally arrived in January. His overlordship lasted until his death in February 1293. This signory thus sprang forth directly from party strife and from party contacts made abroad.

Nearly all the *signori* who succeeded in founding enduring regimes issued from eminent feudal families, rich and powerful in city and country. Usually they disposed of vast estates. In 1259, for example, in the regions around Treviso and Vicenza, Ezzelino da Romano's family had endless possessions, including houses, palaces, castles, shops, mills, forests, mountains, and whole cultivated expanses. With these resources they had no trouble making alliances with other feudatories or distant heads of parties, often by means of select marriages. The Montferrat marquises of Piedmont were this sort of family; so also the Este of Ferrara, the Malatesta of Rimini, the Gonzaga of Mantua, and at Genoa even the Spinola and Doria.

The best setting for successful resistance to the signory was to be found in cities with a strong commercial or industrial base, cities where the old feudal nobility had been decimated or absorbed into the business class. Bologna, Florence, Lucca, Siena, Perugia, and Genoa answered best to this description. Pisa also belonged to this cluster of cities, but the catastrophe at Meloria and the ensuing economic fright pushed the city's big business class into a fatal panic, rendering it unable to govern itself. Venice was a city without a feudal nobility at home. The Venetian patriciate was deeply committed to commercial enterprise. And there is little doubt that Baiamonte Tiepolo's bold but failed *coup* of 1310 would have turned into a bid for signorial power, for the patriciate was too heavily massed on the government's side.

The easiest targets for *signori* were the cities whose commercial indus trial base was small relative to the surrounding rural economy: e.g., Verona, Mantua, Ferrara, Treviso, Como, Lodi, and the Romagnol towns. Here agricultural productivity predominated over commercial exchange and industrial output. Partly as a result of this, the nobility remained an ambitious and populous force which held itself largely aloof from business enterprise. Here noblemen rarely engaged directly in trade; it was somewhat dishonorable for them to do so. The more land-based type of city could not long resist the onslaught of the budding *signore*, the party leader with a large rural constituency and a strong following of urban noblemen. The combination proved to be too much for any union of artisans and merchants.

These observations put Milan, possibly the most heavily populated city in Italy, into a new light. Having a large and vigorous class of artisans and merchants, here was an industrial city at the heart of a rich network of economic and exchange relations. Contrary, however, to what happened to the nobility in the big Tuscan cities, the Milanese nobility retained its separate and strong identity. Maintaining a high birth rate and a pronounced military stance, it continued to be more than a match for the middle classes, particularly after the Motta—the union of lesser knights and rich merchants —abandoned the *popolo*.

In casting around for the causes of the signory, for the conditions attending the takeover by *signori*, we have come up with war emergencies, economic need, the tenacity of violent party conflict, fear, intercity alliances, and the inclinations of the nobility. But within these limits, the concrete occasions that triggered change were complex enough to confound the most sophisticated social science.

SIGNORIAL GOVERNMENT

During the fourteenth century, the signory brought enough pacification and stability to a few cities—chiefly Milan, Padua, and Ferrara—to give rise to the myth that civic peace and signorial government went together.

Strong-arm methods squelched dissent and conflict but failed to uproot the causes of civil discord. Violence might long endure behind appearances. Able *signori*, such as the Carrara of Padua or some of the Visconti of Milan, reaching out in their administrations to the whole community, rose partly above social divisions and could allay frictions by means of balanced policies. Many Lombard and especially Romagnol cities, however, had continuing strife and changes of unstable signorial regimes. It would be difficult to improve on the stories that Symonds retails about the barbarities and fine lusts of certain signorial families.

Until a *signore* obtained recognition via imperial or papal action, every act of his government had its supposed ultimate legitimacy in the orginal transfer of authority, no matter how violent the circumstances connected with his takeover or with the approval accorded by the commune. The regime insisted upon its legitimacy and admitted to nothing irregular—indeed, went out of its way to rally lawyers and judges to its cause. We saw the judge Pietro d'Arpo spearheading the legitimization of the Caminese signory at Treviso in 1283. Matteo Visconti, *signore* of Milan, recruited the support of lawyers in 1313, when the death of the Emperor Henry VII seemed suddenly to undermine his claim to an imperial vicariate. Azzone Visconti procured the public endorsement of two lawyers in March 1330, when his overlordship was confirmed by Milan's Council of Nine Hundred. Again and again *signori* used the slippery resources of the law. Arguably, the more illegitimate a regime, the more ostentatious its claims to constitutional right—no strange spectacle to the twentieth century.

The signory's emphasis on the lawful face of its affairs has often been commented on by historians but not often appreciated. Power relies upon imagination. It was the very legal shakiness of the new *signori* that made them scramble for every legal ruse and device. They used the law to hold the community. Law and order were manipulated to veil the underlying lawlessness—and oligarchies were no less adept at this. For all their original violence, *signori* knew that they could endure only by regularizing procedures and affecting to side with the rule of law. Despite the allegations of historians regarding the growing apathy of citizens in the fourteenth century, the astute *signore* tended to leash his authority. If nothing else, he observed legal forms. His enemies, whether in exile or silently resident in the city, looked on and only waited to overthrow him.

The new lord recognized that the traditional structure of office in the commune had to be, or appear to be, respected. Gradually he gutted the power of the old legislative councils; only the foolhardy tyrant swept them away altogether. This goes to indicate, yet once more, that the alleged apathy of citizens was not so thorough as to ensure that they could be disregarded. On the contrary, the *signore* studied the mood of citizens and offered appropriate responses. He had to pay lip service to practices that he probably disdained, but that lip service helped to make his situation more tolerable.

The major legislative bodies survived in nearly all the cities that fell subject to signorial rule. Milan's Council of Twelve Hundred, reduced to Nine Hundred shortly before 1330, was called occasionally into session by the Visconti. In the 1320s, Verona's Council of Five Hundred met under Cangrande della Scala. Cecco degli Ordelaffi, *signore* of Forlì in the same decade, assembled the communal Council of Four Hundred on a number of important occasions. At Bologna, Taddeo Pepoli called meetings of the Council of Four Thousand in the late 1330s and early 1340s. The Council of Three Hundred at Bergamo—cut to 144 members in the early 1350s—continued to meet even after the commune was drawn under Viscontean-Milanese rule in 1332. Treviso also had a Council of Three Hundred which met under the Caminese *signori*.

As time passed these councils met more infrequently. They might be used to rubber-stamp certain of the lord's major enactments, or they might be called to meet on minor matters only; but they were not dissolved. The council of nine hundred, five hundred, three hundred, or whatever number remained on the edges of government. As a matter of fact, in a number of important instances, such councils took a much more active part than this suggests. Conciliar membership remained, therefore, important. If the large legislative council met less often and if its major powers had been taken away, then we might suppose that the lord of the city took little notice of its membership. Instead, he took a keen interest in it and used a variety of devices to keep the council filled with trusted supporters. This implies that the council had more value than historians have often supposed and that even rubber-stamping was an important operation in the conduct of signorial government.

How the *signore* controlled membership in the large councils reveals his slyness, his mixture of prudence and naked force. It was rare for him to pack legislative bodies by simple appointment. He took a more conciliatory route and had recourse to regular procedures. At Milan, potential members of the large council were reviewed in each parish by a committee of parish "elders." These, in turn, made recommendations to the head of the municipality's chief administrative body, the Consiglio delle Provvisioni, and he made the final choice in consultation with the twelve members of this *consiglio* and the approval of his Visconti master. The twelve were chosen by the lord or by his closest collaborators. Controls at Mantua, Verona, and Treviso entailed similar procedures—review, recommendation, selection, and approval. In this way, a large assortment of citizens seemed to be brought into the processes of election, but there was complete control from above.

Now and then the *signore* let all his weight be felt. At Cremona, under the Visconti, the two old legislative councils of four hundred and two hundred citizens were replaced by one. The members of this council were selected by the *signore* himself, and in 1356, under Bernabò, who was not known for his finesse, the name of the council was changed to "the Council of the Lord Bernabò Visconti and of the Commune of Cremona."

A more devious system of controls, used by oligarchies as well as signories, centered on the practice of filling offices by drawing names as in a lottery. Votes in council, or other checks, eliminated the undesirable citizens and certified the eligible. The eligible names were put on individual tickets and entered into different pouches for the key offices. Those drawn for a particular office and term then saw service. In the process, there was ample room for manipulation.

In Pisa a number of different *signori*, and chiefly the Gherardesca counts, narrowed the basis and operations of government. In 1370 the general legislative council was pushed aside and the fullness of power passed to an ensemble of small councils. Real power, however, remained with the twelve *anziani*, who nominated the members of three small councils. Pisan *signori* therefore sought to control the *anziani*. In 1369, the year before he took covert signorial power in Pisa, Pietro Gambacorta was granted the right to check the names of all citizens listed for entry in the office pouches. He shared this right, which was really the right of veto, with two other men, one of whom was prior of the *anziani*. But in 1373 he alone got this right, which he combined henceforth with the right to participate directly in the designation of citizens for the eligibility rosters. In this capacity he acted together with the *anziani* and a special council of sixty-four *savi* ("wise men"). To make it easier to control, this council was reduced to twenty-eight members in 1377. Furthermore, all the leading members of Pietro's family—four or five men at least—also gained the right to take part in drawing up the lists of eligibility. The *savi* always included one or more members of the Gambacorta family. Pietro turned the *savi* into regular advisers and electors of the *anziani*, then into the chief instruments of Gambacorta rule. They were drawn strictly from among adherents; they were informally organized; they met almost daily; they varied in number; and their advisory functions, reflecting a Pisan tradition of counsel by "wise men," promoted the impression that something of the city's republican-communal institutions survived. Instead, Pietro's hand predominated. In 1377, ten *savi* met to make nominations for the new podestà. Three of the ten were Gambacortas, Pietro and his sons, Benedetto and Andrea.

A departure from the foregoing procedures was the method of cooptation: the members of a given council chose their successors directly or indirectly. This practice or its like went back to the consular commune. In certain cities, consuls had appointed electors, who in turn chose the succeeding body of consuls. In 1334 the chief advisory council at Imola was made up of eight *anziani*. At the end of their term in office each of these nominated four candidates and the *signore* then chose from among them. An overall slate of the eligible citizens had been cleared, of course, by the *signore* or his intimate aides, but a conventional mode of succession was thereby observed.

The emphasis on the *signore*'s regard for forms points to the conditions around him, but does not minimize his power. For the authority originally made over to him by communal assemblies often verged on the absolute. At Treviso, Verona, Padua, and Mantua, he had the authority not only to interpret the law but also to suspend, change, or make it. He could alienate the properties of the commune. And while the power of justice was normally delegated, he could lay effective claim to it, in civil and in criminal proceedings, in capital as in minor matters, and he could also grant pardons at will or overturn the decisions of the ordinary judges. It is difficult to see that anything connected with government lay outside his authority. In the course of the fourteenth century, with the practice of conferring imperial or papal vicariates, this authority was increasingly stabilized. In the Romagna, to turn a *signore* into a papal vicar—the Romagna belonged to the jurisdiction of the papacy—was to invest him with a higher legal authority; now the commune was no longer the sole basis of his governing position in the city. Farther north, as at Verona or Milan, the grant of an imperial vicariate had the same effect. But just as no vicariate could in itself prevent conspiracies or save *signori*, so the lack of one did not necessarily lead to *coups d'état*. The immediate setting decided this far more than imperial or papal titles.

The title of any particular lord might give him the fullness of power, especially in the Romagna and the northeast, but he rarely exercised it in full. Even in the most turbulent of regions, Romagna, he was compelled to accept legislative and advisory councils and to have some regard for collective feeling. For military supremacy, as John Larner has observed, availed "little against the opposition of a united town." Hence Romagnol "*signori* had to rule with a certain measure of representation and consent by their subjects."

Surprising details emerge from one of the most successful of all signories, Milan under the Visconti. Vicariates, for example, did not eliminate the desire for communal confirmation. Having been granted an imperial vicariate in 1329, Azzone Visconti asked, nonetheless, in the following year, for recognition from Milan's Council of Nine Hundred. The council responded to the request of the "lord general in perpetuity" by endowing him with full *dominium* over the city (March 15, 1330), yet in 1331, in view of an imperial vacancy, he also procured a vicariate from the pope. Titles evidently had an aura as well as some practical value. In 1330, the Council of Nine Hundred handed over full legislative and judicial powers—or almost, for they seem not to have surrendered the commune's fiscal autonomy. This was not lost until after 1385, when Giangaleazzo Visconti captured the signorial power by trickery from his uncle, Bernabò. Hitherto, Visconti lords had often sought conciliar approval for new and special taxes. Bernabò, it is true, had governed brusquely and at times cruelly, above all in subject cities such as Cremona and Brescia, but not a single citizen raised a voice in his favor when he was toppled by his nephew. Later, in 1405, the chief administrative council for the municipality of Milan, the Consiglio delle Provvisioni, succeeded in imposing a system of fiscal controls on Giovanni Maria Visconti. The success was temporary. As late as 1427, the same council, composed of twelve trusted supporters of the *signore*, tried to regain control of the city's revenues, but he simply rejected their representations. The power of the *signore* is in full view here. A man like Bernabò would most likely have had the councilors arrested; in the end, however, he was much less effective as a ruler.

The fourteenth-century *signore* governed through a variety of councils, advisers, and aides. The old captain of the *popolo* usually disappeared, his functions absorbed by the *signore*. Where he survived, he was usually turned into a magistrate. But this was more the destiny of the podestà: in nearly all signorial cities he became the leading magistrate.

As of old, the podestà could not be a native of the city in his charge; he often had military skills or some acquaintance with the law; he entered the city with a staff of judges, knights, notaries, and attendants; and he served six months or a year. His knights and attendants carried out police duties. In subject towns, the podestà (or "vicar") was sent out from the capital city, say Milan or Genoa. The courts of the podestà often had full jurisdiction in civil and criminal proceedings, except for cases claimed by the lord or minor cases belonging to the competence of certain guilds. And although there were courts of appeal, the *signore*, in session with his counselors, constituted the highest court. In a few cities, Padua most notably, the podestà and his officials were responsible chiefly for penal justice and public-finance litigation; civil litigation remained with a panel of native judges (thirteen in Padua), drawn from the city's college of jurists.

The podestà, or his equivalent, was also the *signore*'s chief administrative official. At Milan this administrative function belonged to the vicar of the Consiglio delle Provvisioni. Like the podestà at Padua, the Milanese vicar presided in the large council or in other citizen bodies; he relayed and published signorial ordinances or decrees; he accepted complaints or recommendations, kept the city under some surveillance, and reported back to the *signore*.

As we have seen, at least one legislative council—there had often been two—survived the signorial takeover. Selectively filled—bullied, manipulated, flattered, irregularly assembled—this council served to keep and foster contact between the *signore* and the body of citizens. Through it the latter felt him out and he could gauge their humor, for the agitated fourteenth century, with its devastating wars, plagues, and fiscal crises, would often force him to seek their support.

The *signore*'s advisory and administrative councils varied greatly, according to time and place, and a good deal of obscurity conceals the inner workings of the advisory councils. By the late fourteenth century the lord of Milan had a privy or "secret" council, staffed mainly by soldiers and lawyers—all men of extensive political experience. Appointed by the lord of Milan, they were consulted in all matters of high policy. But the administration of Milan itself was in the hands of another council, the Consiglio delle Provvisioni.

Although the Carrara lords of Padua also had a council of advisers, it seems to have been organized much more informally and intimately. There was no such arrangement at Pisa during the Gambacorta signory (1370–1392). Pietro Gambacorta may have gotten his sons and other relatives into the highest councils of state, but the family, unlike the Carrara or Visconti, had no signorial traditions, and Pietro often assumed the manner of "first among equals." He received a yearly stipend from the commune and had no reliable control over the communal fisc. He reviewed the whole slate of citizens eligible for high office and eliminated those who could not be trusted to follow the Gambacorta lead, but he had to work through the small councils of *savi*, who took office in accord with traditional procedures.

The actual power of the *signore* varied. At the moment of overthrowing a government by force of arms, he might well have absolute power *de facto*. But military force aside, signories were stronger and more stable at the end of the fourteenth century than at the beginning. Imperial and papal vicariates helped to provide a thickening patina of legality. Survival itself also assisted the course of change. The Este, Gonzaga, Carrara, Visconti, Malatesta, and a few other such families came to be identified with signorial authority; in the process, a bank of deferential feeling was built up among citizens. Military control, however, remained basic to the enduring success of *signori*. This aspect of signorial government was often represented by a fortress within the urban space, especially in subject cities. When a *coup d'état* terminated Lucca's subjugation to Pisa in 1369, and the imperial *palazzo*, symbol of Pisa's hold over Lucca, was destroyed, the Lucchese went wild with joy. The chronicler Sercambi reported: "There wasn't a man or woman big or small who did not get up on the remains . . . many wept with joy and many others seemed to go crazy and beside themselves. . . . They thought they were in a kind of second paradise."

The continuing success of the signory also depended upon professional soldiers. Now and then, in the thirteenth century, cities had employed the services of mercenaries, but there was a steady rise in this practice and after about 1340 professionals dominated military action all over upper Italy. Small armies—mainly German and French—revolutionized the organization and conduct of war. Hired by signories as well as republican oligarchies, they were allotted short-term contracts, usually for several months. But Italian professionals took the lesson and won the initiative back by 1400. Meanwhile, citizen militias passed from the scene as effective war units. Governments were anxiously concerned to keep arms out of the homes and hands of citizens. Once citizens were disarmed, most cities could be held militarily by a few score knights and several hundred crossbowmen. The professionalization and business of war in fourteenth-century Italy helped greatly to ensure the survival of signories.

The personality of the *signore* was exceedingly important in the workings of his state. He could take dictatorial action or he could bring the commune, or parts thereof, into his consultations. More often he navigated back and forth between these two poles. Surfacing amid the turbulence of civic life but hemmed in by still vital communal institutions, the *signore* of the first two generations (to 1330–1350) could exercise unbounded power when he had the military force and when the city was divided. He could not, however, always rely upon this, and he had to beware of growing discontent in the city, as the billowing costs of war forced him to impose heavier taxes. And so he often resorted to a stick-and-carrot policy, while having to draw upon all the resources of his personality too, as Jacob Burckhardt noticed long ago. Although the commune had developed a complex panoply of political and administrative procedures, it had long been a changing and adaptable society, sometimes afraid in its feelings but not in its actions. In this setting, the *signore* had much leeway for his articulation of a mode of government. A brutal and haughty man isolated himself and could end badly; a more sensitive ruler gained critical support in the community.

The self-consciousness and poise of the capable *signore* are summed up by a set of rules drafted in 1408: Carlo Malatesta's political advice intended for the young lord of Milan, Giovanni Maria Visconti.[1] Mixing a rudimentary Christianity with a strong sense of utility and a rough-and-ready view of the public good, Carlo observed:

> Praise the King of kings and Lord of lords; love your subjects and they will love you; busy yourself with your government; refrain from excessive gifts and expenses, especially in times of war; do everything you can to avoid wars; beware of using cruelty; observe all promises but promise nothing without previous counsel; retain only loyal and trusting councilors, letting no others interfere; let nothing and no one come between you and your brother; insist that all petitions requiring your signature be approved first by your council of advisers or by a trusted servitor, the better to avoid errors; let neither the Council of Justice [Milan's high court], nor any of your agents, ever publish any edicts or letters that violate, directly or indirectly, any of the statutes or ordinances of the city of Milan or of your illustrious forebears; do not let the Council of Justice interfere in proceedings over which it has no right; see to it that your judges always adjudicate justly; beware lest you be deflected from the path of truth or justice by the passions of your servitors, as this can bring ruin; reward the deserving and punish the wicked; let corrupt officials be put to death; keep your fortresses in the hands of foreigners and out of the hands of citizens and local men; show no mercy to confirmed rebels, but punish them in accord with justice; punish those who give aid or counsel to rebels; let no one build castles or forts, and tear down those that are built, keeping only the ones necessary to the public good [*eas que propter publicam utilitatem necessarie sunt*].

The observations speak for themselves. While betraying a persisting climate of distrust and passion, they also show a clean grasp of the problems of power and assurance in getting the job of government done.

One of the most talented of all fourteenth-century *signori* was Giangaleazzo Visconti of Milan (d. 1402), whose able policies appear even in his treatment of subject cities. When he seized Verona, Padua, and Pisa in the 1390s, he had their old communal magistracies reconstituted into provisional governments. These then transferred the right of rule to him. At Pisa, in

1399, he reestablished the prestigious *anziani*, eliminated by the last local *signore* (Gherardo d'Appiano), and even authorized them, when they chose, to bypass his chief agent in Pisa, the ducal lieutenant, and communicate directly with him. Although his officers took control of all fortresses in Pisan territory, he decreed that Pisa should retain her traditional structure of councils and magistracies. Finally, his agents sought to cut expenditures, promises were made not to increase taxes, and interest payments on credits in the Pisan public debt were guaranteed.

Nothing stirred the public passions of citizens more deeply than taxes. All states, signories and oligarchies, had to reorganize their fiscs in the fourteenth century, as government expanded and military costs climbed. Perhaps the most effective fiscal cadre was that of the largest signory, Milan, where public finance was in the hands of well-organized staffs: auditors, bookkeepers, notaries, lawyers, and special officials (*referendarii*) who were regularly dispatched to subject towns to check accounts and local conditions. At Mantua under the Gonzaga the administration of public finance was not nearly so neat. In the later fourteenth century, the personal fiscal agent of the signorial family gradually undermined the jurisdiction of the *massaro*, the chief fiscal officer of the old commune; and no clean distinction was made between communal monies and monies come from the personal patrimony of the Gonzaga lords.

Much of the signory's consolidation of power went on behind the façade of old communal institutions. When all pretense had been dropped and the new political institutions had emerged, the fifteenth century was upon the cities and the landscape of power had been definitively transformed.

CHAPTER VIII

THE COURSE OF POLITICAL FEELING

THE MATRIX: LOCAL FEELING

Political feeling in the Italian city-states around 1300 was rooted in a passionate attachment to place: a city and its environs. Along the banks of the Arno and near the Po, in the Veneto as in Liguria, citizens had a first and fervent allegiance to their own cities, to the local shaping of their own political destinies, and this feeling survived the Renaissance.

In 1300, commitment to the empire—the supreme political entity in name—was an abstraction, acknowledged by Italians only so far as the empire allowed them to be absolute masters of their own local affairs. Italy lay in utter disunity. The intensity of local feeling made for a hundred states rather than one. Visionaries who pictured a unified world empire were few and unheard. In the cities, the course of politics was carried by the force of local feeling and was determined in the councils, in the houses and enclaves of party and class leaders, under the weight of neighborhood pressures, and in the streets, where feeling raged among citizens and could stain the most philosophical views, like a running dye in the wrong place. Dante's dream of a unified world monarchy issued from his very awarenesses of the divisiveness and violence of local feeling.

There was good reason for the tug of local feeling. From the day of the commune's emergence, men had found order and protection by grouping together locally. As the commune expanded, the life of urban residents came to turn more and more around the decisions and fortified buildings of local government. The feeling that men had their earthly and family fortunes tied to the fortunes of the commune became such as to arouse the most intense loves and hatreds, especially in cities where unstable government made for continual fear and uncertainty. In this atmosphere the New Jerusalem seemed to some men to lie only inches away, if they could but take control of government. Citizens driven into exile longed for their native ground with an intensity whose glow could be rendered only by metaphor. Pietro dei Faitinelli (ca. 1290–1350), in exile from Lucca, vowed that if ever he returned to his native city, "I'll go licking the walls all round and every man I meet, weeping with joy."[1] In fury and loathing, Guittone d'Arezzo (ca. 1235–1294), one of Dante's chief lyric forerunners, denied his native Arezzo because it was in the hands of the enemy party, the Ghibellines. Penned in exile, the denial amounts to an emotional high treason which underlines, paradoxically, the force of his attachment:

> People loathsome and low,
> an evil base regime,
> Judges plunged in perfidy,
> a war steely and strange,
> make me hate my land,
> alas, and love another's.[2]

The search for order and protection, and the need of the propertied to cleave to their family base in a time of grievous civil disorder, must suffice to explain the rise and force of local patriotism. Just as citizens fought dangers far beyond their city walls, so, turning to a domestic scene agitated by shaky government, they clustered into groups and fought bitterly over the organization of the political space within the city walls. That space was fatally important, as has been emphasized, because the individual concerns of citizens—fortune, social place, and identity—could not be severed from politics: the urban space was too small for this. And this goes to explain the incandescence of political feeling: conspiracies, insurrections, mass exile, the vengeful razing of houses, the penchant for physical assault on public officials, or the readiness of men to imperil their souls. The fiery cardinal and Ghibelline Ottaviano degli Ubaldini (d. 1273) reportedly asserted, "If I have a soul, I have lost it a thousand times over for the Ghibellines." Dante put him into the company of heretics and lowered him into the burning plains of hell's sixth circle (*Inferno*, X, 120).

The conflict between warring purposes, as isolated in the cardinal's statement, was the central problem for political feeling and thought. That is to say, when the intensity of political passion became such that it could have none but worldly ends, how could it possibly be reconciled with Christian presuppositions? In the absence of native secular traditions of inquiry and under the ruling influence of a clerical intelligentsia, the language of everyday discourse on politics and government was given in part by clerics or by lawyers in holy orders. It was language shaped by religious and moral concerns. When laymen began to write about politics and the aims of government, they turned to the language of religious morality. Contemporaries instinctively assessed political action by the standard of sin and virtue. Political parties and tyrants were described as the enemies of Christ, offspring of the devil, heretics, persecutors of widows and orphans, and perpetrators of every imaginable sin. In like manner, political passion habitually involved oaths, prayer, blasphemy, and religious emblems. Odofredo, the thirteenth-century jurist, observed: "When the lowly commoners want to engage in sedition, they go into a church." And all the armed popular societies took religious names or the names of patron saints: the Credenza of St. Ambrose (Milan), the Credenza of St. Bassiano (Lodi), the Society of St. Prosper (Reggio), the Society of St. Geminian (Modena), the Society of the Cross (Bologna), and the Society of the Faithful (Florence).

Being all-pervasive and hence disposing of a kind of sovereign terminology, religious sentiment seeped constantly into political feeling and political views. Here are some verses in testimony ("Mormora il popol c'ha mal signorato"):

> The people murmur, "wicked government,"
> Yet each always connives at evil,
> And so their grumbling's worth a damn,
> For evil moves from them.
>
> As the sinner springs from sin,
> So is the part related to the whole:
> The finest-seeming man put
> Into power is the worst,
>
> God lets the despot rule
> To hurt and not to help him
> Or to scourge the sinning folk;
>
> Then up He props one even worse
> To dash him into grief
> And show His way of punishment.

Politics is put into a theological framework. The writer was Bindo Bonichi (d. 1338), "one of the worthiest and most representative figures of the big mercantile bourgeoisie of Siena" (Sapegno). He often appeared in Sienese political office right around 1300. The poem's facile connections account for all political maladies and its thinking is entirely typical of the time. The poet takes in the entire field of political action, while also retaining a note of skepticism and resignation. He sees government as a necessary evil. This view harked back to St. Augustine and the late Roman Empire, but is revealing in Bonichi, who staunchly supported the Sienese oligarchy of the Nine and would have fought to keep government in the hands of his party and class. Yet he is able to sit back and see politics as that which brings out the worst in men. The contradiction was easily resolved by the conviction that government is necessary, however attainted, and fully accords with God's arrangements.

Something in this feeling may help to illumine the political ferocity of the age. Bonichi's view could explain any criminal enormity in politics by seeing it as part of the natural and divine order of things; but self-interested imaginations could also easily turn such an explanation into a way of justifying all political behavior. Guelfs could kill Ghibellines with a good conscience, and all political opponents could boast that God was on their side. Ezzelino da Romano must have been alone among the period's despots to go to his death impenitently; there was some hope of salvation in heartfelt penance.

The close connection between the political and religious visions is strikingly brought out in a long poem by the Franciscan Giacomino da Verona, a North Italian of the late thirteenth century. In "The Heavenly Jerusalem,"[3] the poet boldly transfers earthly motifs to heaven and envisages a walled-in city at peace under one ruler, Christ.

The city is laid out in the form of a square with "three beautiful gates" on each side. It is built on a foundation of precious stones and its walls have "fine gold walkways." "Up there stands guard an angel with a sword of divine fire in hand" (ll. 50–51). Public squares, streets, and ways are of gold and silver and paved with crystal. Hallelujahs resound. The houses and palaces are a wonder to behold, made of fine marbles clear as glass and whiter than ermine. A beautiful river flows through the middle of the city, all around which are fruit trees and flowers whose redolence reaches for "a thousand miles and more." No one in the city has any reason to be afraid (l. 75). It is immune from machines for hurling missiles: "Neither catapult nor trebuchet or other can damage the buildings or anything else" (ll. 71–72). For Christ, "that glorious baron" (l. 215), is "duke, lord, and defender of the whole city" (ll. 73–74).

This vision of paradise is a manifest comment on earthly affairs, on the condition of war-torn thirteenth-century cities. It is a simple statement of desire for political and social peace and for less ugliness (even flies are debarred from the heavenly city). But the most striking thing about the poem is that its paradise is merely a perfected and dressed-up North Italian city of the thirteenth and fourteenth centuries. Religious morality might color direct political experience, but experience was putting new stresses on all the traditional molds.

One common political image of the time united family and religious feelings: the image of the chaste mother or woman as symbol of the city. The age was obsessively responsive to the idea of female chastity, for the chaste woman echoed the virtues of the Mother of Christ and represented the essence of honor and respectability in family and public terms: an apt symbol of rectitude. In her honorable chastity, the good mother could hold her head up high before all the world. In a poem ("Magni baroni certo e regi quasi") addressed to the two Gherardesca lords of Pisa in 1285, Guittone d'Arezzo refers to Pisa as "the city, your mother," once splendid and beautiful but now "denuded of her beauty and honor," many of her "dear sons dead or in prison." He urges the Gherardesca to goodness and to restore the city to her glorious state. The Anonimo Genovese wrote two poems in the 1290s built allegorically around a "great lady" and her sons (Genoa and her citizens).[1] She was formerly full of "wisdom and goodness, honor, good customs and courtesy." Peerless in Lombardy, she had "every benediction and was richly endowed with lands, money, and possessions." Her sons grew into riches, power, and honor, but greed and pride overtook them, dividing their ranks. Driven by the devil, they "lay hands on her person . . . tear her dress to pieces" and "strip her of her patrimony." By centering on the image of the dishonored mother, the poet exploits family and religious feelings with an eye to political ends.

Judging by the language of chronicles, statutes, and verse, we can see that in the period up to about 1350, urban folk did not separate questions about the nature of politics from religious presuppositions regarding human behavior. Political conduct was easily decipherable in accordance with conditioned responses about sin and virtue. The tenor and terrible intensity of civic life were, however, straining the old frames of reference: tradition no longer went to explain the totality of feelings and experience. A heavy, guiding sense of sin and virtue persisted in political feeling and thinking, but unrehearsed notions and insights were beginning to surface in discussion.

THE EXAMPLE OF BRUNETTO LATINI

Let us take one of Dante's Florentine mentors and pace the movement of perception and feeling in his political thinking.

Brunetto Latini (ca. 1220–1294), like his father before him, studied to be a notary. He was trained, therefore, in Latin composition, in the varieties and forms of written contracts, and in the redaction of governmental acts and documents. As a practicing notary, he attested deeds, last wills, and business agreements, and he drafted court records, statutes, state letters, or even treaties between Florence and other states. Brunetto's life coincided with the most agitated period of his city's history. The overturning of governments was not quite a commonplace, but he saw four such changes. He also witnessed the triumph of the *popolo*, continual war between Florentine Guelfs and Ghibellines, and the marked decline (1250–1292) of the old municipal nobility. From about 1254, excepting only a period of political exile in France (1260–1266), he began to hold office in the city and became a prominent figure in Florentine public life: as head of the Florentine chancellery, in a number of other key secretarial posts, as councilor and adviser, twice at least as ambassador, and once (1287) as a member of the city's chief executive body. Whether in private legal transactions or in the political affairs of the commune, Brunetto's life was given to practical activity and public service. His bookish preparation was geared to practical affairs, but then these leavened his bookish experience. A confession in *Il Tesoretto* (l.

2561) reveals that he knew himself deemed, in nice understatement, "a little worldly."

Exile, as Dante and Machiavelli and many others were to learn, sometimes worked to convert psychological strain into literary form. Brunetto Latini wrote his important books in exile: *Li Livres dou Tresor*, a French work in the vein of medieval encyclopedias; the unfinished *Il Tesoretto*, a didactic and allegorical work in verse; and the *Rettorica*, a partial translation with commentary of Cicero's *De inventione*. These writings disclose two passions that were closely linked in the author's mind: eloquence and public life, the word and the effect of the word in the political community—interests inseparable from cities and urban ways. For the city was, in Brunetto's eyes, the essential political community, the true form of civilized society. Exaggerating one of Cicero's views, he held that "the supreme science of governing a city is rhetoric: that is to say, the science of speaking, for without effective speech the city would not exist and there could be neither justice nor human company."[5] Hence the Ciceronian myth, fully accepted by Brunetto, that the origin of civilization was the work of a rhetorician who went into the wilds, assembled humanoid animals, and got them to live together in one place and under one law. The outcome was a city. The lawgiver could only be a rhetorician whose distinctive virtues lie in his magisterial command of wisdom and eloquence.

Li Livres dou Tresor was the first encyclopedia to be written for learned laymen. In fact it was directed at burghers. Although it treats theology, history, and the natural sciences, the main concerns of the work are ethics, rhetoric, and city government. The overriding intellectual influences are Aristotle and Cicero, the first of whom helps the author to see the close connections among ethics, community life, and politics, while the second illustrates the importance of rhetoric in the community. But Brunetto was no mere slavish and uncritical borrower. Taking hold of his borrowings in a fresh and vigorous manner, he was moved to borrow only the insights and precepts that squared with the liveliest parts of his experience. Again and again he betrays a preoccupation with the political and moral problems of the urban space. And he discusses the dynamics of trade and money, urban manners, usury, the rendering of military service to the commune, communal office, political authority, and civil justice.

The most important part of the *Tresor*, for our purposes, is the treatise "On the Government of [Italian] Cities," which appears in Book III, next to a sustained treatment of rhetoric and "good speaking." Here Aristotle and Cicero recede into the background or disappear altogether and the matter put before us is one of which Brunetto had much firsthand experience. For he is dealing with Italian cities and their communal regimes during the middle decades of the thirteenth century; more specifically, he discusses the office and functions of the podestà.

This discussion belongs to a genre much seen in thirteenth-century Italy.

The cities produced a flurry of works, now mostly lost, on the procedures and functions of high office in the commune, particularly those of the chief executive and magistrate, the podestà. Brunetto's treatment has affinities with at least three other works written between about 1220 and the 1260s: (1) the *Oculus pastoralis*, (2) a set of official Sienese documents, and (3) the one it most resembles, John of Viterbo's *De regimine civitatum*. But some prototype, now lost, probably stood behind the genre, and Brunetto doubtless used it. His writings offer us a sense of the man as an individual. However, his political perceptions and borrowings bind him to the great problems of his time.

Like other works of its type, Brunetto Latini's "On the Government of Cities" is a handbook of official action and procedure. It opens with two chapters on the origins and nature of government, on the ideal bonds between the podestà and the citizens of the commune, and follows with a series of chapters that are both descriptive and advisory. The subjects include the election and ideal qualities of the podestà; getting information to the podestà-elect; form letters to and from him; his official preparations and approach to the host city; his duties on the day of his arrival; some set speeches; dealing with his staff; his assembling the communal councils; electing ambassadors; his administration of justice; his custody over the rights and properties of the commune; preparing for the election of his successor; and the main things to be done during his last days in office.

Terse, precise, and practical, the treatise broaches theory only when required by the nature of the argument. Thus, for example, on the day of his arrival in the host city, the podestà-elect is urged to begin the morning by hearing Mass. Entering the city, he is met by its knights and mounted burghers and all make their way to the cathedral or major church. There he goes before the altar, and Brunetto advises him to pray fervently. Immediately thereafter or sometime later that day, in accordance with the custom of the city, he must address the assembled citizenry, and the question arises as to the type of speech he should give. Now there is more than a brush with theory, as Brunetto touches on the nature of justice, impartiality, God's will, and the benefits of peace. Even here, however, the treatise observes its commitment to practical instruction: two basic situations are imagined, war and peace, and formulas are provided for the two types of speeches.

Why the genre had a marked pragmatic bent is clear from its purposes. It was a guide literature; it was directed at two parties in the commune, citizens and podestà, and these were meant to read and profit from such works. There is conclusive evidence to show that the authors of handbooks in the podestà genre were moved by the conviction that the government of the commune often included inexperienced people, rich upstarts and rough knights, who needed detailed recipes and instructions on the procedures of podestaral government. In his preamble to the *Oculus pastoralis*, the anonymous author promises an "easy" treatment "because simplicity is the friend of those who are unpolished, to whom I address this, and to those who are not very literate." Works belonging to this genre were usually composed in Latin, but contemporaries catered to the needs of "simple" folk by producing vernacular translations. That the aim was to guide relatively inexperienced men is also taken for granted by Brunetto, who envisages only the most basic situations and procedures, while also presenting examples of set oratory that are simple and much to the point.

Brunetto's treatise has an obvious organization. Opening with some general observations, it moves quickly to the characteristics of the good podestà, and then follows him through a chronological succession of events and duties, up to the time of his leaving office. The work as a whole gives voice to three urgencies: (1) that the podestà adhere strictly to the laws of the commune, almost to the point of his being a stickler; (2) that he be absolutely impartial in the handling of political affairs; and (3) that he cleave to justice in his courts of law. These are the recurring themes; Brunetto cannot emphasize them enough. He does not take it for granted that the man holding the commune's highest dignity will keep to a strict impartiality and observation of the laws. Experience taught otherwise. Italian cities, as we have seen, were so troubled by partisan and class strife, and subjected government to such a barrage of sectarian strains, as to make it impossible for the podestà to rise above politics and partisanship. Brunetto Latini, therefore, could hardly escape the feeling that the essence of good government resided in impartiality. The odious effects of partisanship dictated a manifest solution—impartiality; but the underlying troubles were structural and so far more serious. Any true solution would hinge on the emergence of new forms of government. Either political power was shifted in its social moorings, or the problems of political violence and instability could have no realistic solutions. Consequently, Brunetto's emphasis on impartiality was a giving way to feeling which belonged to the symptom rather than to the cure. It was all right so far as it went, but it did not go far enough.

If the dominant stress in Brunetto's treatise has to do with the crying need for just and impartial government, it also has an array of other feelings and perceptions, giving us a novel perspective on many of the problems already met in the preceding chapters.

Around 1250, certain communes already elected their podestà by drawing lots, in the effort to keep partisanship at a minimum. Brunetto urged that the podestà not be elected by lot, nor by any other means which admitted the element of chance, but rather that he be chosen with "great care and sage counsel."[6] The author was hopeful. The practice of electing officials by a system of lots was stark testimony to the fear of partisanship and duress in the election process. We see the conservative *popolano* in Brunetto, who was a member of the Florentine *popolo*. He was impressed by noble stock and old lineage, but he saw no *a priori* political virtues there; and therefore he advised citizens, when casting around for a new podestà, to take no notice of a prospective candidate's power and lineage. Instead, "consider the nobility of his heart, the honorability of his life and customs, and his virtuous works both at home and in his other podestaral dignities [*segnories*] . . . but if he be noble of heart as well as lineage, then he is certainly worth much more in all things."[7] Next, listing and concisely discussing the qualities to look for in a podestà, Brunetto concludes: "Most people do not consider his habits but rather look to the power he commands or to his lineage or to his will or to the love of the city in which he is. They are, however, deceived, as this is why war and hatred have greatly multiplied among the Italians in our time . . . why there is division among the cities and hostility between the two parties of burghers, for whoever gets the love of one certainly gets the animosity of the other."[8] The image of the strong man and aspiring tyrant—Ezzelino da Romano, Provenzan Salvano, the Torriani, and others—filled Brunetto's eyes, and he abhorred the tendency to choose government heads on the basis of their power within a given party, or their popularity, ambition, or noble stock, or because of the host city's friendly relations with the podestà's native city.

Brunetto's suspicions and fear of strong men entered into his oligarchical conservatism. On the one hand, power should be shared among the experienced, the wise, and the eminent; on the other, it should not be allowed to spread beyond this circle. On the one hand, again, the podestà should make fearless use of the laws of the commune to protect the weak (widows, women, and orphans) against "the wickedness of the powerful"; on the other, he should not go so far in this direction "that the strong are deprived of their rights through the tears of the weak, for you [the podestà] have all people in your custody, the big, the little and the in-between."[9]

In societies heavily marked by the imprint of class, status, and deference, intellectuals often combine the conservative feelings of the upper classes with a special elitism of their own. Brunetto shared the oligarchical views of his Guelf contemporaries, but his education and learning took him a step farther: he distrusted popular passions; he feared any but carefully weighed decisions; he had not much respect, especially in political affairs, for those with little or no education; and he believed that most people are taken in by baubles. In accord with these views, he held that carefully controlled deliberations provided the best counsel and that open discussion was likely to be dangerous.

On the first holiday after taking office, the podestà was to assemble the people of the city and give them a tough, admonitory address. One of the podestaral notaries was then to read out the new ordinances, "and the podestà should suffer no one in [that] general assembly to get up and speak, for if one speaks another would also speak, with the result that there would be a lot of embarrassment and obstruction [*uns gries enpeechements*], especially if the city has two parties."[10] Later, this counsel of expedience, intended to prevent hostilities from flashing forth, is buttressed with advice which again shows our man striving to rise above any contending parties; but, interestingly, it is advice which seeks policies that are shaped neither by one man, nor by the many voices in council, but by the few. Discussing the podestà's need to take counsel in all important matters, Brunetto urged him to sound out the experts, including judges, heads of guilds, "and other good people." In proposing legislation, the podestà was meant to approach his consultative body or the communal councils with proposals that were simple, brief, and to the point. A podestaral notary then read the matter out to the assembled advisers and legislators. Immediately thereafter, "let the podestà get up and restate the need as it is and was," doing so in "bare and simple" terms so that no man could allege bias on one side or the other. Next, just before opening discussion, the podestà was to warn the councilors to keep to the subject at hand, to refrain from praising him or his staff, and to listen carefully to the speakers. Meanwhile, one of his notaries would record the essence, if pertinent, of what each speaker said. "And let it not be tolerated that too many people get up and give counsel." In matters that called for secrecy, a councilor who betrayed the nature of the discussion was to be condemned as a traitor.[11]

From time to time, apparently, the call for counsel and deliberation got out of hand and the presenting of opinions turned into a debate. Brunetto condemned this. His plea for limited discussion and his treatment of the podestà's relations with councilors reveal two different aspects of the communal situation: first, the fear that open discussion could serve no other purpose than to stir up partisan passions and plunge the city into more violent discord; and second, the widespread assumption, among communal authorities and leading citizens, that real political discussion concerned only the few, the experts and authoritative politicians, and that this made for the best kind of city government. The idea of electoral representation was minimal. Those few whose voices were expected to carry weight gave counsel, it was thought, out of their own experience, not by representing what citizens in the different neighborhoods were feeling and thinking.

Representative and personal views in Brunetto's treatise are so perfectly joined that it is next to impossible to sort out what is personal. Even where we think that we detect a purely personal note, further consideration nearly always discloses an attitude that belongs to the age. Thirteenth-century podestaral literature indicates that many contemporaries, not just Brunetto Latini, acknowledged the importance of rhetorical skills in the conduct of government. He was, however, one of the first to see that correct composition and skilled oratory could be used to keep a city's political passions from breaking forth. The art, so used, was a device more than a cure, but it might enable the podestà to finish his term of office without additional tumult in the governing councils. In short, although Brunetto idealized the possibilities of rhetoric, he also saw its importance in the political struggle and sought to harness its capabilities.

We have noted the Florentine notary's emphasis on impartiality in government, his strong sense of the divisions and hostilities in the city, his oligarchical bent, and his belief in the use of composition and speechmaking to keep political passions cooled. He also emphasized rank and ceremony in civic life.

Letters exchanged between the host city and the podestà-elect are meant to be sprinkled with rhetorical flourishes, each full of praise and flattery for the other. Touchiness and tempers abound. Honor and dignity require constant tribute. Thus, as the podestà-elect approaches the host city, the news spreads and on the morning of his arrival all the knights and mounted bourgeois go to the city gates to meet him. If there be a bishop, he also attends and takes his place alongside the new dignitary.

Finding the city in peace, the podestà promises in his first speech to observe the laws, to be impartial, and to prosecute all lawbreakers, whatever their eminence and influence. "I have come," Brunetto has him say, "not from the itch to gain money but to acquire praise, esteem, and honor for me and my staff. Therefore, I shall cleave to the straight path of justice."[12] "But if the city has war within, owing to the discord among citizens," let him say, advises Brunetto, that God enjoins peace and that he would have preferred to find the city in peace. "For harmony elevates cities and enriches the burghers, whereas war destroys them."[13] Clichés bound forth here, summing up, however, much of the political experience of the period.

The bent for political illegality was often in Brunetto's mind. He repeats his warning that the podestà should have no personal friends in the city, as this would lower the podestaral dignity, make him suspect, and aggravate civil discord. The implication is that the podestà would be tempted to help friends, even in violation of the law. Brunetto returns to this and to related themes. "He [the podestà] should guard against selling justice for money, for the law says that he who does so should be condemned as a thief. He should guard against being intimate with subjects [citizens], for this will arouse suspicion and spite. He should guard against taking gifts from anyone subject to his government, for any man who receives a present or service of some kind has sold his freedom of action [*a sa franchise vendue*] and is constrained as if by a debt. Again, he should guard against taking counsel in private from anyone in the city, and let him not ride privately with any man, nor go to his house to eat nor for anything else, for this will stir up against him the suspicions of citizens."[14]

The election of the new podestà was arranged by the incumbent, who saw to it that when the electors "have taken their oath, they meet in a private place until they discharge their functions."[15] Here again the point is to keep influence and party passion away from the electors. The chapter concludes with a sharp injunction to the podestà that he not be tempted to accept a second term in office because it can only end badly.

As we comb Brunetto's treatise and come upon repeated warnings to the podestà, admonishing him to adhere to the law and to avoid all friendships and partisan influence, we begin to realize that civil strife and partisan passion are regarded as the ordinary and obvious condition of cities. Brunetto trusted no one. When a city elected a new podestà, it was exceedingly important to get full, accurate, and precise information to him, for the manipulation of ambiguity was easy and too easily led to a clash. Brunetto agreed that podestàs should pray often and hard, and he endorsed one of the intellectual clichès of the day, namely, that all power comes from God. But even from his exile in Paris, as he reflected on the podestaral office, he re-created the atmosphere of suspicion, fear, and violence that characterized the life of Italian cities. It was as if he feared that every group within the commune was spurred on by naked self-interest and that only the law, and perhaps fear of God, presented a barrier.

But Brunetto feared more than illegality and partisan passion. In one respect the entire treatise "On the Government of Cities" is a plea against one-man rule, for it hedges the podestà in with an imposing list of admonitions: don't accept a second term; don't make friends; don't have personal contacts; don't be indebted to anyone in the commune; don't let yourself be praised in council; rise above parties and factions; always consult the expert and eminent citizens; favor the opinion and counsel of the (controlled) majority voice; keep strictly to the law in all circumstances; and beware of imposing additional taxes or getting the commune into debt, "save for the manifest profit of the city and by approval of the council."[16] Most of these warnings are repeated.

Citizen Brunetto would himself pull with one faction or another once he returned to Florence and active politics. Had he not already suffered from his partisanship, exiled along with other Guelfs? But in the treatise he had to be more detached and assume that it was possible for government to stand above the contending parties or factions. Not above class: he did not for a moment think that government should stand above class in the sense of its insisting upon equality for all. As is clear from his conception of justice, Brunetto accepted the existing hierarchy of classes and inequalities, as he accepted a long line of thought, indeed an ideology, which explained and justified the condition of the rich and poor, the weak and mighty. In this view, inequality belonged to the realm of justice. Driven by sin and wickedness, men had seized and laid arbitrary claim to the goods of the earth. Some had got much, while many more had got little or nothing. The results issued in property and inequality. As a general condition, this was now fixed; so, too, was the principle of property; and now justice also took its place among men. For justice maintains inequality but makes civil society possible. Justice, therefore, is the aim of government, but government can and should deal impartially with all classes, groups, and factions within the commune.

Brunetto's political feeling and thinking were the vital expression of his experience in the commune, even when he came to consider the most abstract questions, such as justice and impartiality. Whatever he took from the intellectual tradition, from Aristotle, Cicero, or St. Augustine, he envisaged in the context of a walled city with grave social and political tensions. He traveled in Italy, Spain, and France, and he lived in the last for five or six years; but the Florentine experience, the image of the fierce struggle between contending classes and parties, remained fixed on his retina. He loved Florence; he was enormously proud of it; and it is likely that Paris confirmed him in the feeling that life outside cities was not desirable. He observes in the *Tesoretto*: "Every man who comes into the world is first born to his father and relatives, then to his commune [*comuno*]." This is immediately followed by the conclusion: "Whereupon I would not want to see anyone in control of my city" (ll. 166–173). "Commune" means "community" in this passage: every man is born into a community. But the moment Brunetto visualizes a community, his mind turns naturally to a thirteenth-century Italian city under communal government. He felt that citizens owe a supreme debt to their city, which had provided them with the amenities of civilized living. The feeling amounted to a full-blown patriotism. "I want you to be honest and loyal to your commune," he urges, "and whatever happens to it, strive to keep it from perishing" (*Tesoretto*, ll. 1939ff.). He returns to the theme: "don't be a provoker of war or civil disorder [*romore*]. But if it should happen that your commune has to take to the field, I want you to conduct yourself with valor and to show yourself above your estimate [i.e., to spend more on arms and horses than you can afford]." Then he cautions against cowardice: "And don't have doubts of any sort about death, as it is better to die honorably than to live being despised on all sides" (ll. 2145ff.). Brunetto is saying, be ready to die for your city and raise no questions, regarding conscience or other matters, that would tend to prevent you from doing so.

With this commitment to *patria* he returns us to the matrix of local feeling. He had gone as far as he could, in the thirteenth-century setting, to free himself from an all-encompassing religious mentality. He extracted his view of politics from a powerful attachment to city and commune and pushed it to the beginnings of a doctrine which sought to validate purely secular feelings. He was a Christian and urged the reader of the *Tesoretto* to worship God, to worry about the state of his immortal soul, and to repent. But when Brunetto thought about politics and society, he was sometimes able to sort these out of the reigning religiosity. Then he was on the brink of saying that city life is an end in itself, requiring no higher validation.

THE VANGUARD OF FEELING

The medieval notion that all political power issues from God was not just an abstraction and a commonplace. It came up continually in public speeches and discourse, was central to a whole conception of humanity, and helped men to get their bearings. The doctrine was enunciated in the oaths of kings and podestàs, who acknowledged the divine origin of their authority. Acknowledgment was also made in the podestà's first address to the assembled citizenry. At least one of the principal implications was obvious enough: namely, that all political activity is in some profound sense a religious concern, subject to an eternal order of values, and that governments, in turn, have legitimate religious concerns. Popes and their publicists would make capital of this. There were immediate consequences for the commune as well: heretics were tried by the Church but the commune executed them. In city after city, the commune annihilated heretics: at Parma in 1279, Bologna in 1299, Novara in 1300, Bergamo in 1301, Padua in 1302, and Pavia in 1303. At Bologna, in May 1299, a crowd rioted in the government square because two purse makers, heretics both, were denied Holy Communion before being put to death by fire. Repenting, the rioters began to go before an inquisitor. Of the 362 people examined, 250 were women.

Guido Fava, an arts professor at the University of Bologna in the early thirteenth century, put together a formulary of letters and speeches for public occasions. Those touching the office of the podestà often bring out the intersection between the political and religious sectors of experience. Fava's model for the podestà's first public address begins with an invocation to God, the Virgin Mary, and all the saints. More revealing is an exchange between the podestàs of two cities. One writes to the other, requesting him to intervene in a case of disputed debt between two citizens from the two cities. The other podestà takes action, secures the contested monies, and replies with a letter which touches upon the foundations of medieval political thought. The appropriate passage reads: "The world sees so much discord and controversy that all people would be happy, and especially those who head governments, if God had granted so much grace to men that they could live contented with His reason and without quarreling. But angels fell from heaven and man from paradise. . . . No wonder, therefore, that earth has both strife and reason, for it abounds in multitudes of sins, which podestàs should wisely work to remove and eliminate." Here are more than intimations of the Augustinian idea of government as a remedy for sin and law as a barrier against the wickedness of men. In Fava's view, podestàs work to help make the barrier effective. He returns to the subject in a model for the podestà's address on the occasion of electing a successor. Urging the relevant council to elect the best man for the office, the podestà speaks of God's grace, of the ever-increasing wickedness of men, and observes that "if there were no one to adhere to reason and punish the lawbreakers, men could not live in this world. Therefore, the peoples of the earth wisely see to it that there be governors and rulers, who maintain justice and truth."[17] Fava promotes a view that appears to have universal application, but it is intimately connected with the myth of man's fall and ultimate redemption in Christ.

If the track of traditional political feeling passed directly through religious considerations, then the mark of any *new* feeling, the vanguard of political feeling, was in its gradual break from a religious captivity. The more political discourse avoided religious metaphors and diction, the more it made a new track for itself. This process of change was not to be completed for centuries. Machiavelli's *The Prince* (1513) shocked Europe, and the seventeenth century still thought seriously in terms of a divinity that hedges kings.

The fertile beginnings of secular political feeling lie in thirteenth-century Italy. The feeling sprang from an ardent attachment to place, to city, and to commune, and it was turned into an unbridled local patriotism. Florence and Genoa, Milan and Bologna, Siena and Padua all seethed with local pride and bluster. The world in which the good life was possible seemed to stretch not much further than immediate political horizons. Podestàs, even as they came into a city and made religious invocations, praised local accomplishments and flattered local vanities. In a model letter of acceptance, Guido Fava has his prospective podestà say: "If it please you, I shall come [to you as podestà] to do those things that touch upon the state and grandeur of your most glorious city." And the *Oculus pastoralis* improves on this: Let my term of office, says the new podestà in his first public speech, redound "to the increase and glory of this glorious city and its citizens, subjects, friends, and allies. If I should want to talk about these matters in some detail and go into the praises of this magnificent city, of its noble knights and the nobility of its *popolo* . . . [if I should] praise the work of its manly government and what it did last year for the good and honor of this city; and if I should point out the nobility of its beginnings, its faith, and its prudence, the day would not be long enough, nor would my mind find the way to put an end to what I might say."[18] Formulas yes, and crude flattery for simple folk, but local feelings had to be petted, and in the course of the century the flattery increased. This condescending judgment about "simple people" was made by the author himself of the *Oculus pastoralis*. The original formulas were most likely developed for the grander communes such as Pavia, Bologna, Milan, Florence, and Genoa; soon enough, however, they also came to be used in more humble places.

The Anonimo Genovese, writing between 1294 and 1311, was possessed of an intense love of Genoa and pride in its history. All his poems touch upon some aspect of the city's life, manners, mores, and worship. He saw politics under the cover of a moral and religious shell, but he could also break away and see the menace of despotism, mainly in terms of law and the will of the citizenry. In his "De condicione terrarum et civitatum," in rhymes that thinly veil the Genoese political situation, he reasons: "A city which tolerates an honor-lusting ruler because of the few, and not by the common will, can never really have peace because he is not a true ruler."[19] Those who oppose him will not be satisfied until they bring him down, so that the city is held on the edge of civil war. The evil few cannot make legitimate one man's dominion over his neighbors, and such a man cannot be rescued from ruin because he rules over what does not belong to him. In fact, he does so much injury to the city that he is "not a ruler but a tyrant." It follows that anyone who wants his city prosperous and justly governed "will want an outside podestà who keeps to the scales of justice, does not make friends, and grants only what is right by reason to big and little men alike." He procures "the common good" by his impartial application of the law. "In this fashion the city . . . prospers and grows in honor." But there is "something else that brings on war, and that's a citizen so grand and proud that he despises statutes, laws, and commands." This hurts others and can throw the city into civil discord. The Anonimo concludes with the hope that God will look after the city. The poem has obvious moral overtones, but religious diction is only twice introduced. With a few swift and direct strokes, the writer (1) puts forth a notion of consensus rule, (2) argues the common good, (3) decries the disrupting power of particular individuals and groups, and (4) insists upon a detached and fair application of the law. Given a new emphasis and a stricter harmony, these views pointed the way to a more worldly analysis of politics in the commune.

The bonds of local patriotism made Brunetto Latini ready to put the commune above every consideration save God. He could almost admit that government had an intrinsic worth, needing no justification, religious or otherwise, outside itself. His amazingly high assessment of the dignity and value of rhetoric sprang directly from its indissoluble connection, at least in his mind, with the government of cities. In these matters, Cicero aside, Aristotle's influence on Brunetto was fundamental. The Greek thinker was the decisive intellectual influence on the vanguard of European political thought in the thirteenth and fourteenth centuries. But the political Aristotle—to separate him from his other works—would have had nothing vital to say to the thirteenth century, if late-medieval urban experience had not squared with so much in his political thought. Conveying something of the atmosphere and outlook of the Greek city-state, Aristotle's *Politics* found its most vigorous response in the world of the Italian city-state. Brunetto, Ptolemy of Lucca, Remigio de' Girolami, Marsiglio of Padua, and others succumbed to its influence, not because of the innate superiority of Aristotle's ideas but because of the Italian point of departure: namely, the form of political authority in the commune. Even Dante responded in kind, in seeking to heal the divisions within and among cities by means of a universal monarchy—a higher, more legitimate and more effective force. He also took the word *città* ("city") "to denote the fundamental and 'typical' form of human association."[20] For him the ideal city provided the setting for the best sort of society. In Canto VIII of *Paradiso*, he holds that citizenship improves the quality of human life, and by citizenship he means membership in the body of those qualified to legislate within the city. Only later, in his imperialist phase, did he go on to think of kingdoms as a basic form of human association.

To see the birth of the state in a divine judgment, or to root it in the nature of man himself without any pejorative suppositions regarding his fallen condition: these were the rival views, even if they were not seen in this guise, and Aristotle best represented the latter. In the first view, the state is a repressive force, as much a punishment as a remedy for sin, and certainly a monstrosity unless circumscribed by a Christian framework; in the second, the state is a positive institution, which not only regulates and protects men but also perfects their companionship and makes possible their most worthy enterprises. In the former view, public service can have nothing good about it unless it is related, in some manner, to the Christian vision of loss and redemption; in the latter, public service is a manifest good in itself, requiring no mystical act of enablement or ennoblement.

In these oppositions, we can begin to see how and why local patriotism, in the invigorating atmosphere of the commune, could gradually result in a more worldly assessment of the state. It may seem remarkable that the change took so long in coming, but this is to underestimate the force of the Christian lexicon. The transition from one view to the other was not in the first instance a process of abstract cerebration, as historians of ideas like to imagine, but one of action and feeling, experience and attitude. The transition involved a community process and a fund of expressive attitudes from which any gifted individual might fitfully draw new insights.

Such a man was the Dominican friar Remigio de' Girolami (d. 1319), a prominent Florentine intellectual who was able to see and esteem the applicability of Aristotle's political philosophy. Yet his idea of the common public good was not necessarily pinned to Aristotle; it had welled up from local feeling and was lodged in the statutes of communes, the speeches of podestàs, and the musings of poets.

Remigio de' Girolami studied at Paris, probably in the 1260s, where he came under the influence of Aristotle's political and moral writings. Returning to Florence sometime in the 1270s, he lectured for the next four decades on ethics and theology at the Dominican *studium*. In Florence he found a familiar environment, having been born to one of the city's *popolani* families. His father, brother, and nephews appeared and reappeared in a variety of leading communal offices, and he himself may have served as an intermediary in certain political crises.

Remigio's writings show an impressive range and a wide acquaintance with early Christian and classical authors. Certain themes recur, among which are a strong love of his native city and a keen sense of the common public good. He feared and detested faction and extolled the benefits of peace. Faction subjected the good of the community to particular interests, subverted the state, and made civilized living impossible. Commitment to peace and the common good was fundamental. He was therefore willing, at least in theory, to base friendship upon the extent to which acquaintances were devoted or not to the common weal. A man unmoved by such devotion was unworthy of friendship.

In *De bono communi*,[21] Remigio develops a view of man in society that has surprised and disturbed modern commentators. Calling on the Aristotelian perception of the relationship between part and whole, individual and community, he puts the good of the community above that of the individual. The argument finds that the individual needs the community, is succored by it, owes all his worldly advantages to it, including even the largest part of his spiritual life. Similes are introduced. As the hand depends upon the structure and function of the whole body, so the individual depends upon the community. Cut the hand from the body, and the result is a lifeless object; cut the individual from his community, and he turns into something less than a man. "Destroy his city and a citizen is like a painted or a stone image, because he is thereby shorn from the vigor and work that he once had." We are led to conclude that the good of the whole precedes that of the part, which cannot stand alone. The same conclusion follows along another route: "He who is not a citizen is not a man, for man is by nature a political animal, as the philosopher [Aristotle] observes."

Occasioned by Florence's political turbulence and mass exiles of 1302, *De bono communi* is a passionate condemnation of factionalism and selfish men. The insistence upon citizenship in effect accuses Florentines of having shed their humanity in their tearing up of the commune. Against a background of war and ruthless faction, Remigio hailed the united community and the supremacy of the state, which alone made possible the conditions for the exercise of virtue. Understandably, he argued that the individual should love the community more than himself and almost more than his own soul. He noted that this idea might appear to bring the individual soul into conflict with the wishes of the community, but he disposed of the problem by means of elliptical arguments and illustrations. Satisfied that the good of the individual is nearly always contained in the good of the community, he imagined, most exceptionally, the possibility of the individual's accepting eternal damnation for the sake of the community.

The common good and peaceful politics are so much a part of Remigio's conception of the community that scholars automatically equate his community with an idea of the state. Well versed in the writings of the early church fathers, and particularly St. Augustine, he retained something of the traditional view, which saw the state as a restraint upon sin. But his emphasis was elsewhere: he looked to an ideal *worldly* state before which the citizen gave way in all matters. If in the established tradition of political thought and feeling, the citizen was a Christian first and foremost, with Remigio, at least in *De bono communi*, the Christian is first of all a citizen. The new Leviathan was not yet born, of course. The vocabulary of Remigio's world was far too religious for that. But it is a measure of the commune's civic density, of its capacity to foster civic ardor, that Remigio could have gone so far in his views. The patriotism and civic commitment of others, of Latini and the Anonimo Genovese, were not so boldly rationalized, but their call for the gratitude of citizens also moved from fresh insights and feelings.

In the next generation, in his *Defensor pacis* (1324), Marsiglio of Padua converted the aggressive and self-willed experience of the communal city-state into a broad statement about correct relations between the temporal and spiritual authorities. He also studied at Paris, but his organizing ideas—he was born to one of Padua's political families—continually remind us of the structure of political authority in the commune. Following Aristotle, in deriving the origins of the state from human fellowship and from the political nature of man, Marsiglio introduces the image of the *legislator humanus*. This "human legislator" is "the university of citizens" and, more specifically, "the better or weightier part" of these (the *pars valentior*). Oligarchy thus enters immediately as a constituent part of the state. The body of active citizens, or *legislator*, is the lawmaker. They represent the will of the community; they make the law by willing it. Consequently, the law no longer reflects a presupposed realm of reason and is no longer related to an eternal order of values. In willing the law, the *legislator* alone decides what is good and what is right. The changing standards of the *legislator* become the measure of right. In expressing the will of the community, the "better part" of the citizens may control and judge the government or *pars principans*, as Marsiglio calls it. The implication is that they can change or reconstitute their government at will. But a prince, a podestà, or a small magistracy may stand at the head of government. We may therefore conclude that a large part of the Marsiglian conception of the state is hardly more than a restatement of constitutional and political practice in the commune. There the councils of active citizens (*legislator*), working together with the executive power (*pars principans*), were so much the lawmakers and could alter things so completely that, as Dante said to the Florentines, "what you weave in October doesn't last to mid-November. How often you have changed laws, coinage, offices, usage, and renovated every part! . . . you are like a sick woman who can find no relief in bed but keeps turning so as to free herself from pain."[22]

CHAPTER IX

OLIGARCHY: RENAISSANCE REPUBLICS

THE REPUBLICAN ENVIRONMENT

Between roughly 1280 and the middle of the fourteenth century, the commune faced such grave internal and external problems that it had to alter its constitution to survive as a small state. In all cases the choice for the commune seems to have been either to put itself under one-man rule, under one family in hereditary succession, or to narrow the ranks of the political citizens. There is no reason to suppose—though the supposition is often made—that one of the two outcomes, the signory, was more natural and inevitable than the other. Going by the communal polity that preceded despotism, by the steely resistance of communes to external conquest, and by internal resistance to signorial rank, we might even argue that a republican outcome, as experienced in Florence, Lucca, and Perugia, would have been more "natural" in a dozen other cities.

Venice, Florence, Siena, and Lucca were the four major republics of the Renaissance. At Florence the old republican councils and magistracies remained vital to almost the middle decades of the fifteenth century. After an interlude of veiled signorial government (ca. 1470–1494), the city recovered and vitalized its republican institutions (1494–1512), then produced a body of leading thought on history and politics, and finally, besieged by a foreign army, went to the wall in 1530, after three years of ardent republican agitation.

In the course of the fourteenth and fifteenth centuries, three other important cities—Genoa, Bologna, and Perugia—passed back and forth between signorial and republican regimes. Later (1528), Genoa made a definitive return to its republican institutions. The importance of these three cities is that they provide additional settings for the tracking of a republican environment.

The seven cities were small states with subject territories. Bologna and Perugia were perhaps the least independent, being subject in theory and at times in fact to papal government. Looking over the seven cities, we find that in significant matters they seem to have little in common: two coastal and five inland cities, all from the upper third of the peninsula. The variations among them were remarkable. Having the largest state, Venice was also the most stable of the seven and very different in this respect from Genoa, the other seaport.

As the peninsula's two great seaports, Venice and Genoa provided their citizens with rich commercial opportunities. They had an enterprising *haute bourgeoisie* and a relatively populous nobility. Economically, the latter were varied and somewhat changeable, much involved in shipping and long-distance trade. The two ports depended upon the traffic from inland industrial and trade centers. Florence's strained relations with Genoa in the fifteenth century are attributable primarily to the Florentine takeover of Pisa (1406) and Livorno (1421), two ports which put Florence on the coast, drawing the flow of Florentine exports and imports away from Genoese shippers.

Geography had accorded the fisherman of the Venetian lagoons protection against massive invasion. As a result, Venetian trade relations with Byzantium and the Near East had a relatively secure development during the tenth and eleventh centuries. By contrast, Genoa's explosive successes, expansion, and riches in the eleventh and early twelfth centuries introduced an early element of instability into Genoese public life. Genoa had a popular movement in the second half of the thirteenth century, but it was not strong by comparison with its correspondents in the inland cities and it was manipulated by the class of big merchants and shipping magnates. Here, as in Venice and Pisa, the lure and profits of the sea worked to siphon off popular energies and to keep social discontent from breaking forth into organized revolt, at least until the late fourteenth and early fifteenth centuries, when, cramped by a shrunken economy, Genoa registered an escalation in the political fervor of the artisans and *petite bourgeoisie*. In the late thirteenth century, even Venice had seen a budding popular movement, but it was stamped out shortly after 1300. The persistence of a popular current in Genoese public affairs was one fact that made for a very important political difference between Venice and Genoa. Another critical difference lay in the character of the two nobilities. Surrounded by mountains, Genoa, unlike Venice, both had and attracted a strong and fertile feudal nobility which was much given to the deep country and the profession of arms. Descending into Genoa, or already resident there for part of the year, they turned to piracy, shipping, and trade, and took over the commune in the twelfth century. But they clung to their rural estates, long retaining something of their feudal habits; and although in time they intermarried with more purely mercantile families, they contributed the habit of disruption to the whole rhythm of

Genoese public life. Occasionally, down to the fourteenth century, they entered the city with groups or bands of loyal rustics (their *homines*), brought in from the outlying rural regions. Such men could be armed. But there was a counterweight: Genoa's rich bourgeoisie. When the principal noble families, in view of their own great shipping and trade interests, actually joined together in political cooperation, while at the same time gaining the support of the city's rich bourgeois, then the manifest polity for Genoa was an oligarchical republic. In fact, sharp divisions within the ruling class, fostered by a stubborn feudal consciousness, often invited foreign rule, with one or another faction in the city thereby winning the advantage. And it was more than two centuries before sectarian ambition at the top was overcome in favor of the cooperation that finally issued in an aristocratic republic (1528).

We have seen that popular movements were weak at Genoa and especially at Venice. The resources and outlets provided by the sea reduced the sting of economic and social discontent. But something else also worked to keep the *popolo* feeble politically: the fact that the richer part of the middle classes was heavily engaged in shipping and maritime trade in the thirteenth century, and families from this stratum were drawn into government and into the patriciate. They thus obtained what in other communes was more likely to be obtained by means of violence. Such accessibility to the ruling class—at Venice down to 1300 and at Genoa to the end of the fourteenth century—obviated the need for a strong movement of the *popolo*, and this, in turn, provided the humbler classes with fewer political models and fewer political occasions. A sufficiently ambitious and disruptive *popolo* was not there to lead the way. At Venice, after 1300, the rise of "new men" was no longer to be on the massive scale seen before, so that fourteenth-century popular stirrings could not have the explosiveness of the early-thirteenth-century *popolo*. Moreover, Venetian police and political controls in the fourteenth century were tighter, more thorough, and more consistent than the like of anything seen in other cities.

The inland republics were five: Florence, Lucca, Siena, Perugia, and Bologna. The last two, torn persistently by internal faction and pressured continually by the papacy, succumbed definitively to signorial government in the fifteenth century. There were two major features common to the five cities: first, all had strong popular movements which altered the makeup of the old aristocratic commune; and second, all managed to impose their authority not only on the field of surrounding feudal magnates, but also on the adjacent districts or even on counties beyond. In neither Tuscany nor parts of Emilia and Umbria did feudal barons win a stranglehold over neighboring towns and cities, as happened in Piedmont, the Romagna, and in the vicinage of Bergamo, Treviso, Ferrara, Mantua, and Verona, where the jurisdictions of a late feudalism were not eliminated. And it is well to recall, speaking of thirteenth-century popular movements, that the *popolo* under-

mined the claims of ancient blood, carried broad trade interests to the forefront of government, and put many more people under the umbrella of the
office-holding class.

These changes had politico-cultural effects that are not easy to pin down.
The memory of events in the commune was tenacious. Word of mouth in
that close environment could endow events with an appeal that might last
for generations. The early behavior of the *popolo* lodged some desire or
hope among certain categories of men, notably the skilled textile workers,
who had no place in the thirteenth-century *popolo* but who became its
spiritual heirs in the second half of the fourteenth century. The revolts of
craftsmen and skilled workers at Lucca (1369), Siena (1371), Perugia (1370,
1371, 1375), Florence (1378), and Bologna (1411) were dramatic episodes
that briefly put humble men into the foreground of politics. Unlike the
popolo's thirteenth-century membership, they did not dispose of substantial
properties and business interests. A few had small shops and a house or two
at best; many had far less; and others owned not even their proper tools.
Theirs was a more daring plea than the *popolo*'s. They argued that they
were overtaxed, underemployed, and not allowed the just right to form
guilds, while yet contributing greatly by their labors to the wealth of the
city. Like the *popolo*, however, they challenged governments with a variety
of bold claims, including the demand for office and for some voice in the
formation of economic policy.

Under a tough and fast-striking signory, or at Venice, where restraints
were sharper and the political ambiguities fewer, there would have been
little environment and no indulgence for the workers' revolts of the 1370s
or for the increased political consciousness of the artisans at Genoa right
around 1400. The fact that fourteenth-century Florence, Lucca, Siena,
Perugia, and even Genoa saw much political debate in both councils and
piazze led certain groups of men among the disenfranchised to try their
hand at revolutionary change. This surviving hope and its attendant conditions were an important part of the fourteenth-century environment for
republicanism. But apart from the Ciompi uprising in Florence (1378), we
know little in any social detail about the fourteenth-century revolts, and the
most summary sketch must suffice to indicate their track in the general
mainstream of the city-state. Only Perugia, Siena, and Florence will be
considered.

The cycle of rebellions began at Perugia, which was ruled by the city's
merchants and rich guildsmen known as Raspanti. They were opposed by the
Beccherini, the feudal-noble faction. Throughout the fourteenth century
the vitality of the commune's republican institutions lay directly in the
needs and custody of the Raspanti. In 1368 Perugia's nobility, largely in
exile, joined forces with papal mercenaries against the Raspanti, and in 1369
they laid siege to the city. The war imposed unbearable hardships on
Perugia's poor, acutely so on the craftsmen and workers in the wool indus-

try, with the result that these rebelled in the autumn of 1370 and forced the Raspanti to sign a peace with the papal legate. Lower-class resentment against the government of rich *popolani* was kindled by the impossible price of bread and a loathed tax on the milling of grain. Frightened by the swelling strength of the papal-noble faction inside the city, the Raspanti also feared the lower orders and sought to disarm them in May 1371, whereupon there was a second uprising, spearheaded again by the wool craftsmen and workers of the St. Angelo district. The Raspanti were driven from the city. The workers had mutinied to better their economic lot and vaguely hoped for some reforms in government. With the flight of the Raspanti, however, power passed into the hands of a papal governor, who was fully backed by the Perugian nobility. There had been no alliance or understanding between the nobility and wool-working plebs, although the latter had probably been manipulated. In 1372 the papal governor ordered the building of an enormous fortress, designed to guarantee military control over the city. But neither fortress nor mercenaries were to save papal strong-arm government. There was no relief for the city's workers, and powerful resentment again built up. The popular explosion finally came in December 1375, with the wool industry's work force yet once more at the vanguard. They besieged the fortress for twenty-four days, at the same time dismantling it almost piecemeal, and in the end the governor, his mercenaries, and the Perugian nobility were forced to surrender and leave the city. Now the Raspanti, returned to Perugia in triumph and power, again bypassed the wool-working "rabble," who had no program, no political experience, and no sense of sustained organization.

In the spring of 1355, after a reign of over sixty-five years, Siena's government of rich and well-placed men, known as the government of the Nine, was overthrown. The Emperor Charles IV's approach to the city occasioned the revolt. For the first time in Siena a mass of workers and "little people," egged on by noblemen, took a main part in dramatic events. Buildings were razed by fire, and among them was the *palazzo* of the wool manufacturers' (Lana) guild, which incited the particular hatred and violence of the artisans and workers in the wool industry. The new government, headed by a magistracy of twelve men (the Dodicini or Twelve) and still holding power for the richer and middle classes, was itself overthrown in 1368. In fact, there were three *coups* in 1368, the second and third uprisings having the appearance of tilting power more and more toward the poorer classes. Yet discontent continued, and in fact was sharply intensified by grain shortages and high bread prices in 1371, when the streets of Siena resounded with the uproar of still another insurrection. Riotous crowds broke into houses that were known to have large deposits of grain. Again the Lana workers and artisans, in bitter conflict with their employers, the guild masters, took the initiative by threatening street violence and demanding reforms. Residing for the most part in one section of the city (Ovile), they had previously formed a neighborhood organization called the Bruco society or company (Compagnia del Bruco). When three of their leaders were arrested in July 1371, the company attacked the jail, killed and wounded several guardsmen, released the prisoners, and then made a successful assault on the government palace. Small shopkeepers and artisans from other trades rallied to their side. Reorganizing the Fifteen Defenders, now Siena's highest office of state, the rebels first took seven, then twelve, of the fifteen places. The remaining three, oddly, were assigned to families which had been represented regularly in the old government of the Nine (1287–1355). The new twelve among the Fifteen, recruited from the humbler classes, were called "Reformers" (Riformatori). But the Bruco rebels had not carried their purge far enough, for the Fifteen were able to organize their destruction. Two weeks after the attack on the jail (July 30), the middle and upper classes, with the support of the Fifteen, sent troops into the city's textile working-class quarter, where, in bloody encounters, they massacred many of the members, and their women as well, of the Compagnia del Bruco. Much of the Ovile quarter was sacked and burned to the ground. Reformed yet once more, the government retained something of its deceptively representative character. Sharper changes came in March 1384, again by means of fire and sword, on the heels of a crisis in foreign policy. The nobility outside the city combined with the Noveschi and Dodicini to expel the Riformatori from government. The Salimbeni, Malavolti, Piccolomini, Tolomei, Ugurgieri, and other noblemen returned to the city, leading 800 horsemen and 2,000 foot soldiers. A new government of Ten was established, which included four Dodicini (men of a middling sort), four Noveschi (rich merchants, bankers, landowners), and two from the *popolo* "of the greater number" (humble men but not Riformatori). This effectively terminated the political influence, direct and indirect, of the mass of poor men and petty artisans connected with the wool industry.

The wave of proletarian agitation in Florence, leading to the famous uprising of July 20, 1378, was connected in part with sharp civil discontent over a war between Florence and the papacy (1375–1378). Florentine political strains and economic distress were acute. But the events of July 20—organized armed assemblies and an orderly march to the heart of the city, culminating in the storming of the government *palazzo*—were not prompted initially by famine and poverty, which then were no worse than they had been in recent years. The immediate causes of revolution stemmed from conspiracies, from the flaring up of open political discussion among all social groups, from several weeks of escalating violence, and from rising bread prices. A mob overthrew the government on July 20, and although the ensuing regime lasted for only five and one-half weeks, political power suddenly came within the grasp of more obscure levels of the population. The main benefactors and pivotal group of the July 20 revolution were the petty capitalists and entrepreneurs of the wool industry—dyers, carders,

shearers, tenders. Small-time employers of labor, they were themselves without the legal right to form guilds and indeed were subject to the wool manufacturers and merchants of the powerful Lana guild. Their fees, production,
and work standards were determined by this guild; and they had always
been denied the right to any voice in government. Now, with the help and
support of four or five renegades come from the rich bourgeoisie, they
seized and held power for a few fleeting weeks. Of some 13,000 newly enfranchised citizens inscribed in the new guilds, fewer than 2,000 were cleared
for high office. Beneath these was the multitude of propertyless workers who
performed the manual labor and who remained barred from political office.
The revolt of July 20 resulted in a government dominated by men from the
lower middle classes, and they brought in a series of reforms. They abolished
the tax on the milling of grain; they halved the salt tax; they ordered all
grain owned by Florentines to be brought into the city; they introduced
measures against grain hoarders; they renewed the campaign to recover the
communal property which had been covertly appropriated by influential
citizens; they set up a commission to audit fiscal records back to 1349; they
tried but abandoned a scheme to suspend interest payments on investments
in the public debt; and as they fell under increasing attack in late August,
they brought forth a proposal to carry out a new tax census and to levy
direct personal taxes.

Although it is true that there were many economic gradations in the
crowds of men who toppled the government on July 20,[1] it is also true that
the next five weeks brought out the "natural" groupings and rifts. What
became frightening and too radical for middle-class guildsmen was not radical enough for the Ciompi, the class of hired, propertyless workers in the
wool industry. On August 28, after much secret preparation and some agi-
tating in the working-class districts, culminating with a demonstration of
more than 5,000 Ciompi before the Church of San Marco, the self-styled
"people of God" marched on the government palace, led by eight of their
number, "the Eight Saints of God's People." They called for a ten-year
suspension of all interest payments on the funded public debt (the *monte
comune*), in the conviction that this fund greatly increased the burden of
taxes because it was exploited for investment purposes by the rich. Again,
being often in debt to their employers and exposed to callous duress and
mistreatment, the Ciompi demanded a two-year moratorium on debts. But
the thunderbolt was their demand that the government priors take an oath
to the Eight Saints (also a two-month elective office, like the Priorate), in
effect recognizing the Eight as Florence's supreme governing body. Negotiations between government and Ciompi continued for the next three days.
The workers were gulled into thinking that everything was going nicely for
them. Meanwhile, the Gonfalonier of Justice and other government leaders
were secretly in touch with the council of war and with the leaders of the
middle- and upper-class guilds throughout the city. They sponsored a

deceptively peaceful demonstration and show of arms on August 31 in the main government square, with the armed Ciompi also present. But as the day wore on, not realizing that there was a conspiracy afoot, some of the Ciompi dispersed, while others, lulled by their belief in the government's good intentions, lost militancy and became careless. Suddenly, in the late evening, the attack was launched by the collectivity of solid guildsmen and rich merchants. Even recent allies turned against the Ciompi. With the guild of butchers leading the armed assault on the workers, the *petit bourgeois* regime bloodied the streets, and many mutineers fled from the city. The government of new priors, taking office on September 1, was purged of Ciompi sympathizers, and for the next three years surviving or suspected Ciompi were prosecuted, fined, exiled, or executed. In the 1380s the dyers, doublet makers, and other petty employers of labor were excluded from government and their new guilds were abolished.

As at Florence, so at Siena and Perugia, the ranks of humble men engaged in wool production had many economic gradations, but critical pressure finally divided them. The dividing line cut between those who employed labor and those who hired themselves out; those who had tools, working premises, and perhaps some property, and those who had little other than their labor. At Siena and Florence, as well as Perugia and Lucca, the 1370s show increased politicization among the lower classes and a flash-point readiness to rush into politics. Soon enough, however, Ciompi and petty employers discovered that politics was more than sudden onslaughts: that it was a matter of careful organization, continuing exertion, and more fully articulated programs.

The revolts at Perugia, Siena, and Florence speak for the environment of republicanism. This was to be found above all in cities with a strong commercial or industrial base. Textiles, shipping, trade, banking, smithery, and a variety of lesser industries predominated. In social terms, the environment called for a large and somewhat diversified bourgeoisie. In demographic terms, populations ranged anywhere from 25,000 to 100,000 or more people. However, once a republican-communal tradition was established, and external circumstances were favorable, then a population of even 15,000 or 20,000 people might do, as seen in fifteenth-century Siena and Lucca, although such numbers made for a permanent insecurity. These two cities often had to call on the help of Milan, the papacy, and other states in order to foil the ambitions of their more powerful neighbor, Florence. In short, the republican environment required a population large enough to endow a city with the human resources to establish a territorial state; the city could then spill over acquisitively into the surrounding and more distant regions. A city smaller than Siena or Lucca was too easily subject to conquest by a larger neighbor.

Since at least two signorial cities, Milan and Pisa, answered fully to the foregoing description, we must look at social conditions more carefully, as these also were decisive.

No republic could prevail against a potent and aggressive nobility, unless that nobility, as at Genoa and Venice, went energetically into trade, shipping, or banking; and Venice, in fact, had a mercantile nobility that did not live from military skills. When the nobility was drawn at least partly into commerce, as at Siena and Florence, the transformation issued in closer ties with the bourgeoisie: old nobility and rich middle-class families got together in joint business ventures. But if the nobility retained attitudes of the sort that were more in keeping with arms, fortified places, and rural vassalage, and if no effective contols were clamped upon those who were overly strong in the streets and political councils, then the arrogance and violence of particular families became a constant threat to government. The results of this were to be seen at Pisa and partly at Genoa. In the twelfth and thirteenth centuries, Venice itself had much trouble with rebellious Venetian magnates in the eastern Mediterranean.

The social environment of republicanism, then, called not only for a populous enough bourgeoisie but also for a weak or defeated nobility, or for one transformed. In such a setting, collegiate-republican institutions could triumph over any particular family or over any small bloc of families of the type which continually angled to monopolize office and control government. But even the most secure of republican states could not always offer safety and civil concord. The Venetian government trumped up charges against a number of political activists and hanged them in 1300. In 1310, Venice faced and defeated one of the most serious conspiracies of its entire history; in 1355, Venetian authorities decapitated a conspiring doge, Marin Faliero, and executed his *popolani* collaborators; and in 1365 they were driven to suppress and destroy all evidence pertaining to yet another doge, Lorenzo Celsi, suspected of carrying on illegal political activity. Again, the important bourgeois families of Florence and Lucca absorbed some of the haughty ways of their feudal predecessors, and they could push their cities to the brink of civil war. Yet a republican polity long survived there, despite violence and disorder, whereas the signory was soon victorious in cities where the nobility continually bullied government.

It has often been held that the signory issued from the *popolo*'s seizure of power. The trouble with this thesis is that it takes things to be what they seem. At Verona and Milan the *popolo* invested its leaders with lifetime dignities, but it did so because it was locked in a bloody political struggle with a swarming nobility that was determined to have its way, as had been so traditionally. It was the very power and exclusive claims of that nobility that drove the *popolo* to the most extreme measures, though these did not succeed and the nobility prevailed. Moreover, in every city won by the signory, noblemen were the first and habitual beneficiaries. Very often their fiscal or other privileges received confirmation or extension; they held office, sometimes sharing it with talented men enlisted from the bourgeoisie; they served in the *signore*'s armies; and they occupied the castellanies and governorships in the signory's subject territories.

A commercial or industrial base of major regional importance, urban populations ranging initially from 25,000 to 100,000 or more inhabitants, a large bourgeoisie, and a defeated or integrated nobility: these were the decisive conditions for the environment of republicanism in the city-state. Without these there could be no republican government in fourteenth-century Italy; with them a republic could hope to survive. We shall see that the fifteenth century brought some important changes. One other condition remains, however, to be added. Venice aside, the republics—Florence, Lucca, Siena, Perugia, and Genoa—tended to retain the conditions for some political and social flexibility in the fourteenth century. This allowed for a vague but persistent popular ideology, wispy and hard to define, yet present in the minds of modest guildsmen and parvenus. The operative force of this is evident in the workers' revolts at Florence, Siena, Perugia, and elsewhere. But the stubborn popular strain in political feeling and thinking had not vanished altogether even under signories, as would be confirmed by the radical phase of the Ambrosian republic.

From the early fourteenth century, with the contraction of the economy and the reversal of the demographic cycle of growth, rural immigrants no longer entered cities in large numbers. Later, after the Black Plague (1348) and for some time to come, Italy saw a shortage of agrarian labor; farms lay fallow and lower-class immigration from the countryside into the cities fell off still more sharply. There was no significant pressure from below to enter into the middling ranks or elite groups at the top. Social classes gradually hardened, but this was not noticeably attested until the fifteenth century. At Siena the five sociopolitical blocs froze; no new blocs came forth to challenge the establishment, nor to ask for a place in it. Something like this—the freezing of the ruling class—had occurred at Venice in the early fourteenth century, but the other republics, Genoa included, had no such development until 1380–1430. New men trickled into government thereafter, but their numbers were so small as to mean little or nothing in historical terms. In fifteenth-century Florence, new men managed occasionally to enter important office with the help and push of powerful families like the Albizzi, Medici, and Capponi, though such success did not ensure a political place for descendants. These were more likely to fail than to succeed. Furthermore, recently acquired wealth was occasionally wiped out by discriminatory taxation.

With the above changes in mind, we can understand why any residual political feeling of a popular sort evaporated in the course of the fifteenth century. The political stability of republics came increasingly to be moored in fixed classes and a fixed patriciate. Oligarchy—the endemic way of communes and republics—turned gradually aristocratic; and the fifteenth century saw the emergence of political views based upon arguments from birth and family antiquity.

THE LESSON OF THE AMBROSIAN REPUBLIC

On the night of August 13, 1447, as the duke of Milan, Filippo Maria Visconti, lay dying, the absence of a Visconti heir rendered the question of a successor enormously uncertain. Rumor raced through Milan and other cities of the duchy. That night too, when the duke died, some of his counselors and an elite of the Milanese nobility met to reach a decision about the succession. Bungling and terribly secretive during the last twenty years or so of his life, Filippo Maria had made no preparations for any government to follow. Astonishingly, the all-night meeting of Milanese notables issued the next day in a republic named after the city's patron saint, the republic of St. Ambrose. It lasted for two and one-half years, to be overwhelmed finally, in February 1450, by starvation and the troops of the *condottiere* Francesco Sforza. The collapse of the republic was preceded by a brief dramatic history which, in just over thirty months, bizarrely reenacted the major vicissitudes of the early commune. Power swung from the ducal curialists and nobility to the richest sector of the middle classes, then on to humbler groups, lesser tradesmen and shopkeepers. Political life was drawn into a vortex of controversy and suspicion. Exile, forced and voluntary, returned; so also sudden arrests and executions. Ideas came to life and real issues were debated, however distressingly. The effects of ideology were rampant. They were exhilirating times for politics, perhaps, but not for many a citizen. In the end, the nobility and a large part of the *haute bourgeoisie* finally defected: they abandoned the republic and chose a *signore*, Francesco Sforza, who brought pacification by simply squelching the pretensions of the bourgeois republicans.

The Ambrosian republic has a double and contradictory value for historians. On the one hand, that it could have been established at all, in view of the fifteenth-century world, was so extraordinary as to seem freakish; on the other, it reveals the presence of stubborn memories of the old commune and a reawakened readiness to return to corporate communal government. But interestingly, historians almost invariably emphasize the former—the abnormal origins and nature of the Ambrosian republic. So doing, they are able to dismiss it as a strange excrescence, something not to take seriously, and this allows for the accepted historical view that popular government— and hence popular political feeling—was dead in fifteenth-century Italy. But though it had been largely suppressed, a strain of popular political sentiment or resentment resisted. Genoa, Florence, and Milan all went through moments of popular political ferment in the fifteenth century; and at Bologna, in 1411, following a Ciompi revolt, artisans took control of government for nearly a year. But disorganized and unfocused sentiment, or mere rage, was no basis for programs or sustained political action.

At Milan in 1447–1450, contrary to all our presuppositions about the fifteenth century, we find a powerful resentment against signorial government, and this in the most successful of all signories: we find the alleged apathy of citizens metamorphosed into militancy; we find a part of the nobility ready to take back all the authority once ceded to the Visconti *signori*; and we find the middle classes, or parts thereof, eager to seize power. But the failure of the Ambrosian republic is also instructive because it will help us to discern some of the limitations and problems of fifteenth-century oligarchy.

Filippo Maria Visconti's death brought relief to Milan. He had not been seen in the city, not even on ceremonial occasions, for fifteen years, and the Milanese neither liked nor admired him. His clandestinity and pederasty gave offense and scandal, but nothing was more condemned than his erratic wars and heavy taxes, despite the fact that much of this burden was shifted from Milan over to the subject cities—Pavia, Parma, Tortona, Lodi, Piacenza, Como, Novara, Crema, and Alessandria. Even before his death and the ensuing sighs of relief, a group of prominent jurists and noblemen, many of them ex-ducal counselors and ambassadors, were planning to establish an aristocratic republic. Celebrated old names immediately took the limelight and the initiative: Lampugnani, Bossi, Cotta, Morone, and Trivulzio. Here was the first big surprise. Long associated with different aspects of ducal government and fully implicated in its policies, they were yet able to cut loose and dream of an aristocratic oligarchy. Probably they looked to Venice, to its lumbering stability and undeniable mainland successes in the fifteenth century. And we may suppose that in a few cases, as a spinoff from their educational exposure to humanism, they also looked to Cicero, Livy, and the Roman republic. At any rate, they stole the initiative from Filippo Maria's generals, who were deeply divided over the succession and jockeyed to put the dukedom into a variety of hands. The leading candidates were Alfonso of Naples, the duke of Savoy, and Francesco Sforza, the soldier of fortune who had married the late duke's only child, the illegitimate Bianca Maria.

Although it is very surprising that a circle of noblemen and the aristocratic college of jurists should have abandoned the cause of signorial government, their turnabout made sense in one respect. Being key members of the political class, having often served the duke and city government, they had much experience of public life; they had a political education and consciousness; and therefore in any general shift of political sentiment, they might well seize the initiative and bring about the first reforms. Florence twice produced a situation not unlike this: in 1465–1466 and in 1493–1494, when the closest and most able collaborators of the Medici went unpredictably over to the political opposition, indeed became its most effective part, and in late 1494 managed to resuscitate the Florentine republic.

In founding their republic, the patricians of St. Ambrose were not without arguments. Richly endowed with legal talent and recognizing the instrumental quality of the law as much as anyone, they took the origins of the Visconti overlordship back through the imperial confirmations (dukedom, vicariate) to a popular vote within the commune. The duchy was no monarchy; the authority of the Visconti was hedged in by no divine right. And since the dynasty perished with Filippo Maria, the fullness of power (sovereignty)—so went the argument—now returned to the Milanese *popolo*.

In fact the new government had little that was popular in its constitution. On August 14, when citizens flocked to the meeting ground of the old communal assemblies, the Broletto Field beside the cathedral, shouting "Liberty! Liberty!" the patricians were strongly supported by heady municipal feeling. That morning and for the next four days, as political reforms unfolded astoundingly fast, the smooth orchestration of events revealed that a circle of men behind the scenes had worked out every detail. Apart from some grumbling noblemen of great rank, the universal approval of citizens seems to have been immediately won. With the highest ducal councils—secret council and council of justice—in suspension, the city's chief municipal body took things in hand. This was the Consiglio delle Provvisioni, consisting of a vicar and twelve councilors. Moving swiftly on the night of the duke's death, they consulted the variety of important municipal officials, the big state functionaries, the college of jurists, the heads of the principal guilds, as well as leading bankers and merchants. Then they established a council of twenty-four men, called the "Captains and Defenders of the Liberty of the Commune," to serve in office until January, and on the morning of August 14 presented this *fait accompli* to an enthusiastic assembly of citizens. They had worked through the night. The commune was born again. Representing each of the city's six gates (administrative districts), the twenty-four captains— four from each district—became the city's supreme governing body. They appointed another small council to take charge of having the parish "elders" in each district (*porta, sestiere*) select four men for a total of twenty-four, and these then more or less determined the membership of the new Council of Nine Hundred by nominating 150 men per district. Possibly the final selection of the 900 councilors lay with the parish elders. At all events, the election of the 900 took place on August 17 and they held their first session the next day.

Pietro Verri and other historians have claimed, on legal and masked ideological grounds, that the twenty-four captains had arrogantly usurped power. Verri calls them sarcastically "a college of heroes," an unwarranted slur. The twenty-four had a stronger legal case than Sforza, Alfonso of Naples, the duke of Savoy, any French prince of the blood, or any other claimant save the emperor, whose power had long been overruled by authority *de facto*. Filippo Maria had left no legitimate heir and designated no successor. His death created an emergency. The Viscontean state fell apart. All but two subject cities—Novara and Alessandria—rebelled. Power devolved *de facto* upon the highest municipal body, the Consiglio delle Provisioni and its advisers. The secret council represented the duke, and he was dead; we cannot say that it represented the state, for this indeed is what was in question. Grasping the opportunity, the Consiglio triggered a series of actions that climaxed, in the course of four days, with the first session of the Council of Nine Hundred. And on August 18 this large legislative body gave its approval to the reforms of the previous four days. Since it was clear that nobody was going to take any notice of the emperor's title to designate a successor, the law as theory was cast aside. Decisive action took control of the scene, set its own rules, and made the law for some time to come.

The twenty-four captains represented Milan's leading groups, the nobility and rich bourgeoisie, although defections would follow in time. In the typical fashion of Renaissance communes and republics, the captains were flanked by a council of advisers. In all oligarchies of the age, as will be shown in the succeeding section, the principal executive bodies tended to be larger in fact than might appear to be the case on paper.

From the very outset the captains confronted enormous, and eventually insuperable, difficulties. Most of Milan's subject cities founded ephemeral republics or preferred to turn themselves over to other overlords. Venice lunged into the Lombard Plain, took Lodi and Piacenza, and rather thought of the whole region as fair game for conquest. There was also the menace of Francesco Sforza, the period's most able soldier, scheming to claim the duchy for himself. Venice, Florence, Naples, and mercenaries all scrambled to decide Milan's destiny. The Ambrosian republic thus had to be wary of the peninsula's leading powers. Beyond this, the twenty-four captains faced an acute fiscal crisis, having inherited nothing but debts and unpopular taxes from the late duke.

The republic hired Sforza's arms but could not dictate his actions, unless the captains succeeded in reforming the fiscal structure and in maintaining unity and massive support at home. This would give them the force to impose some restraints on the soldier. From November 1447 to the end of its life, the republic responded to the foreign peril by enacting stiff laws against traitors and conspirators. Above all there was fear of Sforza's contacts in the city. But the republic's great malady was its inability to find solutions for desperate fiscal needs, the great stumbling block for other city-states.

The twenty-four captains did away with part of the existing tax structure. They destroyed most of the old registers and documents relating to individual and group tax levies. They tried to establish a funded public debt, the treasury of St. Ambrose, encouraged citizens to invest in it, and thus tried to raise 200,000 gold florins. But citizens did not step forward to lend the needed monies for defense and government. The captains then set up a commission of thirty men with the mandate to fix individual and family tax assessments. This also failed. The captains next had the thirty commissioners —among whom were rich bankers and merchants—levy taxes on themselves, but the sum of expected revenue had to be drastically reduced. A public-finance emergency had come to stay.

The chief ailment stemmed from the fact that Milan had lost the bulk of its revenue overnight, in the revolt of subject cities. And yet the city had to field armies, conduct a major foreign policy, and strive to reconquer its lost territories. This called for money and supplies. Other ills also touched the politico-moral nerve system: ills involving social schisms, group interests, fiscal exploitation, and a tradition of privilege. For the oligarchy of St. Ambrose had no intention of redistributing tax levies, of lightening the indirect taxes on goods and transferring a more equitable tax load onto the families rich in movable and real property. Instead, they called upon these to lend money to the treasury of St. Ambrose and then guaranteed returns on investments. In due course, in desperation, the republic was compelled to alienate public land and public rights.

The crisis in public finance, foreign dangers, and the effects of Francesco Sforza's diplomatic and military machinations combined to split the republican oligarchy. There was, from the beginning, a group of noblemen who claimed that only the Holy Roman Emperor had the legal title to dispose of Milan. This group gradually swelled and began to gravitate toward Sforza, as the fiscal emergency became more acute and the *condottiere*, while apparently fighting for Milan, piled up personal successes. Pavia and then Cremona offered themselves to him. He was dubbed "count of Pavia." He took Piacenza away from Venice, and the city was cruelly sacked. Before the end of 1448, four other towns had turned themselves over to him— Novara, Tortona, Alessandria, and Vigevano. The government enacted laws against speaking ill of "liberty" (i.e., republicanism) and prohibited controversial discussions. In the setting, this was tantamount to imposing silence on all important public matters. The republican podestà and captain of the people both received increased powers to ferret out conspiracy. Heavily armed guardsmen, in growing numbers, were brought into the city. Suspicions and fears were such that the government hired three lieutenants to act as checks on the new captain of the people, Carlo Gonzaga, who eventually defected to Sforza.

The year 1448 saw widening rifts among the nobility of middling rank, which had once been the mainstay, together with the mercantile *haute bourgeoisie*, of the republican regime. Tensions resulted in a sharper moralism and severe ordinances against blasphemy, gambling, ornate dress, and sodomy. In October 1448, Francesco Sforza signed the Treaty of Rivoltella with Venice, which committed the Venetians to helping him subjugate Milan and the rest of the duchy, excluding only the cities taken by Venice.

Stunned by his treachery—he was in the pay of Milan—the government fell. At once the Council of Nine Hundred moved to slash the term of office of the twenty-four captains, cutting it from six to two months, the better to control them.

The government of November 1 had a new social complexion. There were no lawyers in the newly elected group, and most of the twenty-four captains came from the bourgeoisie. The nobility's republican ranks were thinning, and before the end of the year nearly all the republic's leading *condottieri* (mercenaries) had gone over to Sforza. Meanwhile, he marched north along the Ticino River and grabbed Milanese territory at will. When his troops began to stop the flow of victuals into Milan, sometime before February 1, 1449, the republic brought in harsh measures against food hoarding and black-marketing. The elections for the new government of January 1, 1449, had resulted in an even more decisive victory for the class of rich bourgeois, who still looked to the nobility for leaders but were dedicated to the republic and were bitterly opposed to Francesco Sforza. Among the most ardent of the captains of the new government were two men whose social identities must have stung part at least of upper-class Milan: the notary Giovanni da Appiano and the craftsman (*artefice*) Giovanni da Ossana. Two months later, reelected to the new government of March 1, these two men were joined among the captains by a baker and a butcher. The government mounted a campaign of repression against the Ghibelline nobles who favored Sforza and worked secretly for his victory. In January the twenty-four had several noblemen arrested and decapitated, including one of the major architects of the republic, the jurist Giorgio Lampugnani, who was tricked into leaving Milan and then eliminated so as to avoid provoking a furor in the city. Having lost faith in the republic, he had in fact connived with Sforza. More executions followed in February and March. At the end of May some 200 citizens, mainly so-called Ghibelline noblemen, were condemned to death for treason and all their properties were confiscated. The condemned included many of the city's grand old names: Visconti (of the bastard lines), Crivelli, Borromei, Dal Verme, Sanseverino, Stampa, Bossi, Lampugnani, Litta, and so forth. The indictment charged: "The accused are guilty of *lesa maiestas*. Driven by a treacherous and ungrateful spirit, they are parricides because they machinated against their fatherland, reaching agreements with the enemy, showing them favor, and conversing with them." Political tensions throughout the winter and spring had been aggravated by famine, caused by Sforza's blockade against the flow of food supplies.

On June 1, whether by intimidation or honeyed prompting, elections in the Council of Nine Hundred again ended in a victory for a group of bourgeois captains. By the end of the third week, however, the 900 councilors were so riven by discontent that the government stepped in, ordaining that they could no longer meet without the consent of the captains. React-

ing sharply in the elections for the new captains of July 1, the 900 returned a government of Ghibelline nobles. Ossana, Appiano, and some
others were arrested forthwith, but the new government was unable to
move swiftly enough to change the direction of ongoing policies. Fearing
what the next election might bring, the diehard republicans—the *popolano*
Guelf faction—staged a tumultuous insurrection on August 31, the day
before the elections for the new captains. They stormed the government
palace, killed one of the twenty-four captains, drove the others out of the
city, sacked their houses, and thus prepared the climate for the next day.
The elections of September 1 resulted in a government of Guelf bourgeois.
Many illustrious citizens now abandoned Milan to join Francesco Sforza, in
the belief that he alone could save the city.

The next few months saw a complete polarization of political and social
forces. Sforza, craftily, did not lay siege to the city but merely tightened the
military noose so as to cut off the trickle of food. The cold of the late
autumn brought wholesale famine to the city, yet the intransigent bourgeois
republicans held out. The government intensified its laws against public
assemblies, private discussion groups, and all criticism of public policy.
Tight curfews were imposed. Men who broke the security and sedition laws
were subject to capital punishment. In January, Sforza set up special commissions in the country districts around Milan, to strike at those guilty of
helping the "illegal" leakage of food supplies into the city. By February,
Milan was on the verge of absolute starvation. The poor fed on roots and
vermin. Food smuggled into the city was dear beyond all measure and
instantly bought up by the richest citizens, among them the middle-class
oligarchy of republican diehards. It took an avalanche of special measures to
keep the great throngs of poor from assaulting the seat of government. In
late February, when the twenty-four captains assembled the loyal remnants
of the Council of Nine Hundred, they continued to believe in their ability
to save the republic and keep a lid on the populace. Instead of which a
frenzied crowd collected outside the assembly (February 24) and then
erupted against the government. The insurrection was led, predictably, by
two noblemen, Gaspare da Vimercate and Pietro Cotta, who were also
professional men at arms. Noblemen from the Stampa, Trivulzio, and other
families joined the raging crowd. They assaulted the government palace and
overthrew the twenty-four. On the next day, at the meeting of the revolutionary government of nobles, there was a group still willing to fight for the
Ambrosian republic; but the pro-Sforza noblemen easily prevailed and
opened the gates of the city. Unarmed, Sforza entered Milan with members
of the provisional government at his side.

The republic was overthrown by intolerable fiscal strains, by the med-
dling and machinations of foreign powers (and first of all, ironically, Venice
and Florence), by the rebellion of cities once under the central rule of
Milan, and by Francesco Sforza's army. But the defeat cannot be assigned to

republicanism as such, for no government could have survived the phalanx of obstacles faced by the Milanese republicans. Lesser troubles destroyed the Carrarese signory at Padua (1405) and brought down the Medici overlord-ship in Florence (1494).

Our real interest here is the manner of the Ambrosian republic's failure: the particular problems which it created and confronted as an oligarchy, in contrast to those associated with signorial governments.

It was clear from the outset that a group of men from the upper classes had resolved to seize the power of government in Milan and its subject territories. Opposed by outside forces, this determination was also under-mined by internal causes: (1) by deepening splits within the ruling group, as it faced graver problems and some leaders lost heart; (2) by its inability to reorganize and redistribute taxation; and (3) by the stiffening desire of middling social groups to share in the exercise of political power. As the course of events unfolded, noblemen and *haute bourgeoisie* decided that if they could not hold the fullness of political authority, then no other class would, and so they plumped for signorial rule. It was a stubborn and su-premely elitist way of evaluating the community's human resources. If they could not rule, then they—no one else—would serve the ruler, the new duke.

The history of the Ambrosian republic reveals that vivid memories of the old commune survived, and political action took this fact beyond mere nostalgia. Citizens nourished grievances against the signory even in the fif-teenth century, so much so that in crisis the antipathy briefly submerged or changed common sense. Yet practical political cooperation between social classes was minimal. There were no traditions to buttress this, and none could be created overnight. Milanese society, like Italian society generally in the fifteenth century, was stratified indefeasibly, in consciousness no less than in external reality. Leaders as well as followers assumed authority to be the "natural" right of some and not of others, of the few and not the many. During the republic's thirty months, no class or group at the forefront of political society was moved by the conviction that power should be shared, except, paradoxically, in the form of seizing it for themselves. Even at its most radical the Ambrosian republic was an oligarchy, not because the Ossanas and Appianos were villains and dodgy politicians but because they were dogged by conspiracies and constrained by the ideological limitations of their city-state world. It had not entered anyone's head that a purposive and watchful electorate could or should be large and varied. Venice, the flowering myth, had a closed political class. The Ambrosian republic's inabil-ity, even in emergency, to reform taxation is the incontestable sign of the fixity in the city's social stratification. The inability was rooted in the hard expectation of privilege, in the intuitive perception that to carry out a serious reappointment of the tax structure was to menace the social order itself, for such reform would have drawn a fiscal noose around the rich upper classes, and no argument, apart from extremist religious ones, could be offered to vindicate this.

Contrary to all expectations, the death of the last Visconti lord elicited passionate republican stirrings among certain members of the Milanese nobility. A large part of this class, at least to begin with, consented to the Ambrosian republic. This quite unexpected reaction is the most baffling aspect of the whole republican interlude. An important scattering of well-educated noblemen, trained in law and attracted to the republican spell of civic humanism, espoused republican ideals. Part of the great nobility, however, never sympathized with the republic. In the end, crisis brought loyalties around to their traditional moorings. From late 1448 and early 1449, the vast majority of noblemen began to pass over to Francesco Sforza.

THE WORKINGS OF OLIGARCHY

Modern democracies have ministerial or cabinet-type governments; communist states are apt to be run by party heads and functionaries; absolute monarchs depend upon advisers and ministers. In this sense all government is oligarchical. But the sense is trivial and the implied comparisons are reckless, for fundamental distinctions are buried under a superficial apperception.

Italian republics of the fourteenth and fifteenth centuries were constitutional oligarchies. Florence, Venice, Lucca, Siena, Genoa, and Perugia all had a restricted class of politically enfranchised citizens who formed the social basis of government. These alone were entitled to occupy the offices out of which men legislated, administered, and frequently adjudicated. There was no legal voice in politics save through the right to hold office. Although the proportion of enfranchised citizens ranged between about 2 percent (fifteenth-century Venice) and 12 percent (fourteenth-century Bologna) of the total population, the figure most often stood at the 2 or 3 percent mark. In practical terms, however, the figure was nearer 1 percent. At Florence and Venice, the large republics, this involved some 200 to 600 men at most. These were the men who appeared and reappeared in the highest offices; here the large majority of their nominal legal-political peers never held a place.

Under republican government, with its variety of short-term executive bodies, advisory councils, and special commissions, the class of citizens rotated through public office. One large legislative council, such as the Great Council at Venice or the Council of Four Thousand at Bologna, might hold the entire citizen class and be a fixed body. The government could assemble it at will. At Venice, in the fifteenth century, the Great Council sat on Sundays. Florence had a near equivalent in its traditional legislature: the Council of the People and the Council of the Commune, which met once or twice weekly or several times a month, depending upon the urgency of pending legislation. Since a term in these councils was for four months and since they held all told only 600 to 700 citizens, they could not hold the whole class of political citizens. But rotation gave every eligible man a chance to sit in these councils for at least one term every sixteen months or so. Many citizens shuttled back and forth between the two. Taken across a period of from sixteen months to two years, these Florentine councils were the repositories of a citizenship that was largely fixed.

Since the workings of republican oligarchy were complex, subtle, and often devious in the extreme, some sustained analysis is required. The ingenuity of Renaissance Italians was not devoted exclusively to the arts; it was invested in politics too.

In the confined urban spaces of the city-state, the instruments of sovereignty could easily be turned either to favor certain groups and families or to devastate them. Members of the political class played for capital stakes; and families schemed to occupy certain offices, keeping their eyes on profit and honor, at Florence, Venice, and the other republics. In the struggle for honors, tremendous importance was attached to electoral procedures, to political eligibilities and disabilities, to relations between vertical and lateral offices, and to behind-the-scenes "fixing." The political system itself depended upon the oligarchy's ability to control the devices employed first to fix the class of political citizens and then to reduce the ranks of the chief officeholders. In this the law was primary. For it provided the props that held up the entire system, the qualifications that denied or extended political privilege.

Small, powerful councils were the most enduring and characteristic institution of the republican system of oligarchy. In one way or another, this was to be stamped upon the civilization of the Italian Renaissance—on education, on literary culture, on the whole range of civic values. From its earliest days the commune—the consular commune—put a magistracy of eight to twelve or more men (consuls) at the helm of government. Soon, other small bodies—judicial, advisory, fiscal—surfaced alongside the mightier consulate and took a substantive part in its everyday proceedings. By 1200, small, short-term councils had become the commune's basic means of rule. The large legislative bodies assembled far less often; they could be somewhat unwieldy; and citizens did not see them as fit forums for the hammering out of policies or the daily tasks of government. Small councils thus pushed into the fore of public life, and such was to be the political way of republics down to the end of the Renaissance.

Whether at the apex of government, just below, or farther down, small councils had an ever-changing membership: terms in office were for anywhere from two to six months or a year, the purpose being to give all members of the political class the opportunity to take office and directly exercise power. Only an oligarchy could have and partly realize such aims.

For the same reason, republican governments also imposed other restrictions: e.g., that at least one or two office terms elapse before an incumbent return for a tour of duty in the same council; and in the case of the highest governing councils, such as Florence's nine-man magistracy (the Priorate), whose personnel changed every two months, an incumbent could not return to the office for two or three years from the expiration of his last term. At Venice a similar prohibition, lasting one or two years, debarred the six ducal councilors and outgoing members of the Council of Ten. If up to about 1260 the policy behind short office terms was to keep power rotating, thereafter citizens also pursued another aim: to keep would-be despots or factions from perverting the functions of powerful office. In an age when North Italian cities were afflicted by a plague of ruling cliques and despots, short office terms and the observance of regular electoral procedures became increasingly compelling.

Republican public life was dominated by small councils: executive, fiscal, and judicial councils; also powerful *ad hoc* committees, councils in charge of subject towns and territories, military councils, currency and mint magistracies, councils on trade and maritime affairs, and so on. These bodies often disposed of the authority to arrest, to investigate, to impose fines, and in certain cases to inflict capital punishment. They regulated the affairs of their jurisdictions and had a direct effect upon policies through their influential recommendations. They worked in collaboration with other councils that sat higher up on the tiers of power and honor, but those near the top could function autonomously, even autocratically. Excellent examples of this are to be seen in the Council of Ten at Venice, the Decem Baliae (war council) and Eight on Security at Florence, and the Balia at Siena. Not rarely these offices resisted or ignored the wishes of councils at the summit of authority.

The dynamics of oligarchy are best understood by examining the anatomy and proceedings of small councils.

Whoever sat in the ruling councils held, in effect, the day-to-day instruments of sovereignty. But how exactly were men elected to these councils? Republics, as already noted, had a small class of political citizens, all of whom qualified in theory for service in the highest councils. But in fact the large majority never saw such service, whereas the rich, well-connected, and "experienced" men occupied the coveted posts more or less continually.

At Venice and Florence, candidates for high office were drawn only from select lists or from among a field of select nominations. This is to say that there were *de facto* categories of political citizenship, and the highest category was the one made up of the men who repeatedly served in the small councils at the pinnacle of government. A man who appeared in such a council only once or twice in the course of his life, as often happened at Perugia and Florence, was not a member of the group at the top. Connections or desire had failed him.

The select lists or select nominations were decided on by vote in the ruling council or in special councils. This touches the celebrated practice of screening or "scrutiny." There was much reliance on this procedure at Florence, Siena, Lucca, and Perugia, but the Genoese also observed it. Periodically, the government called for a scrutiny or review of all the men deemed eligible to hold public office. Such a review was usually held every three or four years, sometimes once in five years. But dissatisfaction within the oligarchy, or sudden changes in government resulting from a *coup d'état*, could easily bring about irregular scrutinies and changes in the favored lists of citizens.

The initiative in the drawing up of eligibility lists belonged to the chief executive bodies. They formed the core of the reviewing council, which included a scatter of officials and spokesmen: usually the formal body of governmental advisers, then a broader circle of leading officials, and the representatives of neighborhoods and of favored groups, such as Guelfs and guilds. Sitting together, these men composed the reviewing council and might number, in all, anywhere from 75 to 300 or 350 citizens. They studied the eligibility lists, but they took particular trouble with the names finally approved for potential service in the ruling councils. A man fit to serve in a minor office or in a legislative body might be wholly unfit, in social or political terms, to serve at the forefront of public life, in the world of high policy and decision making.

Generally speaking, reviewing councils took a vote on every name that came before them. Beginning either with the existing or with new lists, they confirmed or eliminated names and sometimes added new ones, provided, of course, that any new names met the property and tax requirements of citizenship. They voted on each name, but from this point on the all-important details varied from city to city and from time to time. The approval or confirmation of a name might require a simple majority vote, a two-thirds majority, or a three-quarters majority. Moreover, there were marked differences in the mechanics of voting: by ballot, by voice vote, or by standing up. But the critical difference was that between a secret and an open vote, and here again the form of the ballot introduced complications. Ballots —beans, tickets, balls, or whatever—could be cast in ways that made them secret or not. A black or white bean openly rendered did not make for a secret ballot: it could be seen and councilors could be distributed in the assembly hall in such a way as to put every man present under surveillance. In the second half of the fifteenth century, councils at Florence operated in this fashion almost constantly; the Medicean oligarchy made a programmatic use of the "exposed" system of balloting. Other methods of voting, such as by voice or standing up, were all the more subject to psychological duress, particularly as faction and favoritism persisted. At Venice the expectation of electoral fraud ran so high, at all events after about 1400, that the globules used as lots were secretly marked so as to preclude the smuggling in of fraudulent ones. Again, at Venice, very little time was allowed to pass between the designation of an elector and his making of a nomination for office; furthermore, he stood with his back to the whole body of voters and prospective nominees, to keep signals from being exchanged between him and anyone in the assembled body. Yet none of these precautions kept the same thirty or forty Venetians from continually winning elections to the principal offices.

The foregoing controls could be tight or tolerant, according to the needs and fears of the ruling group. Established practice under the so-called "Good Government" of Siena, a regime which lasted from 1287 to 1355, is illustrative.

Here the effective restrictions were drawn more tightly than in anything suggested above. The Good Government's chief executive body, the *concistoro*, was a council of nine men who served two months. Rich merchants, bankers, and a scatter of middling but solid burghers provided the government of the Nine with its social basis. *Nouveaux riches*, lawyers, physicians, and nearly all noblemen were excluded from the regular key offices. The Nine were in direct control of nominations for the general legislative council and for the leading fiscal office, the four Provveditori di Biccherna. In fact, their powers went much beyond this. Up to 1318 the outgoing Nine, the podestà, the captain of the people, and the four heads of the gild of bankers and big wholesale merchants (the Mercanzia), voting in a secret assembly, elected the succeeding Nine. To win a place in the Nine required at least ten of the fifteen votes. From 1318 onward the general council elected the Nine via a complex system of lot-drawing. The names of those eligible for the dignity were, however, designated by the Nine in office. This was not the only control, for the members of the general council were elected by an assembly of the Nine, the podestà, the four Provveditori di Biccherna, the four consuls of the Mercanzia, and the consuls of the knights. The Nine also elected the Provveditori and the podestà. The leading authority on Siena's Good Government has found that certain men served in the Nine as many as eight different times and that at least 10 percent of his sample—despite the fact that records are very incomplete—had no fewer than three tours of duty there. In addition, at one time or another, more than one-third of his sample of 470 men also had close relatives in the Nine. These findings make us "suspect that the law of 1318 which required selection by lot was not effective."[2]

Up to 1318, Siena's Nine were elected by a council of fifteen men, nine of whom were those soon to be replaced by the next Nine. This reveals that the Sienese were very near to using a system whereby officeholders chose their successors, a strict oligarchic device. This type of procedure went back to the early consular communes, where consuls had now and again designated the succeeding body of consuls. Renaissance republics discouraged this practice. However, insofar as nominations made by leading magistracies carried great weight with the assembled electors, the results of this were somewhat akin to those of successive co-optation. In fifteenth-century Venice, each of sixty outgoing senators had the right to make a nomination for the senate of the following year, and these nominations were among the most influential in the Venetian Great Council.

After 1385, Siena was dominated by five different sociopolitical blocs, and whether or not they bypassed electoral lotteries or employed forms of successive co-optation, their control of the state endured.

The pattern and devices were repeated in fourteenth-century Perugia, where the Raspanti, the political bloc of prosperous merchants and bankers, prevailed. Their chief rivals, a vital and militant nobility, spent many years in exile or in exclusion from office, or they were allowed at times to hold only those offices, such as embassies or judicial and advisory posts, that required a certain social bearing and preparation. Perugia's highest ruling council consisted of ten priors who held office for two months. In the early 1300s the ten priors were drawn exclusively from among the guildsmen: one from the guild of bankers and money-changers, two from the rich merchants' guild (Mercanzia), and seven chosen by lot from among the members of the other forty-two guilds, although each prior had to satisfy minimum tax requirements and "never have exercised a servile trade." Guildsmen had at one time elected the ten priors via "a secret scrutiny." Then the guild rectors and the two priors who represented the Mercanzia became the deciding force. Later still, the Ten and the treasurer of the Mercanzia drew up a slate of candidates to be "scrutinized" by the rectors and leading members of the seventeen principal guilds. The approved names were then ticketed and put into pouches for the Ten, and the next term in office went to the first ten names randomly drawn. Every year, eventually, a body of the Ten, choosing in theory from among all guildsmen, selected twelve "wise" citizens for each of the six two-month periods of the forthcoming year. The names were deposited in six pouches and the office went to the first ten drawn in the "lottery" for each period.

When a *coup d'état* swept the Raspanti from office in September 1389, the triumphant nobles had no need of lessons in electoral procedure. For six months a powerful committee of five noblemen (the Cinque dell' Arbitrio) worked with two of the priors, also noblemen, to select the Ten for each tour of duty. Later the Cinque selected a council of twenty to "scrutinize" the eligible names and to revamp the pouches for the Ten. The procedures thus were the traditional ones but the social basis of power was different. In the fifteenth century, although Perugia accorded more recognition and influence to papal governors, the city's autonomy and rights in subject territories remained such that the clamorous rivalry for high office continued unabated. The nobility split into factions and manipulated the eligibility lists, the name tickets, and the office pouches. Before 1500, a powerful old family, the Baglioni, gained the decisive voice in government, mainly by controlling the strategic offices and an emergency war council of ten men. Parenthetically, the Baglioni could sometimes privately muster up to 4,000 armed followers.

In the Perugian development from finesse to crudity, from drawing lots to stacking councils, from a constituency of forty-two guilds to the near takeover of the Baglioni, we see a gradual perversion of the system of electoral lotteries and pouches. Not that the system could make for equity, save in the most ideal circumstances; but in the thirteenth and early fourteenth centuries, under the watchful eye of a more resilient and popular commune, election by lot put many more citizens into important public office. Later, having mastered the system of lots and pouches, republican oligarchies manipulated its devices to preserve a facade, while at the same time pilfering power for the few.

The smooth functioning of oligarchy derived from the particulars of the system, from all the minute procedures and loopholes that enabled ruling groups to hold power and to seem to offer equality to all political citizens. Yet historians have tended, oddly, to neglect the details of the stratagems that raised some citizens repeatedly to high office, while keeping most other citizens out. Only Florentine proceedings have been probed in anything like the desired detail, and they exhibit enough complexity and ingenuity to confound all but the experts.[3]

As the Florentine republic took a sharper turn toward oligarchy in the late fourteenth century, its scrutiny councils narrowed and their membership became more selective. Like some other cities, Florence was quartered into administrative districts. Each quarter or fourth received an equal share of most of the significant public offices; procedures ignored differing population densities in the different quarters. Even the legislative councils were filled by equal numbers of men from each quarter. Florentine practice thus called for a large variety of office pouches, assigned not only to specific quarters but also, where pertinent, to sixteenths (*gonfaloni*). For example, one of two major advisory councils consisted of sixteen men ("standard-bearers"), whose names were drawn for the office from the sixteen different pouches for that office. Hence the approved lists of eligibility were really nothing more than a stage along the way to a hoard of pouches: pouches for the sixteen standard-bearers, for the Twelve Good Men, for the Priorate (the highest executive body), for the Eight on Security, for the council of war (ten men), etc.; and then different pouches for each of these, in accordance with the different districts. Down to 1434, moreover, there were separate series of pouches for the eligible men from the seven major guilds, from the fourteen minor guilds, and from the class of magnates or *grandi* (a decimated nobility), who qualified for the lesser offices.

Numerous name tags or tickets, drawn up from the approved name lists, went into the various pouches. A single name might be ticketed a dozen or more different times to satisfy the demands of a polity which perpetually moved men from one office to another. The intricacies of the system not only made for a wide margin of error but also invited manipulation and ingenious intervention. In an atmosphere of fierce scuffle for political place, the temptations must often have been irresistible, and no one was more effectively placed to understand and profit from the electoral complexities than the leading citizens.

Frequently, as was the case in Florence, the name pouches for the principal offices were kept in chests under lock and key, and these in turn in the sacristy of a church in the neighborhood of the government buildings. The chest for certain offices might go into one or two other chests, one inside another, each with a different lock. The different keys were held by different members of the regular clergy; and if one of these was a Franciscan, the other might well be a Dominican. The chests, accordingly, could be opened only in the presence of two or three clerics, with the chief executive body and the podestà standing by in supervision, so that many eyes were trained on the pouches during the critical moments. And since, needless to say, the clerics and other caretakers had bound their honesty with oaths, an air of rectitude and solemnity clung to the whole cycle of proceedings.

Yet for all this ceremony, the names of some citizens were repeatedly drawn for high office, while many others were never drawn at all. Some names got into none of the pouches, not having been confirmed by the scrutiny council. Many more names, subjected to a second and tougher scrutiny, were omitted from the pouches for key office. At Florence a third control belonged to the *accoppiatori* or pouch officials, who filled the pouches for the Priorate and the highest executive dignity (Gonfalonier of Justice). There was an individual pouch for the latter and several pouches for the Priorate, including a small special one known as the *borsellino*. At the discretion of the *accoppiatori*, names deposited in the *borsellino* and in the gonfalonier's pouch had a much higher chance of being drawn. After 1434, the Medicean oligarchy used additional stratagems to keep the influential offices strictly in the hands of an inner circle of citizens. The favorite device was a special council of ten *accoppiatori*, employed to "reduce" the number of names in the key pouches, thereby multiplying the odds in favor of certain names. On occasion the government resorted to outright election by vote of the Priorate. Although effective, these crude practices produced dissatisfaction among citizens, with the result that the Medicean regime was sometimes driven to bully legislative councils into approving the short-term establishment of special *accoppiatori*.

The pre-Medicean oligarchy had two functional levels: a group of eighty to 120 men who consistently appeared in the principal offices and occasionally in more modest posts; and a larger group, involving some 350 to 450 men, who also appeared in important office but only seldom and irregularly. The ordinary province of this group lay in the secondary and minor offices. The group at the top controlled the state but relied upon clients, supporters, and ambitious people in the second group to carry out much of the supporting and auxiliary work of government. With occasional brilliant exceptions, the ruling group was a conflation of men from the leading old merchant families: Capponi, Ridolfi, Guicciardini, Albizzi, Strozzi, Castellani, Rucellai, Soderini, Salviati, and the like. For many generations these families lodged men in the top tier of the oligarchy. The men of the second tier were a more changing group and at times more vigorously on the make. They had some resources: wealth, solid or helpful marriage connections, a respectable antiquity in the city, or the backing of one of the city's pre-eminent families. A few families of the second tier—e.g., Gaddi, Martelli, Ginori, Pucci, Pandolfini—eventually rose to the top. Yet the fifteenth century was an age of sociopolitical contraction; the dominant families held ever more tightly to their supremacy, leaving no sure place either for up-starts or for other old families.

In examining recruitment for the small ruling councils, the true reposi-tories of power in the republican oligarchies, we have emphasized "scru-tinies," name tickets, office pouches, lotteries, and election by executive fiat. There was more, however, to the councils themselves.

The one or two small councils at the head of state were normally flanked by at least one body of advisers. At Venice, meetings of the potent Council of Ten usually included the doge and his six councilors, in addition to a small number of other advisers brought in *ad hoc*. The doge and his council, in turn, were very often joined by the heads of two other councils and by three different groups of experts known as *savii*. At Florence, two advisory colleges with voting rights, the Twelve and Sixteen, regularly served with the highest council (the Priorate), while the Florentine council of war (ten men) worked closely with the Priorate, with the Eight on Security, or with other leading officials.

The small councils of the executive cluster conducted the capital affairs of state. They might also hear civil and criminal cases in appeal. In times of emergency—occasionally fabricated, as at Florence and Siena—the dominant council or councils had so much discretionary might that they could con-vert it into a temporary dictatorship: suddenly power was exercised abso-lutely. But this anticipates a theme. The prior questions are these: What went on inside the small ruling councils? How did they deliberate, vote, assess the voices of individual councilors, and open or close themselves to varieties of pressures?

Discussion tended to be under the chairmanship of the recognized head —Gonfalonier of Justice, doge, or other titular. Earnest talk, with an eye to making decisions, was the fundamental daily fare of ruling councils. In this connection, the most common of all their practices was to call in advisers and experts so as to hear their views on the major questions of the day. Generally, such men were extremely influential because they had much political experience and were themselves members of the oligarchy's top tier. Ruling councils could summon anyone in the city, but they summoned above all the men already prominent in government circles.

Having heard a panel of views, the given council held its own further discussions, before proceeding to a vote. Normally, as in diplomatic negotiations or proposals for new legislation, conciliar approval required two-thirds majorities. Voices in council did not carry an equal weight, even apart from considerations regarding differing personalities and degrees of eloquence. Except perhaps at Venice, where, as we shall see, small councils had a greater internal equality, the republican environment betrayed social dissimilarities at the political summit. When appearing in the ruling councils, men of the oligarchy's second tier could not match the weight of those who boasted more experience in statecraft, better connections, an older tradition of wealth, and often too a superior education or a more comprehensive vision of human relations. Moreover, the personal, intimate nature of small councils also made for constraint. The context, after all, was oligarchy in confined spaces, the confines of the walled-in city or densely populated port.

Officeholders were not strangers to one another, not in the key offices. They had not entered councils in faraway palaces; and their colleagues in office were not men whom they had never seen before. On the contrary, a familiar and intimate air pervaded the rooms and halls of the government *palazzo*, which had been in every officeholder's field of vision ever since his childhood.

Politics, government office, festivities, marriage, and religious confraternities all provided the occasions for the oligarchy to get to know and judge its members—to know their family history, financial standing, lines of marriage, misfortunes, eccentricities, and so forth. There could not be many skeletons in closets; the surrounding physical and kinship world was too close for this, too sharply defined. One sixteenth-century Lucchese, Gherardo Burlamacchi (b. 1520), made an impetuous listing in his memoirs of every serious crime in which his relatives had ever been implicated. His aim was to prepare an accurate record against any calumny that might in future be circulated against the family. He also went on to say that there were few houses in Lucca without scandal and that "in the great families there is always every sort [of misdeed]."[4] So it was in other cities.

As eight, ten, or twelve men took office in a ruling council, most of them were entering into a group of familiars where relations might or might not be cordial. Virtually all of them would be known personalities. The more experienced of them, looking around the council, could anticipate the dominant attitudes and forthcoming lines of policy. And all knew, moreover, that a particular regard was due to older men who had repeatedly served in that and kindred councils—to the merchant, lawyer, banker, or shipping magnate with one of the city's grand old names. The presence of such men in the council was felt all the more if they happened to have relatives who also appeared in high office. Lucca provided an excellent field of examples: Poggi, Cenami, Trenta, Bernardi, Arnolfini, Guinigi, Burlamacchi, and Buonvisi. By contrast, the men of the oligarchy's second rank were less influential, and their conciliar interventions less weighty. They were heard, of course, and they might even have a persuasive manner, but they lost force in the council's knowledge that they might not again appear in such an office, or not for five or ten years. Indeed, the speaker's own awareness of this must often have made him cautious to a fault, eager to alienate no one and to win the future support of everyone. At the level of high policy-making, the best documented of all conciliar deliberations, Florence's Consulte e Pratiche, reveal that the socially modest men of the oligarchy, the sort who relied upon the patronage of leading figures, often withheld their opinions, sat silently by, parroted the views of others, or even, nagged by vague fears, said one thing in council when in fact they believed something else.[5]

Yet once more we notice the importance of voting procedures. The secret ballot made for fewer constraints. In the 1480s, Lorenzo de' Medici used to stalk into meetings of Florence's main governing council to watch the priors vote by open ballot. This was one of the signs of a "veiled signory." But in the 1420s and 1430s, under "the humanist republic" and before as well, the gonfalonier or an oligarchical whip sometimes got up in the Priorate, raging because a proposal had failed to pass by secret vote: "Let's put this measure to an open vote! Then we shall see who the friends of this regime really are, and who the enemies." And none would dare oppose the bullying call for an open vote.

Venice presented a different picture. There, from 1300, the gradual freezing of the class of political citizens was effected by means of a legal limiting and defining of the nobility. Those entitled to sit in the Great Council—the sole recruiting ground for all other important offices in Venice—were noblemen. No one else was. By about 1350 some thirty to forty family clans or houses held the preponderant place in the state, and this remained so down to the late sixteenth century. For all the meticulous care devoted to secret voting procedures, men from the same leading houses habitually dominated high office. Within the Great Council, nominations for office were made both from "below" (from the Great Council itself) and from "above" (the senate and powerful executive complex). All members of the Great Council drew lots; the thirty-six winners were then divided into four committees, and these made the nominations from below. But the nominations from above were far more influential, and it was exceptional for these candidates to lose elections. At the end of the fifteenth century, discontent among the throng of indigent nobles in the Great Council was strong but unfocused, particularly because private political meetings were forbidden by law. In partial response to the swell of discontent, the ruling group was persuaded to reduce and in some cases eliminate nominations from above. Whereupon a wave of obvious, outright corruption swept the body politic. Henceforth bribery became common; noblemen made secret agreements; votes were crudely bought and sold; and the richest noblemen carried away the prizes. Indeed, for some years in the early sixteenth century, the government actively encouraged the Great Council to vote for the candidates who put up the largest sums of money for the offices in question. The money paid amounted to a kind of buying of the office and went as a gift to the state.

There is little evidence, interestingly, that the Venetian electoral changes of around 1500 had any effect on the essential composition of the city's ruling group. Both before and after, decade after decade, most of the same thirty or forty houses prevailed. Their money, lands, or far-flung business interests endowed them with decisive contacts and maneuverability; and these, united to their political experience, enabled them to get the nominations and attract (or buy) the secret ballots in numbers large enough to win the elections for key office.

The high offices in Venice were regularly occupied by men who were peers both socially and economically. This was unique, for the small ruling councils at Florence, Lucca, Perugia, Genoa, and especially Siena not seldom included men drawn from the solid but undistinguished ranks of society. These men were propertied, sometimes even well connected by marriage, and certainly well off by comparison with the large majority of people in town and country. They could also claim some administrative and political experience. But their status was modest by the standard of the illustrious old names around them in council. And we have seen that this made for psychological imbalances inside the small councils at the head of state. Venice escaped this. Its ruling councils contained, on the whole, a greater equality among members. They all were rich, even if some, now and then, were very much richer. In its key councils, Venice was a plutocracy; and while a given man in council might have more influence and rhetoric than any one of the others, none had any call to be afraid of voting against him or against the putative group around him. Thus, Venice's famed political stability was also in its small councils, perhaps chiefly there. For in 1500 the Great Council (about 2,500 noblemen) circumscribed enormous economic disparities among individuals and families. The crowd of poor and pinched noblemen was a reservoir of discontent, but the inner oligarchy, through its hold on the ruling councils, successfully kept all divisive issues off the floor of the Great Council. No proposal could be introduced there without previous discussion and approval in the senate, which had about 230 voting members. Furthermore, no measure could come before the senate without the previous consent of the Collegio (twenty-six men in all): the doge, his six councilors, the three chiefs of the Quarantía (the main court of criminal appeal), and sixteen ministers (in three teams) who specialized in political, military, naval, and mainland affairs. Indeed, the tacit powers of yet another potent council, the Ten, were so broad in matters touching the security of the state that their disapproval alone could keep matter out of the Great Council and even the senate. Exile or exclusion from office was the penalty used against noblemen who urged controversial legislation.

The full Collegio and the Ten totaled thirty-six men. If we add a few other officials, such as the three "attorneys general" (*avogadori di comun*), we have the top tier of those who effectively governed the Venetian republic. Nothing official entered the senate or Great Council save through this tier, and they, the forty-odd men at the head of state, sat in the places of honor both in the senate and the Great Council. As they rotated through high office, they often passed from one office to another *within* the forty. If the ruling group could maintain political stability among those who tended to monopolize the forty places, then this secured the controls for keeping the larger councils in line. And stability among the forty was achieved by means of an electoral system which consistently staffed the ruling councils with economic peers. Forty men held the key offices, but about 150 men, perhaps fewer, took turns there more or less regularly, and all sat in the senate. This was the crucial peer group in the Venetian oligarchy.

The small ruling councils of Renaissance republics had remarkable discretionary powers, the sort that most Europeans today would think of as dictatorial. It is not merely that they could arrest, try, and even execute people at will; they could also suspend constitutional guarantees. They could bypass legislative councils, declare war, impose taxes, or simply silence the murmuring community by decree. Although only emergencies brought on such action, rigged emergencies were known even at Venice, as in the circumstances surrounding the Council of Ten's deposition (1457) of Francesco Foscari, doge. But ruling councils seldom took emergency decisions without a careful canvassing of advice, and here we see the critical function of the *ad hoc* advisory groups. Since the two or three ruling councils of any republican city constantly relied upon the advice of other officials and eminent citizens, the entire core of the oligarchy was continually on call. If it happened that ten or fifteen of the city's leading public figures were not in office that term (though this was unusual), they were on call all the same. They could be summoned at will. In this capacity, as advisers to the current holders of principal office, they might appear in the ruling councils every day for weeks. There they expressed their views and helped to shape policy. Through them the ruling councils were permanently in touch with the entire core of the oligarchy, so that there could be no misunderstandings in communications between government and social elite.

The institution of the *ad hoc* advisory committee was one of the most ingenious and flexible devices of the whole system of republican oligarchy. By summoning an array of advisers, the ruling councils were able, so to speak, to jam the whole core of the oligarchy of citizens into government;

they were able to present such a formidable front of support that a majority of "responsible" men would seem to have been brought directly into the shaping of policy. This could be eyewash, particularly where faction prevailed; and in any case, generally speaking, only the inner oligarchy was truly arrayed in the *ad hoc* advisory groups. The mere appearance of a broader canvassing, of a deeper sounding out of the political community, was often enough taken for the reality.

CHAPTER X

ECONOMIC TRENDS
AND ATTITUDES

THE LAND

Between about 950 and 1200, the whittling away of the great feudal estates of crown, Church, and big nobility looms as a fact of the first magnitude. Basic historical structures were decisively affected, from demography and property relations to family organization and urban social values. The boom in population, lasting down to nearly 1300, made ever more massive demands on foodstuffs and agricultural production. Swelling quantities of cereals and higher protein contents contributed, in turn, to rising birth rates. The process was circular. Land rose or soared in value, generating a keen hunger for it and attracting much investment. Deforestation, diking, irrigation, drainage, and reclamation from waste opened new lands for farming, and developers introduced more intensive methods of cultivation. Vast tracts of common land were gradually converted to private holdings. In the environs of cities first, then in the deeper country, the dissolution of the great feudal estates was accompanied by the erosion of dependent tenancies and servile labor.

By 1300, in much of Tuscany and Lombardy, this process had gone very far. Serfs and other dependent rustics had bought off compulsory labor services, converting these into rents in kind or coin, or they had successfully made other arrangements. The countryside around many a city teemed with a class of medium landholders and entrepreneurs, of knightly or more humble origin, who consolidated lands, engrossed holdings, organized farming with an eye to profit, and used every device from aggravated usury to encroachment to extend their properties or long-term leases. The leases often turned out to be veiled, profitable purchases. Particularly in the shadow of cities, where such entrepreneurs had citizenship or ties of kinship, agrarian reorganization came sooner. North-central and upper Italy saw the decline of the manorial system, the disappearance of demesne farming based upon serf or dependent labor, and the rise of more flexible tenancies. The transformation was best seen in the rise both of commercial leases at specified rents and of *mezzadría*, a complex form of contractual sharecropping by which the tenant farmer surrendered part of his produce, often about half, to the landlord. But whether achieved by long process or fiat, the emancipation of praedial and personal serfs was not the result of new libertarian values. In the neighborhood of cities, the movement against serfdom went forth in part from the commune's determination to draw increasing numbers of men under its jurisdiction and taxation. Servility also lost out to more profitable arrangements between landlord and tenant because, amid the population boom and the rising demand for food, the new arrangements held more promise for both parties.

The agrarian revolution, as summarized above, altered the vital links between town and country. A continuing tide of rural immigrants helped to fill the urban space down to 1300. Cities depended upon the rural hinterland for food, fuel, labor, building materials, investment outlets, and even markets. Not that the basic dietary needs of large cities could be fully satisfied by local produce, as is well known from the histories of Florence and Milan, Genoa and Venice. The two seaports, in famine and in plenty, always depended upon imports of corn and other foodstuffs. Urban markets occasionally exhausted local supplies of wheat, wine, oil, and fruit, with the result that wholesalers, including governments in search of adequate corn supplies, then had to look very much farther afield.

Relations between town and country were not merely those of agricultural supply and demand. Well before 1300 the "putting out" system of domestic manufacture was already fully attested: certain branches of the urban textile industry depended upon labor from the outlying rural areas around Lucca, Florence, Milan, Pisa, Cremona, Piacenza, Bologna, and little places like Asti and Prato. Again, Genoa, Pisa, and later Venice long depended upon seasonal or emergency drafts of peasants in large numbers to help man their large fleets. The treasury of every city-state, signory and republic, came to bank heavily on the varieties of taxes, direct and indirect, levied upon subject populations both rural and urban. No sooner was fifteenth-century Venice the possessor of a mainland empire than its tax receipts from rural parishes went to help batten one of the most successful fiscs in Europe, from which—emergencies aside—returns of 5 percent were regularly paid out to holders of shares in the Venetian public debt. Country girls were heavily recruited for domestic work in the cities, and the newborn infants of comfortable urban families were put out to wet nurses in the country. The cumulative impact of relations with the countryside was bound to have a profound effect upon the outlook and values of the dominant urban groups. But the main ingredient in this regard was the economic activity—farming, usury, and investment—carried on in the countryside by rich and middling folk from the city.

Citizens invested and speculated in land from the twelfth century onward and ever more increasingly in later times, at Venice dramatically so after 1400. They bought up farms, consolidated holdings, speculated in futures, leased out oxen and farm equipment, and lent money to tenants and country landlords at rates of interest ranging from 10 to 100 percent, often in the range of from 20 to 40 percent. The country became a prime field for investment and enterprise. It was not true, even in the thirteenth and early fourteenth centuries, that the returns from commerce were so high and safe that it was foolish to tie money up in land; it was even less true in the fifteenth and sixteenth centuries, when the Italian business world faced multiplying risks, intensified competition, and a strong resurgence of aristocratic ideals. Wherever records are complete enough, or where representative last wills have been studied, we find the rich and middling families of urban society characteristically possessed of farms or scattered pieces of productive land. Their town houses were stocked with corn, cheeses, wine, oil, meats, fruits in season, or whatever other produce came from their own lands. According to the best advice, these stocks were meant ideally to suffice for periods of up to two years, as in the case of grains, oil, and wine, particularly in the fourteenth and early fifteenth centuries, when plague and military depredation frequently disrupted agriculture. The farms of citizens lay usually within a radius of twenty miles from the city. If they were farther out, it was all the more likely that they were managed as straight investments. In the case of lands farmed strictly for domestic consumption, surpluses were partly stored and the remainder was sold or hoarded, in accordance with fluctuating market conditions. Many a family depended for a part of its ready cash on the piecemeal sale of its grains, oil, wine, and other produce.

The ties between the urban upper classes and the agrarian economy did not make for amities between town and country, landlord and tenant, save in the idyllic hyperbole of pastoral poets and the classicizing attitudes of fifteenth-century humanists, who wrote for an urban audience that looked down on country people. The Renaissance reading public was to be found principally among the class of absentee landlords: citizens who spent two or three months a year in their country houses. Before 1300 the affluent bourgeoisie, whether or not affiliated with the nobility, began to look upon the country as a sort of holiday retreat, and this view came to prevail in the course of the fourteenth and fifteenth centuries. Yet the intercourse between city and rural parish did not draw the two populations together in affection or trust, least of all in their incarnation as landlords and tenants. The urban record public and private, prosaic and literary, is rich in the virulent prejudice of a landowning patriciate which exhibited derision and distrust for the neighboring peasantry and for those who worked the farms of the absentee owners or absentee entrepreneurial lessees.

The thirteenth-century jurist Odofredo was already warning that when a nobleman (*viz.* rich landlord) is with a lone peasant out in the country, however much he may insult or threaten him, the peasant does not utter a word. But if the nobleman should so much as raise his voice against the man when in the company of other peasants, all would turn and knock him down from his horse. Observes Odofredo: for when peasants are together, they are prone to all mischief, "but when they're alone, they're not worth a chicken." In the fourteenth and fifteenth centuries, Tuscan and especially Florentine collections of advice and family memorabilia had much to say about dealings with country tenants and farm workers. The advice to treat with them only when they are alone is often repeated. Landlords are urged to be deeply suspicious, to be on their guard always against their tenant workers, to expect to be cheated by them, to bully them, to summon them into the intimidating city and browbeat them there, to do them no favors and to expect none. Relations between landlord and tenant were a school for antagonism: each struggled to get the maximum of work or concessions from the other. It was inevitable that the *mezzadro* (sharecropper) should strive to hide some of the fruits of his labor so as to surrender smaller portions to the landlord. He had only his labor and cunning to help him and his family against debt, misfortune, bad weather, illness, or the inability to work in old age. Sharecroppers and laboring lessees who could not work were put off the land. Between landlord and peasant there were written contracts, of course, but there was nothing to guarantee them except law and the law courts, and these were controlled by the class of absentee landlords in the city. The English historian P. J. Jones has noted that the law codes of the different cities sometimes express the bias against peasants, variously described as "natural-born inferiors," as "the basest order of society," or as malicious, insolent, stupid, and malign. In much fifteenth-century verse the peasant is a buffoon, a lout, an ignoramus, a cheat. It was not uncommon for rich citizens to marry off bastard daughters—the mothers were apt to be servants or domestic slaves—to men from the country and to give them small dowries, expecting the country to absorb them and to forget, but that was about as far as they wanted their rural ties of kinship to go.

The fourteenth-century raconteur Franco Sacchetti observed, "The city should produce good men, the villa good beasts." The proverb was also echoed by his Tuscan contemporary Paolo da Certaldo: "The villa makes for good beasts and bad men, so don't frequent it; stay in the city and give yourself to a trade or to business of some kind." Although this prejudice against the country would vanish in the fifteenth century, it had persisted among the thrifty, nose-to-the-grindstone part of the bourgeoisie. It went with an image of the beastly peasant and the lawless nobleman caricature. Right through the fourteenth and fifteenth centuries, even in the environs of Florence, a tiny minority of noble citizens (e.g., certain branches of the Ricasoli and Panciatichi clans) frequented the city little and the country much—hunting, hawking, riding, tending their lands, and occasionally receiving homage. There was a rustic strain in such men but also something of a pastoral, aristocratic ideal. This ideal won new converts and got a very much wider dissemination in the later fifteenth and sixteenth centuries.

The cleavage between city and country is deviously expressed in Italian painting of the fourteenth and fifteenth centuries.[1] In countless examples, from fresco as from panel painting, the city haunts the picture space in images of city walls, complicated archways and vaultings, towers, battlements, urban ruins, and architectonic rock formations. Artists and patrons were moved to make statements in pictures about their cities, churches, and neighborhood settings. Now and then the image-statements are an urban fantasy, ruins or fantasticated rock formations. No matter, for the image of the city breaks through. In such representations, emphasis upon the clustered urban space is a testament of "civil life," a muffled rejection of the country as organized space for living. But the rejection may also be more explicit, as in the work of Mantegna, Leonardo da Vinci, the Crivelli, the Vivarini, and many another. Their country views, whether in the foreground or behind, are often stamped with the architecture, geometry, and lapidary textures of cities. The countryside is disavowed. In much fifteenth-century Italian landscape (see Figs. 12 and 13 in insert of illustrations following p. 242), it is this "cityfied" aspect that gives it a luminous and somewhat quaint appearance. In certain views of walled-in cities (Fig. 2), the surrounding rural space is depicted as a sort of no man's land fit for armies and desolation, not for civilized living (*vivere civilmente*). Infected by the arrogance of the domineering city, the artistic imaginaton was also affected by the immediacy of a subjugated countryside, and so it produced fantasticated pictures of the established relationships of power.

The city gave rise to a literature about the country that turned rural folk into thieving louts. Noble shepherds were the brain-spun self-images of a literary elite. But if the deep rural parishes had produced a literature, urban usurers, absentee landowners, and the bailiffs of the great landlords would have figured among the leading scoundrels. These harried not only property-less tenants but also the petty rural landowners, who were squeezed by urban taxes and hounded by debt and usury. In the process many lost land, livestock, home, even farm tools; and the beneficiaries tended to be citizens, bourgeois or noblemen, of the powerful neighboring cities.

The disintegration of the great estates of Church, crown, and feudal nobility was followed after 1350 by a new consolidation and reconcentration of holdings over much of upper Italy—Tuscany, Emilia, Liguria, Lombardy, and Piedmont. Despite the shortage of farm labor for decades following the Black Plague (1350–1425), the value of land rose again, especially after about 1440. More and more land passed into fewer hands. In parts of Tuscany and the Veneto, certain monastic houses greatly enlarged their holdings, but the course of change also turned in favor of the laity—rich bourgeois, noblemen, and feudal dynasties. The Carrara lords of Padua are alleged to have owned, by 1400, a fourth of Paduan territory. This land was parceled out and sold to Venetian patricians after 1406, when Venice grabbed Padua and expropriated the Carraresi. About three-fourths of the land around Parma had returned to feudal hands by the middle of the fifteenth century. At Florence early in the century, one branch alone of the Strozzi clan (Palla di Nofri's) owned vast estates outside the city. "At Bologna in 1496, 63 percent of the population possessed no land at all, 19 percent had only minor holdings, and most property was engrossed by the urban patriciate. At Modena in 1546, 88 percent of all land was held by duke, nobility and clergy."[2] And in 1547 in Lombardy, the peasantry owned less than 3 percent of the plain's fertile zone.

While in the south, even in the eighteenth century, some 65 to 70 percent of land remained ecclesiastical property, in northern Italy, by the sixteenth century, the Church claimed only 10 to 15 percent, in parts of Tuscany more like 25 to 35 percent. The rest was overwhelmingly in the possession of princes, noblemen, merchants, and other big landowners and speculators—a laity eager for land and its returns. Lombardy in particular, in the second half of the fifteenth century, witnessed a marked flow of urban capital into the countryside. According to the historian C. M. Cipolla, in 1500 the net returns from agriculture in Lombardy were rising swiftly, possibly to exceed the net total of receipts from Lombard trade and industry. In the Veneto the massive landed investments of the Venetian patriciate commenced after 1406 and continued to grow throughout the sixteenth century. All over upper Italy, landholdings swelled but the class of landowners shrank. Moreover, there is evidence to suggest that the fifteenth century saw the increase of enforced rural labor (corvées), notably in the regions under princely rule, such as the lordships of Mantua, Ferrara, and Savoy. In many rural parishes, indeed, corvées had never been fully eliminated and much coercion crept into *mezzadría*.

So we have a picture of the domineering, exigent city whose richer citizens bought up the countryside, called upon the labor of the rural population, and imposed a burden of taxation there. Those whose laws governed the rural parishes were those, too, who ran things in the city—oligarchs, aristocrats, or the advisers to *signori*. The effects of this hegemony were not limited to commercial leases, *mezzadría* contracts, and balance sheets; no, the whole quality of life was affected. The patrons and purveyors of culture shut their eyes and dreamed of their farms beyond the city walls or the surrounding waters. Large stocks of foodstuffs and rising incomes from land went to underpin such dreaming. The expense of leisure in the Italian city-state was in large measure the labor of the country.

POPULATION AND TRADE

In the sweep of historical time from the tenth to the sixteenth centuries, the period before about 1320 or 1330 was very remarkable for its social energies. By then the economic upswing, demographic numbers and vitalities, social mobility, and the variety of political forms had already attained their highest or richest levels. The modes of agriculture and virtually all the commercial and industrial techniques that were to characterize the High Renaissance—the "putting out" system, technology in textiles, the bill of exchange, deposit banking, double-entry bookkeeping, and the different types of business partnerships—had all been seen. Thereafter only the emphases and details varied. And thereafter, too, the different parts of upper Italy registered a very much slower rate of change and growth, as well as fitful *tempi* of stagnation and decline. In this purview urban population figures may turn out to be conclusive.

Between 1350 and 1450 no upper Italian city had rises in population that were anywhere near the records set in the period from about 1140 to 1280. Again, between about 1450 and 1500, only Verona and Ferrara recorded rather dramatic increases in population, and this in special circumstances. Otherwise, in 1500, all the major cities were still struggling to regain their early-fourteenth-century population levels, and many would not succeed in this until the eighteenth or nineteenth centuries. The Black Plague of 1348 and waves of succeeding epidemics had carried off from 35 to 65 percent of the rural and urban populations. Most of the following figures and some of the dates are approximate:

City	Date	:	Population	Date	:	Population	Date	:	Population
Milan	1300	:	150,000	1463	:	under 90,000	1510	:	under 100,000
Venice	1338	:	120,000	1422	:	84,000	1509	:	102,000
Florence	1338	:	95,000	1427	:	40,000	1526	:	50,000
Genoa	1290	:	60,000	1400	:	36,000–38,000	1535	:	50,000
Bologna	1320	:	54,000	1371	:	35,000	1495	:	50,000
Siena	1328	:	52,000	1460	:	15,000	1520	:	21,000
Pisa	1293	:	38,000	1427	:	7,500–10,000	1562	:	10,000
Padua	1320	:	38,000	1411	:	18,000	1500	:	27,000
Verona	1325	:	38,000	1425	:	14,225	1502	:	42,000
Pavia	1320	:	28,000	1475	:	16,000			
Mantua	1320	:	28,000	1463	:	26,000	1527	:	32,000
Lucca	1300	:	23,000				1540	:	18,821
Vicenza	1320	:	22,000				1548	:	21,000
Modena	1306	:	18,000				1539	:	15,675
Ferrara	1320	:	17,000				1520	:	41,000

Verona and Ferrara were atypical. Because of special local circumstances, such as a flourishing wine trade, Verona benefited from its proximity to Venice, though the same was not true of nearby Vicenza and Padua. Ferrara, like Mantua, was the capital of a princedom and the site of a brilliant court, continually attractive to tradesmen, soldiers, visitors, and functionaries. It was a center of conspicuous consumption, especially after

1450. Milan's failure to recover in full is noteworthy, in view of the fact that as the political and administrative heart of a large duchy, it attracted merchants, artisans, professional men, soldiers, and functionaries; and doubtless, too, it siphoned people and advantages away from neighboring cities such as Pavia, Piacenza, and Cremona. In the total economy of the northern plain, the gains at Verona and Ferrara could not alter the general picture of stasis and decline in the century from 1350 to 1450. The remarkable upswing at Verona—and it was both economic and demographic—was recorded between about 1440 and 1490, a prosperous half-century for much of the Lombard Plain. But the sixteenth century brought invasion, war, bouts of famine, and material scarcity to Lombardy and even the Veneto. Of the great northern cities, only Venice and perhaps Genoa recorded substantial gains in population during the first sixty years of the century.

Historical demographers and economic historians see a close link generally between their respective spheres. The strongest point against the argument for stagnation in the Italian Renaissance economy has been in the suggestion that the production of goods in the fifteenth century, when taken on a per capita basis, may have equaled or surpassed output in the thirteenth and early fourteenth centuries. If this could be demonstrated, the argument from demography would lose some of its force and the productive levels of fifteenth-century society would have to be readjusted upward. But no adequate figures have been adduced in support of the per capita argument and it is unlikely that they will be, owing to the exiguity of quantitative data for the pre-plague period. In the event, we are obliged to return to the indications of demography.

Parts of upper Italy continued to show much economic vitality in the fifteenth and sixteenth centuries. There can be little doubt of this. In the late fifteenth century, visitors and resident merchants from northern Europe noted and were often struck by the bustle and spectacular variety of goods to be found in Milan and Venice. As Lucca's great silk industry foundered in the late fourteenth and early fifteenth centuries, Lucchese "know-how" spread. Other cities took to producing silk on a large scale: Florence first, then Bologna, Genoa, Milan, and Venice. Lucca itself made a comeback before 1500. These cities issued lines of heavy silks, all extremely expensive, as well as lighter-weight cloths, such as sarcenet, tabby, and *soriano*. Again, when the Florentine wool industry fell into a sharp decline in the fourteenth century, some cities to the north of Florence entered the field and sharply extended their production.

Throughout the fifteenth century, at Florence, Venice, Siena, Lucca, and Genoa, it was still true that young men from the old ruling families were occasionally sent out into the world at the age of fourteen. They engaged in commerce, banking, or shipping, made money, and after many years returned to their native cities to enter politics or to lead more sedentary lives. In the sixteenth century, many Venetian patricians, Florentine aristocrats, and Genoese noblemen continued to give themselves to trade, but they gave less of themselves. As we shall see, a new wind had risen among the upper classes, a new set of values was sifting in to replace the old.

Over the long term, there was a deceleration in the peninsula's productive capacities, a weakening in trade investment and in the upper-class grasp on business initiative, and a decline, at the same social level, in direct personal commitment to trade. Here and there we come on figures in strong support of these observations. Enrico Fiumi's meticulous study of Prato, a town near Florence, plots the Renaissance demographic decline in painstaking detail and shows that in the early fifteenth century, when the population in the town and outlying country was near its lowest point, so also was local trade. In 1428, citizens from leading Pratese families filed tax returns declaring: "I do nothing because I can't do business," or "I do nothing because there's nothing to do," or "I don't ply a trade and I don't know how to ply one."[3] Moreover, from the moment Florence absorbed Prato and its environs (1351), much Florentine capital poured into the Pratese countryside, and this movement continued for the next hundred years, as Florentines bought up farms and estates. Mercantile capital was thus siphoned into Prato's countryside. And when Arezzo, Pisa, Livorno, and other lands fell under Florentine rule, much the same thing happened.

In 1293, in the port of Genoa, tax farmers anticipated the transit of merchandise to the value of about 4,000,000 Genoese pounds; in 1334 the value had dropped to less than 2,000,000 pounds, and totals seldom went above this in the second half of the century. But a gradual depreciation of the Genoese pound in relation to gold depressed values even further. Another set of calculations shows that while fifteenth-century Genoa suffered a 70 percent decline in the global value of its international trade by comparison to pre-plague figures, the Genoese population fell at its worst point (ca. 1400) by not more than 40 percent, with the result that Genoa's trade must be seen to have suffered a marked per capita decline. In fact, the decline was sharper than this suggests, because the intrinsic value of the Genoese pound —a fictional money used only in keeping accounts—declined by about 75 percent between 1288 and 1509.

There are no equivalent long-run figures for the fortunes of trade at Venice, where the problem of decline is more complicated because it is connected, contradictorily, with the rise of new energies too. As Venetian sea power and maritime trade waned in the fifteenth century, the republic acquired a larger mainland empire and bigger armies; it took in large numbers of immigrants and gave encouragement to new and old trades and industries. The result was that by 1570 the population of Venice had been boosted to its all-time peak of nearly 190,000 souls. Where, then, was the decline?

The decline occurred in the traditional heart of the economy, right where the Venetian ruling class had long maintained that things mattered most: in the superior commitment, by both city and upper class, to the sea and to overseas trade. This had made Venice; this had forged a vast commercial and territorial empire between 1190 and 1220 in the eastern Mediterranean; and this had built one of the most populous and exotic of all medieval cities on mere sandbars and a great carpet of piles. Entire forests had been felled to build Venice and its fleets and to supply its shipping with a major export item. By the fourteenth century the Adriatic was faced with a timber shortage. At the beginning of the thirteenth century, the "Commune of the Venetians" could put a swarm of its own sailors and fighting men out to sea for a year or more and then colonize some of the islands and cities of the Levant. Not so later. The turn in Venetian maritime fortunes came in the course of the fourteenth century and became evident at the time of the last war with Genoa (1379–1381), when a Genoese fleet came amazingly close to disembarking within St. Mark's lagoon. Even in 1204, with its far-flung involvements, Venice already relied upon quotas of foreign sailors and fighters for her fleets, but after 1350 this need became acute. Venetian shipbuilding had three or four decades of stagnation after the war with Genoa, and many shipwrights and caulkers abandoned the city. Recovery followed; the shipyards were enlarged; but Venice continued to have trouble recruiting oarsmen, sailors, and fighting men. Then came a sequence of setbacks in the years between 1470 and 1529, when the Ottoman Turks, in a series of stunning naval actions, won islands, ports, and seas, until their empire stretched from Albania on the Adriatic over the whole eastern Mediterranean and back west again over nearly the entire coast of North Africa.

Despite Portugal's opening of a sea route to India, the Venetian spice trade, one of the republic's great sources of wealth, continued to show major profits down to 1570. This was owing mainly to treaty arrangements with the Ottomans. Until nearly 1600, therefore, colonies of foreigners in Venice took the city to be Europe's leading commercial center on the Mediterranean. The energetic expansion of Venetian industry did not, however, stem from the initiative or investments of the patriciate; the prime movers were lesser folk—guildsmen and craftsmen, rich commoners and foreigners. And these, along with the growing ranks of new workers, went to swell the population of Venice in the sixteenth century.

The promise and opportunities of Venice's mainland empire, acquired after 1406, worked a profound change in the Venetian patriciate. Providing it with new concerns, with land, governorships, and other lucrative offices, the mainland lulled the entrepreneurial initiative of the nobility, gradually rendering it more sedentary. In Pareto's classic formulation, entrepreneurs turned into *rentiers*. Almost as soon as Venice grabbed the surrounding mainland, complaints at home alleged that Venetian noblemen were turning away from overseas trade and getting no experience of the sea. Before 1500 the complaint had become plangent. The government toiled to find enough noblemen with the experience needed to command Venetian ships, one of their inveterate occupations. But increasingly in the fifteenth century, instead of taking to the sea at the age of sixteen or seventeen, in well-paid positions ("bowmen of the quarterdeck") reserved exclusively for them, they sold their appointments, and the senate had continually to decree that those appointed should actually go to sea. Set up specifically for the sons of patricians, "the institution degenerated and tended to become merely a hand-out for poor nobles," as the historian Frederick Lane has observed.

The drawn-out retreat from the sea went with an overall shift in patterns of patrician investment. In 1466, Venetians owned roughly one-third of all the land and incomes in the Paduan district and they were buying up estates around Verona, Vicenza, and probably Treviso. Levying a tax on these possessions in the 1450s, Venice saw the returns from this tax quadruple between 1510 and 1582. As the nobility diverted more and more capital into land, less went into trade and venturous enterprise. Alarming crises in public finance during the middle decades of the fifteenth century and again early in the next century dealt serious blows to public confidence in government bonds. Major banks were shaken or went under. The economic historian Gino Luzzatto once compiled a massive listing of the names of some thirty-five Venetian noblemen, most of whom were engaged in business and temporarily resident at Constantinople in the late 1430s.[4] His aim was to underline the vigor of the patriciate's involvement in overseas trade. But the illusory feature of such a catalogue is immediately obvious when we consider that almost any such count for the thirteenth century would have resulted in a tally of several thousand Venetians, that in 1377 decimated Lucca alone had a colony of at least forty-six Lucchese in far-away Bruges, and that the declining curve in the number of Venetians resident at Istanbul (Constantinople) finally led, in 1594, to a mere nineteen merchants, of whom only four at the most were noblemen.

Well into the sixteenth century, Venetians continued to stress the importance of the patriciate's devotion to trade, but historians are coming to detect a note of nostalgia and exaggeration in such emphasis, for by 1510 the proportion of aristocratic ducats canalized into trade was already far from keeping with any putative ideal. Apart from investment in land and a more intense fashion for boastful spending, as we shall see, more of those ducats went into the purchase of public office and into the flourishing business of personal loans. The latter were negotiated through the fictitious leasing of real property so as to conceal the taking of illegal usury.

By the late sixteenth century, notes one historian, "the Venetian nobility's renunciation of trade had become almost general." For about a century, moreover, it had been the custom of many noblemen, possibly a majority, to depend in part or in whole upon the income from public office—judgeships, advocacies, certain governorships, and a myriad of lesser offices. Also to be seen in this light were the perquisites attached to the range of ecclesiastical posts reserved for the sons of patricians.

The gradual change in the outlook and economic underpinnings of the Venetian nobility was accompanied by the growth of conspicuous spending. Thrift came to appear mean and dishonorable, unworthy of gentlemen—which is why, in the sixteenth century's mythology of class, to inherit wealth became one of the fundamental marks of nobility. The self-made man smacked of "avarice." Patricians made their houses larger and showier, the rooms spacious and more ornate. Families took on larger teams of servants. The historian Gaetano Cozzi has observed a growing thirst for banquets, balls, and festivities. There was a pullulation of magnificent country villas: eighty-five at least built in the fifteenth century and more than 250 in the century following. Major art collections were seen at Venice for the first time in the early sixteenth century. And in the generation preceding, noblemen had developed a craze for portraits of self, family, and forebears. The dowering of daughters, already dear and getting dearer in the fifteenth century, turned more and more inflationary. The legal limit on dowries was raised four times between 1505 and 1575, going from 3,000 to 6,000 ducats, but it was absurdly easy to get around the prescribed limits. A few Venetians—e.g., Andrea Vendramin, elected doge in 1476—paid up to 30,000 and even 40,000 ducats of gold in dowries for their daughters. During the middle decades of the sixteenth century, the old dowry limit of 3,000 ducats alone would have paid the full year's wages in the Venetian shipyards of more than sixty skilled craftsmen or 150 to 190 unskilled workers.

Scholars have suggested that entry into big business in the sixteenth century required larger outlays of capital. Competition from abroad was keener, markets and material sources were unstable, and personal industry—which made for "avarice"—had to be unstinting. But all this was already true of the fifteenth century, as is clear from the life of a Florentine silk merchant, Andrea Banchi (1372–1462).

He came from a family of silk merchants. His sons, brothers, father, and paternal grandfather all went into silk. Andrea himself trained a number of young men in the trade. In 1427 he was one of the four or five richest silk merchants in Florence, out of some eighty to a hundred Florentines in the trade. There was a sharp division of labor in the industry, which included not only spinners, weavers, winders, throwers, warpers, dyers, boilers, and other skilled workers but also differences between the specialized weavers who produced brocaded velvets and those who made the cheaper taffetas and satins. As a result, Andrea had to rely upon hired overseers, especially because the system of "putting out" materials to different craftsmen was widespread. Workshops of more than a half-dozen workers were few.

Like all the most capable merchants in the silk industry, Andrea Banchi was involved in all phases of the enterprise. His investments started with the skeins of raw silk. Then he or his agents followed the emerging product, as it went from craftsman to craftsman, up through to the point of sale; but he owned the product all along the way. At the end of the process the manufacturer turned into a merchant, being either a retailer in the home store, where Andrea and his four shop boys sold goods, or a wholesaler abroad, at Geneva, Rome, the Abruzzi, or wherever. For all his capital, ability, and contacts, Andrea had to give his business his constant personal attention. Yet he suffered losses or took in derisory profits in a number of cities—Paris, Naples, Bruges, and Barcelona. There was seldom a steady outlet for his silks. He was continually on the lookout for new markets and customers; therefore he had to have reliable agents abroad: salesmen, actually, to push his cloth, for the competition from other cities was cutthroat. Andrea's biographer, Florence Edler de Roover, notes: "Quality was not enough to find buyers; one must also know the clientele, its tastes and its habits." The most expensive silks—our man's specialty—had, in any case, a very restricted market.

Andrea toiled hard to bring in profits, but bring them in he did. And although he took public office now and again, having been born into the political class, he had little time for politics and was occasionally forced to refuse offices. Between 1427 and 1457—thanks in part to his systematic tax dodging—he trebled his fortune, estimated at 18,000 gold florins in 1460, not including his house, villa, and three other pieces of real estate. The sum was enormous. But we are talking about the man who had become Florence's richest silk merchant by 1457 and one of the city's first ten taxpayers. Though he had worked nearly all his life—and he lived to be ninety—in the greatest of luxury trades, his 18,000 florins fell far short of the spectacular fortunes made by many a thirteenth- or fourteenth-century wool merchant, moneylender, or Venetian spice importer.

Business enterprise, in absolute and relative terms, had become increasingly difficult because foreign competition was keener and markets narrower. It became more difficult, too, because the Renaissance offered more serious distractions to the upper classes. And chief among these was politics. The Italian historian Marino Berengo has pointed out that politics in Italy came to be formally associated with noble lineage for the first time in the sixteenth century. Now men were deemed noble when they and their forebears had a "natural" association with office and public life: in other words, when they were born into a more-or-less fixed political class. As a matter of fact, men had taken this perception rather for granted long before its elaboration into an ideology. The view was turned into law at Venice as early as the start of the fourteenth century. But generally speaking, the fifteenth century offered securer political rewards and satisfactions. Politics in the thirteenth century had unfolded as a corporate enterprise, in friction and conflict between classes and among guilds and parties. But in the fifteenth century, with the emergence of more settled political classes (patriciates), men in politics could be much more certain about office and the moral or material rewards thereof. They constituted a more cleanly delineated oligarchy; they were especially subject to the seductions of politics; they were the very ones—in an age of commercial risk—to court public office, to glorify the name of politics, and to give, accordingly, less and less time to the vocation of their ancestors, commercial enterprise. This countervailing process, which put political and business careers in opposition, made increasing gains in the period after 1450.

For the upper classes the Renaissance also provided other major distractions from mercantile activity, among them fervent literary pursuits, genteel farming, secular artistic interests, an enhanced bent for family life, and a taste for mundane fashion which some contemporaries thought "effeminate." None of these was compelling in itself, but none came by itself; none was isolated. All were linked to the values of the dominant social stratum, and the concomitant viewpoint could be compelling.

PUBLIC FINANCE

The fiscal institutions of the Italian city-states were bewilderingly complex. They reflected the genius of urban politics, with its attendant stresses and deceptions, and they expressed the intricacies and expedients of the urban mind. Commune and city-state were a moneylender's paradise; this affected the institutions of public finance in their essence. Merchants and their many converts among noblemen wanted returns even on their tax disbursements. Wherever possible, therefore, taxes due were turned in large part into loans. By the middle of the thirteenth century, credit and its mechanisms governed the fiscal proceedings of the larger communes; auditing and tax collection were centralized in the course of the fourteenth and fifteenth centuries; and the public finance of the modern state was born.

From about 1150 the leading communes already had significant revenues. Imperial grants and usurpation increased these. Communes boldly chipped away at regalian rights, such as the imperial rights of coinage, the lucrative salt tax, and income from the administration of justice. There were communal imposts on bakers, butchers, and millers; also levies on mercantile goods. Communal properties and local market rights brought in small but important sums. Finally, although the commune began to impose direct taxes (the hearth tax and a personal property tax), these were known as extraordinary levies because crown and empire had collected them very occasionally and only for exceptional expenses.

Throughout the thirteenth century, the commune fought to gain control over the indirect taxes, chiefly tariffs and tolls, that were still collected by others—the bishop, the order of knights and noblemen, the leading feudal family, or the powerful guild of shippers and overseas merchants. The *popolo*, the more exigent part of the middle class, led the struggle to establish the commune's fiscal sovereignty and eliminate glaring tax privileges.

As the commune expanded, taking in more people and subject lands, its revenues and expenditures continually increased. But after 1250, expenses left their graded course and began to climb steeply, owing partly at least to an increasing reliance upon the expensive hiring of mercenaries. Although citizens were paid for their military service, the hardened foreign professionals commanded very much higher rates of pay. Florence, Pisa, Genoa, Venice, Milan, and Bologna all had markedly higher public expenses in the second half of the thirteenth century. In the fourteenth century, Florence, Pisa, Perugia, Genoa, and Bologna endured in a state of sharp habitual debt. Later, in the fifteenth century, Florence and Genoa again, but also Milan and Venice, were pushed into harrowing fiscal crises. They were forced to overhaul their organization of taxes.

By the early thirteenth century some communes—Florence, Lucca, Siena, Pisa—already levied a personal property tax when exceptional need arose. In the beginning, knights and noblemen were often exempted from this tax, known as the *lira*. When claimed by noblemen, landed wealth in the neighborhood of cities largely escaped the *lira*. Later, from about 1250 and with the *popolo*'s victories, the direct property tax (*lira*, *estimo*) was more effectively collected, and now real property, urban and rural, was snared. In this fashion the *popolo* struck out at its major antagonists, the city's old propertied and noble families, while also subjecting itself to the same tax for about two generations. But strong resistance to the tax developed within the popular ranks, even as the *popolo* triumphed. The outcome was that wherever the *lira* or *estimo* was truly levied, repeal eventually followed, as at Florence in 1315, or it was so diminished or so rarely collected that it was ridiculously outweighed by the revenue from indirect taxes on food staples, services, imported goods, and business or property transactions.

Another great source of government funding took on in time the ambiguities of a direct personal tax. This was the so-called "forced loan," the most ingenious fiscal device of urban oligarchy. In the twelfth and early thirteenth centuries, citizen loans to communes were largely voluntary. Such loans became common after 1150, most notably at Genoa, where groups of shipping magnates and big merchants, mainly of noble stripe, made loans to the commune in return for the intake from taxes consigned. Such proprietary control over a tax might be good for a number of years, until the loan had been repaid with interest, often at a rate of 15 percent. But the interest on emergency loans could rise to 30 and 40 percent and even more. In studying Sienese finance during the first half of the fourteenth century, Bowsky repeatedly turned up interest rates of 60 percent. Voluntary big loans to government also attracted high interest rates at Pisa, Florence, Bologna, and Perugia. A Venice the customary interest was 12 to 20 percent. Here, then, was a superb investment outlet for privileged urban groups. In many instances a tax for a given period could be "bought" with a cash payment of only 10 or 15 percent of the promised loan to government, and the outstanding balance was then paid over, according as the tax was collected by the speculators involved. Tax farming and loans to government could thus converge.

The right to such lucrative lending or tax farming belonged only to citizens, but when we come on the names of the big lenders, they turn out to be well-placed men from the top tier of citizens or their relatives and business associates. Although the making of large loans, often by a combine of rich citizens, was seen down to the sixteenth century, the occasion was increasingly tied to emergencies. Genoa apart, such loans were floated less and less often after the mid-fourteenth century. Meanwhile, an alternative form of public financing had appeared on the scene—the forced loan, which was to have a remarkable history.

The origins of the obligatory or forced loan are obscure. At some point, evidently, when the commune's need for monies was desperate and interest-bearing loans to government were seen to be a good thing, credit-minded early merchants, in an astonishing stroke, hit upon the idea of the forced loan, which imposed (!) a profit on a select list of lenders. To begin with, only wealthier citizens were affected and early forced loans undoubtedly earned a handsome interest, owing to the fact that the practice grew out of voluntary loans. Even around 1300 the two types of loans were sometimes confused, because the element of compulsion varied greatly in forced loans. Genoa, just after 1200, may have been the first city to collect forced loans, but Venice and Florence were immediately behind, while Pisa, Siena, and other cities followed.

Venice reappointed her system of forced loans in 1262 and for more than a hundred years paid a steady interest of 5 percent on receipts. Despite higher incomes from commerce and urban rents, Venetians were generally satisfied with 5 percent, and before 1320 the forced loan had become a popular form of investment. Indeed, it took on the character of a negotiable security and became a profitable field for speculators. Although the benefits trickled down in some cases to certain guilds and modest folk, the system was restricted by and large to the well-to-do. In 1379, it took assets of more than 300 ducats to qualify for inclusion among the obligatory lenders. When we consider that the wages of a skilled craftsman came at best to forty or forty-five ducats per year and those of shipyard laborers to between fifteen and twenty ducats, we see how selective the system was. In 1379, with a population of about 60,000 people, Venice listed only 2,128 lenders.

At Siena, Pisa, Florence, and Genoa, forced loans earned a much higher interest than the 5 percent paid at Venice. In his study of Sienese public finance, the historian William Bowsky commonly found interest rates of 10, 15, and 20 percent on *preste* (forced loans). At one point, over a four-year period in the early fourteenth century, the interest rose from 15 to 40 percent. But in 1336, responding to sharp public discontent, the oligarchy finally resolved to hold interest down to a maximum of 10 percent on all loans to the commune, including *preste*. At Pisa, between about 1280 and 1350, interest rates oscillated between 12 and 20 percent for the big individual lenders, while at Florence the range was generally between 10 and

15 percent. Florence fixed a 5 percent rate in 1345, but since interest there, as everywhere, was paid on the par value of the forced-loan securities, rich speculators had little trouble procuring higher real rates of interest by means of manipulative buying. At Genoa, in the late fourteenth century, interest on obligatory loans was in the range of from 8 to 10 percent.

The forced loan was not just a source of income for the well-to-do, nor a mere device for rendering personal taxes more palatable; it became a system of public finance. By making the paying out of interest absolutely foremost, except in conditions of emergency, governments turned the negotiable forced loan into the occasion for consolidating and funding the public debt, and this enabled governments to function in a state of perpetual debt. Now the large receipts from indirect taxes could go into a central fund mainly for the purpose of paying interest or even of liquidating the debt, while ordinary expenditures could be debited against the fund or drawn from other sources. Moreover, short-term loans could be raised against the fund as a whole or against the gradual yield from ongoing forced loans. In 1262, when the Venetians reorganized their system of forced loans, they made a breakthrough: theirs was the first European state to fund the public debt. Florence reformed her finances along kindred lines in 1345. And Genoa, after several attempts at fiscal consolidation, finally executed a major reorganization in 1340, when three series of debts were united and the bulk of receipts from indirect taxes assigned thereto.

The consolidating and funding of public debts, later to become one of the classic modes of deficit financing, failed to solve the fiscal problems of the Italian city-states. Amid a people decimated by successive cycles of plague and famine, public expenses continued to rise alarmingly, eventually to issue, as from the later fourteenth century, in agonizing fiscal episodes. The larger, more ambitious states were the more visibly or dramatically affected—Venice, Milan, and Florence, with their subject territories and daring enterprises. But lesser states also suffered. Lucca, Siena, Bologna, Padua, Ferrara, and Mantua suffered the military encroachments and blackmail of the others. The ordinary expenses of government—salaries, administration, the normal upkeep of roads and defenses—were mild. No large city had any trouble meeting these, which took only a part of ordinary revenues. Although bread and wheat subsidies could be costly in times of famine, when they kept the price of bread down, governments got social peace, an excellent return for their money. The truly staggering disbursements were for military expenditures and accruing interest on the public debt: expenditures incurred in paying off small armies of marauding mercenaries in the second half of the fourteenth century, in wars between Venice and Genoa, Florence and Milan, Venice and Milan, and thereafter, in the late fifteenth and sixteenth centuries, in the wars that put large foreign armies into Italy. Cities under princely rule were burdened, in addition, by the grand style of their princes. Jewels, heaps of silk brocades, banquets, gifts, pensions, and costly religious patronage put a heavy burden on budgets.

The first and chronic victim of Renaissance fiscal crises was the interest on obligatory loans. This put the whole apparatus of deficit financing under a chronic threat. Genoa ended by putting itself, so to speak, into receivership. In 1407, with the establishment of the Casa di San Giorgio, which incorporated the state's private creditors, Genoa put most of its revenues and fiscal administration into the hands of the Casa, in guarantee of the loans advanced to government. At Venice in 1380–1381, in the midst of the Chioggia (Genoese) War, numbers of rich noblemen were compelled to auction off their big town houses to meet their forced-loan obligations. The government suspended interest payments on the public debt. Venetian bonds fell to 18 percent of their par value, rising finally to 67 percent in 1424, only to plunge again to 13 percent in 1474. Interest by this time had been lowered to 1 percent of par—meaning a real interest rate of above 7.5 percent—and even then interest payments were interrupted for many years. Florence carried a massive public debt throughout the late fourteenth and early fifteenth centuries. Despite an overhauling of the tax structure (1426–1427), Florentine tensions came to a head in a mad war of aggression against Lucca (1429–1433), when a terrible fiscal crisis led directly into the political ascent of the Medici house. Interest on and credits in the Florentine public debt suffered. In 1427 the market value of two or three different kinds of government bonds in Florence stood at 20 to 35 percent of par.

The exploding costs of government undermined the institution of the obligatory loan, threatening to turn it into a direct, nonreturnable tax. But the ruling classes at Florence, Venice, and other cities held out tenaciously against this. In their view, money lent, whatever the circumstances, was a loan and lenders had a right to interest, whatever the opinions of canon lawyers. In solvency, governments tried hard not only to pay interest but also to return the principal. Between 1316 and 1350, Venice made remarkable progress in the liquidation of its public debt. Generally, the suspension or lowering of interest rates was a measure of last resort. As a last resort, too, payers of obligatory loans could sell their credit shares on the open market, even if they thereby lost the interest and much of the principal. In such transactions, rich citizens and speculators were far more likely to fare better than poor ones.

All city-states were forced to retain or restore a direct personal tax, scaled in theory according to the taxpayer's assets or income. Florence had occasional recourse to the *estimo* in the late fourteenth century, and later a mode of assessment (the *catasto*, 1427), devised as an obligatory loan, was sometimes collected *ad perdendum*, that is, as a direct tax with no expectation of interest or restitution. Venice introduced an irregular direct tax from the time of the Chioggia War (1379–1381); a regular one was not brought in for nearly another hundred years (1463) and that was the *decima*, a personal tax on all income from real property. Florence, in 1480, followed with its own *decima scalata*. But Genoa, which had long relied in part on a direct tax, the *avaria*, eliminated it in 1490. Evidently the Genoese ran a tighter and more successful operation.

Genoa's public finance was really administered through the Casa di San Giorgio and was therefore in the hands of experts: an aristocratic merchant elite that knew banking, international trade, and investment. And being also the ones at the head of state, or standing close by as advisers, how could they not know the market conditions attending loans to government, and how could they fail to foresee many a major fluctuation? A corresponding advantage lay with the circle of ruling families at Florence, Venice, and even Milan, where there was a close tie between the ducal treasury and the city's big business and financial families. Milanese dukes wisely favored recruiting at least some of their financial advisers and leading fiscal agents from among such families. At Venice and Florence, not all rich men and major holders of government bonds figured among the regular occupants of important office; some, indeed, were seldom seen in office. Conversely, however, nearly all men in the front ranks of politics were wealthy, or at least well-to-do and well connected. At Florence, in the decades around 1400, many small taxpayers chose the interesting right to pay one-third only of any forced-loan levy but thereby lost all claim to any interest or restitution of the principal. Here again was a fiscal device whose resources benefited the rich more than the modest. Fifteenth-century Florence saw a surprising number of rich citizens all but destroyed by discriminatory taxation, but they were the casualties of vendetta and corruption, not the victims of an impartial fisc.

All cities had a relatively large class of what Florentines called *miserabili*, people so poor that they could pay no direct tax or the like, although even beggars were sometimes made to cough up a few forced-loan shillings (*soldi*). Generally speaking, among the listed payers of direct personal taxes and obligatory loans, those most severely affected were the small and middling owners of real property—craftsmen, small shopkeepers, and petty *rentiers*; people of the sort who owned one shop, a house or two, a mill or a farm. Their properties were easily identified and listed. They were also more likely to come under the particular burden of certain excise taxes. If, for example, a small retailer had one or two farms and he produced any wine at all—and wine carried one of the heaviest of duties—it was difficult for him to conceal amounts much in excess of his domestic consumption. But if a citizen, keeping with the habit of the upper classes, had numbers of farms scattered here and there in the subject hinterland, not only casks of wine but also land itself might escape the eyes of tax assessors and fiscal agents. Moreover, the concealing of liquid assets came more easily to big merchants, bankers, and those who invested monies abroad.

Direct taxes and obligatory loans at Venice were based upon property assessments that fell systematically well below the mark of what patricians and citizens truly possessed in movable and real property. Indeed, the underestimation of private wealth at Venice was a matter of unspoken government policy, for the major sources of revenue were not there, as we shall see. Florentine fifteenth-century records, which are much more detailed in these matters, show something else: that citizens routinely submitted fraudulent tax returns. The account books of our silk merchant, Andrea Banchi, reveal that in the period from 1430 to 1458 "he had no scruples about cheating the officials of the *catasto* and understating his income." The Medici, the Rucellai, the Strozzi, the Guicciardini, and their ilk: all the illustrious families of Florence programmatically concealed liquid assets, lands, houses, investments, and merchandise. At least some of them thought nothing of debiting their tax declarations with fictitious donations to churches and religious houses—donations covered by fraudulent legal transfers. Often they kept two sets of account books, one for the tax officials and the "secret" or true one for themselves. Letters, diaries, and primers of advice document the fact that Florentines made a science of concealing wealth from government and even from neighbors. But what the Florentine propertied classes perfected must have been practiced by citizens in other cities as well.

Except where certain noblemen enjoyed tax exemptions, as at Milan and Genoa, the rich everywhere complained of taxes; but the middle and lower classes shouldered the overwhelming burden. A leading authority, C. M. de la Roncière, has demonstrated that Florence stepped up the variety and rates of its gabelles (duties) on foods in the fourteenth century, with the result that by the 1370s all items—bread alone excepted—carried taxes five to ten times higher on the average than they had been early in the century. The tax on oil, for example, went from three to fifteen *soldi* per *orcio*; the value of the tax on salt rose by a factor of twenty,[5] on eggs by a factor of twelve, and on hogs by a factor of seven.

In his magisterial study of public finance at Siena (1287–1355), William Bowsky traced a parallel increase in the varieties and yield of the indirect gabelles, as well as a growing dependence upon them, rather than on direct taxes such as the *lira* or *dazio*. He concluded: "The government did tend to favour the wealthiest and most powerful elements of society—great landowners, merchants, bankers, and industrialists. . . . Increasing reliance in the fourteenth century upon gabelles that burdened the masses of the city and the adjacent [subject] communities most heavily and the extensive recourse to voluntary loans that were very profitable for the monied classes would suggest that the ruling group was not indifferent to its own economic interests."[6]

The veering toward indirect taxation seems to have been a general one. Wherever we look, even cursorily, we come on a similar tax structure. Centers of agricultural produce, or small market towns, garnered most of their revenue from duties on foodstuffs, whereas major commercial centers like Venice and Genoa also took in large receipts from the movement of merchandise. Mantua, a middling city, had its chief taxes in duties on food-stuffs and merchandise. And again, in the early fourteenth century, during the town's final phase as a free commune, little Reggio Emilia, lying between Parma and Modena, saw a marked rise in the number and yield of the indirect taxes, including local highway tolls.

A few fifteenth-century figures will help to point up trends and a course of development.

Milan's rich receipts came mainly from indirect taxes, its own and those exacted from subject cities and lands. Unlike Florence, where the business community sought to hold down gabelles on manufactured and commercial goods, particularly exports, Milanese revenues banked heavily upon the gabelles on such goods. This source of revenue was backed up by others: a variety of city-gate receipts, and duties on salt, milling, wine, meat, fats and oils, iron, fish, white bread, and all items for sale in the public markets. In 1390 the Milanese state showed receipts of some 830,000 gold florins. Milan's contribution (172,600 florins) was about 20 percent of this; the rest came from the cities and outlying regions under the rule of Giangaleazzo Visconti. Some seventy years later (1463), Milan still accounted for less than a quarter of the duchy's global revenues. But more revealing was the ratio between "ordinary" and "extraordinary" returns, the latter being income from direct personal taxes (*taglie*). The figures show a total income of 1,664,750 imperial pounds (a money of account). The "extraordinary" receipts (61,811) totaled only about 2.7 percent of the whole. In moments of grinding fiscal need—three or four times, for example, in the 1430s and 1440s—direct taxes were levied on all property owners and feudal noblemen, including courtiers, amounting to one year's rental or income from all their holdings, but this was not the case in 1463. And if tax and property assessors at Milan worked in the manner of their Venetian brothers, then actual disbursements by direct taxpayers fell far short of true income.

About 1500 the Venetian republic had regular yearly receipts of more than a million gold ducats. In 1463 the Lagoon's part in net contributions totaled 611,600 ducats; the mainland cities subject to Venetian rule brought in 234,800, and the overseas domains 180,000. Only a small fraction of the 611,600 ducats derived from direct personal taxes. However, redeemable obligatory loans, in this time of bad indebtedness, accounted for about 30 percent of the gross returns from the capital city, which was high indeed. A generation later, the republic was showing net receipts of some 1,150,000 ducats, of which 620,000 came from Venice proper, but now just over a fourth of this sum (160,000 ducats) came from direct taxes. Owing to wars, commercial dislocation, and foreign-policy needs, Venice faced one of the worst crises of its history.

Down to the early 1400s the great source of revenue for all city-states was a complex of indirect taxes. Obligatory loans were also important, but less so and mainly in difficult times. The massive weight of public financing rested on the humbler social classes, for the carrying charges—the accruing interest—on obligatory loans inflated the public debt and aggravated the indirect taxes. Ambitious policies aside, some wars were inevitable, to be sure; if, however, you paid for them by tripling or quintupling customs or excise taxes on oil, salt, pork, eggs, wine, and everyday wares, or by taking forced but redeemable interest-bearing loans and securing these against the duties on foods and wares, then you increased the fiscal weight on the poorer classes. Moreover, since families of the richer sort consumed much of their own produce on their farms, they escaped a large fraction of the gabelles on foodstuffs.

But the fifteenth and early sixteenth centuries brought a redirection in some cities, Florence and Venice above all. Periodic fiscal emergencies put such a strain on public expenses that the upper classes had to dig more deeply into their own purses. All the indirect taxes remained high, and governments occasionally devised new or more devious ones. But now, too, direct personal taxes were collected rather more often; government securities lost value; wealthy families—unless they had an established place in public life—could be ruined; and obligatory loans meant a continual leakage of private wealth, unless a family was rich enough to hold on to the titles to such credits for periods of thirty and even forty years.

One conclusion comes almost of itself: private wealth in Renaissance Italy was most likely to endure when combined with a place in the political ruling class, and the more eminent the place the better. Although success in large-scale trade continued to be a mainstay, it was harder to come by. Another source of wealth for upper-class families, high office in the church, also provided the means to make or rebuild family fortunes, but there was clamorous competition for the limited number of lucrative bishoprics, abbacies, curial posts, and other major benefices. Land, again, offered adequate investment outlets but was more easily tax-listed than merchant capital. The overall result was an ever more urgent need to hold a secure place among the leading families in government, particularly as ecclesiastical preferment also depended upon the pressures of ambassadors at the papal court. Venetian aristocrats and Florentine oligarchs did not have their hands in the public till, not at all; but when spasmodic waves of direct taxation broke over them, they were in the best position to have foreseen events, to reshuffle or partly alienate their credits in the public debt, to maneuver behind the scenes, and to serve on (or stand up to) the commissions of tax and property assessors.

Conservative as well as liberal historians—e.g., Cessi, Luzzatto, Fiumi, Cristiani—have taken note of the heavy reliance upon indirect gabelles, while also noting the fierce and prolonged resistance to the imposition of direct taxes. But they have argued that this was less a matter of the "class policy" of rich oligarchs than a "realistic" determination on their part, in view of the menace of taxes, to keep movable assets free for commercial investment and for credit operations. As if this had not the stamp of class! It could be argued much more compellingly that the fiscal onus on subject rural districts harried and destroyed the small farmer, that heavy customs and excises on wares and foods frustrated the industry of the whole class of artisans and craftsmen, and that selective duties, such as on wool at Mantua or on iron at Milan (a metallurgical center), victimized entire industrial sectors. Arguably, too, the wildly unbalanced tax structure of the Italian Renaissance went to arrest social mobility and to produce the conditions that made for economic stasis, unreliable upturns, and decline.

A UNITY OF ATTITUDES

Public-finance policies were bolstered by an underlying unity of attitudes with regard to politics, social views, and moral values. To sum up that unity in a few words, the emphasis should fall overwhelmingly on the city-state's practical and ideological commitment to the maintenance of privilege. This commitment prevailed always, commencing with the aristocratic origins of the commune. Stated thus, however, the perception is trite, for privilege has characterized all Western societies in some important way. The problem is to trace the workings of privilege, to unveil its covert forms and to see its ramifications. To single out privilege is not the end of a problem but the beginning.

The belief of citizens in the necessity and rightness of privilege corresponded to the real situation in the community; it was a galvanizing point in the consciousness of those who held power in the city. In the first stage of the commune, a local nobility exercised authority by right of birth, status, and brass, which were founded in turn upon landed wealth. Noblemen created the urban commune and had no trouble justifying their place in it. Later the *popolo* disputed their authority on a variety of grounds. But the popular claim was self-warranting, for the challenge was also based upon the *popolo*'s sheer ability to mount it successfully. Henceforth any good-looking argument would be used to support the popular claim. Then came a new phase in the vicissitudes of privilege. The *popolo* limited its numbers, clamped tax or property qualifications onto the right to hold public office, laid down long residence requirements, and steadfastly discriminated against certain trades. Here was a new assertion of the principle of privilege: by its mere success in seizing power, the *popolo* was able to convert a usurpation into a state of privilege. Later still, after the upstart *popolani* of the thirteenth century had ruled for several generations, often intermarrying with the old municipal or neighboring nobility, they came to set a special price on tradition, political experience, and politically active forebears, the better to vindicate their control of government. So doing, they turned themselves into a new nobility. Furthermore, they developed arguments to go with oligarchy by elaborating on the claims of political elitism, and they worked those views into their governing constitutions. Venice, Genoa, Lucca, Bologna, Florence, Perugia: all were subject to these processes, while the signories—Milan, Ferrara, Mantua, Padua—never ceased to accord special privileges to favorites and to the enduring old nobility. Many Venetian families deemed to be "old" in 1300 were upstarts in 1150. And most of the "old" Florentine families of 1450 were upstarts in 1300.

Public finance in the city-state rested upon the unspoken assumption that people without political rights, or with little voice in government, should carry the major burden of public expenses. Time turned might into right. The acquisitive city-state grabbed at everything in its horizons and drew it under its rule: lands, townships, castles, people. Vigorous, once independent communes fell subject to it. Taxes were levied unilaterally. Genoa seized her hinterland and developed a commercial imperialism. Venice imposed her trade policies first, later conquering the cities of the Veneto and spilling over into Lombardy. Florence subjected Pistoia, Arezzo, San Gimignano, Volterra, Pisa, and lesser towns. Milan took a score of cities. In the fifteenth century the subject territories of the major city-states returned a surplus of monies in tax receipts: more than sufficed for the ordinary expenses of government. But the ambitious and expansionist foreign policies of Milan, Venice, and Florence made for crushing war budgets. Moreover, in peacetime, ordinary tax receipts went to pay the carrying charges on the public debt, whose biggest beneficiaries were the wealthy citizens and oligarchs. The Florentine republic had an investment fund (the *monte delle doti*, founded 1425) for the dowering of girls. Occasionally, modest families managed to invest small sums in it, thus fostering the illusion that the fund's advantages were generally beneficial. In fact, the great advantage was with the oligarchs and well-to-do, for the interest paid on the fund was drawn mainly from indirect taxation. In his *Della Famiglia*, the Florentine humanist Alberti flayed the city's merchant class for turning government into a base business, into a "shop" from whose profits they dowered their daughters.

In its conquest of neighboring lands and towns, the city-state betrayed a double vision, one for itself and another for its subject territories. To threaten the political independence of Florence, Venice, or Milan was an intolerable outrage in the eyes respectively of Florentines, Venetians, or Milanese. But when they took over a lesser state, as when Venice grabbed Padua or Florence "bought" Pisa, they viewed the acquisition as an act of defense, a safeguarding of vital lifelines, or a restoration of "peace and order." In most cases there was little to support this viewpoint other than the argument of a Milanese statesman (and canon lawyer) in 1420: he held that "right" is in the force of arms (*ius est in armis*).[7]

The fiscal treatment doled out to subject peoples had its moral parallel in attitudes toward the peasant, the derided lout of so much urban literature and urban humor. License for this sprang from the urban patriciate's superior position, and a way of life that called for long holidays in the country but for tough, exacting relations with the peasantry. This toughness, again, was reproduced inside the city, indeed was perhaps more severe there, in patrician relations with lower-class groups, such as the many artisans and varieties of workers. The subject merits sustained observation.

If arms were the final arbiter in controversy between city-states, the organizing power of wealth was the key to controlling the urban space. The *popolo* came forth only when the city had produced sufficient numbers of new men of substance who found, in their economic success and need, the will and ability to create a political organization, a brotherhood. But once their political authority was secure, they swiftly mobilized the resources of government—legislation and armed force—to block the formation of guilds among the lower classes or to keep them feeble and subjugated. At Venice and Genoa the authority and diversified social contacts of the wealthy merchants sufficed to dominate the craft guilds. Efforts to form guilds among workers or among certain categories of artisans were branded as conspiracies. Privilege and the *status quo* coincided. Textile workers and artisans, subject to the guilds of the rich mercers in wool and silk, were especially pinned down by legislation which, in Florence for example, denounced their "brotherhoods" (i.e., guilds, associations) as monopolies contrary to Christian charity and the brotherhood of man. But such thinking did not apply to the cloth merchants' guilds—monopolistic consortiums which dictated wages, hours of work, conditions of work, fines for work infractions, or even torture and prison sentences for subject workers. On occasion they also fixed the base lines of prices. In short, while one type of guild was a conspiracy against the community, the other was no more than part of the hallowed order of social being. Again the double vision.

Before the middle of the fifteenth century, the hegemony of princes and oligarchies was on the whole so solid, so well supported by institutional traditions, that artisanal guilds, as at Milan and Genoa, could no longer pose a threat, even remotely, to the constitutional order. Indeed, in political matters, ruling groups routinely circumvented their own guilds in favor of the standing magistracies and councils.

Renaissance fiscal policies weakened and helped to snuff out the guild movement among the lower classes. In the twentieth century, in countries with a strong tradition of trade unionism, the menace of pauperization has worked to trigger or enhance militancy, although a part of such fervor has been harnessed and transformed by the irrationalisms of national-socialist appeal. But in the Italian cities, with their arch social hierarchies, sharp group provincialisms, structural (i.e., "built in") biases in favor of privilege, and the inexperience of workers in matters of organization, pauperization demoralized the members of the more humble guilds, not to mention those beyond the guild pale. There was little to be expected from the artisanal associations. Unemployment and low wages, for piecework as for day-labor-

ing, topped the list of workers' and artisans' grievances in the later fourteenth and fifteenth centuries.

With wages we touch a sphere which historians are only just beginning
to broach seriously. Yet it will be surprising if current or future research
advances conclusions that depart from the patterns that we have already
traced in the workings of power and privilege. The emerging profile—based
upon hard bits of information from Venice, Milan, Genoa, Florence, and
other parts of Tuscany—seems to be one of a gradual decline in real wages
throughout the Renaissance period. First there was the sharp rise and extension of the indirect taxes on foods and wares, so characteristic of the
fourteenth century. Then, the great textile centers of Tuscany and adjacent
regions suffered industrial depression: unemployment spread, work among
the employed was often sporadic, and wages were scaled down slightly in
the period from the 1360s to the 1380s.

During the fifteenth century, in the more thriving textile regions farther
north, we find much evidence of industrial practices of the sort which had
greatly agitated workers and artisans in earlier times. At Genoa, about midcentury, the wool industry's weavers complained bitterly because they were
usually paid in overvalued goods, rather than in cash. Yet they had a guild,
and this all but tells us that the guildless spinners and washers of wool, most
of whom lived in the adjacent countryside, had even graver wage difficulties. A parallel sector, the Genoese silk industry, apparently boomed in the
later fifteenth and early sixteenth centuries. The weavers in this luxury trade
were highly skilled craftsmen expected to draw superior wages. In fact, they
were paid in an inferior currency (*lire de paghe*), at a rate of fifteen shillings per pound rather than in accord with the true measure of their productivity, the twenty-shilling pound. In other words, a weaver who
produced four lengths of cloth was paid in a special workers' currency
which, in actual exchange values, was equivalent to his having produced
only three lengths. But here again spinners took sharper losses; they were
forced to hire their tools from the big silk merchants, and the rental
amounted to one-half of what they produced, unless they could pay in
cash.

At Venice, in the most strategic of all her industries, shipbuilding, conditions for wage earners were no better. In 1460 one of the highest-paid of all
such categories, the caulkers (they were forbidden to form an association),
complained of their unbearably low wages. They charged that the shipbuild-
ers, gathering in groups of ten or twelve, would agree among themselves
upon a given wage and pay no higher. Moreover, owing to weather conditions, shipwrights and caulkers rarely worked more than half a year, and
ordinarily the working season was shorter. In an exceptional response to the
complaint, the Venetian government ruled that the caulkers were to have a
minimum daily wage of thirty-two shillings of "small money" in the months
from March through August and twenty-two shillings of the same money

during the other months. At the higher rate, these superior craftsmen earned nearly three times as much as rope workers, who drew just over eleven shillings per day, and nearly four times the wage of the shipyard's unskilled laborers, who got only eight to ten shillings daily. If a shipyard laborer was employed throughout the year (some 250 days), which was seldom the case, he earned just enough to survive. There was no question of his trying to keep a family on such a wage, and in the sixteenth century, owing to the depreciated value of "small money," this wage was worth less. Not surprisingly, as from the 1380s, and moving back up now to the better-paid levels of craftsmanship, we hear of complaints against shipwrights and caulkers who deserted Venice, or the industry altogether.

But more dramatic and much more persistent at Siena, Lucca, Florence, Genoa, and elsewhere was the official outcry against the textile industry's artisans, especially weavers and dyers, who in many cases abandoned their cities and roamed widely in search of employment, higher wages, or less swagger in their bosses. Not only did they go off with trade secrets and special skills—so ran the complaint—but their desertion also threatened or further depressed the home city's economy. From time to time, accordingly, as at Genoa and Florence, governments enacted legislation aimed at luring craftsmen back to their native cities by granting ten- or fifteen-year moratoria on their debts and personal taxes. But these were palliatives. The root difficulties were in the social system itself, in the amplitude of rights accorded to power and privilege. St. Antoninus, archbishop of Florence (1446–1459), put his finger on the problem. Censuring employers in general and cloth merchants in particular, he denounced their payment of wages in goods and in clipped or debased coin, which decidedly lowered real earnings. He also accused employers of withholding wages, of late payment, of welching on oral agreements, and of refusing to pay the rates set by common consensus, though even these were insufficient to support families.

The big employers tended to control industrial organization. In the Milanese iron and metalworking industry, for example, the importers and buyers of the iron monopoly controlled the supply of metal. They bought up all the raw material and sold or farmed it out to individual workshops, where the metal was worked up into arms, wares, or whatever. Then repossessing the lot, or buying it back, they were now in position to sell the final product at home or abroad. The controls were tighter still in the textile industry, where the best-off and most skilled of craftsmen, the dyers and weavers of heavy brocades, never at any point owned the goods they produced. Their dependence upon the lots of work and material brought to them by the merchant drapers was absolute. At least in his business affairs Andrea Banchi, the Florentine silk merchant, seems to have been nothing if not hard, and we can easily see why. Of all industrial sectors, as the French historian Jacques Heers points out apropos of Genoa, silk production required the tightest organization and the largest initial outlays of capital.

As a Christian, the rich merchant had a variety of ways to satisfy the demands of his conscience, and all were institutional: he could give much or little to hospitals, convents, and churches; he could provide "a poor girl of good family" with a few ducats of dowry; or, in his civic ardor, he could donate monies for work on the cathedral and for the upkeep of the city gates. At Venice he could route his charity through the so-called *scuole grandi*. But in his role as businessman, employer, and member of the political ruling class, he was exceptionally demanding, which stood in nice contrast to his self-indulgence as a taxpayer. A hoard of surviving account books attest that he often noted every shilling spent and every dozen eggs due him from his rural tenants. His privileges and political authority provided the lineaments of his social identity. He could not yield in these matters save by changing himself, and on the whole he liked himself; he was self-satisfied. Bouts of religious quirkiness—as when a Venetian patrician gave himself over to extreme asceticism—were a rarity and never affected more than an insignificant minority.

The institutions of charity made amends for excessive callousness. As a result, there was very little secular sentiment about the plight of workers or unemployed craftsmen. Preachers gave a voice now and then to the grievances of the city poor, but this did not keep the archbishop of Florence, Antoninus, from comparing labor with other items used in the industrial production of goods, such as tools and horses. The Florentine humanist Matteo Palmieri, in his book *On Civil Life* (1438), argued in favor of a bare subsistence wage: if people from "the lowest orders of society earn just enough to keep going from day to day, then that suffices." Moreover, they should work for the state, and any who refused without good cause should either be forced to work or banished: "the city would thus cleanse itself of the harmful plebs."[8] In a letter on the nature of the "civil family" (1468), Antonio Ivani, a humanist who served in public posts at Genoa, Pistoia, and Volterra, held that people who hire themselves out for wages, such as servants and workers, "should be reverent, obedient and loyal to their masters." But he urged that they be fully fed or properly paid "because being from the lowest orders, to get enough food for their stomachs is almost their only concern."[9]

The Renaissance owes more than we suspect to labor. Current study shows that wages throughout the period remained static in some sectors and slightly declined in others, with the trend possibly on the side of decline, owing to a drop in the value of petty cash (wage money) relative to gold coin. Although the fourteenth century registered tremendous gains in revenue from indirect taxes on foods and goods, the fifteenth century must also have seen a few such gains because of the persistence of billowing budgets. Therefore hidden taxes, too, cut into the value of real wages. Certain categories of workers, notably in the textile industry, were paid a bare subsistence wage. Old people and women were among the chief victims, as in Tuscany, where many toiled for long hours at spinning, baking, and other crafts, in the struggle to stay alive.[10] But the hand of the poor was also present in the building craze, in the grand architectural monuments of the Renaissance. For this busy sphere of activity, geared directly to the needs of the upper classes, offered much work, above all to laborers of minimum skills. Remuneration for such labor frequently took the form of food for the working day or the bare equivalent in petty cash. The great private *palazzi*, villas, churches, family chapels, and public monuments were only the most visible signs of labor's investment. The "surplus" labor of rustics and city folk went not only into country villas and urban *palazzi*, but also into the profits of business and farming, into government salaries, into the indirect taxes that paid the interest on government bonds, and much else. Profits, in turn, were diverted partly into fresco cycles, carved pulpits, costly tapestries, leather-covered walls, and smart panel paintings, and into the hands of the poets and humanists who coursed their way through the princely courts. The images of ragged workers and poor folk in the frescoes of Masaccio, Cosimo Tura, and Filippino Lippi are not fictions: they depict the submerged part of the human investment that went into the making of Renaissance culture.

CHAPTER XI

HUMANISM: A PROGRAM FOR RULING CLASSES

THE PROGRAM

Humanism was the city-state's major intellectual experience. It was a refinement of values that derived largely from the urban ruling groups, but it also needed their confirmation to have any force as a program. Humanism spoke for and to the dominant social groups. It was the concerted study of classical Roman and Greek literature; it embraced the whole field of knowledge from poetry and geography to natural science, but its syllabus was heavily weighted in favor of "the humanities" and its philosophical focus was man in society. Its emphasis on civic consciousness was so strong at first that for decades (ca. 1400–1460) humanism had no sure definition apart from considerations of its place in a social context. Petrarch's arch and dogmatic "What is history but the study of Rome?" is fatuous unless we see that it comes from his eagerness to relate the achievements and miseries of Rome to the circumstances of his day.

Florence, Milan, and Venice put a remarkable number of humanists near the forefront of government; and the lesser cities, republican and signorial, regaled them with administrative, secretarial, advisory, academic, and tutorial posts. Although some humanists were humbly born, their ideals of education, humanity, and political order could be realized only in a society with privileged elites—a society rather like their own. There was no remarkable difference between the humanist image of the educated gentleman and such learned fifteenth-century oligarchs as Palla Strozzi and Francesco Barbaro. A swordsmith educated in the humanist vein was not thereby fashioned into a humanist swordsmith. With the right contacts, he was put on the track to becoming a prelate, an important municipal secretary, a governmental counselor, a courtier, a tutor to princes, or a university professor. In the worst of cases, he might be assumed as tutor to the sons of wealthy men, nobles, or oligarchs.

When Vergerio, Bruni, Guarino, Vegio, and other humanists made a plea for the capital value of the *studia humanitatis*—grammar, rhetoric, poetry, history, and ethics—they had a select readership in mind, as is clear from their dedications, the interlocutors in their dialogues, their references, allusions, and apostrophes. They addressed well-placed people: oligarchs, noblemen, rich bourgeois, princes, prelates, curial officials, administrators, professional men, and other literati. Like Petrarch's remark about Roman history, the humanist call for the ardent cultivation of rhetoric and the classics made no existential sense outside the context of cities, of municipal eminence and rewards, of importance vouchsafed to oratory, and of the vital experience that led citizens to what was relevant and useful in the classics.

Humanism envisaged a course of study and a certain kind of citizen. It was an educational ideal. But it was not designed to issue in pure contemplation or prayer, nor was it meant for the urban community at large. Instead, it looked to a practical life in society and it was meant for those destined to hold leading social positions. This had a decisive effect upon the content and outlook of humanism. One of the most influential humanist treatises of the fifteenth century, Pier Paolo Vergerio's *De ingenuis moribus* (ca. 1402), citing the authority of Aristotle, warned against letting literature "absorb all the interests of life. . . . For the man who surrenders himself entirely to the attractions of letters or speculative thought perhaps follows a self-regarding end and is useless as a citizen or prince."

In the presuppositions of humanist educators, Latin grammar was the fundamental discipline on which all learning and correct doctrine depended. Classical Greek received a good deal of emphasis, but it was nearly always taught through Latin. In his treatise on education (1457), Battista Guarino, the youngest son of the great humanist educator, declared: "Without a knowledge of Greek, Latin scholarship itself is, in any real sense, impossible." But Latin remained the grammatical framework for educated men.

There is no need to dwell on the link between grammatical study and ideology. The connection speaks for itself: as only very few of antiquity's literary works had been translated into the vernacular, the classics could be neither read nor used to underwrite fifteenth-century experience save by students with a strong command of grammar. In fact, in its highest form (philology), grammar was to become a leading weapon in the struggle against the educational establishment. The foremost humanist teachers composed their own Greek and Latin grammars, and these carried the day in all advanced pedagogic circles.

A complete humanistic education took the student up to about the age of seventeen. Yet, generally speaking, even in rich merchant households, as at Genoa, Florence, and Venice, boys entered the family business at thirteen or fourteen years of age, unless they were intended for a career in the Church, in which case their studies continued. In lower-middle-class and artisanal families, boys were usually set to learning a trade at the age of seven or eight. But among the rich and well placed, boys might be sent, at thirteen or fourteen, to a distant city, sometimes overseas, to traffic or to help keep accounts. In occasional pleas to such families, humanists sought to increase civility and to soften the ungainly attachment to profit. L. B. Alberti and Francesco Barbaro, for example, urged families not to force their sons into money-making trades of a "servile" or "demeaning" nature. Lay moralists such as Brunetto Latini and Francesco Barberini had been urging something like this ever since the thirteenth century, but their call had not been issued in the name of an elaborate educational ideal.

The major poets of Rome and Greece held an important place in the humanist syllabus. Homer, Virgil, Horace, Juvenal, and Seneca headed the list, followed by Ovid, later by Terence, and more rarely by the Greek tragedians. More than a source of mere pleasure, poetry for the humanists was a commentary on experience; it was a guide, a shaper of men. Most of the leaders of the humanist movement wrote poetry or produced verse translations. Francesco Filelfo composed large quantities of Greek verse. Poliziano was one of the two or three finest lyric poets of the fifteenth century. And Battista Guarino flatly declared that "the ability to write Latin verse is one of the essential marks of an educated person." Here was an aristocratic—not just a scholarly—ideal, the spirit of which was soon to be taken up by Castiglione and others, to be worked into a model for courtiers and gentlemen.

The humanists loved and valued Dante, despite the fact that his great work was in the vernacular; they loved the Latinity and virtues of the early church fathers—Ambrose, Lactantius, Jerome, Augustine; but they loved Cicero and Quintilian more, at all events in fits and starts. The tradition of Christian literature was not sufficient; it was not the sole repository of experience. As if cramped by the imagery of Christianity and in response to unassuaged demands in their everyday experience, the humanists reached out enthusiastically for the polish, subtlety, and worldliness of the pagan poets. This drew them into polemic with defenders of the established educational order—Cino Rinuccini, Giovanni Dominici, Giovanni da Prato, and others. Soon, too, they clashed with philosophy faculties. All the outstanding advocates of humanism, from Petrarch and Salutati to Valla and Vegio, had to conduct a defense of the pagan poets against critics who argued that the "serpent" of antiquity, present especially in the poets, undermined Christian faith. To refer to God as Jupiter or Saturn could not be good, and it was scandalous to rehearse students in the amorous license of certain of the elegiac and lyric poets. To this the humanists angrily replied that people had been moral before Christianity, that the Bible also had risky books and passages, that the best poetry was divinely inspired, and, in any case, that much pre-Christian poetry could be read for its hidden moral, symbolic, and religious meanings. A number of humanists—Salutati, Caldiera, Landino—squeezed a range of Christian equivalents or messages from the classical mythologies. The historian Charles Trinkaus has rightly made much of the theological poetics of the humanists. How could their movement, however novel its accents, fail to reveal the imprint of Christian values? There was no escape from the world, even in imagined structures. Yet in their reading of Homer, Virgil, and others, in digging for as many Christian meanings as they wished, the humanists could not avoid the surfaces in pagan poetry: the distillation of firsthand secular experience re-created by means of word, metaphor, sound, and meter. Fervent proponents all of the study of eloquence, the humanists believed that nothing moved the passions more effectively than the power of language. This being so, we shall never know—and no doubt they did not know—how far they were willing to use allegorical interpretation as a cover for their immediate responses to pagan poetry. Virgil's Dido could provide a dramatic lesson for Christian women, as Maffeo Vegio alleged, but she was Virgil's Dido first.

When we turn to the other areas of humanistic interest—to rhetoric, history, and ethics—we have little trouble finding the pertinent social moorings. Humanism emphasized the utility of these studies and in so doing said what their political and social uses were.

If the technical foundations of humanism were in grammar, the high aim was rhetoric, defined as eloquence, as the art of persuasion, or more simply as the art of the most effective speaking and writing. Historical writing could also belong to rhetoric, so far as it was meant to adhere to a certain form and style, according to the manner of ancient models. Moreover, insofar as "true eloquence" presupposed wisdom, ethics and indeed philosophy could also be ranged under rhetoric. In humanistic theory, as gleaned from Cicero and Quintilian, the perfect orator combined goodness and wisdom. The perfection of rhetoric was not divorceable from philosophy.

Whatever the needs of private men, the humanists perceived that public men need the art of rhetoric, the power of "bringing conviction to different minds" (Vergerio), in the administration of the state. Hence they urged its study on princes, noblemen, statesmen, and citizens. They also realized that the intimate atmosphere of oligarchical cities imposed the need for correct expression, even in private affairs, on people of high social station. "To be able to speak and write with elegance is no slight advantage in negotiation, whether in private or public concerns" (Vergerio). For the Florentine Matteo Palmieri, writing about 1436, the "best citizen" was the "perfect orator" as represented by Cicero and Quintilian. The humanist T. L. Frulovisi (ca. 1400–1480) observed in his *De Republica* that since "every form of eloquence is necessary to citizens responsible for government," eloquence is even more important for the urban prince, lord of the city. Again, Francesco Patrizi of Siena (1413–1494), in a section on "the excellent citizen" in his *De institutione reipublicae*, maintained: "No quality is of more vital concern to the state than public speaking, especially that aspect which relates to civil discussion. For the ends of the state depend upon the ability of men of affairs to persuade others into or out of a proposed course of action."

Bruni, Guarino, Vittorino, and A. S. Piccolomini (the future Pius II) all insisted upon the civil function of the "humanities" and made eloquence the summit of study, although the final end was purposive action in society. Piccolomini noted, in his *De liberorum educatione* (ca. 1456), that "Eloquence is a prime accomplishment in one given wholly to affairs," meaning by "affairs" politics and the task of ruling. Lorenzo Valla argued, in the preface to the third book of his *Elegantiarum latinae linguae* (1435–1444), that no Italian lawyer could master the science of law "without the *studia humanitatis*," and he was thinking especially of grammar and rhetoric. In the political context of fifteenth-century cities, whether under signories or oligarchies, the humanist plea for eloquence was not just a bookish ideal: it was a direct address to the ruling classes, urging them to broaden and modernize their outlook.

With history we broach an interest that showered the humanists with the opportunity to express fifteenth-century values under the guise of historical narrative. Their very choice of historical subject matter was telling: Rome above all and classical Greece. Here was the true focus of secular historical study. Then came the history of one's own city (e.g., Venice, Florence, Milan) and recent or contemporary history, as in humanist biographies or commentaries on their own times. All other histories—aside from certain historical parts of the Old and New Testaments—were omitted from the course of study. In his essay on education (ca. 1456), addressed to the young king of Bohemia and Hungary, Piccolomini presses the study of Roman history and warns, "Beware of wasting time on subjects such as the history of Bohemia or the history of Hungary, as these would be the work of ignorant chroniclers . . . a clobber of nonsense and lies, without attraction in form, in style, or in serious reflection."

The humanists looked to history for what it could tell them about their own experience. Theirs was a demand for relevance. They believed fervently in the utility of historical study, above all for students destined to be involved in political affairs. They believed that historians—notably Livy, Sallust, Caesar, and Plutarch—taught everything from virtue to eloquence, from wisdom to practical worldliness. They made a constant point of associating the lessons of history with practical politics and government. As a result, they seemed at times to urge the study of history more on rulers and on citizens than on students and scholars. Lionardo Bruni stated, in his *De studiis et literis* (ca. 1405), that "the careful study of the past enlarges our foresight in contemporary affairs and affords to citizens and to monarchs lessons of incitement or warning in the ordering of public policy. From history also we draw our store of examples of moral precepts." If the study of rhetoric led to polished expression, and ethics to the principles of morality, then history offered the specific examples of virtue and vice and provided the outlines of a political science. It is not at all surprising that historical study and the study of statecraft should have been essentially one and the same for Machiavelli, for whom, as for Petrarch, Rome was the light.

If history was to be relevant, a study to be spliced with the living parts of experience, then worldly Rome, or at any rate a history built around cities, had to hold the center of inquiry. This was "civilization"; the rest, in cultural terms, was Gothic barbarism. Nine hundred years of darkness, the "Dark" or "Middle" Ages, lay between Rome and humanism—centuries unlettered and plunged into ignorance. Then came the revival of cities, civil government, the arts and letters. This conception of history, first elaborated by the humanists, erected a bridge between antiquity and the Italian city-state in its "higher" stages. The bridge passed over the "Dark Ages" and linked the two sensibilities.

A self-image haunted the humanist vision of antiquity. The zealous search for guides in classical literature was a way back to fifteenth-century experience. Among the personalities and themes of the ancient world, the humanist preference was for the politics and moralities of urban life, for orators and public men, for eloquence and celebrity. In the life of Greek and Roman cities, they found their own cities; in orators and literati, they found themselves; in public men—rulers, statesmen, orators, professional soldiers—they found their friends, acquaintances, patrons, and again themselves. In eloquence, as we shall see, they found an ideal which could be turned into a recipe for cultivated men of the world, a recipe for ruling classes. And in celebrity—fame, glory, honors—the humanists singled out the highest earthly prize to which they themselves aspired, a prize conferred only in signorial and oligarchical cities, in the form of embassies, university chairs, high office, tax immunities, and literary commissions.

Far from being trivial, the self-images projected back into antiquity were the way to bring it forward; they served to revive classical learning. Looking back to Greece, the humanists saw themselves in the company of Demosthenes, Lysias, Alexander the Great, Aristotle, Alcibiades, Plato, Lycurgus, Pericles, and so on. This was not the company of modest folk. And looking to the history of Rome, they picked the company of senatorial families, eminent statesmen, emperors, generals, celebrated rhetoricians and poets. This also flattered the patrons of humanists. Petrarch, indeed, held imaginary conversations with Cicero. Humanist intellectuals called attention again and again to the fact that Aristotle was tutor to Alexander the Great, that Plato was teacher to the kings of Sicily, that Cicero was an illustrious public figure, and that the versatile Caesar wrote his *Commentaries* while on campaign. The humanists had no trouble relating these and many other like matters to their own lives and to the experience of their reading public. They took for granted their affiliation with power.

But this affiliation could be finer and more historically turned. Committed to oligarchical republicanism, the Florentine humanists praised the literary life and politics of republican Rome and took the historical origins of Florence back to the Roman republican period. However, Uberto Decembrio, Guarino Guarini, and other humanists who depended upon the patronage of princes saved their praise for the achievements and brilliance of the Roman principate. A famous polemic (1435) between Poggio Bracciolini and Guarino turns on an intriguing assessment, for and against, of Julius Caesar's contribution to the Roman environment for thought and letters, but at the heart of the controversy we see Poggio's arrogant siding with the Florentine republican polity and Guarino's grateful commitment to signorial rank, with its resources for more centralized cultural initiatives. Neither saw the veiling effect of his own values. In 1483 the great Lombard humanist Giorgio Merula was commissioned to write a history of the dukes of Milan. This immediately elicited a teasing letter from his friend the Venetian patrician Ermolao Barbaro, one of the most accomplished humanists of the fifteenth century. Barbaro contended that Merula would not be "free to proceed according to your own designs" and that he would find it much harder to render a complete and truthful picture "than it is in free cities." The Venetian did not choose to see that the humanist historians of republican cities—Bruni, Poggio, Bernardo Giustiniani—were also capable of producing historical panegyric that was as ideological, even if in a different manner, as anything issued from a princely court. The courtly intelligentsia had no monopoly on the veils of a *conscience mystifié*.

All humanists, whatever their stripe, made a candid alliance with power. They plumped for the ruling classes, empires, and luminaries of past *civil* times; they also wrote in unashamed praise of their own cities, rulers, and patrons. The marriage with power could also be more devious and subtle. Two illustrations must serve.

One of the outstanding Venetian humanists of the fifteenth century, Bernardo Giustiniani (1408–1489), aristocrat and statesman, held that letters and culture "always followed a great empire."[1] For only mammoth power, riches, and a history of triumphs offer the conditions for a great patronage, supply the requisite rewards and thereby stimulate the will to excellence and glory. Athens and Rome in their prime, and the Babylonian and Egyptian empires, provided Bernardo with the main examples. The opposite condition, powerlessness, led to barbarism and provincialism. In the name of culture and country, therefore, he gave himself to government service and to the furthering of Venetian expansionist policies: empire and civilization were, for him, different aspects of one and the same condition.

In his preface to the six books of his *Elegantiarum* (1435–1444), Lorenzo Valla begins with an invidious statement about empire: "When I consider, as I often do, the achievements of our forbears [the Romans] and those of other peoples and kings, it seems to me that our men excelled all others not only in dominion but also in the diffusion of their language." They excelled the Persians, Medes, Assyrians, Greeks, and many others, in military as in other virtues, but especially in carrying their tongue to distant lands. So doing, they served not only "the greatness and glory of their own city but also benefited the whole human race." In their linguistic imperialism, they "surpassed even themselves and, almost leaving behind their worldly empire, reached the company of the gods in heaven."

Here again, then, if more rhetorically, culture and empire are intertwined. "For the Latin language," Valla continues, "is what educated those [conquered] peoples and indeed all people in the liberal arts; it taught them the best laws; it secured the way to all knowledge; and its effects on them were such that they could no longer be called barbarians." The humanist goes on to distinguish the "divine" quality of language and culture from the merely "regal" quality of arms and government. And although "We have lost Rome, kingdom and authority . . . yet we still rule a large part of the world by this brilliant domination [the rule of Latin]. Ours is Italy, ours France, ours Spain, ours Germany, ours Hungary, Yugoslavia and many other lands: the Roman empire is wherever the language of Rome dominates. Now let the Greeks go and brag about the power of their tongues." Then suddenly turning to his own day and lamenting the barbarous use of Latin in the intellectual disciplines, Valla equates language and city, Latin and Rome, deplores its occupation by the barbarians, and, casting himself as the general Camillus, ends the preface with a clarion call to liberate the city (Latin). His union of power and culture is direct, playful, and poetic; it colors his entire viewpoint, for throughout the individual prefaces to the six books, his language is steeped in the diction and imagery of force, counterforce, and invidious comparisons.

The humanist attitude toward history was emphatically selective, elitist, self-congratulatory, and fixed to a criterion of worldly success. The humanists were drawn irresistibly to the ranks of winners, except when victory went to "barbarism." In addressing their pleas for the study of history to the members of oligarchies and to princes, they were saying, in effect, that the lessons of history could teach them, the holders of power, the way to improve their political *nous*. Appositely, in his *History of the Florentine People*, Bruni presents "a political history in which he asks how decisions are made . . . who makes them, how and to what extent they are effective. He is dealing . . . with the instruments and workings of power."[2]

In celebrating moral philosophy over science and metaphysics, the humanists put the problems and tasks of civil life before all other philosophic concerns. This emphasis was, however, more characteristic of the first half of the fifteenth century than of the second half, when the ideal of the contemplative life began to win more praise. If Plutarch's public worthies and Aristotle's *Ethics*, with its stress on the virtues of civil action, dominated humanistic moral values early in the century, later on "the divine Plato," with his larger tribute to pure contemplation, often got higher marks. In their most militant phase, when first taking their program to their host of upper-class readers and listeners, the humanists were driven to extol the life of action and social usefulness. By such means they satisfied their own needs and those of their audience. Later, as humanism gained acceptance, its moral accents could change somewhat, even in favor of a more bookish life of reflection.

But whatever the accents, the moral vision of the humanists remained aristocratic. In their view, the highest worldly good was in study and in outstanding political activity. The attainability of these ends belonged to the purview of the legally constituted class of citizens, to the humanists themselves, and to princes and their advisers. In short, the highest humanist good resided with the happy few, with those who had the political rank for grand action or the virtues and economic resources for leisurely study.

When and where humanism gave prominence to traditional Christian values, its concept of the good was of course more universal: here artisan and oligarch could find validation for their ways. But as an educational and intellectual undertaking, humanism could not escape its union with privilege because of its necessary insistence upon long years of study. What is more, the humanists did not generally regard their ideals of study as preparation for the lucrative professions, law and medicine. On the contrary, in their more arrogant moods they looked down upon these as "mere money-making pursuits." Humanism, instead, was a preparation for life: a life of study and public service. And when it was felt, in the later fifteenth century and afterward, that one of these could be sacrificed, public service was the more likely to give way in theory, although in practice most humanists born into the political class remained active in government and politics.

Let us see how the fifteenth century turned eloquence, the core of humanism, into a program for the ruling classes of the different cities, oligarchical or signorial.

Recent scholarship has insisted that eloquence was the guiding aim of humanism, above all with the first two generations of humanists. Beginning with Petrarch (d. 1374) and quickening with the humanist movement of the early fifteenth century, Italy saw an advancing array of men who were ready to restore rhetoric to something of its preeminence in the ancient world, where it was long the pivotal educational discipline and where oratory was a school for statesmanship. Petrarch and Coluccio Salutati (d. 1406) were key figures in the revival of classical rhetoric, and although they feared that it could be perverted if it was not anchored in true (Christian) wisdom, they seemed at times on the brink of according it parity with philosophy. But with Bruni and a later generation of humanists, rhetoric became a worthy match for philosophy. Indeed, for Ermolao Barbaro it was at its best only when united with philosophy, as observed in the life and works of Plato and Aristotle. Lorenzo Valla went so far as to rank eloquence above philosophy, so comprehensive and exigent was his conception of rhetoric.

Far from being a narrow technical discipline, the pursuit of eloquence was turned into a way of life. It was not a goal for specialists. Although taking in logic and philosophic study, rhetoric also went beyond these. It could render the technicalities of the philosophers in more ordinary speech. It drew precepts, pointers, and examples from poetry, history, and direct civil experience; and it made vital use of these in discourse that might range from intimate letters and conversation to public oratory and debate. It aimed to move, persuade, excite, or educate listeners and readers. Owing to its very nature, it was turned toward the practical and recreational needs of people in civil society. It therefore qualified as the instrument *par excellence* for the reshaping of men. So viewed, as C. Vasoli and E. Garin have argued, eloquence—and here it also subsumes philology—could be turned into a fine cutting edge. It could help to change the foundations of learning and to reorient culture. Valla's brilliant critique (1440) of the forged *Donation of Constantine* was not only the first really dramatic use of the new philology; it was also a vigorous rhetorical and polemical attack on the Church's worldly claims.

A startling conclusion follows. To promote the foregoing ideal of eloquence in the fifteenth-century setting was to seek to put a powerful device into the hands of princes and ruling elites. Legitimate political opposition was out of the question; it became conspiracy. Structurally, as the preceding chapters have shown, there was no viable outlet, in republics or in signories, for truly contrasting political voices. The major exception to this occurred at Milan in 1447, with the establishment of the Ambrosian republic, and then only because the upper classes temporarily defected, passing from loyalty to signorial government to a fleeting oligarchical republicanism. But they soon rejected the experiment. The "humanist" conspiracies of Stefano Porcari at Rome (1453) and Olgiati-Lampugnano at Milan (1476) ended miserably, having no social backing of any sort.

As conceived by the humanists, the ideal of eloquence could soar in importance and take a leading place in education and culture only with the help and encouragement of power; without such support, it could be no more than a bookish desire.

The ambitious scope of humanist eloquence, with its disciplined core and ideal worldly ends, depended upon an elaborate schooling of the spirit. Touching a theme that swiftly became a commonplace, Bruni said of humanistic studies that "they are called the *studia humanitatis* because they make the complete man." And again late in the century, in Ermolao Barbaro's "many letters and lectures to his pupils, one dominating conviction was hammered home time and again: *humanitas* is not a matter simply of externals, of ornament; it is a spiritual entity which produces in man the true man, the citizen, man in his totality."[3] But this was not every man: it was the citizen. Fifteenth-century historical reality imposed its conditions. The ideal of eloquence and *humanitas* could not touch more than the few because the required preparation presupposed the advantages of birth (i.e., the rights of citizenship), as well as the disposable time and income. The "scholarships" provided by the Church went largely to well-connected families and their protégés. When Battista Guarino, in his *De ordine docendi et studendi*, advocated the study of Juvenal and Terence because they give "not only a copious and elastic vocabulary but also provide us with a store of sound and dignified judgments," he was evidently not thinking of shopkeepers and little pawnbrokers, artisans or country people. Even semiliterate Venetian or Milanese noblemen were beyond the pale, except insofar as they represented what to avoid or had sons who might be schooled to eloquence and *humanitas*.

In the world as it was, the humanist pursuit of eloquence, shying away from specialization, turned into an ideal for Renaissance gentlemen, from which Castiglione's *The Courtier* was to draw so much. In addition to being prepared in classical letters and having the readiness to apply the lessons of the past to current problems, humanism's perfected product was meant to be a man of the world—versatile, accomplished, and socially at ease. This is why humanist educators—Vittorino, the two Guarinos, Vegio—accorded great emphasis to voice, gesture, intonation, and phrase. In aiming for the perfection of eloquence, they could not fail to concentrate also on social effects and social bearing. They stressed the habit of reading aloud, to help pupils develop self-confidence in public speaking. To round out the curriculum and thinking particularly of pupils who came from the knightly nobility, they also called for a routine of physical exercise, such as running, leaping, and hunting, with an eye to future martial requirements.

Matteo Palmieri, Guarino, Frulovisi, and other humanists made a plea for talented boys from poor families. They believed that rulers should encourage such boys to pursue a humanistic course of study. But nothing in this belief departed from the organizing values of the program for ruling classes. In the city-state environment, an obscurely born youth with a humanistic education was all the more likely to cling to the values of those whom he had been trained to serve. In this regard, suffice it to cite the examples of Bruni, Poggio, Guarino, Vittorino, or even Tommaso Parentuccelli, who rose to become the humanist pope Nicholas V.

THE ORIGINS OF HUMANISM

If we have learned anything from modern European sociology, it is that historical and social interests, not systems of logic, determine what shall count as knowledge.

The point may be tersely illustrated. If tomorrow the West should learn and believe that the Second Coming is to take place in our time, the interest in nuclear physics would falter and the support for science would crumble.

The system of mathematics that has enabled us to probe the universe might still retain its internal validity and its bearing upon the movement of sub-atomic particles, but soon it would no longer count as knowledge, as it fell away from our interests and concerns.

The Italian Renaissance brought a major shift in interests. Its identifying characteristic lay in a new consciousness, in new ways of interpreting experience. The shift was connected with advancing elements *in* experience, important elements that could no longer be adequately "processed" by the old forms of consciousness. Humanism, one of the innovative forms, won the attention of men not by going through the established bulwarks of higher learning first, the universities, but by moving around and outside them. It advanced by way of state chancelleries, as at Milan and Florence, and princely courts, as at Mantua and Ferrara. It entered the scene by means of propaganda, official history, and panegyric, and via the consciousness of those patricians—e.g., Palla di Nofri Strazzi (Florence), Leonardo Giustini-ani (Venice)—who craved a larger view of things and more consistency in experience. These men were few to begin with but their place in the for-tunes of humanism was critical. They sought a deeper understanding and a more timely justification of their worldly commitment to public life and its psychology.

One of the traditional and widely held views was well summed up by the Milanese "master of grammar" Bonvesin de la Riva (ca. 1250–ca. 1314), in his *Libro delle tre scritture*:

> Wealth, exalted place and worldly honors
> Are naught but a dream dreamed by sinners.

This view of the marriage between sin and the world persisted. Yet the call for a different "reading" of experience had been in the making since the thirteenth century, when literature on the office of the podestà and men such as Brunetto Latini, Rolandino Passageri, and Remigio already found virtue in citizen obligations to the worldly city. The members of the legal profession, jurists and notaries, also voiced positive attitudes toward public service. These attitudes, however, won no large audience; they were not teased out to become the basis of a comprehensive and manifest ideology. Myth-making, in short, had failed to occur.

The universities—Bologna, Padua, Pavia—might have been the starting points for the march of humanism. But this was not to be. Humanists began to hold university chairs in Greek, rhetoric, and moral philosophy around 1400 and after, when patricians and other important political people, as at Florence, Pavia, and Padua, worked directly for the appointments of Chrysoloras, Guarino, Vittorino, and Gasparino Barzizza. Later, from the 1420s and 1430s, there were more university posts for distinguished hu-manists and Greek scholars. By then, however, recognition and the early campaigns had been won. The fact was, paradoxically, that Italian universities in the thirteenth and fourteenth centuries had been excessively geared to practical ends: they produced jurists, physicians, teachers, and a few philosophers, usually clerics, who carried on the tasks of instruction and reflection. But abstract thought catered to the needs of the clergy, not to a laity caught up in an intense civic life. Legal study turned increasingly practical in the thirteenth and fourteenth centuries, when university lectures on Roman law made frequent reference to the current law codes of cities, as well as to contemporary cases and decisions.

There remain the arts faculties of the universities, the teachers of grammar and rhetoric who prepared students for the higher faculties or for the formularies of letters and contract law (*notaría*). Here, finally, the link with humanism was joined in a line of literary notaries. But even here the triggering force came from outside the universities; it came from the experience of notaries who were deeply involved in politics and public affairs.

The role of the university in the origins of humanism has been deemphasized in order to make way for a more difficult analysis.

A shock of events often brings about fundamental realignments in the history of ideas. But Italian humanism was not a response to a shock of events. The late fourteenth and early fifteenth centuries, which saw the full emergence of humanism, record nothing dramatic enough for that. A civic culture had been in the making for more than 200 years. To see humanism as a major current in the developing civic culture is to see it as a phase of consciousness, of upper-class consciousness. Some of the main lines of humanism were drawn into place at the end of the fourteenth century, as a spinoff from the clamorous wars of expansion and consolidation between Florence and Milan, oligarchy and signory. In this perspective, the finer details of biography are irrelevant and groups count for more than individuals. Petrarch, therefore, need not stand out in this analysis, save insofar as he had much appeal for the humanists who came after.

Humanism represented one phase of a civic culture which involved a rich variety of forms. Thus, between about 1180 and 1330 a forest of new parish churches had sprung up in the different cities and the life around these was explosively intense. The churches were a treasury of art forms, and artists won local or more universal acclaim. Communes left their mark in the castellated walls and braggart towers of their main government buildings. The display of vital energy went into vernacular poetry, too, and into storytelling. Lacking a font of native vernacular traditions, urban verse was moved to borrow forms and attitudes from the Sicilian and Provençal poets, as well as from a school of ribald Latin versifiers, but the results were characteristically urban and Italian—as in the finely wrought and yet moving preciosities of the *stilnovo*, or in the burly and biting diction and perceptions of the comic realists. Finally, at the edges of formal cultural activity, in local codes of law, in chronicles, in short administrative treatises, in prose formularies, and in the occasional sermon, apostrophe, early memoir, or fleeting philosophical passage, we come upon strongly positive statements concerning the civil community, the state, or the duties of citizens. And when this civic feeling, infused with an enhanced worldliness, became forceful enough to find a self-image in the passion and swagger of classical rhetoric, then humanism came forth full-fledged.

The critical figures in the origins of humanism were lawyers and notaries, the most literate members of lay society and among its most active in public affairs. The training of notaries varied greatly: from that for the type of man who learned all his Latin and the different forms of public instruments as a notary's apprentice to the training of those who attended a university for two or three years. The latter heard lectures in Latin on rhetoric, dialectics, and the elements of law. The courses in rhetoric emphasized correct writing, particularly in epistolary composition, but also touched the art of speechmaking. With training of this sort, the notary with literary inclinations might go on to read more Cicero, some Virgil, and even some Seneca, but more especially certain of the late Latin writers.

In the thirteenth and fourteenth centuries, the bulk of the written business of government was in the hands of chancellery notaries. Most private business transactions of any real importance came under notarial seals. And down to the early fifteenth century, the middling levels of administration and politics usually included a scatter of notaries. The short treatises on communal administration, produced in the thirteenth century, issued from this circle. Brunetto Latini was a notary. Nearly the whole school of Paduan pre-humanists hailed from the administrative-legal profession, and the two leading figures, Lovato Lovati (ca. 1237–1309) and Albertino Mussato (1261–1329) were notaries as well as politicians.

The rise of pre-humanism had its chief vehicle in those notaries whose livelihood depended largely on communal administration. But they were in no position, standing as an independent group, to remake the foundations of education and learning. They were involved in government more than were other occupational groups; their education provided some preparation for dealing with ideas; and since they performed the tasks of a secular intelligentsia, they were the obvious candidates for bringing about a major reorientation of thought. But this vanguard—for a vanguard of men is what we are talking about—had no historical force until it was able to call upon the larger force of the groups behind; and this backup support was too feeble or fragmentary during the thirteenth and fourteenth centuries. So long as the administrative literati, in the give and take of daily discourse, were not driven and stimulated by the citizens around them, driven toward a fresh view of the virtues of political activity and worldly pursuits, so long would that vanguard of men fail to find enough social utility in any garnerings from the literature of antiquity; so long, too, would they have trouble drawing education, politics, eloquence, and classical antiquity into a coherent intellectual program. It would be very odd indeed to suggest that the pre-humanist (Latini, Lovati, Mussato, Ferreto of Vicenza, or Convenevole da Prato) was unable to enjoy Virgil and Cicero in the quiet of his study, when he could enjoy and appreciate them only thus. But he could not convert his enjoyment into a vision for living men and argue that the classics should be made the basis of all education and learning, unless he had a lively sense of that which counted for his contemporaries and unless he could link the bookish values in his consciousness with something urgent in theirs.

There could be no humanism without literary intellectuals, but neither could literati edge their way toward humanism, toward a new cultural program, and then "impose" it on their times, unless they did so with the help of a favorable moral climate, a responsive public, and a generation of students. The less the reciprocity between the pre-humanists and their upper-class world, the more fragmented their emerging literary-civic ideals and the more difficult the advent of the new educational program. If humanism was a phase of consciousness, of upper-class consciousness, then the suggestion here is that by 1400 the urban governing classes had reached a stage in their historical development where a particular kind of consciousness was the most likely to provide upper-class citizens with a sense of unity and direction in their lives. And this was a consciousness oriented more frankly toward worldly ends. Sin would have to be de-emphasized and morality redefined. Otherwise citizens risked having to live lives of extraordinary tension.[4] The pre-humanists and humanists moved sooner and more fully toward a psychological consciousness that was more in keeping with worldly goals. But humanism could have no social reality, it could not surface historically, until the demands of worldliness were taken in, absorbed, and became the psychological consciousness not only of literati but also of the social groups at the top.

Upper-class society was slow in responding to the pre-humanists because of deeply ingrained resistances in everyday life. The medieval emphasis on otherworldly ideals was pertinacious, and contrary views were easily enough discounted or made to ride a place along the borders of heresy. Learning itself came under the seal of the Church: in the university cities, doctoral degrees required the confirmation of the local bishop or archdeacon. At the level of preparing boys for the pursuit of trade, primary education encouraged the traditional mystic values, while also teaching the basic tools of commerce—arithmetic and elementary Latin. Right through the fifteenth century, humanists had to defend their program of study against the charge of its spreading pagan ideals and undermining Christianity.

Two other points remain to be made, concerning the interplay between ideas and social structures.

The great contests over the distribution of power within the city-state were largely resolved in the course of the fourteenth century. In the wake of these resolutions, political and social life became more settled and stable. Ruling classes became more secure, their membership rather more fixed and more distinctly profiled; and the social or group identities of men at the top were less and less subject to challenge. Now such men were ready to look for flattering self-images, and they were ready to deck out their preeminence with myths and with sustained argument. Possible consciousness—the demands of worldliness—was more easily converted into psychological consciousness.

Dozens of celebrated humanists—Petrarch, Salutati, Bruni, the Decembrios, Loschi, Poggio, Guarino, Vittorino, Valla, Filelfo, Poliziano, and others—were "outsiders" in the sense that they won patronage or major public posts in cities to which they were not native. They sprang from families of a middling sort, often professional, rather than from well-established upper-class families. Some recent scholarship has elected to call them "professional rhetoricians" because they depended upon income from chancellery offices, professorships, patronage, and even (e.g., Petrarch, Poliziano) ecclesiastical benefices. With the possible exception of Petrarch's, their pens were out for hire, scandalously so in Francesco Filelfo's case. Such economic dependency did not, however, divorce the "rhetoricians" from the values of their patrons, protectors, and employers. Whatever their politics, whether turned favorably toward oligarchy or toward princes, the professionals were in profound agreement about the vital importance of the humanist program. This cut across political lines. Generally speaking, they had difficult personalities. They were avidly ambitious, socially mobile, proud, touchy, and combative. And they clung to the ideal of eloquence not only from inclination but also because it was their major endowment, the skill that won celebrity and took them up in the world. As Petrarch himself confessed in his most Christian moods, as in his *De vita solitaria*, eloquence was a thing of cities: an exercise best for throngs, governments, and worldly ends.

The professionals saw first and saw deepest into the grounds of praise for the earthly city: praise for politics, for men in civil society, for secular history, riches, worldly accomplishments, and the pursuit of glory. In cleaving to eloquence as a function of moving up from middling social positions, they did much to elaborate a view of the world which flattered and validated the life of the groups at the forefront of society and politics. This view was much more in keeping with the acquired or wished-for status of the professionals than with the social positions from which they had started. Sooner, therefore, and more faithfully than men to the manner born, the professionals—new men, men on the make—were able to articulate the values of the elites which they had entered, or to which they aspired, or in whose service their pens were arrayed.

Arguably the social mobility of the professionals endowed their vision with a larger scope; but fundamental social trends—such as the century's deepening stress on birth, class, and privilege—also had the effect on them, as parvenus, of intensifying their touchiness, snobbery, and esteem for the intellectual virtues. Poggio, for one, was greatly pleased to marry into the old Florentine nobility. The "common opinion" was not for them. They despised "the crowd" and the lower orders and they affected disdain for all "mercenary" trades, from petty shopkeeping to medicine and even the practice of law. In contrast, humanists born to rich or distinguished old families could afford to be more relaxed. Such at Venice were Francesco and Ermolao Barbaro, Leonardo and Bernardo Giustiniani, Gerolamo Donà, Bernardo Bembo, and many another; and such at Florence were Roberto de' Rossi, Palla Strozzi, Giannozzo Manetti, Donato Acciaiuoli, Alamanno Rinuccini, and the proud oligarch Bernardo Rucellai. These men and the renowned professionals most approximated the age's image of the humanist gentleman. The ideal of eloquence, with its emphasis on social presence and public life, could not be easily squared with the modest status of the tutor or schoolteacher. As Vegio observed in his *De educatione liberorum* (ca. 1460), many rich families neglected their children's tutors: "They will not greet their boy's tutor, nor even acknowledge his existence. They pay him as little as they can and that, too, with the air of someone who is losing an eye or a tooth."

THE PROBLEM OF OBJECTIVITY

The danger of treating ideas in a social void is that we blind ourselves to the processes that veil the presence of social interests or self-images in ideas. But the danger of treating all ideas as mere ghosts of the social system is that the assumption which underlies such a treatment may invalidate the treatment itself. If ideas are no more than the ghosts of social structures, then this analysis is *ipso facto* a fantasy. A corrective is called for—namely, to list the "objective" humanist contributions that broke out of the locks of time and place. The point will be to see how social values, fashionable ideas, and critical methods sort themselves out in humanism.

The humanist movement favored certain topics and ideas that fail to qualify for any list of objective contributions because they were directly related to current issues and were heavily laden with the transitory values of the age. When those issues or pressures died away, so also did the applicability and importance of the ideas. The wisdom of Christianity versus the paganism of the ancients has not made for a serious subject of discussion since the seventeenth century. The morality of the classics, so much defended by the humanists, lost all meaning as a question. The demands of public life on the class of citizens gave rise to a controversy over the respective merits of the active and contemplative lives. This controversy also passed out of fashion, though it persisted at Venice to 1600 and beyond. The historical debate on the significance of Julius Caesar was a roundabout debate on the comparative merits of monarchy versus republicanism. So far as this preoccupation passed over into the seventeenth century, as in Venetian political theory, it stemmed directly from political realities and was subject to the duress of contrasting interests and ideologies. A medley of other fashionable topics in the compass of humanism centered on the liberality or parsimony of princes, on the moral worth of riches, and on the question of how to define true "nobility." These topics reflected timely social interests and touched the problem of relations between humanists and ruling groups.

In grappling with the literature of antiquity, the humanists hit on strategies and developed insights that entered into the basic legacy of scholarship both in the literary and social sciences. The political scientist knows, for example, that when he studies the writings of Marx, Rousseau, Hobbes, or Machiavelli, much of the job of understanding requires that he strive to see the texts in the contexts of their time. This principle may seem obvious but it was painfully won and is easily violated; and it was introduced into the stream of Western thought by the humanists. In their zeal to master classical Latin, they came to see and to study the departures from it, the growing accumulation of "barbarisms" across the centuries. So doing, they recognized the historicity of language, as Dante already had apropos of the vernacular, and they began to develop a view of its different stages. This could not, however, be restricted to language; the view involved a conception of civilization and went with a sense, politically and linguistically, of the different periods of Roman history.

Petrarch, Boccaccio, Salutati, and others were acutely aware of the fact that much was missing and much had been deformed in the literary monuments that came down from the ancient world. In their enthusiasm, they sought ever more authentic texts, especially of works dating from the age of Cicero and Augustus. All the humanists were driven by this interest: to get at pristine texts by comparing manuscripts and by learning to peel away the accretions of copyists and translators. Florence, from about 1400, and Milan and Pavia, in the 1420s and 1430s, were the scenes of heated discussion about the meaning of Latin words, their historical character, and changes in grammar and syntax across time. Lorenzo Valla, the outstanding humanist of his generation, benefited from his close contact with these circles. His exposé (1440) of an infamous forgery, the supposed *Donation of Constantine*, rested mainly upon his brilliant philological performance. His *Notes on the New Testament* (1449) apply the emerging philological method to Holy Scripture and reveal his command of Greek. But his phenomenal grasp of the Latin language and literature is evident above all in his *Elegances of the Latin Language*, which distinguishes different historical periods and goes beyond words, grammatical structures, and literature to become history and historical criticism. The new methods of textual and historical criticism were again brilliantly demonstrated, late in the century, by Angelo Poliziano and Ermolao Barbaro, whose textual work combined philology with archaeology, geography, epigraphy, numismatics, and a *on the Dignity of Man* (ca. 1486), when the voluntaristic strain was exceptionally strong. The resulting portrait of man is entirely in keeping with the manner, outlook, and accomplishments of the urban ruling families. Passages in the pertinent works, especially when touching questions of wealth and government, provide the diction and tropes that tie the idealizations to the elite groups. (2) If we study the language of the works in question— Manetti, Pico, Ficino—at the points where they discuss man's achievements, we are struck by the incidence of the verbs of domination and voluntaristic acquisitiveness. The linguistic patterns suggest the force of ruler over subject, of possessor over thing possessed. (3) The theme became an intellectual fashion; it peaked and passed away in two or three generations; so if we seek an explanation, we are driven to concentrate on the times and their stresses, rather than on the philosophical tradition. The middle and later decades of the fifteenth century are the very period when the Italian urban elites enjoy an unchallenged, secure, and stable hegemony for the first time in their history. But the French invasions (1494 and after) will bring an end to this and the heroic belief in man's dignity will evaporate. (4) Finally, in discussions of the *topos*, man's dignity is often made to pivot round his alleged freedom of choice, his ability to make and reshape himself. This also is revealing and puts us on our guard. For in the fifteenth-century world, such optimism, with its sharp worldly emphases, was not the product of monasteries or feudal castles; it issued from cities haunted by the effects of power, class, wealth, and caste. Pico, Ficino, and even the republican Manetti were halfway to being courtiers. Rich oligarchs at Florence and Venice, or men in the ruling circles at Milan and Ferrara, could well make an idol of their freedom, but theirs was far from being the general condition of humanity in Italy.

However general the heroic view of man's dignity, however much it purported to depend upon a notion of human potentiality, none came closer to realization of the ideal than the men with the resources for learning, culture, patronage, and the *trained* capacity for enjoyment of the world's goods. This is so obvious that it seems trivial, yet in surveying the age, historians constantly suppose, like the humanists themselves, that the heroic vision spoke for all men. Not at all. It spoke for an elite, and to ignore this is both to get the Renaissance wrong and to show that we do not see the forces and social interests that lie behind our own values.

CHAPTER XII

THE PRINCELY COURTS

PERIMETERS

The importance of the princely courts for this history is in the fact that they were centers for the union between power and privileged culture. Here, at the level of society's ruling groups, consciousness was most driven to create or seek images of itself in the world around—and had the best means to do so. In their patronage of letters and the arts, the courts made a marriage, occasionally a brilliant one, of power and imagination. After 1440, for a hundred years and more, the vigor and self-indulgence of the courts were such as to give a distinct direction to much of the peninsula's elite culture. But in other ways the course of change was infelicitous. For the political leadership of the courts, as shown in Chapter XIV, was to be catastrophic—leadership lost control—and that catastrophe had its sublimated expression in culture. Giulio Romano's braggart and fanciful Palazzo del Te (1527–1534), built for the Gonzaga lord of Mantua, is a just celebration of the brassy successes of a dynasty which survived every emergency only by constantly putting itself at the service of the most powerful: the papacy, France, Spain, and the empire. The Gonzaga recognized no principle save that of power and political success. The same may be said of the Este lords of Ferrara. Appropriately, in its Italian phase, Mannerism was in part a plea for refinement against the most cynical social values; but in much greater part, it was a quest for overidealized and strange forms in a world in which the order of perceived reality had slipped from the control of society's "natural" leaders. Italy was overrun by foreigners.

The prince—pope, duke, marquis, cardinal, tyrant, or papal vicar—was a powerful magnet: he attracted and repelled. He attracted throngs of people in search of jobs, favors, patronage, honors, and prestige. Others, instead, he repelled in the sense that his powers generated fears and enemies. His authority could be destructive, and so people drew away, fled, seeking cover and protection; for within his domain—and at times beyond—he could crush at will. By this definition, there was something of the prince about the Magnificent Lorenzo de' Medici (d. 1492), and in Florence the space around him, where he doled out favor and injury, was a magnetic field, a princely court. He had enough authority and influence to dispose of public honors and offices, and he also wielded influence abroad. Letters rained in on him from neighboring lords and states, requesting judicial posts, military commissions, and the like, for their protégés. By contrast, Agostino Chigi of Siena (d. 1520) was not a prince except in a metaphorical sense. He was a rich papal banker resident in Rome, a patron to artists and literary men, but also a private citizen who disposed of no public authority, except perhaps as a tax farmer. And if Pope Leo X chose to accept any of Chigi's recommendations regarding a governmental appointment, this was Leo's doing; it did not follow from any title belonging to Chigi. The essential difference, then, lay in the contrast between public and private. Chigi was a rich favorite. Lorenzo, as Florentines used to say, "had a bit of the state." He was a veiled prince in a republican oligarchy, which made his position ambiguous and difficult, especially as political Florence jealously guarded its republican trappings. The difficulty was put to the test by Lorenzo's son, Piero, forced to flee from the city in 1494, after he demonstrated, in some grave political blunders, that he had lost the bourgeois touch—the readiness to play at modesty—of the early Medici.

Down to 1500 the major princely courts, rather in the following order, were the courts of Milan, papal Rome, Naples, Ferrara, Savoy, and Mantua. Papal Rome had resonant international standing as the capital of Western Christendom, but in Italian power politics, before about 1500, it had less clout than Milan and less than half of Milan's fiscal income. The peninsula's northwest corner had three principalities, the first of which outranked Ferrara and Mantua in revenues but not in cultural élan: the duchy of Savoy (100,000 ducats per year) and the little marquisates of Saluzzo and Monferrato, each with its own court. These were often overrun militarily during the age of the Italian Wars (1494–1559).

The fundamental changes in power as in high culture came after 1500, when papal Rome, both in ambition and resources, became the leading Italian court. Naples and Milan fell under foreign rule, first French and then Spanish; they were edged out of the picture as native Italian courts. And although the imperial governor of Milan, Ferrante Gonzaga (d. 1557), was an Italian nobleman, his entourage was a mixed, international company. After 1500, accordingly, the main line of patronage and Italian upper-class culture passed through the papal court, Ferrara, Mantua, Urbino, and Florence under the Medici dukes. Of republics, Florence's brief luminosity aside, only the oligarchies, Venice and Genoa, remained great centers for the joining of power and imagination by means of selective patronage.

But the lines between courts and oligarchies were not always sharp. One of the foremost writers of the day, the Venetian patrician Pietro Bembo (1470–1547), was more at home in courts than in Venice, and late in life, when he was made a cardinal, he entered easily into that princely mold. Caterina Cornaro, queen of Cyprus, held court at Asolo and Murano under the sway of the Venetian republic. At Genoa the rank of families like the Doria and Fregoso was exalted enough to surround their leading branches, as in Florence the Medici, with a courtly aura. Such families had ties of blood with princely dynasties. The Fregoso were related to the Montefeltro lords of Urbino, and two of them figure prominently in Castiglione's *The Courtier*, Europe's first real catechism for "gentlemen." They were sent to Urbino to be trained in the ways of courts.

Italy was a honeycomb of princely courts. The Papal State alone had a number of lesser courts, chief among them the court of Urbino, rendered famous by Castiglione's handbook. The duchy of Ferrara was also, legally speaking, in papal territory, but the Este lords of the city enjoyed such dynastic eminence and so complete an autonomy that they ranked as independent princes. Rather more under Roman dominance were the courts of papal vicars: the Malatesta of Rimini, the Manfredi of Faenza, the Sforza of Pesaro, the Varano of Camerino, the Ordelaffi of Forlì, and the Bentivoglio of Bologna. "Court" may not be too definite a term for the space and personnel around the Baglioni of Perugia, also in the heart of papal territory. At Rome the powerful Colonna and Orsini clans had their courts, not only in the space around their cardinals—and there was one in almost every generation—but also as a function of their vast feudal estates, where they administered justice, collected taxes, enacted local laws, and raised small armies. Farther south, in the kingdom of Naples, a similar position was held by some fifteen or twenty great families in their feudal baronies. In the north, the counts of Carpi and Correggio had little states of their own, while the duchy of Milan had feudal magnates, like the Trivulzio and Borromeo, powerful enough to raise armies and rebel against the ruling Sforza.

Cardinals held the rank of prince: this was the custom of the age. In all public ceremonials, they ranked with dukes and were preceded only by the pope and by kings. They were not allowed to appear in public save in state, accompanied by a train of servitors. Most of them had one or more episcopal courts of law under their jurisdiction, and all the richest ones held feudal estates. From about 1460, down to the end of the Renaissance and beyond, a strain of cardinals was recruited from princely houses: Gonzaga, Este, Sforza, Medici, Colonna, Farnese, Pallavicini, Trivulzio. They were great lords and lived to the style. Their entourage of "familiars" might number up to 300 servitors, ranging from armed gentlemen and companions to secretaries, cooks, and stable boys. At the beginning of the sixteenth century, cardinals Ippolito d'Este, Ascanio Sforza, Giovanni de' Medici, and Sigismondo Gonzaga also retained musicians, buffoons, poets, painters, and dwarfs. To see these princes entering or leaving a city was to see a grand cavalcade of liveried gentlemen and servants. Lovers too of the most prized of all courtly pastimes, they organized hunting parties of hundreds of horsemen and they returned from their sport to the sound of trumpets and fifes, as Roman crowds ran out to gape at them. Theirs was the world of courts, intrigue, and high politics, of state marriages and royal processions. Like any prince, they distributed both hurt and preferment.

At its strictest, a court was the space and personnel around a prince, as he made laws, received ambassadors, dispatched letters, gave commands, decided cases, made appointments, took his meals, entertained, and proceeded through the streets. At its most elastic, a court was—in an age of princes— the space and people around any dignitary who wielded some public authority in his own right, a feudal lord or even, in certain instances, a leading oligarch. As satiric poets noted, Italy teemed with *signorotti*— princelings. The doge of Venice was a prince, and recognized as such by Venetians. But of course he was hemmed in by the power of the senate, the Council of Ten, and his advisers.

Toward 1500 the princely court became a main reference point in the organization of upper-class consciousness. Noblemen and aspiring bourgeois could find their different identities by means of it. A European ideal of conduct rose from it, from the social and mental world of "the courtier," and a set of mystifications as well. Power and wealth collected increasingly around the courts and remaining oligarchies. Princes were thought to sit at the summit of the wheel of fortune. They held the world's prizes. Literature, art, and ideas were deeply branded by the courts. As political thinkers, Machiavelli and Guicciardini were certainly so branded. The love lyric itself carried the mark, as we shall see in Chapter XV.

THE COURTLY ESTABLISHMENT

The key is power: the magnetic force radiating out from the prince, organizing people and space into relations of service and overlordship. Public authority, in part or in whole, reposed in the prince—duke of Ferrara, marquis of Mantua, or duke of Urbino. He was also the city's richest citizen, drawing income from his great landed domains and from a wealth of taxes, some of which were assigned to him personally. Drawing on a variety of indirect taxes, the Bentivoglio lords of Bologna built up a magnificent income after about 1470, until Pope Julius II ran them out of the city in 1506.

The most brutal and obvious manifestation of the prince's power was his residence in the city: a fortress designed to withstand riot, revolution, or war. Whether he lived in it or nearby, as did the Este dukes, there it was with its stately rooms and company of mercenaries, ready to receive the court at any time. At Milan the residence of the Sforza was the castle in the middle of the city, a walled-in fortress with moats, sixty-two drawbridges, and, in 1499, some 1,800 "machines of war." Here were lodged from 800 to 1,200 mercenaries, and many more in times of war.

Arms and politics were fused together for princes like shoulders and head. Throughout the Renaissance period all the Sforza, Este, and Gonzaga lords—and most of their brothers legitimate and bastard—were trained in swordsmanship and mounted combat. And if the Moro, Ludovico Sforza, showed no inclination this way, he was rejecting a preparation received. A serious effort was also made to fire the children at court with the learning of humanism; but horses, hunts, arms, and luxurious display soon overwhelmed books. In the late fifteenth and early sixteenth centuries, the following combined the dignity of prince with the stipends of *condottieri*—they captained large papal, Venetian, or other armies: Ercole and Alfonso d'Este, dukes of Ferrara; Guidobaldo da Montefeltro and Francesco Maria della Rovere, dukes of Urbino; and Francesco and Federico Gonzaga, marquises of Mantua. They and their like were sent away from home to train or to be perfected in arms: to the Neapolitan court, to Milan, to a free-lance *condottiere*, and even to Germany, France, and Spain. Leonello d'Este (d. 1450) spent several years with the mercenary Braccio da Montone; and his half-brother, Borso (d. 1471), was trained at the court of Naples. Ferrante Gonzaga, brother to Federico, marquis of Mantua, served the Emperor Charles V in Spain in 1524–1527 and in 1530 was general of the imperial army that laid siege to Florence. Again, in January 1524, the author of the best-known handbook for courtiers, Castiglione, was already thinking of sword-and-buckler lessons for his eldest son, Camillo, who was not yet seven.[1] He was looking to the boy's future service in courts.

Theoretically, all Italian princes were feudal lords who owed military service: the dukes of Milan and marquises of Mantua and Monferrato to the emperor; the dukes of Ferrara and Urbino and the Aragonese kings of Naples to the pope. In cultivating military skills, they were looking to a tradition, to their states, and to their own safety. Therefore, training in arms was even more imperative for petty princes: the Malatesta of Rimini, the Manfredi of Faenza, the Baglioni in the towns around Perugia. For as the expenditures of these lords constantly exceeded their ordinary revenues, they were forced to seek outside military commissions (*condotte*): to put their men and arms out for hire to Florence, Venice, Milan, the papacy, or to one of the miniature republics, Lucca or Siena. Furthermore, there were demands on princes from their own captains, in addition to the pressure to keep soldiers loyal, hence to keep them in arms and money. The smaller a prince's body of troops, the less his prestige. And here we touch a question that tormented all the courts—the plangent need for money.

Fiscal income derived largely from a rich and complicated assortment of indirect taxes: gabelles on goods of all sorts, especially food staples, duties on exports and imports, and taxes on mills, salt, and contracts. In the princely states, the yield from direct taxes on property could rarely be satisfactory because of the tax immunities enjoyed by many noblemen and favorites. The first Sforza duke of Milan, Francesco (d. 1466), managed to build up the duchy's shattered finances by his military brilliance and *condotte*. But a grandiose diplomacy, costly wars, and a burst of luxurious display drove his sons and grandsons into debt and still more unjust taxes. A kindred fate overtook the lords of Mantua, Ferrara, Urbino, and Romagnol, and other princelings; with the result that they were driven to scurry around for military commissions, to seek better stipends, and to keep up their military skills. The life of such a prince could be "consumed in the details of contracts of service, differences over pay, changes of allegiance, and war."[2] And if he gambled, as princes did, the cry was for more money. The Este and Gonzaga survived by means of a ruthless *Realpolitik*, but other princes went down: the Malatesta of Rimini, the Sforza of Pesaro, the Riario of Imola, the Bentivoglio of Bologna, the Della Rovere of Urbino, and of course the lords of Milan and Naples. And all, as they fell, were in grave financial difficulties.

In the early sixteenth century the jewels of the Marchesana of Mantua, Isabella, were continually in hock to Venetian moneylenders. Once or twice the money was needed to buy a cardinalship. The jewels of the Este, Ferrara's ruling house, were repeatedly pledged. In 1495, Ludovico Sforza turned to Venice for a loan of 50,000 ducats and offered jewels in pledge for three times the value. Princes also borrowed money by farming out taxes or by simply promising one of the gabelles for a given period. They put their jewels out in pawn only as a last resort, though they were often at last resorts. Still another way to borrow was to buy items on credit, as from small-fry merchants and craftsmen, and then to take many months to pay, sometimes even years. Pleading letters from artisans and artists are testimony to this princely practice of the Gonzaga and Este. There remained at least one other major economic resource: the varieties of obligatory labor (corvées) due mainly from certain classes of rustics and available to all *signori*. This was labor called upon for the maintenance of roads and ditches, fortifications, irrigation, or even to help put up new *palazzi* and country villas, like the magnificent Sforza retreat at Vigevano, where Ludovico combined hunting lodge, villa, experimental farm, zoo, and center for animal husbandry. The least studied of all surplus values due to Renaissance princes and feudal barons, obligatory labor was doubtless the major investment in the great Este villas outside Ferrara. In 1471, Borso d'Este ordered the building of an artificial mountain by means of such labor.

Auditors and treasury officials kept separate accounts of the income due personally to the prince, such as that rendered by his lands and *condotte*, and that which was due the state. Yet in practice, popes, cardinals, dukes, and marquises treated all unencumbered income as their own: i.e., all monies not already assigned to specific matters, like the payment of troops and official salaries, or not already committed to tax farmers, moneylenders, court favorites, or benefactions. The prince's power over the state's purse was in some sense unlimited, but only a peculiar blindness would hold back the pay of soldiers in order to reward a mistress or buy a famous jewel. As Ludovico Sforza said in his political testament to his sons, "the solidity and preservation of states consists in two things, soldiers and the respect for fortresses."[3]

Of the major courts, Milan and Urbino were the two extremes between rich and poor in ordinary revenue, until the papal court overtook and surpassed Milan about 1500. Naples, Savoy, Ferrara, and Mantua figured somewhere between. Romagnol and other courts had more modest establishments. Let us look at a range of expenditures.

Ludovico Sforza's political testament (1500) is a memoir on critical questions of security, administration, and succession to the dukedom. In it he prescribed a salary of 500 ducats per year for the highest officers of state, the secret councilors. Money was tight and these dignitaries had other perquisites, including occasional gifts from the prince, but Ludovico was also preoccupied about the loyalty of leading officials and knew that he had to set a yearly stipend large enough to keep them in the style of one of Europe's most extravagant courts. In 1484 the cardinal-prince, Ludovico's brother, Ascanio, had a basic yearly income of 13,500 ducats from assigned ducal revenues, and this was apart from his escalating ecclesiastical income. When Francesco Gonzaga, marquis of Mantua, died in 1519, his daughter and son-in-law, lords of Urbino, were in exile, having been driven from their court by Pope Leo X's soldiers. They had already sold or pawned much of their plate and jewels. The marquis settled 6,000 ducats a year on them for as long as they remained in exile, in addition to which they had the use of a Gonzaga *palazzo* in Mantua. The sum and house were large enough to keep the princely couple in a certain state. At the time, to use a suggestive comparison, real-estate values show that the houses of noblemen in Mantua, generally speaking, ranged in value from 1,000 to 2,500 ducats, the latter attaching to very large structures. On the other hand, the house of a highly skilled artisan in a luxury trade, a weaver of velvet, might fetch eighty-five ducats.[4] But all these figures are dwarfed by Federigo da Montefeltro's reported disbursement of 200,000 ducats, in the third quarter of the fifteenth century, for the construction of the Palace of Urbino (though we must wonder what part of this took the form of forced labor). Calculating wage labor at the rate per man of fifteen ducats per year, we find that the palace represented the wages for one year of about 13,300 men. Federigo (d. 1482), however, also had an imposing palace erected at Gubbio, one of his subject towns; and he had an accumulated investment of about 50,000 ducats in plate, furnishings, and famous tapestries, and another 30,000 in a library. These figures came to something less from the 1490s, when the Italian Wars made money scarce and the cash value of objects and real property fell.

Interest rates at Ferrara went up to 30 percent and even, in some cases, 90 percent. Already in 1490 Caterina Sforza, countess of Imola and niece to Ludovico, begged the Milanese court for a loan of money so as to avoid being driven to accept, she said, 4,000 to 6,000 ducats for property— probably jewels and perhaps some land—that was worth 25,000 ducats.

We cannot say what proportion of total yearly revenues, in any of the princely states, went into the courtly establishment and its largess, into sinecures, new buildings, food, dress and jewels, donations, travel and stables, not to speak of marriages, births, and deaths. No doubt much of this could be viewed as ordinary and necessary expense. But if we estimate a varying figure of 12 to 20 percent, we may not be far wrong, all the rest going for regular government expenditures—administration, salaries, upkeep, troops, and fortifications—and into the interest on public debts.

One order of extraordinary expenditure requires some words apart because, like war, it could make for fiscal havoc: special occasions—marriages, state visits, and the purchase of titles and legitimacy. A minor event of this sort was Borso d'Este's purchase (1452) of a ducal title for a yearly disbursement of 4,000 ducats and a jeweled collar valued at 40,000. His imperial fiefs, Modena and Reggio, were raised to the status of a duchy by the Emperor Frederick III. But the reinvestiture of a later Este duke, Ercole II, and guarantees of the succession, cost the duchy 180,000 ducats, paid to the pope in 1539. We do not know the cost of Borso's trip to Rome in 1471 to be created duke of Ferrara by Pope Paul II. He flashed his way to the city with a train of more than 500 mounted noblemen, many hundreds of liveried servants, and 150 pack mules, and spent twenty days on the road. A very rough idea of the cost of such a trip may be gleaned from figures relating to the duke of Milan's brilliant and much larger cavalcade to Florence in the same year, a spectacle that first awed and then scandalized the Florentines. He led a company of thousands in a train that included 2,050 horses, 200 pack mules, 5,000 pairs of hounds, and twelve covered carriages. Everywhere were gilded horse trappings and cloth of gold, silver, and velvet. The reported cost, doubtless exaggerated, was 200,000 ducats. In 1493, Ludovico Sforza made a trip of this sort to his father-in-law's Ferrara, and although the train went with only 1,000 horses, he and his young wife made it a point of honor to overwhelm the Ferrarese court by their splendor. Lucrezia Borgia's bridal journey from Rome to Ferrara (January 1502), at the head of a cortège of 700 courtiers and servants, was debited to the papacy. Our information concerning the dowry is more precise. She took 100,000 ducats in cash to Alfonso of Ferrara, about as much again in lands pilfered from the diocese of Bologna, another 75,000 ducats in jewels, plate, clothes, linen, and tapestries, as well as a reduction (from 4,000 to 100 ducats) in the annual tribute due from Ferrara to the papacy. Only one dowry of the age surpassed this: the 400,000 ducats for Bianca Maria Sforza, niece to Ludovico, on the occasion of her marriage to the emperor-designate, Maximilian; and she got another 100,000 ducats in jewels, plate, and other fineries.[5] The dowry was payment for Ludovico's accession to the duchy of Milan, making him the first Sforza to receive imperial recognition and titles. In 1491 another of Ludovico's nieces, Anna, took a dowry of 100,000 ducats to Ferrara, in addition to thousands more in eye-catching fineries. The Este themselves, however, and the Gonzaga in this period, bestowed dowries in the range of from 30,000 to 40,000 ducats.

If arms and money were the front line of the courtly establishment, there was then all the life behind, arrayed around the prince and his family.

During the third quarter of the fifteenth century, one of the smallest of the important courts was at Urbino, under the government of Count Federigo da Montefeltro, who was raised to the ducal dignity by the great nepotist Sixtus IV, in partial reward for Federigo's agreeing to marry off one of his daughters to a nephew of the Holy Father. The court of Urbino had a staff and household numbering about 355 people.[6] Among these were forty-five counts of the duchy, seventeen lesser noblemen and gentlemen, five major secretaries, twenty-two pages, nineteen grooms of the chamber, nineteen waiters at table, thirty-one footmen, five cooks, fifty stable hands under five masters, and more than 125 other servitors and lackeys. Batista, Federigo's wife, had seven ladies-in-waiting. The contemporary biographer Vespasiano da Bisticci noted that the court had 500 mouths to feed—probably no exaggeration, in view of Federigo's reputation for hospitality. Political advisers to Federigo, as well as his lawyers, ambassadors, and captains, figured among the listed counts and gentlemen. Craftsmen, artists, musicians, and others were a staff apart, only partly included among the unspecified group of 125 because others of their sort were also hired temporarily or for particular jobs.

A clever *condottiere*, Federigo served as captain general to three popes, two kings of Naples, two dukes of Milan, and several Italian leagues. He added much to his ordinary revenues by his military stipends, collected over a period of thirty-four years. About 1510, during Castiglione's years at Urbino, the reduced grandeur of the court continued to put a heavy burden on its fragile economic foundations.

In the 1520s and 1530s, Mantua, a court of medium rank, had a staff of 800 people. Since an estimate of the 1540s found that a saving could be made of 3,500 ducats per year by discharging 450 of the 800,[7] a saving which averaged just under eight ducats per head, we may suppose that most of the 800 "familiars" were servants with minimal skills—footmen, pages, and other liveried helpers.

Figures for the richest of the courts, Milan, are sketchier than those for Urbino but still suggestive.[8] In the 1470s the Sforza stables had 500 horses and mules for the use of court personnel. About eight were reserved for the duchess and her retinue. The duke alone had, "for the service of his person," forty chamberlains (as against nineteen at Urbino) and more than ten supplementary and still other sub-chamberlains. As some of the noblemen at court served him in this capacity, the duke was clearly surrounded by a whole hierarchy of attendants. Hundreds of servants were attached to the kitchen, dining hall, and stables, with the result that a little world of hierarchies was to be found in each of these. Lowest of all were the runners (*galoppini*), who raced around doing chores and commissions. The dining hall had stewards, servants in charge of the silver service and majolica, table setters, and dispensers of food. The domain of the falconers was elsewhere, among the leopard keepers, dog handlers, and lackeys for the ducal hunting parties. The cruel and violent Galeazzo Maria (assassinated 1476) was a glutton for music and retained thirty-three singers from northern Europe, one of whom, the renowned Giovanni Cordier of Bruges, boasted a salary of 100 ducats per month—a phenomenal sum, considering that he could in theory have retired on an investment of six months' wages, giving him a yearly return of thirty ducats at a modest 5 percent. Most workers and many an artisan lived on half of this. In the 1490s, Ludovico seems to have made economies by simplifying the organization of service, but he retained musicians and a large choral group, stepped up the ostentation in dress and jewels, and added a company of Mamelukes captained by a count. His first secretary, Bartolomeo Calco, an able and learned functionary, commanded a team of thirty men: eight secretaries, seven assistants, a keeper of seals, four recorders, and two archivists, as well as treasurers and doorkeepers. This cluster of men was entirely separate from the secretaries and clerks attached to the duke's high council of state, the secret council. Accordingly, when we say of a rich and powerful oligarch, Lorenzo de' Medici, that he was a prince, we should keep in mind the great differences in power, ritual, and pomp that divided him from Ludovico.

Courtly life was organized around the prince. Everything went to serve him. This meant not only the physical fact that he was flanked by teams of servitors and servants, but also that consciousness itself was turned his way. Men were there to carry out his wishes: they had no social identity apart from the one profiled in the fundamental relation at court, that between service and lordship. This condition was envied because it was joined to that of the prince, than which there was no higher identity. The basic lexicon on the one side was in the vocabulary of obedience and adulation, on the other in that of command and expectation. From this, from the subtle play between the two, a whole courtly literature took its rise. The more we look into the princes Este, Gonzaga, Sforza, Medici, and Montefeltro-Della Rovere, the more we come on individual and dynastic egotisms that knew no bounds. But this was a luxury dearly paid for. The judgment of princes was often impaired by flattery, and since princes liked to be liked, the easiest if most dangerous way for them to be liked, as Ludovico frankly noted in his political testament, was to open up their hands and give—like Borso d'Este on his royal way to Rome, "throwing handfuls of silver coins to people as he entered and left cities."[9] Normally, the lion's share of the prince's largess went into the grasping hands of courtiers.

Court favorites got their rewards, but the next tier of servitors farther down was less well satisfied, and the tiers below these, again, saw the insecurities and burdens multiply. Fiscal shortages were immediately reflected in the suspension of pay, notably at the lower levels, often for months on end, and this affected all servants who lived out or who had outside dependents. A musician might suddenly be sent back to his remote village for playing dissonantly. In 1475, in the middle of a letter about other matters, the duke of Milan casually ordered a tailor thrown into prison because he had "spoiled the doublet of crimson silk" belonging to one of his courtiers.[10] Duke Ercole of Ferrara, in 1480, commanded one of his ambassadors, in the name of service to the duke, to stop mourning his spouse's death, adding that he, Ercole, would find "fresher flesh" for him—a new and younger wife. Isabella d'Este, marchioness of Mantua, got a brilliant young scholar, Niccolò Panizzato, to transfer himself to Mantua in 1492 to tutor her in classical literature. He was offered a stipend of three ducats per month, plus family allowances. But no sooner had he arrived in Mantua than he was dismissed because Isabella decided that she was, after all, too busy to resume her studies. The young man was bitterly disappointed. On an earlier occasion, while on a visit to Ferrara, she terrified a painter, Luca Lombieni, by twice threatening in letters to have him jailed in the dungeon of Mantua if he failed to finish a particular commission before her return, or if he failed to satisfy her. "Perhaps this will make you more anxious to please us in the future."[11]

In 1503, when Castiglione left the service of the marquis of Mantua for the court of Urbino, the marquis, although he had coldly granted his permission, was so angry that for some years Castiglione did not dare enter Mantuan territory to visit his mother. In December 1505, even with the credentials of an ambassador, he was forced at the Mantuan border to turn back to Urbino. Years later, having finally forgiven the courtier, the Marquis Francesco picked a spouse for him from the house of the Torelli counts of Mantua.

A different aspect of the play between service and lordship, especially as it pivoted on the egotism of the prince, appeared in relations between Titian and Francesco's son, Federico, the first duke of Mantua. Thanking the artist in 1531 for a picture of St. Mary Magdalen, Federico declared: "I recognize that in this magnificent work you have tried to express both the love which you cherish for me and your own excellence. These two things have enabled you to produce this incomparable figure."[12]

The prince's anger knew no laws. Francesco Maria della Rovere, when seventeen years old, killed his sister's lover; later, as duke of Urbino and again with his own hands, he killed a cardinal—and got away with it—for alleged abuse to his honor. On occasion, lawyers lost their offices in the state for moving legal action against favorites. Goldsmiths might find themselves in prison for failing to satisfy their lords. Alfonso d'Este, duke of Ferrara, once had the eyes crushed and face trampled of a notary who had sought to have a lawsuit transferred out of Ferrarese territory to Rome. And in 1508 he had one of his soldiers assassinate a leading courtier, the lame and much-scented Ercole Strozzi, who seems to have encouraged an exchange of sympathies between Alfonso's wife (Lucrezia Borgia) and brother-in-law, the marquis of Mantua.

In all these instances the prince justified his action on grounds of honor or the service and loyalty due him. These matters were paramount, and transgressing servitors or subjects might be deemed worthy of the most brutal punishment.

Power radiated out from the prince, but the process was not altogether one-sided. By their importuning flattery and self-interest, courtiers and favorites spurred the prince on to grab what he could, to bestow favors and graces, thus at times disrupting the course of justice. Accordingly, though the prince was the animating force of the courtly establishment, courtiers exercised some force upon him, and this made for a more complicated dialectic.

A PARADISE FOR STRUCTURALISTS

The prince was the centerpoint of the courtly order of consciousness. Around that point (lordship) all life revolved (service), all the dominant forms of thought, passion, and entertainment. If we know how to find the radii, how to read the variety of relations that ran between circle and center, we shall see that courts were a paradise for structuralists.

The fifteenth century was an age of strident self-assurance for the governing elites. Lorenzo de' Medici and his circle bullied and swaggered. The first duke of Ferrara, Borso d'Este, tried to build a mountain. The oligarchical core of the Venetian patriciate looked upon all Italy as fair game. Popes reconstituted their authority in Italy. And Ludovico Sforza believed that he could manipulate the leading powers of Europe. Never before had Italian ruling groups owned so much faith in their ability to control the perceived reality of the surrounding world. In this psychological environment, the interest in self-images, at once direct and devious, became one of the leading pleasures of the day, nowhere more than at the courts. The *richesse* of painted and sculpted portraits was only the most obvious sign of this interest. Painters at court spent much time executing portraits of princes, of the favorites of princes, and of their favorite pets, mainly dogs and falcons, more rarely horses; here already there was an entry into the realm of roundabout self-images. The striking of commemorative medallions—those sharply incised profile portraits of princes and lesser worthies—affords another example of the interest; they were usually cut to celebrate a triumph. The taste spread to rich bourgeois circles with humanistic or aristocratic pretensions, but it began or first prevailed in the strutting courts of the Este, Visconti, Malatesta, Gonzaga, and others. In imitation of Roman models, the profiles were occasionally crowned with laurel wreaths or given Roman shoulder and neck dress, thus associating the portrait (a self-identification) with the power that was Rome and so converting even Rome into a round-about self-image. But the biggest self-image of the age, in company with Michelangelo's unfinished tomb of Pope Julius II, was promised by Ludovico Sforza in the gigantic equestrian statue commissioned from Leonardo da Vinci for the main Milanese square. It was a statue of the dynasty's founder, the *condottiere* Francesco Sforza, Ludovico's father. In November 1493, to celebrate Bianca Maria's marriage to Maximilian and to impress the German visitors, Leonardo's clay colossus was raised onto a triumphal arch and set in the piazza before the castle. The lyric praise of poets followed. But as the duchy was heaving toward deep financial difficulties, the statue, meant to be cast in bronze, was never finished; and after Ludovico was overthrown, his enemies destroyed the clay model. Here, art in our terms was hated propaganda in theirs.

Next, there was the rich scatter of refracted self-images to be found in the objects around: in court tapestries, playing cards, decorated earthenware, embroidered silks, wedding chests, engraved arms and armor plate, and even a variety of sugar confections for special banquets. Courtiers saw images in these of hunting parties, lush gardens and exotic animals (akin to those collected by certain princes), cavaliers and ladies, battle scenes and mythological cycles, such as the Fall of Troy or the Labors of Hercules. Standing before the latter, princes could imagine mythological ancestors and the Este lords with the name Ercole (Hercules) could playfully seek themselves. And if they were short in imagination, adulators were not. As the satirist Panfilo Sasso (fl. 1500) observed, even parvenus were ready to claim descent from Priam, Pyrrhus, and Alexander the Great.[13] Faience and sets of cards depicted sainted knights, patron saints, fortified cities, fair Justice holding her scales, and armorial bearings, as well as personal devices and mottos, a fashion then much in favor with princes. The margins of Lascaris' Greek grammar composed for the child Gian Galeazzo Sforza, later duke, were decorated with colored Sforza devices and heraldic bearings. Borso d'Este once dressed his pages in livery adorned with a motto about "fidelity." "Alpha" and "Omega," in Greek lettering, said the motto on the suit of white satin and gold brocade worn on a famous occasion (Rome, 1512) by the twelve-year-old heir to the Gonzaga titles. His mother, Isabella d'Este, was flashing her allegiance to humanism. Ludovico Sforza's wife, Beatrice d'Este, was enamored of a dress cut from a brocade (price about eighty ducats per square meter) embroidered with the two towers of the port of Genoa. The image was very much to the point, for in his political testament, her husband, lord of that city too, declared, "Genoa is of the highest moment, not only for [the sake of our] reputation but also for the preservation of this, our primary state [Milan]." At major banquets the courts often produced sugar confections done up in the shapes of cities, castles, birds, and animals: the very devices that symbolized the lordship and hunting interest of princes. These devices were also much depicted in painting at court after about 1420 or 1430.

Humanist programs for frescos caught fragments of self-imagery. In 1522 the humanist Mario Equicola suggested that each of the five roundels in the bedroom of his warrior lord, Federico Gonzaga, be adorned with pictures of Victory, Virtue, Bellona (goddess of war), and Hope, while the fifth and big roundel in the middle would depict Fame. Evidently the program was intended both to summarize Federico's qualities (a flattery) and to be a spur.[14]

The courtly quest for, and delight in, self-images was endless and could take the most circuitous routes. When Pope Alexander VI died in 1503, the marquis of Mantua, who was with the French army just outside Rome, wrote to his wife saying that "his funeral was such a miserable thing that the wife of the lame dwarf of Mantua had a more honorable burial than this pope." That is to say, a lowly dwarf—whose wife alone was lower—was the exact opposite of a prince, the very image of power and grandeur. Thus, with an oddly perfect taste, the Gonzaga had introduced dwarfs into their court and in the sixteenth century ordered built, in their own residence at Mantua, a famous suite of miniature rooms. This game, however, of opposite but twin images also fused the two, for the stunted creatures were dressed, like their masters, in lush cloth of silver and gold. When in November 1515 the Venetian ambassadors to Milan passed through Mantua, they found the Marquis Francesco, disabled by syphilis, lying on a couch in a richly adorned room. His favorite dwarf, attired in gold brocade, attended him. Three pages stood nearby, as well as three of his pet greyhounds. Some of his falcons, reined by leashes, were also in the room; and the walls were hung with pictures of his favorite dogs and horses. In short, the room was a cache of turned, circuitous, and refracted self-images. Some years before, his head had been shaved clean to help heal a battle wound, whereupon his courtiers shaved their heads to keep him in countenance and to reflect his. The damaged image of the prince had its consolation in reflections. At Milan, instead, such mimicry was for prize falcons, which were shown off, as if in imitation of the prince, wearing "a little hood trimmed with some pearls and with one much larger on the peak," said the ambassador from Ferrara.[15] The cardinal Ascanio Sforza had a different sort of petted bird: a parrot (price 100 ducats) able to recite the Credo entire.

Imaginative literature at court was on the same track, where power turned all things into figments of itself or into symbolic scraps of the things that were central to its interests and delights. We need only mention the

torrents of accolades in verse produced by poets, among them the best of
the age: Poliziano, Boiardo, Bembo, Ariosto, and Tasso. From doggerel of the
sort occasionally written by Bellincione at the Sforza court, up to the sustained encomia in *Orlando Furioso*, there is a stream of honeyed words and
adoring sycophancy for princes, their wives, mistresses, favorites, and for all
the best-placed around these, not excluding pets. Ludovico Sforza commissioned the poet and courtier Gaspare Visconti to write verses on the death
of a favorite falcon. The best-known of such poetizing was occasioned in
1512 by the death of Isabella d'Este's little bitch, Aura. The marchioness
grieved, and commemorative elegies, sonnets, epitaphs, and epigrams, in
Latin as well as Italian, poured into Mantua from different parts of Italy, and
many survive in manuscript. The equivalent in stone was the sumptuous
tomb designed in 1526, by none other than Giulio Romano, for one of
Federico Gonzaga's dead pets, also a bitch.

The method of tracking self-images, as a way of delineating the operations of consciousness, shows that we should be on the lookout for the
impact of power even in the most unlikely or *prima facie* innocent activity.
Not, however, that Duke Ercole d'Este's "seeking of his fortune" was innocent. Once a year he went around Ferrara with cap in hand, humble airs,
and a crowd of courtiers, begging food at the doors of citizens. Whatever he
gathered—pies, capons, gamebirds, and cheeses by the hundreds—was given
over to feed the city's poor. The exercise made a candid use of power, but it
was interestingly combined with a self-image turned upside down, as in the
pairing of prince and dwarf. The prince put on mock airs and became a
beggar. Power became theater and ritual. But all the provisions collected by
the begging Ercole went to prop up his magnanimity: a weak if sincere
gesture that could not make up for an oppressive fiscal machine, as Ercole
(d. 1505), in the course of his reign, stepped up his political ambitions and
splashed his resources around on grand building schemes.

The courts cast a perfect profile in their orgiastic splendor. All public
occasions allowed for a display of luxury. Marriages, births, funerals, state
visits, the reception of ambassadors, carnivals, special fêtes, and religious processions: these were occasions for the courts to dress up and show off their
splendor. Princes, courtiers, and their ladies went forth in cloth of gold and
blazing with jewels. At their best, in an Este expression of the period, they
thought they looked "like angels from heaven," never suspecting that they
imagined angels in their own image. High points in the march of finery were
the Aragon-Este marriage of 1473, the Este-Sforza marriages of 1491–1492,
Ludovico Sforza's visit to Ferrara in 1493, Bianca Maria Sforza's marriage to
Maximilian late in 1493, Lucrezia Borgia's arrival at Ferrara in 1502, festivities for the king of France at Milan in 1507, and the coronation of the
emperor at Bologna in 1530. A half-dozen other marriages and state visits
were not far behind in their pomp. And marriages often went with the
raising of triumphal arches, where again we see the self-glorifying taste of
the courts.

All the grand occasions drew great crowds of people, among them many from the country. They came to gawk at ornamented horse carriages, chariots, and long files of caparisoned horses; at collars of chained gold on the necks of the rows of gentlemen; gold-fringed sleeves worth thirty ducats each; accessories of hammered, filigreed, laminated, and scaled gold; dresses —Lucrezia Borgia's—striped with fish scales of woven gold; other dresses valued up to 5,000 ducats; headpieces and coronets with assemblies of jewels; and cascades of diamonds, pearls, rubies, and emeralds.

There was a meaning to all this finery that went beyond the mere show of wealth. None knew this better than the actors themselves. More than once there was competition between courts, each yearning to show off the heaviest collars of chained gold. Chroniclers were impressed. Letters were dispatched with precise estimates of the collars in ducats. In a letter to her husband on Lucrezia Borgia's first arrival in Ferrara, the Marchesana of Mantua (an Este) said, underscoring her own father's luster, that seventy-five of Duke Ercole d'Este's gentlemen "wore golden chains, none of which cost less than 500 ducats, while many were worth 800, 1,000 and even 1,200 ducats." When Beatrice d'Este went to Venice in May 1493, on an important mission for her husband, Ludovico Sforza, she took her most resplendent jewels and dresses, aiming to dazzle the hardheaded Venetians. Noting their reaction at receptions and in the streets, she mimed it in a letter to Ludovico: " 'That is the wife of Signor Ludovico. Look what fine jewels she wears. What splendid rubies and diamonds she has!' " He was delighted.

The display of wealth peaked in the exhibition of the prince's treasure, a practice best exemplified at the Sforza court but also observed in Venice. Ambassadors and dignitaries, who were likely to report what they saw, were taken by Ludovico to see the ducal treasure: a store of more than a million ducats in gold, gems, plate, and statues of gold and silver. Visitors came away stunned by the marvels seen.

Luxurious ostentation at the courts was a display of power. Without such an exhibition, there was somehow no sufficient claim or title to the possession of power. Therefore the need to show. At the same time, to show was to act out a self-conception: I am prince and I can show it. The more I show it, the more I am what I claim to be. It was a dialectic of ambition and being. Luxurious ostentation was converted into an identity essence. But it was also the naked swagger of power, all the more so in that the mime took place—a deadly serious mime—within sovereign cities whose close spaces magnified pageantry. Princes went so far as to make no secret of borrowing silver plate and tapestries of satin and brocade for the grand occasions, so eager were they to strike the eye.

The fifteenth century was, we have noted, an age of vigorous optimism and tremendous self-assurance for the ruling classes. Paradoxically, these were the very qualities in princes that could make for insecurity as to legal titles and the preservation of power. Sigismondo Malatesta once set out for Rome to kill the pope. Este brothers and bastards at Ferrara were ready to take power from close relatives, and so they had to *show* power through pomp. At Urbino the Montefeltro and Della Rovere took their start from bastards and from upstart, nepotist popes; hence they also had to show. At Milan the Sforza were a new dynasty, not recognized by the empire until Ludovico's purchase of the ducal title, and even he pushed a nephew and grandnephew out of the way. Therefore the Sforza showed. The Borgias, made by the papacy, never stopped showing. And hemmed in by grandeur, the Gonzaga also hit on a more flattering identity in the practice of showing.

The self-assured readiness for political adventure injected an element of insecurity into the life of the courts and turned ostentation into an identity need. But there was another front of pressures that also drove the ruling groups toward unprecedented luxury: the growing concentration of wealth, the slow rigidifying of the social order, and the gradual freezing of the groups at the top. This process of hardening encouraged luxury as a means of calling attention to status in a world of deepening social differences. Of course princes could favor whom they pleased, so that there was always an insignificant rise of new men into the elite ranks of government, but their descendants rarely endured, or they were absorbed into the aristocracy. In any case, the vast majority of leading political and ecclesiastical posts went to the rich old families, which did much to help keep them rich.

The show of riches and the pursuit of self-images, and the show of riches *as* the acting out or miming of a self-image: these operations, working around the prince, gave a centralized structure to the whole range of activities at court, a paradise for structuralists.

Ritual too was brought to bear: it went to frame and amplify the power of the court. Public occasions meant the sound of trumpets, cannon, drums, pipes, and the air trembling with bells. Duke Ercole produced eighty trumpeters for Lucrezia Borgia's arrival in Ferrara. At Milan the major public festivities began with the duke's arrival, the rolling of drums and the sound of trumpets and pipes. In the late 1480s, when Duke Guidobaldo da Montefeltro and his new wife, Elisabetta Gonzaga, visited their subject towns of Cagli and Gubbio, they were greeted by trumpets, bells, cannon fire, and rows of children in long white dress, shouting, "Duca, Duca! Gonzaga, Gonzaga!" Milan's bells rang for days on the occasion of the birth of Ludovico's first legitimate son. A joy to the prince was a joy for his subjects.

When the French invaded Italy in 1494 and again in 1499, Italian princes and courtiers were surprised and repelled by the "disorder"—the lack of ceremony—in the French court. Cardinals were not shown all due respect. The king's counselors ate, played cards, or casually sat around in his presence. He was swayed too easily and without ceremony. There was chaos and filth in the stables. Instead, the Italian courts were sharply conscious of rank, protocol, and organized households that made for tidiness. The kissing of the prince's hand was *de rigueur*. Ludovico Sforza insisted upon the epithet "Illustrissima" for his wife when she was still the duchess of Bari, not yet of Milan. There was a punctilious use of titles in letters between brothers, between children and parents, and between husband and wife. Castiglione always addressed his mother as "Magnificent and honored madam, my mother." The first duke of Urbino, Federigo (d. 1482), specified three degrees of hospitality for the three orders of visitors: great, middling, and of small account. He also left a volume of rules touching the conduct of court ladies, the ducal table service, and the dress and cleanliness of servants. In the 1460s the Gonzaga were astonished by the bad manners of German noblemen and ambassadors; but they were cool realists in matters of power, and though they would not bend the knee to the powerful upstart Sforza family, meetings with them were a choreography. Regarding a forthcoming meeting at Reggio in June 1465, the Gonzaga marchioness of Mantua wrote to her son Federico: "I think it well to warn you how to behave. First of all, as soon as you see the Milanese party approach, you and your wife must dismount and advance to meet them with outstretched hands and courteous reverence. Be careful not to bend your knee before them, but salute the illustrious duke and duchess, and shake hands with Filippo and Ludovico [younger sons], and also with Galeazzo [Maria, the eldest], if he is present and offers to shake hands. Dorotea [Federico's sister] must also give him her hand and curtsey to him, but if he does not come forward, let her not move a step. Then we will take the duchess up in our chariot and you must all three of you pay her reverence."[16] Instructions are also given regarding Dorotea's dress.

The scene speaks for itself. Direct contact with power required ritual, a tribute paid in gestures. Publicly, power itself was also expressed through ritual and thus magnified. There was an appropriate language too, seen never so much as in letters addressed to princes. The glossary of ritual terms highlighted loyalty and flattery, and centered on the notions of service, obeisance, and self-sacrifice. Here are two expressions: "My life is at your service." "I live only insofar as I am in your excellency's graces." Another: "Nothing in the world pleases me more than your commands." And another: "The sum of my every desire everywhere, always, and in every respect and turn of fortune good and bad is to carry out whatever your most illustrious lordship commands." The variations were innumerable, and some crystallized into formulas. Courtly language also invaded literature and spilled out into more workaday human relations. In the 1520s and after, satirists began to attribute the fashion for deferential expressions and the runaway use of the epithets "lord" and "lordship"—claimed, it was said, by every lowborn adventurer—to the cursed impact of the Spanish hegemony in Italy. But this was moralism, not analysis. The fashion sprang from Italian society itself: with its ailing economy, widening social differences, enhanced emphasis on status, and accelerating *rentier* or courtly consciousness among the ruling groups. From this changing society and changed upper-class identity had come a seductive educational idea, first fully enunciated by Castiglione. He wrote to his mother from Rome on April 26, 1524, urging her to get his son of six years, Camillo, to close his letters to Castiglione with the phrase *"obedient son and servitor*, so that he shall learn from an early age to be courteous [*humano*]."[17] In context, *humano* (echoing humanism) meant polite, courteous, courtly: a condition which, whether in service to the prince or not, recognized and paid tribute to rank.

Power girded itself with ritual to exact obeisance and to seem more imposing, more overbearing. Taking a leaf from the papacy's notebook, the Italian courts would have raised ritual to a science. They combined it with pageantry—spectacle of the sort which serves, especially in difficult times, to captivate the senses and cloud the critical faculties. In this too the princely courts excelled.

Leonardo's equestrian giant, commemorating Francesco Sforza, had promised to be the boldest self-image of the age. There was a contender, also never finished: Pope Julius II's dream of his own tomb—sculptor, Michelangelo. And here we touch upon the Renaissance rage for building.[18]

Art historians bury the *why*—and hence the sociology—of buildings by their excessive emphasis on questions of form and style. Most of the great building projects of the Italian Renaissance, whether commissioned by a Cosimo de' Medici (oligarch-prince), by Stanga counts (Cremonese aristocrats), or by a Pius II, had behind them the urge to exhibit now: to exhibit an identity, to show the power or piety of the man and his family dynasty, and to carve out a space in the city that would belong to that name, that individual and dynasty, for all times. In Ludovico Sforza's time the church-monastery of the Certosa of Pavia, started by the Visconti a hundred years before, was so clearly his ward that no visitor would have failed to associate the Sforza name with it. At Ferrara, having battened on the corrupt fruits of office, the rich ducal councilors from the Strozzi, Trotti, and Taruffo families fired the city's hatred for them by building grand *palazzi* where they entertained princes. At Rome, about 1450, certain men in Pope Nicholas V's entourage already noted the ideological power of "majestic buildings" and advanced the view that papal patronage could thus be used to catch the admiration and fidelity of the unlettered multitude. Pope Sixtus IV (d. 1484) spread the attendant benefits by establishing the right of rich clerics in Rome, chiefly cardinals and leading curialists, to build and bequeath houses to their heirs—which triggered a building boom in the city.

All princes who could afford to do so—and many who could not—were big builders. They erected residential palaces, villas, fortresses, new government buildings, churches, and convents; they also restored and renovated. Thus the Visconti and Sforza, Sigismondo Malatesta, Federigo da Montefeltro, Borso and Ercole d'Este, Federico II Gonzaga, the Farnese and Medici in Rome, and princelings like the Correggio, Stanga, Bentivoglio, Ghisilardi, Bottigella, Trivulzio, and Borromeo. Men of this stripe felt so compelling an urge to build that, taking the few for the many, writers and architects came to believe that the desire to build on a large scale sprang from a basic human instinct.

The swagger of grandiose building was the dance of wealth old and new, and at the courts, it was a mark of power held and dynasty prolonged. In the fifteenth century, when power in the cities was secure beyond any precedent, elite contact with perceived reality was self-assured, with the result that taste in grand architectural activity lay closer to a criterion of use and practical reason. It was an age of manifest achievement. But in the sixteenth century, after the sovereign controls over political reality had been torn from the hands of the big builders, then, in compensation and evasion, princes won by losing: they boasted in their building projects. The architectural accent became pompous or ultra-refined, showy and with a bent for the irrational. A kindred transformation was to be found in much upper-class art and literature; the latter emphasized status and romance. But there was also a strong undertow of literary satire, which focused on the chaos and cynicism in government and leadership.

The foregoing review of courtly life has traced self-images in portraits and in surrounding objects such as tapestries, playing cards, sugar confections, dwarfs, pets, ostentatious luxury, the pageantry of public occasions, and the compulsion to build grandly. It remains to consider a few other interests that served the egocentrism of the courtly space.

Art collections entered nicely into this space because they required large outlays of wealth and were a special kind of looking glass: expensive hobbies to while away the time, subjects of polite conversation (Castiglione), and repositories of novelties and antiquities that reflected signorial tastes. The Medici, the dukes of Urbino, Ludovico Sforza, Isabella d'Este, and the first duke of Mantua, Federico II, were among the chief collectors of the time. There were also a few private collections, or their beginnings, among connoisseurs at Rome, Florence, and Venice. Art objects were an ornament, shown to the best advantage in the rooms of princes and rich collectors, in effect much like the fashionable plaquettes cut by leading goldsmiths, such as Caradosso, to be worn by gentlemen on their luxurious caps. When Piero de' Medici fled from Florence late in 1494 and the Medici collection was threatened, Ludovico Sforza quickly had his ambassador there make inquiries, particularly about the objects that had been in Lorenzo the Magnificent's personal study: "precious and portable things, that is, cameos, carnelians, medallions, coins, books, and such like gentilities [*gentilezze*]."[19] A generation later, at a sumptuous banquet given by the younger Ippolito d'Este in Ferrara, the host drew things from "a silver boat" and gave out "necklaces, bracelets, earrings, scented gloves, little scent boxes, and other *gentilezze*."[20] Gentilities: a revealing use of the word, meaning small objects fit for people of refined taste and gentle blood. But the objects in Ludovico's list above were collected together with pictures, sculptures, and well-wrought glass, as in Isabella d'Este's famous apartments. All these and princely libraries too—since books could also be *gentilezze*—were an ornament used to affirm a lordly identity. As it happens, after the death of his wife, Beatrice d'Este, Ludovico Sforza always used an official seal engraved with her image, a carnelian.

The main amusements at court, apart from the antics of buffoons, were cardplaying, chess, a game of ball, music, hunting, and more rarely jousting. The preferred courtly songs, sung to the lute or to other stringed instruments, were often drawn from Petrarch's sonnets; hence they were love songs of elevated, delicate, and at times playful sentiment. The joust was an urbane war dance done with horse, lance, and sometimes sword. At its best it kept courtiers fit for mounted combat, which was, in tandem with statecraft, the true office of the prince and courtier. At its worst, jousting was little more than the occasion to dress up in gleaming armor and brilliant colors: a mime of war that gratified and flattered the court, while it dazzled the assembled crowds.

Hunting was the best-loved pastime, done during as much of the year as possible, often in large parties that rode out to special grounds and villas. These were appointed to impress and delight distinguished visitors. Women as well as men took passionately to the sport. The Este and Sforza sometimes rode thirty miles in a day. They employed falcons, hunting leopards, and scores of dogs, as well as nets and great sheets of tough cloth. They killed boar, wolves, bear, stag, deer, goat, hare, quail, and varieties of large birds. The sheets were used to cut off and direct the course of fleeing animals. In bourgeois Florence and Lucca, hunting on horseback was seen as the signorial sport *par excellence*. Done as at the courts, it could be nothing else. It required horsemanship, training, much time, and great expenditure, all of which would have been time and capital filched from the countinghouse, shop, and craft. As in their passion for jousting, accordingly, the Medici after Cosimo enhanced their lordly ways by their love of hunting, but even Lorenzo the Magnificent's hunting cavalcades were very modest exercises compared to expeditions at Milan, Ferrara, Mantua, and Rome.

Any well-dressed horseman seen bearing a falcon on a gloved hand was almost, by that fact alone, a *signore*: lord, courtier, or gentleman with estates in the country. For falconing, deemed the most "noble" part of hunting, had a rich nomenclature, a place for well-paid experts (falconers), a ritual, and a variety of specialized hawks, such as *peregrini, lanieri, astorelli,* and *altani. Alfanechi* were imported from as far away as Russia and the Near East. The imagery of falconing penetrated courtly verse. Something of the falcon's soaring grace, speed, and fierce eye made a vivid appeal to the courtly self-image.

It would be odd indeed to draw parallels between princes and birds of prey, or to make moralistic comments about the court's callous attitudes toward poverty, its expenditure on game preserves, and its severe laws against poaching. To moralize would be to fail to see the element of necessity in social identity at court. Princes and courtiers could not be other than they were. One observation, however, needs emphasis. There was a tight, organic link in consciousness between the self-centered, domineering outlook of the court and its spontaneous assumption that the goods of the earth existed first and foremost for its own enormous appetites and delectation. As Beatrice d'Este said to her sister, the marchioness of Mantua, in a letter of March 18, 1491, written from the Sforza hunting ground at Villanova: "Every day I am out on horseback with dogs and falcons and never do we return, the lord [Ludovico Sforza] my consort and I, without our having had infinite pleasures falconing. . . . There are so many hares, leaping up from all sides, that sometimes we know not which way to turn to have our pleasure, *for the eye is incapable of seeing all that which our desire craves and which the country offers us of its animals.*"[21]

The age had another speciality: bastardy.

The fifteenth century in Italy has been called the golden age of bastardy. It might more accurately be called the age of golden bastards. Niccolò III d'Este (d. 1441) is alleged to have peopled Ferrara with them; he acknowledged more than twenty. Francesco Sforza had at least twenty-five; his son, Ludovico, four at least and very likely more. Such children were often brought up at court, together with the children born in wedlock. They sometimes appeared in group portraits and came into substantial estates or handsome life incomes. Honorable and occasionally brilliant marriages were arranged for them. Otherwise, for the boys, there were rich benefices and a career in the Church. The treatment accorded to the natural children of princes and well-placed men goes yet once more to point up the fifteenth-century's psychology of flaunting self-assurance at the level of the upper classes, where courtiers and rich men happily acknowledged bastards and often had them legitimized by papal dispensation. But major honors went to the offspring of princes and rich aristocrats because this is where the titles and estates were; also because the shameless parading of power proudly singled out the bastards and thereby the potency of the father. Princesses and court ladies had no such license, reaching for which they faced the penalty of death. And if Ludovico Sforza's mistress, Cecilia Gallerani, was honorably married off to Count Ludovico Bergamini, a feudatory from the Cremonese, the whole world knew that she went to him with jewels, estates, and the hard promise of continuing favors. The fidelity of women was all, but power and money, come from the prince and filtered through courtly pomp, could work the miracle of toleration and the alchemy of repristinated honor. Something like this, though without the mysteries, also took place in middle-class circles, when a poor girl, got with child by a bourgeois of "good family," was dowered and put out in marriage to a humble working man in the country.

Bastardy, however, was no substitute for the guarantees of legitimacy.

Although courtly life and pleasures circled around the prince, the courtly establishment had its security in marriage, in the promise of legitimate heirs whose existence eased the succession and promised the continuation of the dynasty. Marriage also made important friends and helped to solidify the existing rule. Indeed, the forging of political alliances was the fundamental fact about princely marriages in the fifteenth and sixteenth centuries. Never was marriage arranged with a colder eye for political and dynastic interests. Parents and guardians disposed fully of their children and wards. Frequently the prince made the dowry arrangements and chose the spouses of courtiers and their daughters or nieces. In this fashion he also sealed loyalties and looked to the dynasty's future servitors.

Isabella d'Este's marriage to Francesco Gonzaga was the binding together of two old houses and two neighboring states. Her sister's marriage to Ludovico Sforza lent the burnish of an ancient house to the ambitious and "illegal" Sforza,[22] but in return the Este picked up a powerful ally, or so it very much seemed in 1491. They had also made a strong bond in the south, with Duke Ercole's marriage (1473) to Eleonora d'Aragona, eldest daughter to King Ferrante of Naples, though this was to wrench Ferrara's ties with Venice. Pope Julius II bought respectability and distinction of stock for the Della Rovere upstarts in the marriage (1509) of his nephew, Francesco Maria della Rovere, duke of Urbino, to a princess of the Gonzaga house; the purchase price was a cardinal's hat for Sigismondo Gonzaga, brother to the marquis of Mantua. And Ludovico Sforza bought Milan's ducal title with a dowry of 400,000 ducats on the occasion of his niece's marriage to the emperor designate, Maximilian. But the most methodical use of marriage was made by Alexander VI and Cesare Borgia, for whom Lucrezia, respectively daughter and sister, was an instrument in the Borgian carving out of a state for Cesare. In the sixteenth century, in response to the shock and insecurities of the Italian Wars, Italian princes aspired to stonger alliances still and so to ties of marriage with the French and Spanish royal houses.

Of all the court's occasions and activities, marriage was the one most strictly determined by the interests of the prince; it was the fulfillment of an inherited self-image. Here the prince stood in his most distinguishing guise, the holder of power, taking the first real step towards preserving the dynasty and transmitting that power.

CHAPTER XIII

ART:
AN ALLIANCE
WITH POWER

PATRONAGE AND PROPAGANDA

Art and power in Renaissance Italy went hand in hand. Pictures and sculptures were made for patrons, not for an open market. As late as the 1560s, an artist was likely to lose face and standing if he produced and sold unsolicited works. The important patrons, lay and ecclesiastical, came largely from among the urban ruling groups. Architecture, the *voie royale* of patronage and the umbrella art for the "lesser" arts, was for the monied taste of popes, princes, oligarchs, and rich men; for the state, and for organized groups of the sort that drew men of substance together in leading guilds and religious confraternities. Even Carpaccio's famous cycle of the life of St. Ursula (1490s), executed for one of Venice's more modest confraternities, the Scuola of St. Ursula, had the patronage of Nicolo Loredan—born to one of the city's richest and most illustrious houses—and the cycle shows his family arms, family portraits, and the *ex voto* ciphers of his patronage.

One can say of cities, "Tell me how their space is distributed and I will tell you who governs or owns them"; and one can say of Italian Renaissance cities, "Tell me who owns the imposing *palazzi* or let me study the family chapels in the different churches, and I will tell you who the princes, oligarchs, and rich men are and who their patron saints." Masaccio's tenements (Fig. 4 in insert of illustrations) are the backside of the fifteenth century's "ideal cities" (Fig. 15). Articulation of the urban space was dialectical, a question of relations between wealth and poverty, churches and lay dwellings. It was also a question of other social balances: of where the prepotent families were concentrated, of where they had their houses, churches, or waterfront. Powerful bishops had once been a decisive force in the layout of the urban space. When Cosimo de' Medici, after about 1436, began to move out of his quarter of the city to offer massive charitable support for the restoration of religious buildings in other parts of Florence, he roused fears and envies. Whatever his private motives, his actions seemed the stealthy movements of an aspiring tyrant. The psychology of eminent men was a datum in Florentine spatial arrangements. Cosimo's activity posed a threat to the controls of other old families in the private chapels that had long belonged to their patronage. More was involved than the saying of Masses for deceased kinfolk: the manner of the banker's patronage prefigured a shift in the axis of Florentine political power. However, a change in patronage rarely involved anything so far-reaching. Domenico Ghirlandaio's great frescoes in the Tornabuoni (choir) chapel of Santa Maria Novella (1485–1490), which cost about 1,100 florins, got there by conventional oligarchic means: the chapel had long been the property of the once prominent Ricci family, but Giovanni Tornabuoni hired Ghirlandaio to decorate the chapel, and then managed to get it associated with his own name by means of money, tricky promises, cleverly placed armorial bearings, and influence in one of the Florentine courts. Giovanni was closely related by marriage to the Medici.

Looking back to the fourteenth and fifteenth centuries from modern times, we sort out a segment of experience and call it "art." The men and women of the early Italian Renaissance did not look merely to art, often not at all. Their eyes were primed to find a religious meaning, and the subject matter of Italian Renaissance art was overwhelmingly religious. It was, in the truest sense, propaganda—that which was to be propagated. A religious picture might serve not only as a profession of faith but also to help convey doctrine, to prop up belief, to remind sinners of their obligations, or even as a voice in defense of the Church. The fact that militant Protestantism turned violently against the imagery of the old Church, and so against religious painting and sculpture, shows that communities instinctively recognized the educational and propagandistic intent of religious art.

The deep-rooted habit of *reading* the products of the figurative imagination will be a point to keep in mind, for patrons and viewers did not abandon it with the entry of ever more worldly themes into the subject matter of Renaissance art.

When a chapel, a fresco, a statue, or a church facade was made on commission from an association of merchants or a religious confraternity, as was common down to 1600, it was distinctly associated with a group. Here already, in the bonds between piety and the pride of an organized group, was the visual affirmation of a special interest. At Florence, in the first half of the fifteenth century, the big cloth merchants, working via their guilds, openly asserted their dominant place in the community. They controlled the public monies earmarked for work on the cathedral and Baptistery (the patronal church), and they took major decisions in the most important artistic projects of the period—Ghiberti's bronze doors, the statuary at Orsanmichele, and Brunelleschi's dome.

Corporate patronage of a different sort belonged to the state, as when the

1. "Magdalen Master," *Madonna and Child with Saints*, c. 1270.
Yale University Art Gallery, University Purchase from James Jackson Jarves.

2. Simone Martini, *Guidoriccio da Fogliano*, 1328.
Palazzo Comunale, Siena.

3. Masaccio, *Adoration of the Magi*, 1426. State Museum, East Berlin.

2

3

4

4. Masaccio, *St. Peter Healing with His Shadow*, 1427. Brancacci Chapel, Church of the Carmine, Florence .

5. Masaccio, *Tribute Money*, 1427. Brancacci Chapel, Church of the Carmine, Florence.

6. Masaccio, *Trinity*, c. 1425. S. Maria Novella, Florence.

5

6

9

8

7. Donatello, *St. George*, c. 1415-17. Bargello, Florence.

8. Jacopo della Quercia, *Cain and Abel*, c. 1434, Porta magna, San Petronio, Bologna.

9. Francesco di Giorgio, *Flagellation*, 1470s. National Gallery of Umbria, Perugia.

12

10. Perugino, *Christ Giving Keys to St. Peter*, 1480-82. Vatican, Rome.

11. Piero della Francesca, *Flagellation*, c. 1450s. Ducal Palace, Urbino.

12. Anonymous, *Healing of Cripple* (from *San Bernardino Cycle*), 1473.
National Gallery of Umbria, Perugia.

13

14

13. Francesco del Cossa, *St. John the Baptist*, 1473. Brera Gallery, Milan.

14. Uccello, *Battle of San Romano*, c. 1445. National Gallery, London.

15. Anonymous, *Architectural Perspective View*, c. 1470. State Museum, East Berlin.

16

17

16. Melozzo da Forli, *Sixtus IV Appointing Platina*, 1474-77. Vatican, Rome.

17. Mantegna, detail from *Gonzaga Family and Court*, 1474. Camera degli sposi, Ducal Palace, Mantua.

18. Raphael, detail from *Mass of Bolsena*, 1512, Vatican, Rome.

18

19. Gentile da Fabriano, *Adoration of the Magi*, 1423. Uffizi Gallery, Florence.

20. Mantegna, *St. Zeno Altarpiece*, 1456-59. St. Zeno, Verona.

21. Carlo Crivelli, *Annunciation*, 1486. National Gallery, London

22. Mantegna, *Madonna of the Stonecutters*, c. 1484. Uffizi Gallery, Florence.

Florentine government invited Michelangelo to sculpt *The David* (1501) or when Giovanni Bellini, in Venice, took charge of pictorial decoration in the hall of the Great Council. Governments could at any moment commission works of art. David in Quattrocento Florentine art—young man pitted against brute giant—symbolized a republican stance against despotic rule. The story of Judith and Holofernes, occasionally represented in painting and sculpture, had similar accents.

Yet another order of patronage and control belonged to rich families and oligarchs, who spent large sums on private chapels, tombs, frescoes, and religious panels, thus exhibiting their ascendancy through their piety and vice versa. In 1448 the rich Antonio Ovetari put up 700 gold ducats for the frescoes (now mostly destroyed) of St. James and St. Christopher in the Ovetari chapel of the Eremitani church in Padua. Mantegna and another artist carried out the work. The impact of the individual art patron was increasingly felt in the course of the fourteenth and fifteenth centuries. Pride of time and place goes perhaps to Enrico Scrovegno. Son of a rich and notorious Paduan usurer, he commissioned Giotto's *Lives of the Virgin Mary and Christ* (1302–1305) in the Arena chapel at Padua. The elder Scrovegno had been forced to make partial restitution of usury in order to ensure Enrico's rights of inheritance, and Enrico himself was compelled to enter a lay religious order. Giotto's frescoes served, accordingly, both to help expiate sin and to reinstate the moral worth of the Scrovegni in the Paduan commune, though the entire city-state world was tainted with usurious wealth.

In the early 1470s, when Lorenzo de' Medici sat down to figure out the principal expenditures made by his family between 1434 and 1471, he did not even bother to distinguish the disbursements for architectural and artistic commissions from those for charity and taxes. All were lumped together because all served the one end—the grandeur of his house and its power in the state. Far from regretting the astounding total (663,755 gold florins), he concluded: "I think it casts a brilliant light on our estate and it seems to me that the monies were well spent and I am very well pleased with this." If this candid observation is related to a declaration made by the painter Domenico Veneziano in a letter to Lorenzo's father in 1438—"I promise that my work will bring you honor"—the unity of interests binding patron and painter flashes forth at once: the one provided employment and opportunity, while the other toiled to enhance the reputation of his patron, although the success of this depended upon the finished work. In the early 1490s, on commission from Ludovico Sforza, Leonardo da Vinci modeled a horseman in clay or plaster some twenty-four feet high, intended to be cast in bronze: an equestrian statue that would celebrate the élan of the first Sforza duke of Milan, Francesco (d. 1466). And before we daze ourselves with notions about the period's universal love of art, let it be remembered that popes Julius II and Leo X used artists such as Raphael and Michelangelo to glorify themselves personally, their families, and their office. Power sought self-images, or their destruction. In 1511, in rebellion against the imperious pope, the Bolognese destroyed Michelangelo's fourteen-foot bronze statue of Julius II, which had been posted, three years before, in a niche above the central portal of San Petronio. They melted it down to make a cannon.

It remains to mention the countless orders for small works placed by humbler patrons—modest clerics and people from the ordinary bourgeoisie. A marked distinction has already been drawn, by implication, between influential and ordinary patrons. If the taste of major patrons remained conservative to 1440 or 1450, as at Siena, or even regressive, as at Genoa and Venice, taste must have been even more backward-looking among stay-at-home folk with more limited means. We infer this from much of the work done in country towns, from the productions of popular workshops, such as those of Bicci di Lorenzo in Florence and Giovanni di Paolo in Siena, or from the nature of pictorial decoration on wedding chests (*cassoni*). But there was a category of important patrons, individual and corporate, whose demands and needs opened the way for a new style. And in Arezzo, Orvieto, or other small towns, where we find monuments in the style of the artistic vanguard, say by Piero della Francesca or even by the lesser artist Luca Signorelli, we shall be on to a taste that was first fashioned in the great centers or for leading patrons. It is no mystery when provincial taste follows a more cosmopolitan one: ambition makes men ready to imitate their imagined betters.

SOCIAL POSITIONS AND MOBILITY

The question of the social position and mobility of artists in Quattrocento Italy is not an idle exercise for social historians. It holds a central place in efforts to decipher the social notation in the art of the period. For the artist's receptivity to the demands of patronage depended in part on his place in the social system, on his position vis-à-vis patrons (hence on *their* position), and on the nature of the "wares" made up for them. The goldsmith who exhibited a few rings, belts, and necklaces for a small open market had to keep in mind the fashion and taste of his customers, and he continually took orders to rearrange old gems in new settings. Artists and patrons were forced into an even closer and more vital rapport.

Scholarship has established, rather conclusively, that artists belonged to the order of craftsmen down to the sixteenth century. Their training and work relegated them to the ranks of small shopkeepers and petty merchants: to the world of those who held the obscurer levels of the middle classes. And if certain artists, such as Masaccio and Castagno, died young and poor, while others—e.g., Ghiberti, Tura, Verrocchio, the Pollaiuolo brothers—built up small fortunes, many more of them ended somewhere between, the owners of a small house or two, or a bit of land, but far from rich. In the 1450s, Donatello still rented a house and workshop. The Sienese sculptor Jacopo della Quercia was knighted by Siena in 1435, and this, although extraordinary, points to a changing consciousness. After 1500 the most fashionable artists lived like affluent gentlemen: Leonardo, Giorgione, Raphael, Giulio Romano, Titian. Yet one of the great and busiest Venetian painters of the sixteenth century, Tintoretto (1518–1594), died on the edge of poverty, not because he lived beyond his means but because he took in modest earnings and kept a large family. Luca Signorelli (ca. 1441–1523), who straddled the two centuries, lived, said Vasari, "rather like a great lord and gentleman than as a painter." Others—Brunelleschi, Mantegna, Ghirlandaio—lived as comfortable bourgeois.

The Quattrocento was the age of transition for the social status of the artist. Donatello (d. 1466) refused to wear a splendid cloak and matching undergarment given him by Cosimo de' Medici because the effect was too fine for him. Brunelleschi and Baldovinetti, born into established Florentine families, elected—most exceptionally—architecture and painting. Their sort, by a kind of ironclad social law, nearly always took up more respectable pursuits. But up in Genoa, between 1425 and 1450, there were already two noblemen from Pavia, the count Donato de' Bardi and his brother, Boniforte, who had fallen on bad times and were forced to live by their painting, although they had originally learned the art *per puro diletto dello spirito* (from sheer love of it).[1] The humanist Alberti designed several buildings but was primarily a theorist. Not having a craftsman's background, far from it, he approached art through his amateur's love and was known as a humanist, nobleman, and well-placed cleric. No craftsman would have thought of him as a fellow artist. Architects, goldsmiths, painters, and sculptors came generally from among the multitude of craftsmen and other petty bourgeois; a few were born the sons of notaries, some sprang from simple country stock.

Florence, the most republican of all cities, at all events in the mythology, can provide one example only of a fifteenth-century artist who held a public office of any note. The exception was Brunelleschi, born into the class of political citizens: he once served in the Priorate (1425). A family of great fourteenth-century painters, the Gaddi, "made it" in the fifteenth century by abandoning art for trade and then banking. At Venice the social distance between artists and political authority—between, say, the Bellini or Carpaccio and public office—was simply unbridgeable. Yet they could be the underwriters of political values. Hired to paint the pictures of doges, and battles and other historical scenes in the hall of the Great Council, they celebrated the Venetian past and so were propagandists for the republic.

The formal education of the artist stopped at the elementary level: he learned to read, to write, and to calculate. In some cases he developed the latter to the point of being able to manage relatively sophisticated problems.

The writings of Piero della Francesca reveal this. Vasari claimed that Mantegna, too, had planned to write a treatise on perspective. Probably Francesco di Giorgio and Jacopo de' Barbari could have managed one. A few artists received a smattering of Latin. But none is known—Mantegna's case is doubtful—for whom even the rudiments of a humanistic education may be claimed. Heavy full-time training in the workshop routinely began before the age of twelve—Michelozzo was casting bronze at fourteen—and often boys were already being trained at eight or nine, the very years when they were meant, in the literary or professional track, to secure the foundations of grammar and rhetoric.

This somewhat static picture of the social position of the art craftsman must be followed by a recognition of his dynamic promise. For in this respect the fifteenth century was pivotal; and an exceptional man, born to a modest family around 1450, could end his life as a "gentleman." Such were Signorelli, Mantegna, Giorgione, Raphael, and Leonardo. Later, Titian and Michelangelo could afford to thumb their noses at noblemen and clamoring patrons; but Tintoretto failed to break out of the neighborhood world of the petty craftsman.

The artists most in fashionable demand were decidedly better off at the end of the fifteenth century than at the beginning. Their fees and profits rose; their basic expenses probably did not. The social mobility of the artist was not, however, a function solely of pecuniary gain. More decisive were the changing and growing needs of the important patrons. Their consciousness, as a process grounded in a social structure, had telling effects. As the identity and self-image of the upper classes changed in the course of the century, taking in sharper mundane accents, such as the demand for larger houses, more brilliant marriages, greater show in personal wear, and more preeminence in government, the needs of their patronage also changed. Rich patrons required more images of themselves and their world in figurative representation, and they put more and more "works of art" into their houses. Increasingly, the aims of Renaissance patronage came to lie in the affirmation of a social identity. In the process, which involved nothing less than a transformation in the outlook of the upper classes, the artist-craftsman entered into a new and closer contact with influential patrons. This raised his social position.

Giotto, Arnolfo di Cambio, Ambrogio Lorenzetti, and other artist-craftsmen of the fourteenth century were associated with major enterprises, fresco cycles, and building projects. They won fame and material rewards—though Giotto's name is not even mentioned in payment documents on the Arena chapel—but did not alter their status in terms of the upper-class presuppositions of the day. They labored with their hands, and this was demeaning. Celebrity did not raise their skills from the mechanical to the liberal arts, the arts "suitable for free men." Nor, again, was the Renaissance rise in the status of the visual arts owing to the impact of humanism, for humanism was itself a vanguard current in the evolving consciousness of the upper classes.

Most cities had competing *botteghe* (workshops) with small teams of artists, but there were individual workshops as well. The larger shops allowed for some specialization among the different craftsmen; apprentices and the less dexterous workers were often assigned to the more decorative parts of commissions or to the painting of chests and banners and the gilding of saddles. Two or three well-known workshops in Florence specialized in the production to order of ornamented wedding chests and seem to have done little else. Others concentrated on small devotional pictures of a relatively inexpensive sort, done usually in a very traditional idiom. Popular or fashionable artists, like the Ghirlandaio in Florence and the Bellini in Venice, by taking in more commissions and profits, could also enlist more assistants or apprentices, with the result that their *botteghe* turned out a larger volume of work. Architects and sculptors engaged in a good deal of sub-contracting, which took care of the more menial or routine parts of their commissions. Casting in bronze, for example, was not often done by the sculptor himself.

The traditions of the late-medieval workshop prepared craftsmen for a rich variety of jobs, and the age produced tremendously versatile men who might combine goldsmithery with sculpture, painting, and a knowledge of engineering solutions. Versatility was a measure of the artist's eagerness to satisfy patrons and make a name for himself.

Allowing for flexibility in the following categories, we discern three types of artists: the itinerant worker, the sort who stayed at home, and the worker at court. The "courtiers" are the easiest to single out: Pisanello, Mantegna, Tura, Cossa, Roberti, Piero della Francesca, Raphael, Leonardo, Michelangelo, and others. But most of these men also traveled, the last four extensively, and worked in more than one court. Among the more successful "nomads" were Gentile da Fabriano, Donatello, Jacopo della Quercia, Signorelli, the Pollaiuolo brothers, and Perugino. But these too break ranks: the Florentines, Donatello and the Pollaiuolo, spent long years in Florence. Ghiberti, Fra Angelico, the Bicci, Giovanni di Paolo, Botticelli, Giovanni Bellini, and the Ghirlandaio all answer more to the description of the stay-at-home artist, though, again, some of these executed major commissions abroad.

Travel was exceedingly important for the fortunes of fifteenth-century art in that it diffused style and artistic manner. No artist could finally say, therefore, that he was unaware of the incoming or dominant trends. And this was no less true of important patrons, who also did much traveling.

If we try to compare the material success of the three different groups—and there was much overlapping—the victory goes to the "courtiers." Attachment to a court, when it lasted, brought continuous work and some kind of security, even when compensation was grossly in arrears. Leonardo and

Raphael, and later Giulio Romano, were handsomely rewarded. But there was no discernible difference in overall earnings between the travelers and the more stay-at-home bodies. Often the former were keenly sought after; they had reputations and could attract commissions from afar. Some more sedentary artists, like Ghiberti and the Bicci, had enough work at home for many years. But the artists who failed to obtain commissions at home either suffered or were forced to go abroad, even if they were unknown. The essential thing was to work, and leaving home to do so, for years at a time, could be the lot even of artists of the first rank, such as Masaccio, Donatello, Domenico Veneziano, Perugino, the aging Carpaccio, and many others. Besides, when the call came from a great patron, such as a pope, a duke of Milan, or a merchant prince, it was best in all ways to accept the invitation.

The life of court artists did not necessarily fall into routines and well-defined activities. There were too many needs and changing whims at court. The "courtiers" worked in fresco, on wood, and on canvass; they did portraits, devotional pieces, and large mundane groups in elaborate architectural settings; they painted flags, banners, furniture, stage settings, arms, and horse trappings; they designed festal decorations, costumes, masks, and other accouterments; and they made designs for textiles and for woven or embroidered fabrics to be used as bench covers, bed quilts, and door curtains. At Ferrara, Cosimo Tura made models for goldsmiths and worked as a decorative sculptor in the Este villa of Belriguardo.

All in all, then, artists scurried around to obtain commissions. Exceptionally, Lorenzo Ghiberti and Giovanni Bellini were most successful at home; indeed, the former—a shrewd toady with superiors and probably a bully with those under him—was also influential in the assignment of Florentine civic commissions. But on the whole, it was the modest men who tended to stay at home, where they handled small local jobs. The more ambitious and able sought major commissions at home and abroad, usually being more successful abroad. Security, fame, and honor were chiefly to be garnered at the courts. And if modest talents had to cater to the local taste of people with small sums to spend, it follows that leading artists, on a major commission that might require several years' work, had to be responsive to the wishes of their patrons. Working under very strained relations must have been, after all, unusual. Like Jacopo della Quercia, artists sometimes fled from a job or were simply dismissed. But at the princely courts service was the keynote: you did what was expected of you.

The power of patronage in Renaissance art—its power to influence, to decide, and to reject—has not been stressed enough in scholarship. Most art historians, for better and worse, have made an occupation of concentrating on artistic personalities. This emphasis has been so pronounced at times as to make us believe that one artist—e.g., Pisanello, Leonardo, or Giorgione— could *impose* his manner on a princely court or on the taste of a generation. Arguably, the movement of taste is just the other way around. Communities seize upon an idea, a style, a manner or a point of view, and give it a visible existence by their acceptance of it, thus enabling it to surface *as* history; but they seize and accept it only when it endorses or flatters vital interests and group identities.

SOCIAL IDENTITY INTO ARTISTIC STYLE

The critical point in the sociology of art centers on the way in which artists convert social experience into a figurative language. It is what happens when a way of seeing, as a function of social structure and social change, finds its expression in style. Art is what we have always thought it was, but it is also a mysterious social language.

From about 1300, with Giotto and his followers, the direction of painting, as it advanced from the early to the high Renaissance, was in the so-called imitation of "nature" (*il vero*). The aim along this track was to depict everyday things more or less as they seem to present themselves to the eye. But this entailed incalculable difficulties, for the enterprise required learning how to create the illusion of space in the picture, modeling rounded figures and planting them firmly on the ground plane, watching the sources and play of light (chiaroscuro), understanding foreshortening, and giving more care to the study of human anatomy. Beyond this, the quest for *il vero* depended upon the ability to render movement and emotions via gesticulation and vivid facial expression.

Change of this magnitude presupposes a fundamental change in perception and only comes, evidently, with the historical emergence of a new view of reality; it comes with the decline of one social order and the ascent of another. For our subject is not only a radical change in artistic style but also the larger underlying transformation, the overturning of a whole structure of assumptions.

Down to the third decade of the fifteenth century, the main opposition to the imitation of *il vero* was another, more traditional style. This was based upon the heavy use of symbolic color (chiefly blue and gold), the hieratic placing of figures on a more or less flattened picture space, determination of the sizes of figures and objects by their symbolic values, and then, as from the later fourteenth century—in the style's International Gothic phase—on a spiraling fluidity of linear forms and swaying rhythms. But neither style was pure, neither the emerging new one nor the one which adhered to the old conventions. Each had elements of the other. Tradition in the art workshop was deeply rooted; subject matter was almost entirely religious—hence set to a conservative key—and the vanguard of development had to await the fifteenth-century changes in social consciousness.

The visual revolution brought in by Giotto's generation belongs to the victory of the city and commune in the life of the age. Thus the popularity in religious narrative of urban scenes and scenes just outside cities. More particularly, the Giottesque style caught the self-assurance and practicality of those who lived by trade, stood at the head of the commune, and reached out in aggressive control over the countryside. Their eye was keyed to a religious symbolism, but now it also desired and took delight in everyday images. This was the revolution of Giotto's time. His human forms and those in the *oeuvre* of his followers are the *popolani* of the communal age at the summit of its economic and demographic expansion. The leading patrons of art in Giotto's time—guilds, rich individuals, religious corporations, and communal chieftains—wanted the lessons of religion illustrated in a more mundane fashion and they wanted to see more of the Christ, more of His life story. It was no longer enough to illustrate religious mysteries by means of symbolic, "essential," and flat forms; now something of the life around had to be got into the picture space. This mime is what struck contemporaries and what fifteenth-century observers saw when they turned to the work of Giotto and his school.

Frederick Antal argued that the new taste was the result of a rationalist view of the world, more specifically of the *popolano*'s tendency, particularly as seen in the merchant bankers at the head of the commune, to de-emphasize irrational or mystic elements in the conditions of existence, in order to have a field of apprehension that was more understandable and controllable. It remains to add, rather changing the emphasis, that the new taste was also a function of the *popolano*'s vigor, of his will to bring the message of Christ into a closer, more practical contact with urban life. This meant a line of roundabout self-images, notably in more *popolano*-like madonnas and saints, rather than the old idiom for rendering the hypnotic and static essences of the Italo-Byzantine style, the *maniera greca* (Fig. 1); it meant scenes from urban life more than hierarchies of angels. The bold new painting of about 1290 and after had an upper-class "optic" because it stemmed from a triumphant revolution in perception, and triumph in Florence, Siena, Bologna, and some other cities belonged to the merchants, bankers, and big guildsmen who had won the great thirteenth-century social struggles for power. Appropriately, the new way of seeing involved an optimistic and more worldly Christianity, fully articulated in the monumental and dramatic forms of the Giottesque style. Art historians have often referred to Giotto's "heroic" manner: this is a strikingly apt characterization of the social calligraphy of the style.

By the outset of the fifteenth century, figurative expression had gone beyond Giotto (in Maso, Avanzo, and Menabuoi) in the representation of three-dimensional space and the modeling of forms in the round. In sculpture the freak accomplishments of the Pisani had not again been matched.

John White has demonstrated that the exploration of pictorial space remained a challenge for fourteenth-century painting, that spatial perception made a gradual advance, and that most effective solutions relied upon the use of architectural borderings, such as the interiors of large rooms, arcades, or a framework of buildings and city streets: what in effect amounts to urban space from the viewpoint of this study. The understanding and mastery of three-dimensional space proved to be remarkably difficult and came slowly.

Although most patrons around 1400 seem to have been satisfied with the curvilinear rhythms and swaying forms of the International style, there was also a demand for more rounded space and solid, weighted forms. At Florence, about 1410, this was expressed in the work of sculptors—Ghiberti, Donatello, and Nanni di Banco. Then, rather suddenly, the 1420s saw a surge of new plastic forms and a finer, more rationalized grasp of spatial values in painting and narrative bas-reliefs: accomplishments associated with the names of Donatello, Brunelleschi, Masaccio, and Masolino. The supreme achievement of this breakthrough was the representation of the human figure in an amplitude of space, in such a manner as to heighten its qualities and dignity.

Between 1399 and 1427, thirty-four over-life-size statues of prophets and saints appeared in the heart of Florence, in the most eminent niches of the cathedral and Orsanmichele.[2] At least fifteen of the thirty-four may be ranked as vanguard pieces, the first in a full Renaissance style, and these have been associated with the conditions of a drawn-out political crisis: the Florentine republic's all-out resistance to the advancing armies of despotism, sent first by the Visconti (1390s–1402, 1420s) and then by King Ladislaus of Naples (1409–1414). Intended for public view at two of the city's three main points and commissioned almost entirely by the leading guilds, "the race of heroes that populated the center of the city" gave evidence of the concentration and energies of the Florentine citizenry. The statues at Orsanmichele were "the guardians of the guilds in the maintenance of the Republic, and its spiritual defenders in the battle for the survival of free institutions. As such, they partake of the *virtus* and *probitas* which were the ideal of the Florentine citizen." In this view, Donatello's powerful vision helped to alter the course of painting in the 1420s, which saw the sudden emergence of the new style, partly in Gentile da Fabriano but especially in Masaccio and Masolino, with Angelico, Lippi, and Uccello following fast in the 1430s.

Interestingly, although cast in a thoroughly idealistic mode, the foregoing argument finds the origins of the Renaissance style in a political crisis, and more particularly in the republican ideals adduced by Florence to face and fight tyranny. The dignity of Donatello's freestanding statues and the controlled (perspective) viewpoint of his St. George bas-relief go to embody the ideal of individual freedom, and this too was a central point in Florentine republican ideals, as enunciated by the humanist Leonardo Bruni. By implication, therefore, the rise of the individual portrait, the portrait bust, the new amplitude of space in three-dimensional painting, and the birth of one-point perspective all go back in their immediate origins to Florentine republican ideals.

This astonishing interpretation may not be so far-fetched as it is likely to seem in this summary, if we substitute *ideology* for the more idealistic notion of *ideals*.

Whatever the slogans coined by Florence and her humanist chancellors in the struggle to keep Tuscany from being dragged under one-man rule, the city's mercantile oligarchy was driven to save itself, to preserve its own supremacy both in Tuscany and the city. The cynicism of the republic's chancellors[3] was matched by the oligarchy's cynical policies toward Pisa and republican Lucca, and later on toward the Ambrosian republic. But in rousing support for its political struggle, one so costly that the city's fiscal machine reeled nearly out of control in the 1420s and early 1430s, the Florentine ruling class naturally put its claims in the best possible light. Since when do oligarchies go around confessing to their narrowest interests? At the critical moments, the most callous oligarchs believed in their fine rhetoric and the rectitude of their awakened passions. Emergency generated illusionary ideals that aimed at uniting a divided and troubled Florentine community.

The Renaissance statue and the statuesque in Renaissance painting, with the concomitant mastery of pictorial space, were born in part from ideals and feelings gathered around a struggle for the survival of the Florentine patriciate. All leading guilds and one at least of the lesser ones—the armorers who commissioned Donatello's *St. George*—were deeply affected by the wars against the Visconti and Ladislaus. The city's political schisms were healed in the visual language of the sculpted "race of heroes," whose religious themes and strong civic overtones seemed to put community ideals and energies above faction and disagreement. During much of the period between 1393 and 1434, the city was a turmoil of political feeling. The array of statues pointed up the will and focused ardor of the guild community in its final display of political resolution. Guilds in Florence would never again have political clout. Their assertive civic activity, as expressed in their support of the period's great architectural and sculptural commissions, was their swan song. Caught in a series of hauntingly expensive wars in defense of "republican liberty," government and oligarchy found and brandished ideals, however illusory and self-interested, that stimulated humanism and art.

Although a spontaneous cluster of ideals was a major force in the sudden emergence of the Renaissance style, the style's fecundity and the requirements of patrons moved it immediately away from its ideological moorings and adapted it to other tastes and more enduring interests.

Our subject is, in effect, the identity of the Florentine ruling class, its self-awareness and state of mind during a generation of emergency which subverted Florentine political institutions. For the rise of the Medici house came out of the fiscal and political nightmares of the 1420s and 1430s. Using the solvent of a republican ideology, the oligarchy stood up to the dangers, external and internal; and in the tight topography of the city's small urban space, the array of "heroic" statues, like Masaccio's brooding forms, could take on the aspect of self-images, mirroring the idealized self of the city's leading groups. Indeed, sometime in 1426 or 1427, in the same Carmelite church that holds the *Tribute Money* (Fig. 5), Masaccio seems to have executed a group portrait of contemporary oligarchs, in a fresco destroyed by fire in the late eighteenth century. Within a decade Alberti enunciated the dictum that man, as anatomical figure, is the measure of all things within the picture space. At a stroke, symbolic size and hieratic essences had been swept away.

As in humanism, so in Renaissance art Roman classical motifs and themes became prominent. This involved the imitation of classical heads and stances, as in Masaccio's *Tribute Money*; bolder forms, as in the new statuary; and the depiction of pediments, triumphal arches, columns, pilasters, cornices, and coffered ceilings. Art and humanism at the princely courts found ways to draw upon classical antiquity and especially upon imperial Rome. But the art prepared for the republican upper classes, first at Florence and then at Venice, also longed for association with an eventful and glorious past. Republicans sought sanctions, precedents, and principles in classical antiquity as a way of clarifying and asserting their identity as leaders; so also the men in princely courts.

Since the birth of the Renaissance style has been linked in part with an ideology, it will be well to restate the case.

1. In a time of great political and social distress for Florence, guilds and patriciate plunged into the vigorous support of major commissions: thirty-four over-life-size statues, the Baptistery's bronze doors, the cathedral's cupola, and the Foundling Hospital. All were produced or started in an atmosphere of civil tension and fiscal sacrifice, and all involved the civic pride of the Florentines, who soon boasted about them.

2. Using the dignity of the state and exploiting traditional animosities, such as against Pisa and Lucca, the ruling group sought to unify Florence, while being itself often divided in its views of foreign dangers, taxation, and the Florentine middle classes. The result, as in the chancellors Salutati and Bruni, and less coherently in simpler folk, was an ideology of militant republicanism with a note of universality that could have no basis in social reality. Exaggerated idealisms are inevitable in times of momentous stress and need, when government is forced to call upon the larger community.

3. Florence was caught up in the fusionist process of having recourse to ideals that seemed to overcome rifts in the body politic and served to defend the community from external threat. Artists also were caught up in the civic fervor. Whereupon turning to earlier models—e.g., Giotto, Roman sculpture—that buttressed intuitions of the new direction, a few artists made

the breakthrough. They developed techniques for catching images, frequently idealized, from the pantheon of daily life. The celebration of earthly existence, whether through religious or secular imagery, could now be complete. And soon enough, in Filippo Lippi and a host of others, representations of the Madonna would be little more than more graceful versions of the daughters and young wives, at times the mistresses, of contemporaries. But the breakthrough came by way of a mystification: an anxious puffing up of ideals whose supposed universality was negated in oligarchic realities.

Donatello's *St. George* (Fig. 7, 1415–1417), vanquisher of the beast, idealizes the period's republican ideology, and we glimpse the Viscontean serpent in the tail of the dragon. Ghiberti's *St. John the Baptist* (1412–1416), Donatello's *St. Mark* (1411–1413), and Nanni di Banco's *Four Martyrs* (ca. 1413) capture also in idealized form the independent spirit, force of leadership, and dignity of sacrifice in the Florence of those years.

In that decade too, Brunelleschi, Donatello, and perhaps others rummaged through the ruins of Rome, studying fragments of classical sculpture and measuring columns, arches, and cornices. Like their wealthy patrons, they were testing themselves against Roman models, eager to imitate the things that seemed to bear tellingly upon their own experience. We saw this in the humanists. And like them, Donatello, Brunelleschi, Masaccio, Ghiberti, and many others found classical Rome in themselves; they found their own aspirations in their conception of Rome. Both Christ and the self-association with the power whose triumphs rang down the ages are underlined by means of the hypnotic arch and coffered ceiling in Masaccio's *Trinity* (Fig. 6), which shows against Corinthian pilasters the profiles of the two donors, Lorenzo Lenzi and his wife. Lorenzo (at left) wears the dress of Florence's supreme executive dignity.

Quite possibly the most influential painter of the fifteenth century, Masaccio was associated with everything that made for the new style: man-based proportions, one-point perspective, nudes, portraits, deep modeling, gesture, and smart effects of foreshortening. All spoke for remarkable control of his medium, and, like Giotto, he worked with great rapidity. He executed a life-size nude man and woman which Vasari saw in the house of a Florentine patrician, Palla Rucellai. Another lost work, already mentioned, a fresco once in the Carmelite church, linked artists and oligarchs in a procession on the occasion of the church's consecration. Brunelleschi, Donatello, and Masolino were the masters shown; the statesmen were Felice Brancacci, Niccolò da Uzzano, Giovanni Bicci de' Medici, Bartolommeo Valori, and Lorenzo Ridolfi; "and not only did he [Masaccio] draw all these notable men from life but also the door of the convent and the porter with the keys in his hand" (Vasari). His *Tribute Money* (Fig. 5) in the Brancacci chapel, done in a time of acute fiscal distress for Florence, is so austere that it must have been unsettling and may well have driven off prospective patrons: Masaccio was seeing too incisively, too truly. Christ tells Peter to find the tax money in the mouth of a fish in Lake Galilee and commands him to pay it to the Roman tax collector. The fresco is a sermon on paying to the state what is the state's; it may also be suggesting that the Church should make contributions to government to help defend the community. In making such an unusual commission, the patron of the chapel, Felice Brancacci, a respected political figure, was evidently moved by a strong sense of civic feeling, but he balanced the theme of payment to the state with other frescoes in the same chapel, showing the distribution of alms to the poor and St. Peter healing the crippled with his shadow (Fig. 4). As the scenes hauntingly suggest, Florence had a large number of paupers and unemployed people, known as "the wretched" (*miserabili*) in the famous Florentine tax census of 1426–1427.

Late in 1428, Masaccio himself died in debt and poor in Rome. He had failed to attract the necessary commissions in Florence. Why this was so must forever be conjecture, because the record is silent. But there is plausibility in the argument that his work was not pretty enough, not elegant enough, not acceptably enough idealized in its treatment of faces and themes. He had all the mastery and craft needed to flatter, to play, to delight the eye with baubles, gold, and rich trappings. He performed this way at least once, probably on demand, in parts of the Pisa polyptych (1426), particularly in the *Adoration of the Magi* (Fig. 3), with its portrait of the donors. But that which Masaccio would not or could not do, others, learning from him, were ready to carry out—Fra Angelico, Fra Filippo Lippi, Mantegna—and their patrons were well pleased with them.

Arnold Hauser's well-known distinction between the middle-class and courtly styles of Renaissance art has some utility. It also raises problems, the major one having to do with the overlapping or crossing-over of tastes. Renaissance Italy had a marked degree of artistic cosmopolitanism, as illustrated, for example, by Gentile da Fabriano (d. 1427), who painted for princes as well as for republican oligarchs. Much the same may be said of Jacopo della Quercia, Piero della Francesca, Perugino, Signorelli, the Pollaiuolo, Raphael, Michelangelo, and Titian. But once we have attached an artistic manner to a social identity, "courtly" or "bourgeois," how do we explain in *social* terms any fusion of artistic manners?

If in the realm of militant political ideas, basic points or emphases are borrowed between mutually hostile camps, as when national socialism took the principle of mass organization from the communists, all the more so in art may aspects of style be borrowed from one taste to serve the aims of another. This does not mean that the two tastes converge and become one. It means only that they have points in common. Though tastes may issue from differing group identities, patrons from different groups are likely to share a common viewpoint *in some matters* because they live in the same social universe.

Florence's artistic revolution came out of conditions of extreme political and social stress, but once it was launched, it could be and was mediated to satisfy contrasting tastes, including taste at the princely courts. As mediation, the marmoreal heroics of an artist such as Mantegna served the boastful aims of taste in the Gonzaga court of Mantua. The new style was resourceful: drawing upon the art of antiquity because the Quattrocento found images of itself there, the new style now commanded the panoply of resources required to reshape architecture and cater to the varied demands of patronage.

The fundamental fact for the sociology of Renaissance art was the changing identity of upper-class groups, a changing constitutive consciousness. This process centered on a view of themselves and the world; it involved a transformation in both self-awareness and outlook. The claim that elite identity was fundamental to the fortunes of Renaissance art presupposes two other claims: that the activity of the upper classes was decisive for the production of art, and that we must plot changes in consciousness in order to get at the direction of artistic style. The first of these has already been treated; the second follows.

The transformation in upper-class identity was keyed to changes in society. The fifteenth century recorded a growing concentration of wealth; more land and capital ended in fewer hands; entry into trade required larger disbursements of capital; credit was tighter and business risks increased. Patterns of marriage became more conservative, as exemplified in the trend toward later marriage and the upper-class demand for bigger dowries and stronger, more endogamous marriage alliances. In government and politics, the groups at the top planted themselves more firmly, drew increasingly away from the middle classes, and developed a deeper self-assurance, threatened only in moments of danger triggered by war. This overall process of social crystallization went with an intensification of the claims to family antiquity and lineage, with the result that the elite groups experienced an ever stronger sense of their being special, different, more elevated.

The fifteenth century brought a boom in the construction of family *palazzi* (palaces). At Florence the upswing started in the later fourteenth century. From about the 1440s the princely courts also entered into a long-lasting cycle of major building or rebuilding schemes, involving both older *palazzi* and new villas, but here the resolution to build on a large scale went back for a generation or two. Outside some of the cities, as in the Bolognese, old castles were occasionally converted into hunting lodges and villas. It was a time of stability, especially after midcentury. Recent scholarship has noted that in the 1400s, Florence alone was the site of about a hundred new *palazzi*. Even if reduced by a third, the figure is astounding when we consider that in 1427 the city had only about 10,000 taxpaying households. Signs of the building craze were evident elsewhere, too, as at Ferrara, Siena, Bologna, Milan, and Venice. And private wealth in the last two cities exceeded the like of anything seen in Florence. At Milan the families Borromeo, Vimercati, Parravicini, Fontana, Marliani, Atellani, Dal Verme, Pozzobonelli, Grifi, and

Simonetta all built new *palazzi*. Among the new palaces built in Venice, suffice it to list those of the Foscari, Contarini Fasan, Corner Spinelli, Marin Contarini (ca d'Oro), Dario, and Vendramin Calergi. Equally important in identifying the new consciousness is the evidence of widespread redecoration and renovation in old family *palazzi*, as in the addition of new rooms, new wings, or the reappointment of the internal space.

The flaring desire for more ample and ordered household spaces was not a mere quest on the part of the rich ruling classes for increased physical comfort, unless things are merely what they seem. In the twelfth and early thirteenth centuries, the nobility had erected soaring towers to serve their military needs, but they were also an effective visual propaganda and mode of self-assertion; they were the nobility's testament of energy and dominance, and the matter of comfort in them was an afterthought or no thought at all. So, in the fifteenth century, the search for comfort as such was not foremost. Urban upper classes know how to procure this. And comfort is, in any case, relative.

The Quattrocento building and rebuilding craze was the very process of elite consciousness, redefining itself in terms of new needs, new pursuits and satisfactions. In this process, the needs of an emerging new identity were primary: they took the form of a growing resolution to remake or reshape the things around, and first of all the old domestic interiors and exteriors, the great blocks of stone inhabited by the upper-class groups. In effect, this was a quest for greater control over immediate environments. Princes, oligarchs, and rich men desired to rearrange the main objects in their field of vision. They sought to affirm themselves by means of more imposing *palazzi*, more organized and splendid facades, wider and higher internal spaces, a display of finer manual work of all sorts (from marquetry to hammered metal and leather), a higher finish to things, more rounded edges and polished surfaces, and larger accumulations of objects. There was an escalating taste for grander arches and doorways, carved chimney pieces, coffered ceilings, polychrome ceramic floors, wall hangings, marble plaques, armorial bearings on polychrome enameled terra-cotta, new kinds of sideboards (*credenze*), racks for caps and headpieces, and colorful earthenware (*maiolica*). These new furnishings and decorations were, taken in their entirety, the outward signs of inward change. They accorded perfectly with the sharp rise, in the fifteenth century, of fancier and fussier styles of dress, which required finer handiwork. Social classes work the signature of their identities into their possessions and surroundings. And the changing social identity profiled above was one ever more intent on its authority and on forms of display; it was turning more worldly, more refined, more ostentatious, more boastful. We call this "secularization," that near-synonym for the Italian Renaissance; it was the processing of experience along more worldly lines, the process itself of elite and upper-class consciousness.

By the 1480s, princes and wealthy men were collecting maps of countries, as well as paintings and drawings of different cities, such as Venice,

Paris, Genoa, Cairo, Jerusalem, Florence, and Rome. This aspect of the new worldliness was yet another, if more roundabout, manifestation of the higher certitude and increased assertiveness of the urban ruling groups, as they looked around themselves in rivalry, envy, curiosity, self-satisfaction, and acquisitive bent.

The changing identity of the upper-class groups could have no other form than that of an altered consciousness. Filtering through patronage, it transformed art by making new demands on it.

The portrait was the key subject of the new consciousness. Patrons longed to see themselves and those important to them. The demand grew. Every major sculptor and painter produced portrait busts and portraits, sometimes groups of portraits in fresco. In the fourteenth century, profile portraits of donors were occasionally entered, very subordinately, into religious pictures. The equestrian statue of Cangrande della Scala (1330s) stuns us by its remarkably early date. After 1420, portraits edge their way toward the center of religious narrative, as in works by Masaccio, Gozzoli, Fra Filippo, Perugino, Piero della Francesca, Pinturicchio, Botticelli, Ghirlandaio, Carpaccio, and Raphael. There was also a rising and then rocketing demand for individual portraits and portrait busts. The second half of the century saw a traffic in portraits of dignitaries and princes, done on wood and canvas. The latter could be rolled around a rod and easily transported.

The advancing edge of change in art, the vanguard vision, was in the imitation of everyday reality. This is why the portrait was the key subject: in its resolve to copy "nature," portraiture provided the standard of reality and roused the impulse to catch the immediate world around the sitter. The young Donatello built his fame on his realism. Masaccio, Ghiberti, Uccello, Pisanello, Fra Filippo, Domenico Veneziano—most of the vanguard masters of the age—were portraitists of the first rank. This was more strikingly true—Michelangelo being perhaps the only exception—of the masters of the High Renaissance. But in the fifteenth century, the portrait was the attempt *par excellence* to capture the face of contemporary reality; it was a pragmatic coming-to-terms with actual appearance and surfaces. It depended upon a vision of things that did not, however, come forth in isolation. The vision was related directly to the new domineering view of reality;[4] it was related to the growing concentration of wealth and power, which went to enhance the self-confidence of the upper-class groups; and it was part of the building and renovation craze, as princes, oligarchs, and rich men enlarged and reappointed their domestic environments, at the same time moving out, with their larger *palazzi*, to claim more and more of the urban space. The attendant view of reality—as glimpsed, for example, in militant humanism—was poised, optimistic, and imperious. In epistemological terms, it was a view that took reality to inhere in the everyday world of affairs and manifest sensations. Nature, *as that which is looked upon every day*, was deemed benign by the groups at the top. It was to be considered so until about 1500, when the concussion of foreign invasion shattered the reigning view of reality and the track of upper-class consciousness veered again.

Next in importance to the portrait, in Quattrocento painting, was a more general subject already stipulated in detailed contracts of the second quarter of the century. Patrons desired images or views taken "from life," such as cities, domestic interiors, street scenes, rivers, and mountains. Although an effort to render these had been made by earlier painting, there had been no real program for getting the artist to work "from nature," as is clear from the formula for invented landscapes in Cennini's *Il libro dell'arte*.

The call for portraits and for images of the life around confronted the artistic imagination with such specific demands that the Renaissance style, with Florentine events as the trigger, was born in this way. No matter that the main themes in painting and sculpture remained predominantly religious; the manner of representation became ever more lifelike. For the source of decisive patronage, the changed consciousness of the upper-class groups, was, as we have found, strongly assertive and self-confident, above all with regard to its place and authority in the world. This explains the remarkable surge of imposing new houses and villas—the true triumphal arches of the victors. In the full Quattrocento world, princes and oligarchs, the rich as well as the privileged, exhibit a heightened hope and confidence in the surrounding world. They believe in their ability to govern and enjoy it, even to impose their will upon it; and so they call for images of themselves and *their* world, the city and neighboring countryside. This self-assured view of reality has its expression—for all their differing manners—in the luminous clairvoyance and hyperorganized rationalism of Uccello, Castagno, Veneziano, Piero della Francesca, Mantegna, Perugino, Antonello, Giovanni Bellini, and Carpaccio. Frederick Hartt has said of Piero, apropos of the Montefeltro portraits, that he "shows man in complete control of nature." This is particularly true of the famous *Flagellation* (Fig. 11), with its cold and radiant geometry. In one way or another, all the designated artists show man in control of nature. For perhaps two generations (ca. 1440–1500), princes and ruling classes shared a kindred vision of the world; it came forth from their bold self-confidence and it imbued humanism with the passionate belief that men could truly imitate the achievements of antiquity and draw positive, applicable precepts from the lessons of history. And the artistic reminiscences of classical Rome, whether in the stances of painted figures or in architectural motifs, served to glorify the present, the *us* of the present, by linking *us* to an impressive and much-admired past.

The history of Renaissance art tracks the changing consciousness of the social groups at the forefront of urban life.

MANNER AND STYLE

We have seen something about how social views and values may be so altered as to have decisive effects upon artistic content and style. Social identity is the mediator: it transforms social views into an imaginative geometry, or finds correspondences in visual and literary imaginings.

The advancing art of the Renaissance will be considered here in terms of one style and a variety of manners. In this view, Masaccio, Piero, and Mantegna worked within the same general style but had different manners, reflecting differences in time, circumstance, and personality.

Down to about 1500 or 1510, the advancing style had its lineaments in the endeavor to get close to "nature"—to imitate, replicate, or mirror it. By 1520 a new style had emerged, centering on the desire to rival or even to improve upon nature, but often distorting it and in any case drawing away from it, away from an easy or assured commitment to the shapes and surfaces of the everyday world. In the Quattrocento, on the contrary, the leading masters' commitment to nature as quotidian reality set the general guidelines. This is why art historians have often referred to the "pedestrian realism" of much Quattrocento painting. Writing his *Speculum lapidum* in 1502, C. Leonardi inadvertently summed up the leading fifteenth-century ideal: "Mantegna has demonstrated for posterity every rule and kind of painting . . . he can, in the twinkling of an eye, draw the figures of men and animals of every age and kind, as also the customs, dress and gestures of various peoples in such a way that they almost seem to move." To the artists and theorists of the middle and later sixteenth century, such painting was dry, prosaic, and literal-minded.

If we see the commitment to ordinary appearance (*natura*) as providing the standard for the advancing style of the fifteenth century, then what do we say about Sienese painting before 1440, or, for that matter, about painting and sculpture at Venice, Bologna, or Genoa during the first half of the fifteenth century? Such questions misconstrue the aims of this discussion. The unconscious focus of many art historians is the conscious center of attention here: the artistic vanguard, the advancing edge of change that began at Florence with the generation of Donatello and Masaccio. This is an attempt to explain the process and direction of artistic change, not traditional or dilatory taste. The upper-class transformation of identity was in process, and some cities or groups of men went through it sooner than others. In most cities the traditional views and tastes long persisted, or gave way only in part to the new and more purposive vision of quotidian reality.

Down to 1440 and beyond, with some exceptions, taste and painting at Siena looked back for models to the great Sienese masters of the fourteenth century and to the graces of International Gothic: to color symbolic and expensive, to an elegantly curving line, an inchoate pictorial space, and mystical subjects mystically treated (e.g., saints bigger than trees or city walls). In the hands of Giovanni di Paolo and Sani di Pietro, perspective became decoration rather than a means of charting objects in space. As a school for art, quotidian nature and appearance did not easily win the certification of the Sienese ruling groups. The four or five political blocs in government were too heterogeneous and unsure of themselves, overly subject to decisive pressures from Florence and especially Rome, forced to cleave to cautious policies, and always confronted economically by the business establishments of Lucca and of larger cities, like Florence and Milan. The plastic dynamism and heroic idiom of the sculptor Jacopo della Quercia (d. 1438) were out of place in these circumstances. We need not doubt the allegations concerning his difficult and proud personality. His true competitors were in Florence. He returned from Bologna to his native Siena, probably to be ill at ease, and perhaps it took a knighthood to hold him there. The Sienese used his talents but converted the ardor and power of his forms (Fig. 8), one suspects, into a compensatory heroism. Appropriately enough, as John Pope-Hennessy has observed, "Sienese painting in the fifteenth century developed under an external stimulus and not under an impetus provided from within."

Arguably, upper-class Venice should have held the front line of changing consciousness and worldly taste. Powerful, successful, and ruled by a proud nobility preoccupied with the building of a mainland empire, Venice was the most suitable ground for an optimistic encounter with "nature," whether on the sea, in the conquered Venetian hinterland, or in the city, which was built on sandbars and piles. In Venice, if anywhere, despite the advance of the Ottoman Turks, the ruling class could afford to glory in the world it had made and controlled. Something like this was in fact to be seen, but in a roundabout, devious fashion. The purposive force which had shaped much of Venice remained attached to a religious grammar. That force was a patriciate which had managed, with a ballast of strong religious ideals, to scour the seas, to turn every chance to profit, to keep a singleminded vision, and to preserve devotion for the large family unit. A traditional religious faith worked, paradoxically, to license commercial and political ruthlessness, and there was no reason to discard that which had always worked.

The dilution of the Venetian nobility's religious grammar—the transformation of identity—came in the fifteenth century. Very gradual to begin with, the process was best seen, at first, in the humanism of members of the patriciate, as they turned to antiquity and the literary classics for a divergent ideal, a new civic perspective, a more mundane Christianity. After 1450, the change proceeded with great swiftness, and within a generation Venetian art and humanism "caught up" with accomplishments at Florence. At Venice, however, the frank encounter with reality as everyday appearance lasted hardly more than a generation: it is in evidence in some of the better-known pictures by Gentile Bellini, Carpaccio, and Giovanni Mansueti. Then the artistic and more fasionable imagination swerved off into pronounced degrees of idealization, as in the work of Giovanni Bellini, Giorgione, and Titian.

Quattrocento Genoa presented a spectacle of political vacillation and instability, as it passed back and forth between French and Milanese hegemony. Right up to 1500 the Genoese nobility was too weak, too divided, to hold unquestioned authority. The major art commissions went to outsiders, above all to Lombard masters who worked in a conservative and traditional vein. Then, in the second half of the Quattrocento, with Vincenzo Foppa, Giovanni Mazzone, and Carlo Braccesco, monied Genoa inclined increasingly toward the marmoreal surfaces and lapidary "realism" of the North Italian courtly manner. Not until the resurgence of the nobility in the early sixteenth century, and with the coming to Genoa of Raphael's pupils, Giulio Romano and especially Perin del Vaga, was Genoese upper-class taste seen to turn emphatically worldly. The turn, however, favored mannerist forms—rhetoric, grandeur, ultra-idealization, and technical brilliance. These were the compensatory solutions, pitched on an aesthetico-moral plane, to the horrendous political strains that gripped the peninsula's upper classes in the age of the Italian Wars.

Siena, Venice, and Genoa illustrate the power of local resistance to the vanguard style of the Quattrocento. Traceable in a line of artists from Donatello to Raphael, the style converted the reality of everyday forms and surfaces into a guiding standard. Masaccio, Mantegna, and Carpaccio, for example, worked very close to the standard; others, such as Piero della Francesca and Perugino, worked only a little farther away. But all took their bearings from it; all worked *in* the style: Donatello and Ghiberti (in their bas-reliefs), Masaccio, Fra Filippo, Gozzoli, Mantegna, Piero della Francesca, Pinturicchio, Verrocchio, Perugino, Antonio Pollaiuolo, Melozzo da Forlì, Antonello da Messina, Domenico Ghirlandaio, Gentile Bellini, Carpaccio, Mansueti, and Raphael (e.g., in the Doni portraits).

These artists have different manners, in some cases very different manners, but they also share a vision. They all executed portraits and provide glimpses of contemporary life; all studied the sources and modulations of light in the picture space; all render surfaces in high relief (*gran rilievo*), seek the contours of three-dimensional space, and have an eye for the governing value of the human body's proportions; finally, all strive for clarity and coherence. They suffer, if at all, from a kind of hyperorganization: a view of the world in which objects are perhaps too clearly depicted or too rationally disposed. And here at once we see that Fra Angelico, Domenico Veneziano, Francesco del Cossa, Botticelli, and the early Giovanni Bellini also belong to the list above.

If the Renaissance style of the Quattrocento is not easy to pin down, the age's variety of artistic manners may seem to present insuperable problems. Not so; but a finer mode of analysis is needed.

Characterized above all by its candid acceptance of everyday visual "truths" as the guiding standard, the Renaissance style was an expression of the vanguard currents in upper-class consciousness; it was the expression of a changing identity in an age when the groups at the top could afford so much self-confidence, as in the program of humanism, that they surrounded themselves boldly with self-images and pictorial reflections of their urban world. Boldly, too, they demanded more living space in their town houses and villas; and they set out to rearrange their field of vision, as well in their domestic interiors as in the beginnings of urban renewal. Their confident, humanizing Christianity held the implicit assumption that the world could be turned into a limpid and rational place, and thus be made more easily subject to the control of mind and authority, as in Venice's readiness to rearrange the political map of Italy or Ludovico Sforza's belief in his ability to orchestrate political destinies, and precisely as in the ordered clarities of the artistic style which reveals the identity of the ruling groups. All in all, the view was unflinchingly optimistic.

This confidence existed in the work of Gentile da Fabriano (d. 1427) and his pupil Pisanello (d. 1455), both of whom combined fresh interests with a late allegiance to the International Gothic style. Gentile's altarpiece (Fig. 19), done for a rich Florentine oligarch, Palla di Nofri Strozzi, teems with the images of cities, travel, cultivated fields, exotic animals, exotic dress, hounds, falcons, golden spurs, attendants, lowly grooms, ostentatious brocades, and a splash of gold-leaf paint: all the trappings of nobility, power, and money. Passages of bravura foreshortening point up the symbols of noble rank: richly harnessed horses, spurs, and birds of prey, while cities and their spectral power—the "signs of civilization"—appear everywhere. There is a similar assembly of aristocratic self-images in Pisanello's *St. George and the Princess*, painted for the Pellegrini chapel in St. Anastasia, Verona: hounds, foreshortened horses with resplendent harnessing, a striking elegance of line along the forehead and imposing headpiece of the princess, a hovering city with white towers, and in the upper left, hanging prominently from a gibbet, two corpses beside a turreted mass of urban masonry— as if the looming power of the signorial city had not already been asserted. The advancing style of the Quattrocento would take these scenes and do a more direct projection of them, in accordance with the new order of perception that drew its models from quotidian nature. In this enterprise, the group portrait was a subject always very near to the main guideline: thus, for example, Fra Filippo's *Obsequies for St. Stephen* (Prato, Duomo), Mantegna's fresco of the Gonzaga family (Fig. 17), Gozzoli's *Procession of the Magi* (Florence, Medici Palace), Cossa's portrait of Borso d'Este and his courtiers (Ferrara, Schifanoia), Melozzo da Forli's fresco of Pope Sixtus IV and his nephews (Fig. 16), Botticelli's *Purification of the Leper* (Vatican, Sistine Chapel), Gentile Bellini's *Procession in the Piazza San Marco* (Venice, Accademia), Domenico Ghirlandaio's frescoes in the Tornabuoni and Sassetti chapels (Florence), and Carpaccio's *A Miracle of the Relic of the True Cross* (Venice, Accademia). Even passages in Raphael's *Mass of Bolsena* (Vatican, Stanza d'Eliodoro), notably the group portraits on the right (Fig. 18), are amazingly close to the standard of Quattrocento realism.

The problem of "manner" remains. If we emphasize impersonal social processes, while yet allowing for differences among artistic personalities, how do we account for the variety of manners in Renaissance art? Here again we return to social identities, to their disguised or transmuted forms in artistic expression. The dominating Renaissance identities are, of course, upper class: "courtly," "aristocratic," "bourgeois." But there are also profiles that are more or less oligarchic, older or more parvenu, more land- or more trade-oriented, provincial or cosmopolitan; and all draw upon elements from the dominant identities, for the influence of these is strong and often decisive.

The Renaissance style of the Quattrocento is first fully delineated in Masaccio's Brancacci frescoes (Figs. 4, 5); but the manner is severe, direct, penetrating, vigorous—compelling and lyrical without being in the least rhetorical. In the 1420s, such realism was astounding for the few who understood but very likely baffling and even repellent—the idiom was strange—for most people even in Florence. The vision was an upper-class one: intellectual, rational, bold, an articulation in full control of the visual cone. It designated a clear and firm hold over the world that lay before the eyes of contemporaries. These qualities were linked in consciousness to the most enterprising, traveled, and self-confident part of the Florentine community, the political and commercial upper class. But there was nothing as yet aristocratic or courtly about this vision/style: for it did not include enough that was traditional and hence comfortable; it was too austere, that is, not playful, not dressed up, not "correctly" idealized; nor did it obviously flatter the patron, like the manner in Gentile da Fabriano's Strozzi altarpiece.

But the resources of the style were instrumental; in other hands, they could result in a flattering and fetching manner. Focused perspective, controlled light, modeling, studied anatomies, and right proportions: these were the means to project self-images. Masaccio himself titillated clients in his *Adoration of the Magi* (Fig. 3), where in the center right we see portraits of the patrons, the rich Pisan notary, Ser Giuliano degli Scarsi, and his son. To the display of horses and many spots of gold, the artist added late Gothic touches, as in certain heads and the gently elongated bodies of the two Pisans and standing magus. From between the heads of two horses, one groom strains flirtatiously to catch our eyes, really the painter's eye, as if also trying to catch his own reflection in a mirror. The effect, in a work of 1426, must have been startling.

The next generation of Florentine painters tamed the new style by softening its austerities and mixing it with more conventional accents. Fra Angelico, Fra Filippo, Uccello, Gozzoli, Baldovinetti, and Domenico Veneziano can manage Masaccio's sculptural modeling, controlled light, and three-dimensional spaces. They also, however, adduce a cheerful luminosity, dainty idealizations, and strong traditional elements, such as pretty Gothic heads and suavely elongated forms: the lot calculated to satisfy a rich clien-

tele's taste for optimism, for more conventional and familiar pieties, and for
the contours that were *necessarily* appealing because they reflected partly,
and partly idealized, an enclosed urban world which that clientele ruled and
enjoyed. Cosimo de' Medici (d. 1464) doled his favors out to Fra Angelico
and Fra Filippo. His son, Piero (d. 1469), who was no less astute, hired
Gozzoli, Uccello, Veneziano, and probably Baldovinetti. These were artists
of the first rank; history has judged them so; but they worked to taste.
Uccello's use of perspective went toward ornament; his orthogonals turned
into erudite entertainment. The three large panels of his playful and gay
Battle of San Romano (Fig. 13) ended quite rightly in the master bedroom
of the Medici palace. His *Hunt* (Oxford, Ashmolean) might also have ended
there, as did a picture on the same subject by Pesellino. Jousts and hunting,
celebrated by contemporary poets too, were among the most diverting pastimes of the Laurentian circle. Uccello's *Battle* and *Hunt* could be read as
social breviaries; they were also pure pleasure for Lorenzo, one of the earliest collectors to theorize about delight as the true end of painting.[5] Lorenzo
possessed portraits of the duke of Urbino, Duke Galeazzo Sforza of Milan,
the *condottieri* Francesco Sforza and Gattamelata, and a tapestry of the
duke of Burgundy on a hunt. Here were reflections, direct and devious, of
Lorenzo's preoccupation with power. In the 1470s and 1480s, he was the
near-lord of "republican" Florence.

By the 1450s the style invented in Florence was being adapted to courtly
and aristocratic tastes. The Italian upper classes were on an aristocratic
course, in republican as in signorial cities,[6] and it was natural for them, in
their self-assurance and deepening worldliness, to turn to the new style for
images of themselves, their surroundings, their patron saints, and their en-
throned Madonnas done up in lush brocades, precious stones, and attitudes
of refined detachment. This refracted or filtered quest for suitable self-
images gave rise to a varied manner especially fit for princely courts, for
merchant-bankers and oligarchs (who often numbered aristocrats and
princes among their friends), and for small-town noblemen (e.g., Perugians,
Marchigiani), who occasionally appeared at some of the courts.

Of the Quattrocento painters who gave much time to working for
princes and courtiers, Mantegna and Piero della Francesca—Leonardo da
Vinci apart—must count as the leading masters. Piero spent about three
years working for the Este at Ferrara and completed major works for the
lords of Rimini and Urbino. Mantegna was for forty-six years court painter
for the Gonzaga at Mantua. A group of lesser masters—Tura, Cossa,
Roberti—executed important fresco cycles, now mostly destroyed, at the
Este court of Ferrara. After 1470, Cossa moved on to serve the Bentivoglio
of Bologna, a lordly family, as well as the Griffoni and other prominent
Bolognese families. In Umbria and Tuscany, Pinturicchio, Signorelli, and
Perugino catered in part to the taste of smaller courts, eminent noblemen,
and rich merchants. They also executed major commissions for the papal

court. Finally, there was the provincial-aristocratic manner of masters such as Carlo and Vittore Crivelli, who painted hundreds of pictures in the Marches and farther north. A throng of lesser craftsmen also worked in the aristocratic-courtly vein.

Variations in accent aside, the aristocratic-courtly manner after 1450 has a strong predilection for highly finished surfaces, meticulous detail, sharp contours and edges, and a line tending to break or jerk as it curves. These traits often go with an all-pervading clarity and a fondness for luminous coloration or brilliant light, as in the famous San Bernardino cycle (Fig. 12) and Piero's *Flagellation* (Fig. 11). Marmoreal or lapidary textures predominate—of garments, surroundings, and even flesh. In the hands of the leading masters, the picture space is likely to be thoroughly organized: geometry takes over. A taste abounds for bravura passages of perspective foreshortening, though this passes into cuteness or provincialism when overdone. At times, even in work of the highest quality, the picture is crowded with objects and rich decoration—arches, thrones, other architectural elements, *putti*, floral and fanciful patterns, garlands of fruit and flowers, polychrome marbles, and luxuriously embossed fabrics. The favorite subjects are religious—Madonnas, patron saints, and stories from the Bible. There was also, as we have seen, a heavy demand for portraits and, later on, for mythological scenes. Finally, content and manner are often combined with a plethora of Roman imperial ingredients (a figurative ideology of grandeur), with heroics (e.g., St. George, St. Sebastian, Hercules, the Flagellation of Christ), with elegance of stance and gesture, and, in the provincial schools, with a medley of self-conscious mannerisms.

The aristocratic-courtly vision betrays such a firm and almost hypnotic grasp of detail, so confident a control of spatial relations, and such optimism in its preference for an all-pervading luminosity that the viewpoint—the identity in question—speaks for itself: it is the window of a palace, and the resulting view is for those in command of things, for those who dominate their environment. The luxury in this view belongs to two features: to a pronounced decorative element which borders on symbolism, and to the near-hypnotic grasp of detail, as in pictures where objects are microscopically observed (Figs. 13, 21, 22). The devotion to detail is a late-medieval touch, found in northern Europe too and often given symbolic overtones or ascribed to a love of nature; but it is also a mode of playful self-indulgence. The eye is invited to dwell on strikingly observed surfaces; in other words, the love of detail is also part of the larger demand for ornamentation. Here is a vision of space as surplus, space for sensuous enjoyment rather than for use, and in this respect it departs completely from Masaccio's manner and economy.

The Renaissance theme of "the dignity of man" belonged to an upper-class vision. It was the slogan for an age when princes and ruling elites had so much faith in their own leadership that they could also think of themselves as lords over "nature." The same viewpoint is present in art, in the aristocratic-courtly manner. Nothing better illustrates this than one of the most salient and persistent motifs of Italian painting in the second half of the fifteenth century: the imagery of strange rock formations—architectonic, fantastic, lovingly delineated (Figs. 12, 13). These forms appear as background or flanking landscape, usually in the vicinage of a city. Again and again we find, on close scrutiny, that we cannot tell whether the oddly mannered constructions are natural geological formations or the ruins of ancient structures and urban sites. The guiding vision is intensely urban, the forms often resembling or suggesting bits of city. When it looked to the rural space outside cities, this taste drew away from endowing it with an air of naturalness. Rather, the countryside had to be altered to hint at the grand surroundings of princes and oligarchies, with their great masses of cut and shaped and arranged stone, the proud *palazzi* and churches under their possessive patronage. This was self-confidence of a sort prepared to remake the face of nature. Precisely this is why Borso d'Este, lord of Ferrara, was not mad when he decided to have a mountain built on the flat Ferrarese landscape, in January 1471. All the peasants of the region were put under a decree of forced labor; ships, wagons, and carts were employed to haul earth and rocks to the site; and the enterprise was pursued, despite much complaining by the populace. Borso's extravagant gesture sums up the special consciousness of the age, the absolute self-assurance in the upper strata of society and the complaining but coercible docility below.

The *oeuvre* of Andrea Mantegna (1431–1506) throws light on the social calligraphy of the aristocratic-courtly manner. He was not, perhaps, the ideal court painter, being too passionate and intellectual. Yet there is more candor in his vision than in the work of lesser court masters. The main figure in his *Madonna of the Stonecutters* (Fig. 22) is put up against an explosion of stone; in the right background we see little men cutting into the huge mass and quarrying stone, sections of which have already been turned into part of a clearly rounded column and base. It is as if raw nature is to be transformed into a city before our eyes: again, a triumphant, domineering vision. The motif is repeated in his Copenhagen *Christ on a Tomb*, showing, in the right background, some stonecutters, a recently carved statue, and again a half-made column; or is this, under the hill of Calvary, an archaeological site? Specialists associate these images with Mantegna's keen interest in Roman antiquity. Of course. But classicizing attitudes were easily joined to the militant self-assurance of Quattrocento ruling elites: the Renaissance will to remake the natural environment, and the imitative enthusiasm for the élan of antiquity, were different expressions of the same self-confidence. Antiquity was used to dress up the robustness of Mantegna's upper-class world. And there is no doubt as to where his aspiring identity lay: he longed to be a nobleman, obtained a Palatinate countship from the Gonzaga marquis of Mantua, and built a stylish house as soon as he could afford it.

The Gonzaga cherished the feats of Julius Caesar and had Mantegna celebrate these in a lost cycle, probably in fresco. He executed a series of the deeds of Hercules, now also lost, in one of the Gonzaga castles. The elements of spectacle in the nine panels at Hampton Court, *The Triumph of Caesar*, reveal Mantegna's heroic manner and catch a self-image of the Gonzaga court. Art historians find "a hard, masculine world of valour, discipline, and leadership" in Mantegna's view of imperial Rome. His life-size group portrait of the Gonzaga family in the *Camera degli sposi* (Fig. 17) was "done in the grand manner." The low optical viewpoint makes the figures loom up, magnifying their stature. E. Tietze-Conrat has observed that their "self-assured power" was originally more striking, "before repeated restorations softened them to the taste of a later public. A less reworked portion, such as the *Death of Orpheus* on the ceiling, bears witness to the sheer brute strength of the original painting." The artist turned his decorative assemblies into political statements: space as pleasure and surplus was pointedly associated with authority.

Mantegna's cosmopolitan intellectualism was put entirely in the service of power, and religious themes were not allowed to get in the way of this. His manner was flattering, heroic, propagandistic, and highly decorative but astringent too. Just before moving to the court of Mantua in 1459, he completed major works for Venetian aristocrats: Gregorio Correr, the rich abbot of San Zeno in Verona, and Giacomo Antonio Marcello, governor of Padua. The social moorings of his manner are already evident in the *San Zeno Altarpiece* (Fig. 20), commissioned by Correr. We look upon a closely packed assembly of figures, books, fruits, garlands, ornate frieze, medallions, piers, clouds, and patterned marbles. There is scarcely a passage untouched by ornamentation. Such visual wealth doubtless made for a satisfying altarpiece, but the idiom would have been strange in Florence save to the most aristocratic and traveled part of the bourgeoisie. The emphasis on luxurious surfaces and intricate detail responds to the patron's self-satisfaction and to his taking for granted of such surroundings; it also draws attention to the man's ability to hire fine craftsmanship on a grand scale. The result is that Mantegna's control of the picture space threatens to crack under the massed weight of so many objects and ornaments. Control and ostentation conflict: the *San Zeno Altarpiece* dramatizes the concealed social oppositions between rational enterprise and unfettered expense, between space for use and space for ostentatious enjoyment. Mantegna's art somehow joined—but did not transcend—conflicting social identities.

In Carlo and Vittore Crivelli, we get a provincial variation of the aristocratic-courtly manner. After some troubles in Venice and a stint in Dalmatia, the two brothers settled in the Marches in the late 1460s. They lived and worked separately in and around Fermo and Ascoli, serving a small-town lay and clerical nobility.

Carlo's well-known *Annunciation* (Fig. 21) uses the virtuoso perspective of the Renaissance style in a setting of overstated elegance and fastidious detail. Absolute spatial control is foiled by the clutter of decoration. The result is a ludic effect, a hard but candied surface. Geometry's invitation to the mind is neutralized by the assault of ornament and precious detail.

The Crivelli tend to turn aspects of the aristocratic-courtly manner into stereotypes. In keeping with the manner, they favor a clear light, an incisive line, touches of costly decoration, marbled surfaces, and an assured spatial control. But they fuse these with a regressive provincial taste: swathes of gold-leaf paint, rich Gothic-type frames, crowded ornamentation, the heavy use of direct traditional symbolism, and, in their representation of Madonnas, a colder and more detached figure (the late incarnation of a fourteenth-century or even Byzantine type). To these elements the brothers brought an ideal of refinement which often slipped over into cliché: as in finely cracked floors or parapets, sinuous tresses of hair, fine-grained wood, heads titlted downward in studied foreshortening, the elegantly lipped wounds of Christ, and strikingly long fingers and hands, sometimes a choreography of these, all smoothly curved to win the viewer's admiration. The result was a mannered elegance joined with fuss, achieved mainly by means of cliché, and loved by a clientele that was not overly sophisticated. The Crivelli inundated the Marches with hundreds of their Madonnas.

The imperious feature of the aristocratic-courtly identity had a perfect instrument in the much-favored low optical viewpoint, which made figures seem to tower in importance (Fig. 17). Melozzo da Forli's *Sixtus IV Appointing Platina* (Fig. 16) works in this fashion, while also fixing the personalities in the steely outlines of the individual portraits, just as in Mantegna's handling of the Gonzaga group. The manner of these painters—Tura, Cossa, Pinturicchio, and the Crivelli also come to mind—had a persistently static note, whether in its chiseled line, candied surfaces, preference for the profile portrait, exaggerated detail, or the frozen postures of figures. The fixed note came out of the aristocratic-courtly identity as a function in part of the emphasis on social caste, the arrogant belief in the control over "nature," and the aural effect of the prince as the end or culmination of all social mobility. Caste, the dominant view of reality, and the effect of the prince: these contributed to a certain rigidity of perception or outlook, and more so in the provinces, where tradition was stronger, than in the cosmopolitan signorial cities. Moreover, after 1450, the upper-class approval or validation of everyday reality went far enough to encourage the artistic conversion of surface appearances into "essences"—another reason for the fascination with marbled surfaces, blinding detail, hard profiles, and an adamantine line. These "essences," rising up from a self-assured command over the surrounding environment, were the projected ghosts of a haughty and bullying elite in the provinces, the courts, and the narrowing front ranks of urban oligarchy. Only the shock of prolonged foreign invasion would shake up the dominant identities after 1500.

At Florence, upper-class identity was organized around politics as well as commerce and profit; hence it was more yielding, more adaptable and practical. Style here, accordingly, throughout the century, was more searching, less predictable, often more intellectual, and the result was a more innovative manner.

Venice, with its fixed tiers of citizen and aristocrat, had long provided an environment of stability and an ideology of order and supposed justice. The ruling class had marked distinctions political and pecuniary, but within their tiers aristocrats and citizens had a strong sense of their social identities. A stream of Venetian protraits tell us that they were a self-satisfied lot. They knew themselves to be powerful in Italy, but powerful only in their collectivity. This explains the great importance to them of their integrationist ideology. In the 1420s they were already having the hall of the Great Council decorated with individual portraits of every doge and with large mural paintings of the celebrated events of Venetian history. By the 1470s they considered this hall "one of the foremost showpieces of our city." In their private life and intimate tastes, however, there seems to have been little need for the artistic rhetoric of heroism, at all events not until the humiliating encounter with the Ottoman navy at Zonchio (1499) and the harrowing defeat at Agnadello (1509). The call to see and to show themselves in portraits had started in the 1460s or 1470s and soon became fashionable. From about 1450, as is evident from his sketchbooks, Jacopo Bellini had longed to experiment with the geometry of complicated architectural constructs and the placement of figures within more ample slots of space. This was a turning toward the urban realism of the Renaissance style. But his conservative clientele avoided this route. It was only around 1470 that the vanguard of taste in Venice broke decisively out of the old forms. Then Jacopo's sons were among the first to profit from and reflect the turn in consciousness.

Venetian emphasis on the collectivity is evident in the processions and group portraits done by Gentile and Giovanni Bellini, Carpaccio, Mansueti, and others. Here were the self-images of groups, and art historians have held that this form was especially favored by the men of the big and officious religious confraternities (*scuole grandi*), whose active membership consisted mainly of high-ranking citizens and patricians. Later, there was a taste for family groupings, often of the males only, but individual portraits also catered to the worldliness of the Venetian upper class. At first there was a preference for the sharp, limpid spaces and crisp detail of Antonello da Messina's oils and Giovanni Bellini's work to about 1490. Taste then inclined toward the late Bellini's atmospheric manner, in portraits as in larger pictures and altarpieces. Giovanni's workshop was the largest and busiest in Venice around 1500.

At the end of the fifteenth century, Venetian artists worked in a variety of manners: that of the Vivarini, for example, was regressive, hard, ornate—rather Mantegnaesque; in Carpaccio the manner was prosy and clear; in

Bellini, tonal values were foremost, making for a filtered or atmospheric effect. But these manners also had much in common: modeling in high relief, clear outlines (save for the late Bellini), luminosity of color, more or less clarity of detail, an assured handling of three-dimensional space, and a moderate to higher degree of ornamentation, depending upon the occasion and private taste.

The different manners pivoted, in short, on a basic commitment to urban realism. This allegiance, like the certitude present in the accent on order and clarity, catered to the self-confidence of the upper-class groups and to belief in their ability to rule the environment. Entering Venetian painting in the course of the 1460s and 1470s, urban realism immediately triumphed. But by 1510, throughout Italy, the determining, underlying confidence was collapsing, owing to foreign invasion, war, and a chain of political earthquakes. Giorgione's superlative dreaminess, hinted at even in the late Bellini, played around an evasive mode and already gave expression to the oncoming retreat from quotidian reality.[7]

SPACE REAL AND IMAGINARY

Perceptions of the urban space changed in the fifteenth century, and artists were there to register the change. They "encoded" it in style. Their works bear all the marks of the change, but it can be rendered back into the idioms of social experience only by means of special analysis.

We have seen that the dominant social groups solidified their authority in the course of the Quattrocento, as the political apathy of the lower classes deepened, while the middle classes, already much weakened economically, were more harried fiscally. The groups in command underwent a change in consciousness and in identity. We tracked the change in their building of new *palazzi*, in the renovation of their old *palazzi*, the reappointment of their domestic interiors, and in their groping out for an array of new furnishings and decorative fittings. Francesco di Giorgio Martini (1439–1502) —the Sienese engineer, architect, painter, sculptor, and writer—was one of the first observers to urge that the houses of merchants and small tradesmen be constructed with a clean separation between the rooms intended for family use and those for the conduct of business. But Francesco was theorizing. Moreover, as a working architect, he was writing not from the standpoint of the petty tradesman but from that of the groups at the top. Here were the patrons for architecture, and he was voicing their needs and new inclinations. Indeed, when writing his architectural treatise, *Trattato di architettura civile e militare*, in the later 1470s, he was employed at the court of Urbino. In the economics of the fifteenth century, new buildings belonged to the initiative of the powerful and rich. The middle and lower classes would go on living, as always, in the crowded conditions that joined home to workshop, to store, or to warehouse. These conditions were far more realistic than spatial arrangements predicated upon the family's reduced productivity, which tradesmen could not, in any case, afford.

The passion for building and redecoration, especially noticeable after 1440, had its interpreters. Looking to their peers and patrons, the humanists disseminated an ideology of magnificence, according to which wealthy and powerful men flashed their high status or proved their virtue by showing liberality and spending lavishly on architectural projects such as churches, chapels, *palazzi*, villas, and new public buildings. In this argument, borrowed in part from Aquinas and Aristotle, the humanists were doing little more than bringing Ciceronian Latin and classical allusions to a feeling that was already strong among rich men and princes. They lent their Latinity to the glorification of worldly success. By 1460 a number of major building projects answered to the new ideology, and later on there would be hundreds more—projects associated with the Medici, Rucellai, Pitti, and Pazzi families of Florence, the Bentivoglio of Bologna, the Raimondi and Stanga of Cremona, the Este lords of Ferrara, the Gonzaga of Mantua, the duke of Urbino, the new duke of Milan (Francesco Sforza), and the Sienese nobleman become Pope Pius II.

Thus the urban drive for grandeur and for more ample living spaces sprang from the new needs and wishes of the commanding social groups. As the political and monied elite spread out and preempted more urban space, all others had to be content with less. When about 1500 Duke Ercole d'Este greatly extended Ferrara's walls and tripled the enclosed area, more urban space was created *ex novo*, but this was rare. Few princes had the revenue or resources in forced labor to turn their capital cities into showpieces. Instead, the building boom required some urban clearance: many old houses and shops were torn down to make room for the new *palazzi*.

Such was the setting for the first treatises on architecture in modern history. And from the first, the theorists—Alberti, Filarete, Francesco di Giorgio, Leonardo—conceived of urban space as a totality; they reflected upon the nature of urban sites and contemplated the construction of whole cities. Alberti and his successors took much guidance and material from *De architectura* by Vitruvius, the Roman architect of the first century B.C.; but this text had been looked at occasionally and even studied during the Middle Ages. In effect, the rediscovery of Vitruvius was grounded in Quattrocento experience: in upper-class demand, in the building craze, the ideology of magnificence, and the rising awareness that elites could reapportion or remake the urban space if they so willed. So was born the Renaissance interest in "the ideal city." Here power and imagination united and the ensuing vision of space was domineering, moved by a faith in men's ability to control the spatial continuum.

Appropriately, therefore, Renaissance treatises on architecture are profoundly class-conscious. They distinguish carefully among the kinds of residences fit for noblemen, for professional men, for rich merchants, and for petty tradesmen. Country dwellings are also treated according to social rank. Moreover, in their conception of improved or ideal cities, the theorists have definite views concerning the most fitting sites for the hierarchy of trades and occupations. Thus, because of the attendant sights and smells, tanners and butchers were not to be allowed to concentrate in the "more honorable" parts of the city—namely, the main thoroughfares, the principal public squares, and the areas adjacent to the seats of power. These sites were more appropriate for the luxurious silk trade (Francesco di Giorgio) or for those who served expensive tastes, like the goldsmiths (Alberti). Leonardo imagined a city on two levels: the upper one, turned to the sun, for the upper classes; the lower—with its streets backing onto the upper streets by means of stairs—for the workers and "crowd of paupers." Palladio, in the sixteenth century, took a softer line: he wanted special streets only for animals and for work carts. But the great humanist Alberti planned a city (ca. 1450) which divided rich from poor, so as to keep the important and dignified families away from the noises of petty tradesmen and from the eyes and evil influence of the "scoundrel rabble." In its more extreme form, his circular plan called for two walled cities, one held concentrically inside the other. The poor were to be enclosed within the inner city (*De re aedificatoria*, Bk. V, Chaps. 1, 6).

Francesco di Giorgio and Alberti flatly declared that human society, to exist at all, requires social divisions and varieties of skills, wherefore some men are naturally dominant over others, the few over the many, mind over body. Indeed, certain men are born to rule.[8] This way of reasoning—a classic ideological formulation—was meant to justify the claims of princes, particularly in their need of arms and fortifications, but the argument also turned fully in favor of urban oligarchy.

It follows that the new perception of space—living space, urban space, imaginary space—came forth from "material" realities and was filtered through social consciousness. The changing identity of the dominant social groups, tracked in their buildings and patronage, had a decisive effect upon architects and artists, more than has ever been supposed. Any plan to reorganize the urban space, however dreamlike its goals, was bound to favor the urban elites, unless it also looked to fundamental social changes. For no ideal city was possible, nor could the space of the existing cities be reorganized, save by a relocation of the urban population. But unless the relocation accorded more meterage to the humbler social classes—and this presupposed an improvement in their lot—the redistribution of space would go overwhelmingly to the service of grandeur: to vast public squares (à la Perugino, Fig. 10), wider and straight streets (Fig. 15), and larger buildings or spacious interiors (Mantegna, Antonello, the Lippi, Raphael, and others). This was signorial space: impressive and triumphal voids. Social preconceptions made it impossible to plan the restructuring of cities except by allotting more space to the powerful and less to the powerless. Architectural theorists and visionaries were not radicals: they dreamed in accord with the realities of the day, and these were stacked in favor of power and the class of important patrons.

The "ideal city" of the Quattrocento was politically a deeply conservative conception. It was a response to the rising demand, voiced by princes and urban elites, for grandeur and show, order and ample spaces, finesse and finished surfaces. Where reliable information is obtainable, we find artists and writers whose political and social views are indistinguishable from those of their patrons. In fact, being socially ambitious, like Mantegna, Signorelli, Raphael, Giorgione, and many another, artists could be brusquely committed to "class." In a letter written about 1501 to the Elector Frederick, duke of Saxony, the Venetian painter Jacopo de' Barbari, who had a keen interest in perspective and urban cartography, urged that he declare painting to be the eighth liberal art and that only those men schooled in the seven liberal arts and "noble both by birth and money" be allowed to practice it. Barbari emphasized the intellectuality and loftiness of painting. Painters should work for praise, not profit.

Validated by the groups in command, the dominant perception of space emphasized number, measurement, and proportion. Articulate contemporaries held that arithmetic and geometry gave the way to understand and dominate space. Eugenio Garin has stressed the fact that "we find a great confidence in the power and virtue of man in the 15th century."[9] All the period's writings on architecture are buoyed up by a sense of technological and intellectual triumph. We detect the note of self-assurance even in the perspective sketches of artists such as Paolo Uccello and Jacopo Bellini, and the architectural drawings of Francesco di Giorgio and Giuliano da Sangallo.

If the concern for signorial space had touched architects only, this discussion would be complete, but it also affected the painters and sculptors of the vanguard. Much of their most interesting work betrays a preoccupation with the frozen spaces of the ideal city—that is to say, with unified geometrical compositions, always on an architectural base or within a broad architectural framework, and usually in or beside the confines of a city. We have only to think of Donatello's perspective bas-reliefs, Jacopo Bellini's sketchbooks, Mantegna's destroyed Ovetari frescoes, the perspective *Annunciations* by Filippo Lippi and Carlo Crivelli, the *Flagellations* by Piero della Francesca (Fig. 11) and Francesco di Giorgio (Fig. 9), Antonello da Messina's *St. Sebastian* (Dresden), Perugino's *Christ Giving the Keys to St. Peter* (Fig. 10), and Raphael's *School of Athens*. All these illustrate the ideal city's aristocratic voids: vast organized spaces, or spaces more neatly boxed and absolutely controlled. We see spacious *piazze*, sharply receding perspective views with flanking buildings, crisply organized architectural constructs, or arches and columns looming in the near background and suggesting a monumental, marbled city all around. These spatial concerns appear even in the work of artists whose lyricism supposedly turned them against the lapidary structuring of space: Botticelli, for example, in both his Uffizi and his Washington, D.C., *Adoration of the Magi*.

The rational analysis of space in Quattrocento art is not just space seen geometrically from a single viewpoint, perspective; it is also urban space, inseparable from the architecture of cities; space delineated by stone pavements (the perspective or reticulated platform), large rooms with coffered ceilings and checkered floors, angular views of monumental rectangular forms, and a rich variety of architectural members. In the early Netherlandish masters, the introduction of buildings and receding streets into rural backgrounds "to stimulate the illusion of space . . . is connected with the embarrassment which these masters experienced in developing pure landscape from the point of view of perspective."[10] And in Italian painting, many a rural background—by Uccello, Mantegna, Cossa, and even Sassetta and Giovanni di Paolo—is hardly more than a fanciful urban environment. In 1425, Brunelleschi, possibly the first man to work out the geometry of focused perspective, plotted his views from Florence's two principal points: from just inside the main entrance to the cathedral, looking out to the Baptistery; and from one corner of the main government square, looking toward the great *palazzo*, the seat of power. Samuel Y. Edgerton has argued that the preoccupation with linear perspective was an integral part of the moral quest to match the tidiness and mystic harmony of "God's geometrically ordered universe."[11] In other words, in line with the central argument of these pages, the commitment to linear perspective moved from a sense of having discerned the nature of God's mastery and was at the same time an effort to imitate His grand design. Men would be gods.

We return, accordingly, to the domineering city: to the viewpoint and tastes of those who ruled it. The perfected forms of the imaginary ideal city—grand, symmetrical, proportioned, in fixed optical recession—went forth from a wish for control over the whole environment and from the implicit assumption that this was possible. The quest for the control of space in architecture, painting, and bas-relief sculpture was not analogous to a policy for more hegemony over the entire society; it belonged, rather, to the same movement of consciousness. Behind the two different enterprises was the same drive to comprehend the environment: to convert the surroundings, urban and even rural, to a "known" field. With an astonishing appropriateness, accordingly, the Vitruvian texts suddenly sprang to life and the human body, in keeping with those texts, was turned into a standard for proportions in architecture and painting. Human head and body, for example, were capital and column; or the body might be laid out along the outlines of a church design; and the tips of a man's arms and legs, when spreadeagled, became guiding coordinates for the supposedly "perfect" forms, the square and circle. The confidence and self-glorification of the fifteenth century flash forth here, in the stress on planning and on the human body as universal standard. Historians see this "heroic" vision as a general characteristic of the period down to about 1490. Not so. We should guard against ascribing to a whole society that which pertained only to the upper class, above all to its leading groups. The same mistake is usually made in praise concerning "the dignity of man." Though humanists sometimes credited all men potentially with this, neither the tone of triumph nor the cult of self-glorification can be explained save by reference to the consciousness of the dominant social groups.

The Christ figure aside, the reigning images of Quattrocento art are those of saints, princes, courtiers, oligarchs, and rich men. The pagan gods, toys for the playful and educated fancy of upper-class audiences, were only just beginning their pictorial fortunes. We have taken note of the muted desire to remake the urban space in accord with the demands and self-esteem of the social groups in command. With the elimination of symbolic size and color from painting, pictorial composition became the means to indicate importance. Space also was a means: the cubic illusion which invested each figure with its proper dignity. We have only to study the articulation of space in five of the century's greatest masters—Masaccio, Mantegna, Piero della Francesca, Antonello da Messina, and Leonardo—to see that it was used to single out, to point up, or to encircle and "hold" the most important figures. Up to the beginnings of Mannerism, amplitude of space was a cipher for power and dignity; it possessed a symbolic virtue, as in representations of Christ, Pilate, the Madonna, St. Sebastian, St. Jerome, and Hercules. So also, in numerous pictures, the space that went around princes, oligarchs, and rich patrons served to enhance their presence. For the stately rooms of much Quattrocento painting, the vast squares envisaged by Perugino and Raphael, and the great crystalline or resonant spaces of Cossa, Signorelli, Antonello, Leonardo, Giovanni Bellini, and others are not living spaces for humble men but rather for a society of upper-class saints: the members of an urban elite, including the worldly heads of rich churches and convents. So we get back to self-images or, rather, to the appropriate settings and spaces for the prestigious self-images of the age. And if rich parvenus also commissioned pictures with such spaces, this is because the history of "high" culture in the Italian Renaissance was in the domination of a few social identities, and new men were ready to change, ready to exchange one identity for another.

CHAPTER XIV

INVASION:
CITY-STATES
IN LIGHTNING
AND TWILIGHT

THE MAIN LINE OF EVENTS

The life of the Italian people, as a story cast around self-determining city-states, came to an end in 1494. In the autumn of that year, Charles VIII of France, in command of an army of 30,000 men, marched through the Savoyard Alps and descended into the peninsula to claim the kingdom of Naples. His serried ranks of Swiss infantry, heavy cavalry, and forty pieces of artillery awed the Italians, who rushed to meet his demands. The few naval encounters also went in his favor. Four years later the new French king, Louis XII of Orléans, claimed the duchy of Milan by right of his descent from a Visconti princess and took it by force of arms in September 1499. By April 1503, large parts of Italy, in the north and south, lay in the hands of governors French and Spanish. For the next half-century, French, Swiss, Spanish, and German soldiery made a bloody bid for political mastery on Italian soil.

In its diplomatic and military scope, the factual history of Italy in this period is best told by a computer, so many and tangled are the treaties, negotiations, and battles that make up the basic chronology. The experience of the Italian Wars colored all of life—most especially that of the dominant social groups, because they were stricken in their leadership.

Ever since the eleventh century, Europe had produced large numbers of men who were ready to bear arms for hire. Late-thirteenth-century Italy already drew many such men from distant places. But the sixteenth century provided richer prey and more adventure. A swelling population produced a flood of ready fighters. The recruiting grounds for the foreign armies of the

Italian Wars were Switzerland, Gascony, Burgundy, Castile, Aragon, southern Germany, Austria, the Rhineland, and Flanders. From these regions came rough and hungry men, often the unemployed or even the rejects and fugitives of society; and their commanders, better in name if not in spirit, were petty noblemen as well as great barons. The sight of Milan, Padua, Florence, Genoa, Rome, and Naples inflamed their ambitions.

In his longing for Naples and dream of a crusade against the Turks, the young Charles VIII was egged on by lords of the realm, by Neapolitan exiles around him at court, and by French commercial interests that looked to the rich cities of Italy for profitable trade advantages. French dynastic involvement in Naples, borne by the princes of the house of Anjou, dated back to the 1260s. This claim had never been allowed to die, but the Hundred Years War and the rivalry with Burgundy had blocked any sustained effort in pursuit of the title. With the extinction of the Angevin house (1481), the Neapolitan claim passed to Louis XI (d. 1483); and Charles VIII, his son, soon let it be known that he took seriously the French claim to the kingdom of Naples. As early as January 1484, he was encouraged by Venice, then at war with Milan and Naples, to make good this claim as well as the Orléans' claim to the duchy of Milan.

In 1494, no contemporary could gauge the dimensions of the external dangers faced by the peninsula. In the course of the fourteenth and early fifteenth centuries, the Italian states had sorted themselves out into five major entities by means of usurpation and arms. The larger had acquired the smaller nearby: Milan, for example, had conquered Lombardy and Venice had grabbed the cities of the Venetian hinterland. This process had been aided by a schismatic and weakened papacy, which began its reconsolidation only in the 1420s, with the pontificate of Martin V. By the middle of the fifteenth century, the remaining smaller states, such as Ferrara, Mantua, Savoy, Siena, and Lucca, tucked in among the bigger ones, could survive only as clients of the latter. A balance of power had been achieved among the five dominant states: the Venetian republic, the duchy of Milan, the Florentine republic (or veiled signory), the Papal State, and the kingdom of Naples. This balance was formally recognized, after the Peace of Lodi (1454), with the formation of the Italian League (1455). Florence's war with Pope Sixtus (1478) and the War of Ferrara (1482–1484), which pitted Venice against Milan and Naples, threatened to destroy the balance, but there was little in these disturbances that prepared the way for the political earthquakes that began in 1494.

In the early 1490s, Naples was ruled by Ferrante of Aragon (d. 1494), whose father had conquered the region in 1442. Cut loose from Spain, this dynasty had been integrated into the Italian system of states. Ferrante, accordingly, feared King Charles' pretensions. He also feared the diplomacy of Ludovico Sforza, uncle to the duke of Milan, because Ludovico was angling to push aside his incompetent nephew and seeking for himself the imperial investiture to the duchy. Since another prince, the duke of Orléans, brother-in-law and cousin to Charles VIII, was also known to be yearning for the duchy of Milan in right of his descent from the Visconti dukes, Ludovico endorsed Charles' plans for the conquest of Naples, hoping thereby to enlist Charles' support against the duke of Orléans' designs on Milan. To save himself, Ludovico was ready to send Ferrante to the wall. In this fashion, two of Italy's five major states tumbled into feverish diplomatic activity, then into military preparation.

But elsewhere in Italy, political aspirations were no less opportunistic. In 1493–1494, Pope Alexander VI dithered nervously between France and Ferrante, between Ludovico and Ferrante, straining to find what would be best for his own sons and the patrimonial interests of the Borgia house. Venice, instead, was rather warm to Charles' plans for an Italian expedition and looked to benefit territorially from such an enterprise. A sixteen-year war with the Turks (1463–1479), resulting in the loss of parts of its eastern empire, had turned Venice's ambitions around to a more acquisitive mainland policy, as shown in the republic's savage onslaught on Ferrara (1482–1484). The Venetian nobility did not see that it had any stake in the peninsula's status quo. Another republic, Florence, was reverting to full republican status (1494), as the impolitic Piero de' Medici alienated most of the leaders of the old Medicean oligarchy. Florentine politics fell into focus in the antithesis between the Medicean establishment and the revived republic. And whatever religious excitation—the Savonarolan movement—did for the restoration of the republic, it was a source of marked instability for Florence in foreign affairs.

Among the lesser princes, Duke Ercole of Ferrara, for example, applauded the coming of Charles VIII because he hoped, in the ensuing disarray, to regain the lands of the Polesine di Rovigo earlier lost to Venice (1484). And in Italy's northwest corner, the duchy of Savoy and the marquisates of Monferrato and Saluzzo were too weak to do other than welcome the French invaders.

The French occupation of Naples (1495) did not last six months. King Charles had moved into a confused, divided Italy. Cities opened their gates to him. Feudal barons—Colonna, Orsini, Sanseverino—rose up in his favor. The Genoese fleet was put into his hands. Abruzzese peasants took up his standard. And on February 21, 1495, with the Neapolitans shouting "France! France!" he entered Naples. One Aragonese king followed another in swift succession: Ferrante died on January 25, 1494; Alfonso II abdicated a year later; Ferrante II (Ferrandino) died on October 7, 1496, and was succeeded by his uncle, Federico.

Scarcely had Charles entered Naples than an anti-French alliance was signed in Venice (March 31) "for the protection of the Church and the defense of the Holy Roman Empire" (!). The alliance included the pope, Emperor Maximilian, Ferdinand of Spain, Venice, and the duke of Milan.

Commines, the French ambassador in Venice, was astonished by the news and asked dazedly if his king would be able to return to France. "Certainly," replied the doge, "if he comes as a friend to the league." From this moment on, sudden reversal, governed by the strictest self-interest, became a characteristic of Italian diplomacy. The indecisive battle of Fornovo (July 6, 1495) permitted Charles to scurry back into France with the part of his army which had not already been eliminated by an epidemic of syphilis. In October the worried Ludovico Sforza made a separate deal with the king; he was still grasping for a way to secure himself against the duke of Orléans, who detested the peace and would have marched gladly on Milan. Venice, meanwhile, had seized the Apulian ports of Trani, Brindisi, and Otranto, while Ferdinand of Spain, who already held Sicily and Sardinia, took other strongholds in Calabria and Apulia.

The next surge of activity was released by the death of Charles VIII in April 1498. Ludovico's old enemy the duke of Orléans became King Louis XII and lost no time negotiating accords with England and Spain in order to free himself for Italy. In April 1499 he made an agreement with Venice, the Treaty of Blois, which partitioned Milanese territory; in October, disposing of about 30,000 men at arms, he was in Milan. Venice's share—with 15,000 men—was Cremona and the Ghiara d'Adda. Ludovico Sforza, now a fugitive in Germany, had been unable to command the loyalty of the Milanese, and even his soldiers had failed to rally to his defense. Soon feeling the weight of the French occupation, Milan rebelled (February 1, 1500), and within days Ludovico was back in the city, but he had to flee again in late March and was taken prisoner at Novara in April. He spent his remaining years (d. 1508) a prisoner in France, reading Dante and, toward the end, scratching quaint drawings on the walls of his dungeon at Loches.

Fortune for now was with another house, the Borgias. Pope Alexander's son, Cesare Borgia, was in Milan to celebrate Louis XII's triumphant entry into the city. More than acquiescence, papal underwriting of Louis' desire for Milan and Naples was obtained with a French commitment to help Cesare make a state for himself in the Romagna. The timing for Cesare's state-building was perfect: Venice and Florence, the major neighboring states, toiled with their own urgent problems. The Venetians were at war again with the Turks (1499–1501), and the Florentines were riven by controversy over a narrowing oligarchy, by the menace of a Medicean restoration, and by desperate efforts to reconquer the breakaway colony of Pisa. With the help of the papal treasury and French troops, Cesare took Imola and Forlì late in 1499, Cesena in January 1500, then Rimini and Pesaro and still other cities and their districts in 1501 and 1502.

Louis, meanwhile, made for Naples, first clearing away the diplomatic road barriers. In November 1500 he concluded a secret agreement with Spain and Venice, aimed at partitioning the kingdom of Naples: he was to get Naples and the Abruzzi; Spain was promised the southern part of the kingdom, including Apulia and Calabria; and Venice was to hold on to the

Apulian ports. The treaty was finally published in June 1501 and billed as an offensive pact against the Turks. Pope Alexander was also a signatory. Deserted by his baronage, Federico, the king of Naples, was easily overwhelmed, and the French occupied Naples in August 1501. This liquidated a line of kings. Pope Alexander tried to use the occasion to finish off his great enemies, the Colonna lords, allies of the defeated king.

Ferdinand of Spain (Aragon), king also of the islands of Sicily and Sardinia, had set his heart on Naples and his soldiers within striking distance. Only Louis XII's troops stood in the way. In a series of campaigns, beginning with the capture of Taranto (March 1502) and ending with the fall of Gaeta (January 1504), Ferdinand's brilliant general Gonsalvo de Cordova cleared the way. Two battles of 1503 decided the issue: Cerignola (April 28) and Garigliano (December 29), both ending in terrible losses for the French, in troops (Swiss and Gascon pikemen) as in artillery pieces. Louis was now compelled to acknowledge Spanish mastery in the south, but in northern Italy he remained "the boss of the shop" (*padrone della bottega*), in one of Cesare Borgia's nice ironies.

European diplomacy had never been so intense, nor war, at least for Italy, so real and cruel. Alexander VI died in August 1503, to be succeeded by an interim Piccolomini pope, Pius III, and then, on October 31 of the same year, began the pontificate of a passionate and self-willed man, Julius II, whose whole school and style was power politics. The first big victim of the changes in the Vatican was Cesare Borgia. Bereft of the papal treasury and opposed by Julius, an ancient foe of the Borgias, Cesare saw his Romagnol state fall apart. Venice was there to snatch up the pieces: town after Romagnol town passed into her grasp. It was land, mainly fiefs and vicariates, that belonged to the overlordship of the papacy. And Pope Julius, angrily set on rebuilding the Patrimony of Peter, now made preparations to smite the aristocratic republic by entering into an anti-Venetian alliance (Blois, September 1504). This treaty allied him with the Emperor Maximilian and Louis XII, between whom there was only a truce, for Maximilian was not resigned to Louis' holding a fief of the empire, the duchy of Milan.

The pressure on Venice mounted until it was compelled, in 1505, to give up some of the lands formerly held by Cesare Borgia; but having copious Swiss and Romagnol mercenaries in their hire, the Venetians were strong in the field and could insist on holding on to certain Romagnol cities. Julius, faced with major problems in Bologna and elsewhere, and still gathering his resources (1506–1507), was unable to move against the Venetians again until 1508. Having humiliated the overconfident Maximilian, who had lunged into an ill-advised war against them, the Venetians swiftly despoiled him of Trieste, Gorizia, Pordenone, and Fiume, and even took some territory in Hungary. At this point Julius and Maximilian had no trouble marshaling anti-Venetian sentiment, and the result was the famous League of Cambrai (December 1508), which allied all the major powers of Western Europe. The allies aimed not to destroy Venice but to make it disgorge recent and ancient conquests. Ravenna and the Romagnol cities were to revert to the papacy. Maximilian was to get the Veneto and its urban centers, plus of course the lands recently lost; to Louis would go the Venetian possessions in Lombardy; Spain's share, predictably, was the Apulian ports; Savoy could have Cyprus; the lords of Ferrara and Mantua were promised the territories taken from them by Venice; and even the king of Hungary was to repossess his ancient lands in Croatia and Dalmatia. Weak Florence had no part in the league but would have been overjoyed to help pope and foreigner dismember the Venetian dominion.

On the battlefield of Agnadello (May 14, 1509), where the Venetian forces were dealt a stunning defeat, the allies seemed to realize their aim. Venice, momentarily, was thrust back to her lagoons. Now there occurred one of those reversals—the work of Pope Julius—so characteristic of the diplomacy of the age. Losing Treviso first, then Padua and Vicenza, all in the course of 1509, Maximilian was yet determined to press on with the war against Venice and struggled to win the wavering Louis XII to his view; whereupon Julius, seeing France encamped in Italy and noting Louis' enormous influence in domestic politics (as at Florence and Ferrara), suddenly resolved that the French were the great enemy. He turned against the king of France and raised a cry to clear "the barbarians" out of Italy—which did not prevent him from making military alliances with other "barbarians," such as the Swiss and Spanish.

But Louis was not to be easily cast out, and upper Italy now suffered several years of war. He went so far as to use schismatic councils to threaten the explosive Julius II with deposition. King and pope had known each other since the days when Julius, then Cardinal Giuliano della Rovere, had labored in France to stir Charles VIII up against Alexander VI, urging him to march into Italy. Julius responded to Louis' threats with the formation of a coalition against the French, the so-called Holy League (October 5, 1511), which allied the pope, Spain, and Venice; collateral arrangements also included England and the Swiss as active partners. There ensued a sequence of military campaigns and encounters in Lombardy, the Ravennese, the Romagna, and the Veneto. At Ravenna (April 11, 1512), in one of the major engagements won brilliantly by the French, the allied forces numbered 16,000 or 17,000 men, against some 23,000 on the victorious side. Nevertheless, France lost Milan and continually lost ground, driven back by Swiss, Venetian, papal, and Spanish troops, even after Venice defected to the French side (Blois, March 1513). After Julius died (February 1513), his successor, the Medici pope Leo X, renewed the Holy League, which included Maximilian but not Venice, now ranged in the enemy camp. The allies pressed the war hard, in the Veneto piercing as far again as the Venetian lagoons (July–October 1513), until Louis was made to renounce his claims to Milan and Asti (September 1513) and to reach a truce with Ferdinand of Spain (May 1514).

In the preceding course of events, there was abrupt swiveling again of the sort dictated by the tightest self-interest, as in Venice's defection to France. The aristocratic republic was eager to reclaim the territories which she had held in Lombardy and the Romagna before the League of Cambrai. Maximilian hesitated between his claims in the Veneto against Venice and imperial rights over the Milanese duchy. Popes Julius and Leo maneuvered to hold Bologna, Perugia, and the Romagna but also advanced old claims to Parma, Piacenza, and Ferrara. The Swiss got an Italian canton for their blood and troubles, as well as many sacks of hard cash, and they proposed to determine the political fate of Milan on the basis of their alleged military invincibility. At Florence, patriciate and bourgeoisie seemed resolved to commit suicide rather than live without Pisa as their colony, which was finally regained in 1509. Then the republic passed back to Medicean rule, in response to the threat of Spanish troops (September 1512), and the Medicean oligarchy would have collaborated with the devil, let alone with the French or Spanish, to retain control of Florence. Kings Ferdinand and Louis were also ready for any alliance and expedience in order to guard and enlarge their holdings in Italy.

Italy had become the playground of the most cynical game that Europe had ever known. No wonder that Machiavelli and poets such as Berni, Folengo, and Aretino came from its midst.

The death of Louis XII (January 1, 1515) brought the coronation of Francis I, a new spasm of troubles for upper Italy, and the end of puppet rule in Milan, where a weak son of Ludovico Sforza, named after his godfather, the emperor, had been the shadow of power for the body of Swiss infantry since 1512. Allied with the Venetians, Francis quickly repossessed Genoa and took the field in Lombardy against the forces of the anti-French league, which included the Emperor Maximilian, Ferdinand of Spain, the Swiss cantons, Maximilian Sforza, and (as from July 1515) Leo X. In September, Francis won a remarkable victory at Melegnano (Marignano) against cavalry, artillery, and an army of 22,000 Swiss pikemen.

The French reentered Milan and the myth of Swiss invincibility was demythified. Venice regained most of the lands she had lost since 1509. Maximilian Sforza was retired to France with a nice annual pension. And Francis was able to conduct separate negotiations with Spain, the Swiss cantons, and Pope Leo, from whom he took back Parma and Piacenza to reunite with the duchy of Milan. In 1516, Milan saw the movement, not far from her walls, of no fewer than 16,000 Swiss troops in the pay of the proud and angry emperor, who had got nothing from the changes of 1515 and who burned to punish the French and Venetians. But Francis I had also hired Swiss infantrymen—12,000—and these were more trustworthy than the emperor's and more highly disciplined. In the end the emperor had to back off and accept the new situation.

After 1494, and especially after the lessons of 1498–1499, the power to make and break states in Italy issued from outside the peninsula. From 1503 on, it was obvious that France and Spain were the dominant forces in the reconstitution of Italian states and that a genuinely independent papacy, however astute and vigorous the pope, was next to impossible. In striving to cleave to a line between the two great powers, the papacy had to lean heavily now one way and now the other. The moment of perfect balance belonged to pure logic; it was a diplomatic pipe dream. And after Agnadello (1509), even Venice, the most independent of the Italian states, had to hedge its autonomy and recognize that its interests both in Italy and abroad could not be safeguarded except by means of alliances with France or Spain and the Empire. Venice was compelled to fit itself into the design of foreign conquest in Italy.

Much of the celebrated rivalry between Francis I and the Emperor Charles V was fought out in Italy. Already governor of the Netherlands, Charles succeeded his maternal grandfather, Ferdinand of Aragon, to the Spanish throne in 1516 and in 1519, favored by his Hapsburg blood and Fugger money, was elected emperor. Even more than his grandfather (Maximilian of Hapsburg), Charles resolved to possess the duchy of Milan, while already holding Naples, Sicily, and Sardinia as king of Spain. But Francis I had no wish to be circumscribed by Hapsburg power in Spain, the Netherlands, Austria, and Italy, and by many squadrons of Spanish pikemen and German *Landzknechts*. Milan was a major link in the Hapsburg chain. It also gave access to Naples and Genoa, jumping-off points against the expanding Turks and Barbary pirates. Thus the importance of Milan for Charles; moreover, it was an imperial fief and his title to it was unassailable. In the coming wars the papacy offered little guidance: the two Medici popes, Leo X (1513–1521) and Clement VII (1523–1534), were to spin like weathercocks in a raging tempest.

War broke out in 1521 on the borders between France and Spain (Navarre) and also in Lombardy, where the imperial-papal forces won Milan and in 1522 seized Genoa, though not yet the fleet, with the support of the city's Adorno faction. The papal interest lay in getting Parma and Piacenza back. A series of sanguinary engagements reaching up as far as Marseille resulted mainly in victories (Bicocca, Romagnano) for Charles V's armies and led the way to the awesome French catastrophe at Pavia (February 24, 1525), where more than 8,000 men on the French side perished. Francis I himself was taken prisoner. From this time on, nothing seemed able to overturn the supremacy of the imperial forces. The League of Cognac (May 1526), the new coalition formed against the emperor after the release of the king, was headed by Francis I, Pope Clement, and Venice, but it lost one battle after another, although early in 1528, after retaking Pavia, the French commander, Odet de Lautrec, led his troops far enough south to besiege Naples. In 1529 the French made one more serious effort in Lombardy, only to be routed at Landriano.

In rural devastation, in political disorder, and in the overturning of private fortunes, the 1520s were among the most horrendous of a time in which the Sack of Rome (1527) was only the most resonant low point in the conduct of undisciplined, sick, and predatory troops, for these were also years of disease and famine. Nor were the armies of the Holy Alliance more disciplined. If they had been subject to any organized leadership, they would have had little trouble interrupting the imperial commander's ragged march on Rome. In upper Italy, noblemen arrived or fled in the wake of defeated or triumphant armies, and large rural estates changed hands as a result of local political faction or violently contested privileges and offices. In the south, in 1528, when the Viscount Lautrec's drive on Naples failed, the Angevin barons who had sided with the French were crushed and their estates given out to trusted servitors of the emperor and even to Genoese speculators, after the naval commander Andrea Doria bolted from his alliance with the League, gave up the blockade of Naples, and carried the formidable Genoese fleet over to the imperial side. In this *coup* for the emperor there were major rewards for Genoa, owing to the city's banking and trade connections with Spain and the Hapsburgs. Meanwhile, Venice had swiftly hauled in Cervia and Ravenna and whatever else was free for the taking, while Alfonso d'Este, duke of Ferrara, took back Modena and Reggio, now that Pope Clement was down.

It seemed a time for grabbing, until the settlements of Cambrai and Bologna (1529–1530) confirmed and pointed up the imperial hegemony. These settlements made clear that the power to reconstitute Italian states was no longer in Italian hands.

First of all, Duke Alfonso of Ferrara was compelled to give up Modena and Reggio. Charles V, however, the designated arbiter in the dispute between duke and pope, then determined that although Ferrara was a fief of the papacy, Modena and Reggio were imperial fiefs and that Duke Alfonso was to be the holder of all three. Practically speaking, the duke's claims were upheld. Other decisions were also taken and implemented. The duke of Urbino, Francesco Maria della Rovere, had lost his duchy but his claim was recognized, to the dissatisfaction of the pope, and it was now returned to him. Charles raised the marquisate of Mantua to the status of duchy. Siena and Lucca, surviving Tuscan republics, were confirmed in their republicanism. The duchy of Milan was put into the hands of the seriously ailing second son of Ludovico, Francesco Sforza II, another puppet, but it was laid down that on his death the duchy was to pass directly to Charles. Venice was forced to surrender her seizures—Ravenna, territories in the Romagna, and even the dearly coveted Apulian ports. In Tuscany, after a nine-month siege of Florence, an imperial army toppled "the heroic last Florentine republic" (August 1530), and Charles here too became arbiter, in this case of Florence's government. In October he raised Alessandro de' Medici to the rank of duke and in May 1531 published his decision making Alessandro lord of Florence with the right of succession. The legal aura of Charles' arbitration was enhanced by his coronation in two different ceremonies at Bologna (February 1530), making him both emperor and king of Italy. Pope Clement did the crowning.

The arrangements of 1529–1530 struck observers of the more innocent and hopeful sort as the start of a new era of peace. Charles had renounced Burgundy, while Francis I had given up all rights to Naples, Milan, Flanders, and Artois; he had also promised to abandon his allies, Florence and Venice, to their fates. In fact this seems to have made him and Pope Clement all the more fearful of imperial predominance. The marriage in 1533 of a Medici princess (Clement's grandniece, Catherine) to Francis' second son was no gesture of friendship for the emperor. When Francis invaded and occupied Piedmont early in 1536, it was the outbreak of the third war between the two sovereigns. The poisonous rivalry between them was caught by Charles' explosive reaction in Rome on April 17, 1536, challenging Francis to a duel and betting Milan against Burgundy, "although even this belongs to me." He concluded: "But if the king wants neither peace nor a duel, then let it be war. Let us gamble everything. Let it be the ruin of one or the other. Let Christianity itself fall into the hands of the Turks or infidels." Europe was shocked. The imperial army in Italy in 1536 numbered 20,000 Germans, 20,000 Italians, and 10,000 Spaniards. Francis was left holding Savoy and much of Piedmont, but he was still far from Milan. The Truce of Nice (1538) was followed by a fourth war (1542–1544), which ended in much the same way.

There was to be no true settlement until the Treaty of Cateau-Cambrésis (1559), and then only because France was stricken by a generation of religious civil war. It is sometimes alleged that Pope Paul III (1534–1549) ardently sought a neutral line between Charles and Francis. In practice, he was long in the emperor's camp because the French crown needed alliances with the Turks and Protestants and because, as chief of the Farnese family, Paul needed the emperor's collaboration in the service of nepotism, as he set about constructing a state for his son, Pier Luigi Farnese, to whom he granted Parma and Piacenza as a duchy and fief of the Church (1545). During the last years of his pontificate, Paul tried to swing toward France and to stiffen Venice against Charles, with no success. In September 1547, at the instigation of Ferrante Gonzaga, the imperial governor of Milan, Pier Luigi was murdered by some of his own aristocratic subjects and the contested duchy went to his son, Ottavio, who sympathized with and indeed was also son-in-law to the emperor, though he turned to France for help: such was the incredible tangle of interests in upper Italy. Thus ended Paul III's obscure and late efforts to build up a Farnese state as a bulwark against imperial pressures.

At the beginning of 1547, the year of Francis I's death, there was a major but unsuccessful uprising in Genoa against the Dorias and hence the emperor. The rebels, led by a Fieschi, had the aid and support of the French dauphin. Italy north and south experienced a good deal of anti-Spanish feeling in the later 1540s, after Milan had been assigned to Philip II of Spain (1540, 1544), and the French were well aware of this. In 1551, Francis I's son, Henry II, dispatched troops into Piedmont and the invaders got as far as Parma. Henry struck at the bishoprics of Metz, Toul, and Verdun in 1552, and occupied them with the aim perhaps of using them as barter for Milan or Asti. Also, in 1552, a combined Franco-Turkish fleet took Corsica away from the Genoese, allies of the Spanish and Charles V. When Siena rebelled against the imperial garrison in 1552, Henry ordered troops into Tuscany and the Sienese were able, with military help from beyond the Alps, to hold out against imperial and Florentine forces until April 1555. At the same time, French forces advanced in Piedmont, while neutral Venice and the papacy stood by as onlookers. Then, looking to the expulsion of the Spanish from even Naples, Henry concluded a secret agreement (1555) with the new pope, the Neapolitan Paul IV (1555–1559), who hated the Spanish. But in 1556–1557 the duke of Alba, viceroy of Naples, marched a Spanish army into the Papal State and Paul was forced to break his alliance with France. On these affairs the abdication as such of Charles V (1556) had little effect and there followed the enduring settlement of April 1559.

Catcau-Cambrésis had about it no diplomatic genius. It merely confirmed and gave international status to a situation that had been opened and closed by the force of arms. Steel, not quills, had prepared the script for the negotiators; the seals would be provided, in a sense, by the French Wars of Religion (1562–1598). France renounced Milan and Corsica, cleared out of Savoy and Piedmont, but retained five strongholds in the latter for three years and held the marquisate of Saluzzo until 1588. Spain, instead, retained Milan and Naples; her possession of Sicily and Sardinia was a foregone conclusion, and Corsica was restored to the aristocratic republic of Genoa and to the great Genoese Bank of San Giorgio (satellites of Spain). Philip II let Cosimo de' Medici, the grand duke of Tuscany, integrate Siena into the duchy, but Spain got territory and fortresses along the Sienese coast, including Piombino, the Argentario promontory, and the island of Elba, to be used as bases for action against the Barbary pirates, the Turks, and the French. In the north, again, Duke Emanuele Filiberto, a former general in Charles V's armies, was returned to his domains—Savoy, Piedmont, Nice, and adjoining lands. The Farnese, now creatures of Philip II, got Parma and Piacenza, while the Gonzaga of Mantua got confirmation of their title to the marquisate of Monferrato, first secured through a marriage in the 1530s.

A conclusion may be drawn by observing that Philip II's Supreme Council of Italy, founded in 1563, was charged with the direction of Spanish government in the peninsula but had its seat in Madrid. Now most of Italy was subject in some respect to the first power of the age.

THE MAIN LINE OF FAILURE

The temptation to read the nationalism of the modern world back into the sixteenth century must be resisted. Italians—Neapolitans, Genoese, Milanese, Florentines, Mantuans, and others—fought for France, for the empire, and for Spain against one another, but without any sense of betraying a homeland. First they were Genoese, Milanese, Florentines or the rest, and next they swung to the other extreme to become cosmopolitans—men who could look to serving larger and more powerful political units, whatever the language of service. Castiglione's courtier was trained to serve princes, not nations or homelands. Yet in a time when France and Spain were edging toward a sense of nationhood, this cosmopolitanism—moving, contradictorialy, from strong regional attachments—ended by putting the fulcrum of Italian political and military authority into the hands of others. There was a transfer of leadership and a corresponding loss in the power locally required to reconstitute states. Many Italians saw and lamented this, many from among those born or risen into the peninsula's traditional ruling classes, where leadership and privilege had been the *raison d'être*. Ariosto, Machiavelli, Antonio Cammelli, Castiglione, and Guicciardini come to mind, and even two of the chief accomplices themselves—Ludovico Sforza and Julius II, who did as much as any Italian to help transfer power. Such men deplored the abdication in leadership, but their knowledge was foiled by passionate, short-term regional or local commitments. Upper-class Italians could not overcome the pull of immediate interests enough to unite against the invaders, save for a few brief months in 1495. The cry of rage and pain against the "barbarians" had both literary precedent (Petrarch) and urgent political springs (invasion), but there was no reality, social or political, equal to the task of expelling the barbarians.

Foiling the cry were the social realities that prepared and fostered *The Horrendous Wars of Italy* (a book of the day): the antagonistic and oppressive relations between rulers and ruled, between capital cities and subject cities, upper classes and middle classes, lord and peasant, prince and nobility, or prince and bourgeoisie. Here was the main line of failure, in the divisions that revealed the vices of inadequate government: Machiavelli's obsessive theme. For when the horrendous wars were upon them, governments in Florence, Milan, Naples, Rome, Genoa, and the Romagna could not command enough support or loyalty from the subject communities to have any firm faith in survival. External danger made for internal threat. The ensuing insecurity and fear in government made cooperation with neighboring states difficult or impossible. If you could not trust your subjects, then other states, with a simple nudge, could bring you down. The result was not merely more repressive government, but also feverish diplomacy, duplicity, tergiversation, and shifting alliances.

When Charles VIII entered the kingdom of Naples with the ease of an ambassador (noted one of his advisers), political collapse had preceded him. Alfonso II had fled in fear. Some of the great barons of the kingdom—e.g., the princes of Salerno and Altamura, the count of Ariano—had taken up arms against him and his father, King Ferrante, in the mid-1480s, and those who took refuge in France frequented the court, conspired, and descended joyfully into Italy with Charles. That 15,000 Abruzzese peasants went on the rampage and rebelled in favor of the French denotes the swelling of violent discontent among the humbler social ranks, and with good reason. The weight of taxation was felt most acutely here, and it was growing. In the second half of the fifteenth century, the Neapolitan crown increased its revenues by about 25 percent, but interest on loans to government also took a large toll, as ruling-class Italy veered toward more sumptuous living styles and a more expensive diplomacy. The main taxes were on salt, sheep, foods, and certain staples, and these had to be high to make up for the fiscal immunities of the rich barons, lesser feudal lords, and holders of the kingdom's forty-three ecclesiastical fiefs. Yet such privilege had not satisfied the barons, and they again deserted the ruling dynasty when Louis XII marched on Naples in 1501. Crown, nobility, and an exploitative fisc eroded allegiance to the civil order and undermined receptivity to existing authority, thus preparing the way for the foreign takeover.

On the eve of Charles VIII's invasion, most of the lands under the direct or indirect rule of the papacy—the Papal State—knew no steady, stable, or effective enough government. The major exception, Ferrara, had completely escaped from papal rule, and the Este lords there turned for survival to French support and sponsorship. Revenue from the Papal State had the first importance for the papacy, amounting by the 1470s to something like one-third of all Vatican income. In the course of the fifteenth century, the tax yield doubled (to about 300,000 florins), owing mainly to reorganization and the repossession of lordships in Umbria and elsewhere, and doubled again between 1492 and 1525. But centralization of authority was not the same as unity of administration,[1] and the papacy was very far from even the former. From the southern Sienese littoral to the borders of the kingdom of Naples, law and order were in the power of the great feudatories, the Colonna and Orsini and their lesser copies and allies, the Crescenzi, Gaetani, Savelli, and Santacroce. These clans could be a law unto themselves, never more than in emergencies. Popes had to pet or ruthlessly punish them, for Orsini and Colonna were capable of pursuing independent foreign policies and could put popes with their backs to the wall. In May 1494 the Colonna rebelled against Alexander VI, took up the French cause, and seized Ostia as a base for military operations against the king of Naples. In the Romagna, where the different regions were held as papal fiefs and vicariates, governments were often, according to the testimony of contemporaries, not much more than lawless little despotisms, where violence and flagrant injustice were commonplace. This in part was why Machiavelli and Guicciardini admired Cesare Borgia's Romagnol exploits: at least he imposed a modicum of order and justice. And if even neighboring Venice eyed nervously the civil strife and changing faces of despotism there, we can imagine the fears and anger of popes Julius, Leo, and Clement. The Romagna was the major Italian recruiting ground for crack infantrymen, who could easily batter local authority in insurrectionary circumstances. This military fact helps to explain the incidence of unrest and violence in the lands under supposed papal hegemony. Here hundreds of *condottieri*, great captains as well as petty squadron leaders, found that they could ill afford to live without mercenary contracts, lest their incomes plummet and their men become a civil peril. War was big business in the Papal State, where industry was, in contrast, a mean and paltry thing. Yet war made for a deadly bitterness among the lowly rural folk, who suffered special war levies and forced labor (corvées), as at Rimini under the Malatesta. Finally, elsewhere in papal territory around 1500, Perugia and Bologna were arenas for the unreined ambition and bloody feuds of the principal families—Baglioni against Baglioni, Bentivoglio against Malvezzi and Marescotti—which made those cities unreliable allies of the pope, or even enemies of papal policy whenever this promised some advantage in dealings with foreign powers.

The situation in Florence at the start of the Italian Wars presented problems of a different sort. In 1493–1494, Lorenzo the Magnificent's son, Piero, lost the backing of important Medicean oligarchs because of his political naiveté and their desire for a bigger share in the state. This internal schism and Charles VIII's arrival on the scene brought the government down. But then a divided Savonarolan republic (1494–1498) had to beware (1) of Medicean conspirators, (2) of the menace of aristocratic oligarchy, and (3) of the rabid discontent produced by the loss of Pisa and by enforced payments to the crown of France. The republic had to guard against internal and external conspiracy until its overthrow in 1512. It was driven to call upon French help to get Arezzo back from Cesare Borgia (1502) and to reconquer the rebellious Pisans, who solicited support from Venice, Genoa, Lucca, the papacy, and from anyone else who would come to their aid against Florence. In short, from 1494 on, Florentine government was harassed and intimidated by major voices from within the Florentine community, mainly aristocrats and Medicean malcontents. With such antagonists, a republican government was in no position to conduct a leading diplomacy where the military might of France and Spain had been unleashed. But neither could a Medicean state do any better, being absolutely dependent, after 1512 and again after 1530, upon Medicean popes and papal or imperial armies, for the Medici also faced major antagonists both in the city and outside, in the legion of armed political exiles.

The failure of Florentine government was its inability to content enough voices from the opposition to be able to concentrate greater force at home and abroad, and this failure sprang in turn from the pressing bloc of irreconcilable group and class interests in Florentine society.

Milan, the "shield of Italy"—as the imperial governor, Ferrante Gonzaga, called it—was also the political gateway. Here a callous fisc, flashy courtly expenditure, a grandiose diplomacy, an ambitious and fractious nobility, administrative disorder and corruption, and Ludovico Sforza's stealthy usurpation had made for a profundity of discontent that weakened government in its vitals. In 1493-1494, the marriage of Ludovico's niece, Bianca Maria, to Maximilian of Hapsburg cost a dowry of 400,000 ducats, about one-half the duchy's ordinary yearly income, and this to buy the title to the duchy for the bride's uncle. Thereafter Ludovico had to disburse many thousands of ducats to Charles VIII, to the duke of Orleans in war reparations, and to the Emperor Maximilian for a military buildup against the French claim to Milan. When Louis XII's army invaded Lombardy in 1499, under the command of a Milanese exile (Gian Giacomo Trivulzio), part of the duchy's population favored the invasion. The capital, the subject cities, and Ludovico's soldiers refused to fight, despite a system of strong fortifications feared by even the French, and Ludovico was forced to flee into exile. In 1500 his Swiss troops also refused to do battle for him. Many of his functionaries and captains, including supposed favorites, defected to the French. Violent controversy erupted among the Milanese nobility, running along ancient party lines. The stakes were office, favor, and profit under the French, as well as vast feudal estates, which were granted out as hereditary fiefs and whence private armies could be raised. In emergency, the overriding concern and labor of mighty families—Trivulzio, Borromeo, Pallavicini—was not allegiance to the Sforza, or to any prince, but confirmation of their fiefs and privileges.

Faithless protégés, powerful feudal enclaves, discontent with an iniquitous fisc and with corruption in government: these did as much as French arms to overthrow Ludovico's state. Yet his heirs failed to heed the lesson. In just one year (1514) the hedonistic Maximilian Sforza, who was restored to Milan by Swiss soldiery, ran up expenditures of 30,000 ducats for the ducal wardrobe alone. The summer of 1514 was all masked balls and banquets. Francis I soon put an end to these.

Of all the Italian states, the Venetian republic was able to muster the most effective force both at home and abroad. Whatever the long-term causes, Venice had coherence and continuity in government at home and did not provoke the deadly discontents that went to wreck states elsewhere. Divisions within the aristocracy were conscientiously sealed or ruthlessly concealed. Furthermore, the republic had a formidable fleet, a defensive body of water, protective sandbars, and a colonial empire which did much to satisfy the ambitions of the patriciate. But the catastrophe at Agnadello (1509) released all the tensions of the republic's mainland territories, and there local nobilities turned against Venice because their political power had been clipped, even though they retained privileges and were much favored in local courts. The lower classes, on the other hand, and particularly the peasantry, took up the Venetian cause, not from love of the republic but from hatred for local noble castes. In the aftermath of Agnadello, the Venetian patriciate momentarily feared the plebeian class in Venice proper, as if somehow the conditions for an uprising obtained even within view of the lagoons. The real danger, however, was on the mainland; but conflict broke out among the allies, which alone saved Venice from having her Italian possessions amputated.

Venice had used every means to expand at the cost of its neighbors. In the Veneto, in Lombardy, and in the Romagna, the city consistently used arms and alliances to divide and conquer. In the far south, looking to the wealth of cereals there, it picked off the Apulian ports, and in Tuscany, Venetians made a policy of stumping Florence by succoring Pisa, Lucca, and Siena. It has sometimes been argued that, with the spread of the Ottoman Turks, and with France, Spain, and the empire throwing their weight around in Italy, Venice had to expand to survive. Venetian policy was, in this view, one of necessity as well as muscle. But the republic's conduct in peninsular affairs was also very much a matter of Venetian upper-class identity, a psychology which could tolerate nothing less than to be at the head of a rich and first-rate power, even if at the expense of the whole system of Italian states.

If Venetian might did much to hinder the consolidation of the other major states, the papacy did even more to keep the peninsula in turmoil. In crisis, as if by instinct, many Italians looked to Rome for signs of guidance, only to find that Renaissance popes were more interested in power politics, in the promotion of self and family, than in the care of souls. And the perception of this was as sharp a point in the consciousness of the upper classes as it was in the poets and scribblers who delighted Rome with anonymous pasquinades against popes and cardinals. The age saw the large-scale entry into the cardinalate of men from princely and eminent families: Sforza, Este, Gonzaga, Medici; then Carpi, Trivulzio, Pallavicini, Piccolomini, Fieschi; and of course, from Rome, Colonna, Orsini, Savelli, Conti, and Farnese; from Venice were Barbo, Zeno, Michiel, Foscari, Grimani, Cornaro, Pisani, and still others; and from Florence, Soderini, Pucci, Salviati, and Ridolfi. The men who bore these names formed power blocs in the college of cardinals and used their influence to promote dynastic or regional political interests, as in Ascanio Sforza's stratagems for his brother, Ludovico, or Ippolito d'Este's handiwork for his brother Alfonso, duke of Ferrara. Cardinals of this stripe opposed or supported popes, gave their backing to kings French or Spanish, and worked for or against alliances and treaties. They were the hands in the Vatican of their families and states. The more influential of them required yearly incomes of not less than 10,000 or 12,000 ducats to cut an acceptable figure in Rome, where they kept the style of princes: households of 300 to 500 familiars, between secretaries, stewards, attendants, men at arms, servants, cooks, grooms, huntsmen, and what not.[2] Lesser or obscure cardinals with modest incomes had a modest influence, if any at all, and did better to avoid shame by staying away from ostentatious Rome.

Coming directly out of this setting, where the style was also set by the papacy itself, Renaissance popes (Adrian VI excepted) were destined to be worldly men and worse: wily princes and venal compromisers, fervently concerned with their own secular authority and with elevating relations, friends, and favorites. They looked with a sharp eye to papal income, to their armies, to the enlargement of the Papal State, to sowing trouble in neighboring states, and to pitting and balancing French against Spanish, or Venetians against Milanese, except when family interest dictated the favoring of one over the other. The political morality of Renaissance popes had its most characteristic expression in their nepotistic policies. Papal nepotism saw the world as an arena for social advancement; it saw the possessions and dignities of the church as forms of private property; and it flaunted its commitment to the worldly success of blood relatives and friends. Italy thus was morally captained by popes whose policies spoke for a devotion to power, wealth, pleasure, and continuity of blood: the self-same values of Venetian and Florentine patricians, and of the dukes of Milan, Florence, Ferrara, Savoy, Mantua, and Urbino.

Nepotism reached dizzy heights with Alexander VI, who could be almost hysterical with joy when hearing of the successes of his children. But other popes were not far behind, for every pope after Nicholas V (d. 1455) set relatives up as territorial dynasts. The humanist pope from the Piccolomini family, Pius II (d. 1464), was far behind in that he elevated only one Piccolomini to the cardinalate and installed another, who also held the dukedom of Amalfi, in two papal vicariates. Francesco della Rovere of Savona (Genoa), Sixtus IV (1471–1484), the first great nepotist, all but turned Rome over to his family. He had his sisters transfer themselves to the city, where he established them in princely style. He appointed one of his nephews prefect of Rome and had him married to a bastard daughter of King Ferrante of Naples. Three other nephews he turned into cardinals: Pietro Riario, Giuliano della Rovere, and Raphael Riario-Sansoni. For yet another, the troublesome Girolamo Riario (assassinated in 1488), he bought Imola, which Girolamo later used as a jumping-off point to take Forlì and to plot brash conquests far beyond. This man was married to Caterina Sforza, a bastard daughter of the duke of Milan, Galeazzo Maria. Finally a fifth nephew, Cardinal Giuliano's brother, was given the vicariates of Senigaglia and Mondavio (which had rebelled against Antonio Piccolomini) and was joined in marriage to a daughter of Federigo da Montefeltro, who obtained, in exchange, a ducal title from Sixtus.

The main details of Sixtus IV's attachment to his family indicate the perimeters of nepotism that were to become common under popes Alexander VI, Julius II, Leo X, Clement VII, and Paul III. As Leo said in a letter to his brother, Giuliano: "God has given us the papacy—let us enjoy it." And enjoy it they did. From the moment Cardinal Alessandro Farnese took the name Paul III (1534–1549), his relatives began secretly to arrive in Rome. He was known to be a man of "immoderate affection" for his family. Straightway two of his grandsons became cardinals. His son, Pier Luigi, was accorded fiefs and put in command of the papal army. The duchy of Camerino went to his grandson Ottavio as an hereditary fief, and Ottavio was married to a natural daughter of the Emperor Charles V. To Orazio Farnese, a little later, went the prefecture of Rome. And in 1545, as already noted, Paul, defying Charles V, turned Parma and Piacenza over to Pier Luigi as an hereditary fief and duchy.

"Immoderate affection" started with the plundering of the Church's dignities and riches but ended by spreading turmoil in the Papal State and adjoining lands. In this manner papal nepotism went to fuel the Italian Wars. It entangled Sixtus IV in a war first with Florence, then with Naples and Ferrara. It drove Alexander VI to open the Romagna for conquest, which in turn excited Venice, spilled Caesar Borgia's Italian and foreign troops into Tuscany and Umbria, and made for Alexander's complicity with the Italian plans of Charles VIII and Louis XII. Nepotism produced one of the most military and power-oriented of all popes, Julius II. It brought down, in its Medicean incarnation, two Florentine republics (1512, 1530). Under Leo X, it used the foreign military presence to try to create a state for Giuliano de' Medici out of Modena, Reggio, Parma, and Piacenza; and later on it tore Parma and Piacenza away from Milan, thereby occasioning major alarm throughout northern Italy in the later 1540s.

Time and again the needs of papal nepotism made for the movement and increase of foreign armies in Italy.

Four infirmities have been noted in the Italian confrontation with foreign invasion: (1) the inadequate and exploitative nature of government, to which communities responded with grave discontent, revolt, or simple lack of allegiance; (2) the ensuing nervousness and fear *within* government, making impossible, over the long term, any solid interstate cooperation against the "barbarians"; (3) the divide-and-grab policy of Venice; and (4) the nepotism and power politics of Renaissance popes, chief spreaders of disorientation and disarray, owing to their supposed lofty moral authority.

All the major Italian states were ready, equally with Venice, to pursue a policy of divide-and-conquer as far as their resources allowed. But deeds have more weight than wishes. Venetians, moreover, were in a unique position in that they had both less reason and more than other Italians for having a nervous and fearful government: less because the Venetian state had more domestic coherence, resources, and power than the others; more because Venetian possessions in the east were menaced by the advance of the

Ottoman Turks. And this double and contradictory condition made Venice especially perilous to its neighbors.

The four infirmities, as numbered above, give no idea of the waves of wreckage cast up by invasion and war. The imperial sieges of Florence (1529–1530) and Siena (1554–1555) inflicted enormous hardship and economic losses both urban and rural; farms for many miles around were owned mainly by urban landlords. Five years after the Sack (1527), Rome was still a spectacle of destruction: building activity had stopped. Brescia was horribly sacked by the French in 1511; so also were Pavia in 1528 and Genoa, by the Spanish, in 1532. Industry at Como was permanently stricken after 1507, when the danger of war drove out the resident colony of German merchants. Vigevano—the apple of Ludovico Sforza's eye—was nothing but "ruins and desert" in 1529, as were a number of other small towns. In the Milanese countryside, convents and monasteries were often attacked by soldiers, their lands ravaged, and their peasantry terrorized or eliminated by disease and want. Wherever the passage of armies was frequent, as in Savoy, the Lombard Plain, the Romagna, and at times the fertile parts of Tuscany, there suffering and agrarian disruption were deep and persistent.

Fernand Braudel has said that "the Italian Wars did not cut deeply into the health of the Italian economy."[3] Parts of Italy—Venice, Mantua, Verona, Livorno, Ancona, Naples, and possibly Genoa—showed vitality in the sixteenth century. Rome, however, and some of the celebrated centers of trade and industry had definite drops in population: thus Milan, Florence, Como, Brescia, Pavia, Cremona, and Siena, while Bologna and Padua had only very slight increases. But our concern at this point is not with long-term economic lineaments; it is with the effects of disaster on consciousness. People who lived in fear, whose lands were devastated, who were condemned to political exile, or who fled in terror were not—nor were their neighbors—cheered by the thought that the Italian economy retained vitality. For them and for two generations of neighboring observers the experience or fear of ruin was the felt reality.

Consciousness also recorded the impact of foreign invasion in other matters: in the painful surrender of power, of offices lucrative and authoritative; in the growing weight of taxes to pay for war, reparations, and a frenzied diplomacy; and in the substantial loss of control over the administration of justice. Every change of regime brought changes in government personnel, in administration, in the parties favored by local justice, and in the structure of patronage. We noted the crushing of the Angevin barons in the kingdom of Naples: they were stripped of their feudal estates. The like was repeated in the Papal State (how many lords met their destruction in Cesare Borgia?), in Piedmont and Savoy, along the western frontiers of Venetian rule, and in the duchy of Milan, where the state had many different masters between 1499 and 1525.

Of political earthquakes attributable to foreign invasion or its effects, even a partial listing suggests the magnitude of instability. The following saw violent or sudden changes of government.

Florence: 1494–95, 1512, 1527, 1530
Milan: 1499, 1500 (two changes), 1512, 1513 (two), 1515, 1521, 1522, 1524 (two)
Naples: 1495 (two), 1501, 1503
Cities subject to Venice: 1509 (two changes in certain cases)
Rome: 1527
Bologna: 1506, 1511, 1512
Urbino: 1502 (three), 1503, 1516, 1521
Pisa: 1494, 1509
Savoy, Piedmont: alternating masters between 1494 and 1559
Romagnol cities: changed hands many times between 1499 and 1530
Genoa, Pavia, Brescia, Novara, Cremona, Parma, Piacenza: changed hands many times between 1499 and 1540s

This concentration of tremors was centered on the most advanced part of Europe. A civilization that had been four centuries in the making now suddenly faced naked superior force. The centers of authority took the heaviest concussions, and a vast instability was sensed. Italy was hit where it was most likely to react with a change in historic consciousness: in the consciousness of the ruling classes. The culture reacted. Writers, artists, and thinkers responded at every level of sensibility. The idea of Fortune, as a tempestuous and unpredictable force, was raised to one of the reigning concepts of the age. There was a crisis in language, a "language question." A crisis in art: with a measured grasp of the world (classicism) disintegrating into one that was more arbitrary and recherché, often in straining for elegance (Mannerism). And there was a crisis in religious feeling. Many writers retreated into imagination, seeking ideal models, perfect solutions, alternate worlds, or merely building castles in the air. They dreamed of valor, elegance, beauty, and high-minded love. Some found a refuge in quietism or in religious conversion. Others turned to the ardent study of history, struggling to understand the present. And others still rushed headlong into hedonism or boisterous cynicism. But all these responses—varied, nuanced, often contradictory—were held together in the same social universe, the same general consciousness.

CHAPTER XV

THE HIGH RENAISSANCE: A DIVIDED CONSCIOUSNESS

THE KEY EXPERIENCE: CONTRADICTION

Now and then in history the process of contradiction invades a society's major institutions. Social oppositions escalate, making for so much tension that something must give way. The field for such antagonisms is consciousness and its most nimble part, imagination, no less than social conditions and the institutions themselves. Historical crisis is at once in the mind and outside it.

Around 1500, Italian society entered a period of flaring inner contrasts and oppositions, some of which, as in the religious and political realms, had started their way toward crisis in the late fifteenth century. But foreign invasion and war aggravated the tensions and produced new ones.

The most spectacular contradiction loomed up in the practice of religion, in the conflict between what the Church professed and the life of its leaders. With the pontificate of Sixtus IV (1471–1484), the Renaissance papacy went over to sanguinary nepotism, worldly splendor, and power politics in a manner that was to contaminate the whole hierarchy of the Church in Italy for nearly a century. The glaring disparities between doctrine and conduct, between responsibility and the neglect of parishes, generated confusion and dismay, and if the Protestant Reformation was one of the consequences in parts of Northern Europe, the fragmented outcome for Italy was in mysticism, prudent silence, tiny pockets of fervent reform, extremes of cynicism and hypocrisy, and finally in the backlash of the Inquisition and Counter Reformation. The failure of the Church in Italy was the failure of the Italian upper classes.

Although less eye-catching than those in the religious realm, the growing oppositions in social and economic life were just as serious and far-reaching. The continuing concentration of wealth resulted in more luxury at the top and misery at the bottom. A widening gulf separated privilege from institutional disability, and this increased suspicion as well as dislike between social classes. There was a greater emphasis on status over achievement, and a bullying new importance was attached to the claims of noble blood and antiquity of lineage. These towered over the "natural" inferiority of common folk and particularly over the stigma of anything that smacked of manual work. The sixteenth century produced a literature rich in eulogy for the virtues of "gentle" blood, thus marking a corresponding loss in status for those whose hands, or whose parents' hands, were tainted with work or new money. From the second half of the century, even in Venice, the most prosperous of cities, the economic pinch and the turning away from "mere" trade worked important changes in the old patterns of marriage, dowering, cohabitation, and family alliances.

The incandescence of conflict was in politics. The heightened tensions in economic and social life were converted by the middle and lower classes in many a city into the cry "France! France!" when Charles VIII invaded Italy. Italian rulers and ruling groups found that they could not count upon the loyalty of their subjects. Less obviously dramatic was the contradiction, in the face of foreign invasion, between short-term and long-term ends, that is, between immediate local interests and the interests of the peninsula as a whole. Again, contemporaries noticed the enormous disparity between the arrogant ruling claims of princes and oligarchs and their striking incompetence or servility when confronted with war and foreign dangers. The disparity was much commented on by writers such as Niccolò Franco, Anton Francesco Doni, and Ortensio Lando. Yet another urgent antithesis was summed up in the alternative between naked force and law, which Italian rulers would often be compelled to face, after the tumult strewn by nepotist popes, Cesare Borgia, and foreign armies. Should rulers have an easy recourse to force or govern their states more in accord with the dictates of law and tacit consent? Naked force frequently won out. Once the pontificates of Alexander VI and Julius II were over and the barbarians had scaled the Alps, how could anyone in Italy believe that craft and brute force had no fortune or future? Much of Machiavelli's political science was shaped by queries arising from the opposition between the promise of force and the claims of law, custom, or tacit consent.

The discontent of subjects generally, the religious malaise, the initial readiness of many Italians to acclaim the foreign invaders, the clash between plebe and nobility in the Venetian hinterland, in Milan the open struggle between factions, as well as the revived political hope of the upper bourgeoisie when the Sforza were overthrown, and finally the new flash of democratic republicanism in Florence (1495–1498, 1527–1530): these movements of feeling raised for Italian culture the question of relations between rulers and ruled, between dominant groups and subject groups. In thinking about politics, contemporaries often put this question in terms of an outright conflict between elites and populace, but the consciousness of this opposition, as we shall see, was not limited to the realm of politics—it was a problem *in* consciousness and therefore in culture.

In the cruel setting of the Italian Wars, the contradictions in religion and politics, in society and the economy, made for wavering perceptions of reality. During much of the fifteenth century, upper-class groups in the leading cities had taken the everyday world to be both the form and measure of reality.[1] But in the turmoil of the Italian Wars, reality turned suddenly into a problem: the question of what it was, or where it was, lurched forward to perplex men. The testimony offered by literature and art is conclusive. While certain writers and artists sought to work near the standards of a practical realism,[2] others drew away from quotidian reality into marked degrees of idealization or even fantasy.[3] The culture fostered a spirited opposition between two differing perceptions of reality: one more ideal in its lineaments, the other more down to earth. But more revelatory was the fact that a like polarity, with its ensuing tensions, was evident even in individual writers and artists. Pietro Aretino produced savage social satire and pornography, as well as works of a pure religious and devotional nature. Bembo, most of whose verse was done in a refined and idealized Petrarchan mode, also wrote obscene mottoes in which lust, as in Renaissance comedies, is the form of physical contact between men and women. In art the contradictory views of reality lay in the classical and anticlassical styles, an antithesis caught, for example, in the work of the late Raphael and early Pontormo. Machiavelli's political writings wind between stabbing perceptions of mundane reality and perceptions of overneat patterns, between the need to understand real situations and the need to get behind them to their universality or formulaic modes. *The Prince* is a strangely disturbing alloy of realism and idealism, of romance and hard-boiled cynicism, of mad hopes that are turned into probabilities and probabilities that lapse into caricature, as in Machiavelli's pessimistic assumptions about the nature of man. The tension in his political writings lies in the anxious play between realism and modes of idealization or exaggeration. His tense prose style goes to pin down tough realities as well as fantasies. The velleities of a romantic wield the pen of a realist.

It is easy to see why writers and thinkers in an age of crisis were moved to study the contours and innards of political and social reality. Italian control over Italian events was slipping, or had slipped, away; and sensible men desired to see deeply into the causes of failure. But why did Italy not produce a larger number of social and political thinkers of realist stripe? The reply takes shape in the question itself: most observers and thinkers inclined toward idealization. And the reason for this lay in the nature of the crisis itself. The malady was too serious; the contradictions in reality were both too deep and visible; the shape of reality, as something subject to the control of a ruling class, had got out of hand and was too daunting or disturbing. There were no easy solutions, or possibly none at all, because first of all historical reality itself had to be reshaped. Only the boldest sensibilities could bear a sustained analysis of events at the level of near despair. Guicciardini's detached melancholy is evident in page after page of his great history and in every page of his worldly reflections, the *Ricordi*. Machiavelli was saved from despair by his taste for paradigms and his spasms of hope.

The fervor that might have gone into unflinching political and social analysis went, instead, into bitter satire and moral indictment. Here, certainly, the assessment of events had a dimension of sturdy realism. The splendor of popes and prelates, the insolence of foreign armies, the dismantling and reconstitution of states, the Sack of Rome and lesser cities, the rasp of poverty, the arrogance and avarice of the ruling groups, the cynicism of the upper clergy, the evidence of wholesale disloyalty to government, and the rule of force: this world gave rise to a host of satirists and moralists. We need only mention Antonio Cammelli, Antonio Tebaldi, Pietro Aretino, Ludovico Ariosto, Francesco Berni, Pietro Fortini, Matteo Bandello, Pietro Nelli, Giovan Francesco Straparola, and a group of popular writers or proto-journalists known as "polygraphs" (*poligrafi*). They lashed out angrily at the evils and vices of the times, but their indictments rarely went beyond questions of morality and wickedness. The triumphant image was Fortune's wheel gone crazy: a perfect symbol for the widespread feeling among Italians that they had lost control over their lives. The age was a nursery for moral and religious critics, but it held out a deeply disturbing reality to other kinds of writers, unless these could filter that reality through idealization. And this, the process of idealization, was the principal operation at the basis of highbrow culture in sixteenth-century Italy.

The crisis of the High Renaissance derived from the aggravated contradictions in social reality. The perceptual form of the crisis lay in unstable and negative views of reality, and in the branching off into idealizations, where there was much leeway for fantasy and exaggeration. In place of the optimism, audacity, and self-assurance of the fifteenth century, the aristocratic High Renaissance brought doubt, discontent, caution, and bouts of self-delusion; in place of a clear and crisp artistic style, it favored idealization and grandeur (classicism), which passed immediately over to more fluid forms and open compositions, and next to outright departures from and challenges to "the natural" (Mannerism).

The driving contradiction in the High Renaissance mode of idealization was in the conflict between recognition of the unsteady, menacing face of worldly reality and the protective impulse to reach out for a more durable, attractive face via the operations of idealization. Writers could tend one way or the other.

In would-be realists, such as Bandello, Folengo, and Berni, the prevalence of disorder and moral anarchy is given its due: they turn the world into an arena for chaos and the whirling of irrational Fortune, or they dismiss its traditional scale of values. Thus for Berni, peaches, urinals, needles, second-hand garments, playing cards, and gelatine become fit subjects for solemn poetic eulogy. In Bandello's stories, happy men are inexplicably struck down; they are ruled by Fortune or by a dark, unpredictable explosiveness in themselves. And Folengo's hero, in the mock-heroic *Baldus*, a bastard grandson of Charlemagne, is a combination of violent ruffian and innocent, accompanied by a strange and scurrilous band: a first-class scoundrel (Cingar), a half-dog-half-man (Falchetto), a giant (Fracasso), a centaur, a pirate, a poet, a buffoon, and so on. The literary scholar R. Ramat has called the poem a hymn to chaos and its macaronic "the poetic language of the world as chaos."[4] In effect, the realists can bear reality only by caricaturing it.

In the best-loved poem of the century, Ariosto's epic romance *Orlando Furioso*, reality is wild, mysterious, magical, and unpredictable. It is the reality of a lushly imagined alternate world: a refracted image of the disarray in the world of the Italian Wars. The hero's moving passion is mad love; his brains eventually turn up on the moon. Yet throughout the work the poet makes continual contact with his own times, not only to catch and delight his courtly and upper-class readers (his intended audience) but also to impart moral lessons. He never loses sight of the opposition and harmonies between real and imaginary worlds.

In the writers and artists of idealist stamp, worldly reality is presented under the guise of perfected models. The sixteenth century is the age *par excellence* of an avid taste for works—mainly in dialogue form—that treat the ideals of perfect beauty, perfect love, perfect manners, the perfect state, the perfect world (utopia), the perfection of honor, and the perfection of a literary language. The disturbing image of the world as it is, a most imperfect reality, is always introduced into the discussions, but it is brought in as an inferior reality. Hence it is made worthy of censure and is somehow less true, or even less real, than the perfected *model* of reality. Suddenly we understand why the age was drawn irresistibly to Platonism, with its cleavage between the realm of perfect and eternal forms and the realm of mere shadow or inferior replicas, as represented to the senses.

The perfecting of a given reality by means of idealization seems simple enough as a process of thought. The results, however, are likely to be exceedingly complex, owing, in any discourse, to degrees of refinement, to ease in hair-splitting, to the twists of imagination, and to the influence of concealed pressures from outside the discourse proper. Yet the possibilities are finite, for consciousness, collective and individual, is keyed to a social structure, and this means that the products of idealization and imagination bear a traceable relation to that structure, a traceable relation to historical reality.

PATRONAGE IN DANGER

At the end of the fifteenth century the legal profession in Florence was attracting an increasing number of men from among the patriciate. Speaking of the first half of the sixteenth century, Carlo Dionisotti has observed that of one hundred writers of some importance, more than fifty were clerics or drew their incomes from ecclesiastical sources.[5] Twenty were bishops or cardinals; twelve were in regular religious orders; and twenty others were beneficed. Among the latter were writers who, like Ariosto, figured among the servitors and were in the pay of rich prelates. There is a good deal of evidence to show, moreover, that from the late fifteenth century onward, more of the peninsula's well-established and noble families made a determined effort to enlist sons in the clergy, with an eye to capturing the multiplicity of lucrative posts and absentee incomes.

Although economic opportunities were not broad before 1494, the fiscal strains of the Italian Wars made matters worse. The rocketing fashion for luxury and ostentation added greatly to the burdens of family finances, and very much larger sums of capital were doled out in the form of dowries. Especially among families from the ruling social tiers, or among those still striving to establish the credentials of gentility, aristocratic trends became sharper and disdain for active trade—not for business investment—came to be more widespread. The century of Italy's humiliation imposed a need for show and for compensatory heroics on the ruling classes, as in the mania for dueling, for big architectural undertakings, and for "honor and honorable pursuits." The fifteenth-century building boom had been the articulation of a new self-assurance and a domineering social identity. After 1500, the boom continued but its springs changed: the upper-class groups now sought in architecture what they had lost in leadership and politics—undisputed sway over the peninsula. The best places for income with honor were four: the princely courts, the profession of arms, the Church, and the law courts. However, when the Italian Wars, with their "innumerable horrible calamities" (Guicciardini), menaced place, pension, and sinecure at the courts, the Church and the legal profession promised a safer ground for careers. Besides, a talented cleric or jurisconsult was usually free to accept a call to one of the princely seats of power, whether as administrator, adviser, professor, or raconteur. And this touches a major sore, the vocation of regular cleric. Most of the writers numbered among the regular clergy were long estranged from the community life of their religious orders: Bandello, Firenzuola, Folengo, Doni, Lando, and others. An entertaining storyteller, the Dominican friar Bandello, much preferred courts and the company of grand people, and he was warmly sought out by them. The times and the condition of the Church made for a keen dissatisfaction with holy vows—one of our paradigmatic contradictions.

The beleaguered situation of the courts put patronage in danger, because they were pressed for cash and plagued by fears real and imaginary. Seeking grandeur, princes turned to a self-image which called for splendor in the aims of patronage, but the expense of grandeur was also a long train of unfinished works. We need look no further for the major reasons behind much of the work left unfinished by Leonardo, Michelangelo, and others, although the romantic view prefers to find the flaw in genius. Overambitious patrons moved artists around from one unfinished commission to another. Time passed and patrons died, or they or their monies were swept away by invading armies and political emergencies. When Ludovico Sforza was overthrown by Louis XII, a whole corps of artists and writers was abruptly dispersed. The like happened at Urbino in 1501 and again in 1516, when two different dukes were driven out of the duchy by arms and the close relatives of popes. As Cesare Borgia streaked through the Romagna, he attracted writers, among them well-known figures such as Serafino Aquilano and Calmeta, but his even more sudden fall made for another scatter of talent. The overthrow of Florentine republics in 1512 and 1530 resulted in numerous victims and exiles. Machiavelli was one, and the experience forced him into writing and study. Michelangelo, in 1530, lay temporarily under a sentence of death. Guicciardini fell victim to political events of the later 1520s, and his writings reveal the scars of the experience.

Because of political and military difficulties, as well as their ostentation, the Gonzaga and the Este were repeatedly in arrears in stipends due their lettered servitors and artists. At Rome the ambitions and magnificence of the High Renaissance popes served to lure talent and fill the city with genius. This in itself, however, produced waves of uncertainty, not because of the rivalries and odium among competing personalities but because the death of every pope left unfinished monuments and provoked sudden anxieties and new rivalries. This is why the death of the sybaritic Leo X (1521) and the advent of Pope Adrian VI, a "barbarian" of modest origins known for his austerity and rectitude, stunned the Roman curia with anger and distress. Writing from Rome during the tense weeks of that interregnum, Castiglione, trying to explain his state of mind to his mother, admitted to being seized by a tumult of confusion and ill-defined fears, so "that it seems to me I am in a new world and that Rome is no longer where it was."[6]

In the second half of the sixteenth century, Italy's social and economic difficulties, as recorded along the track of patronage, were summed up, arguably, in Torquato Tasso's bouts of insanity. The greatest Italian poet after Ariosto, he had seen his father hounded by financial difficulties, charged with treason in the kingdom of Naples (1552), and forced to flee in exile. Forcibly separated from his mother and sister at the age of nine, owing to his father's need of patronage, Torquato could not bear afterward to be dependent on the patronage of the court of Ferrara, where he had rooms and a stipend. He took the court's every oversight to be an insult to his person and genius and, breaking forth into fits of violence, was put into chains.

There was no more courtly poet than Tasso in sixteenth-century Italy, not even Niccolò da Correggio or Bembo, but also none as tormented, irascible, restless, and mad.

The conditions of patronage touched all the peninsula's ranking artists and writers, even those who were wellborn or rich in their own right, and the reason for this was in the fierce pursuit of honors. Although the beneficiary of a large private income,[7] Castiglione never stopped exerting pressure, wherever he was, whether at Mantua, Urbino, or Rome, to obtain higher posts, incomes, and ambassadorial honors. Eventually, he took holy orders, became a bishop, and by the time he died (1529) he was doubtless aiming at a cardinal's hat. The Venetian aristocrat and dictator of literary fashion Bembo managed to attain this dignity—which he had coveted desperately—thanks to the efforts of his powerful patron, Cardinal Farnese. Ariosto, who expected to garner a place from Leo X and even dared to hope for an episcopal appointment, was acutely embarrassed by the cold reception accorded him in Rome and never forgot the injury. The historian and political thinker Francesco Guicciardini—lawyer, courtier, papal governor —losing the support and patronage of Pope Clement VII, was cast into melancholy, having, he boasted in his *Oratio accusatoria*, maintained a house "full of tapestries, silver, and servants . . . and never riding forth with a guard of less than 100 or 150 horsemen."

The insecurity of patronage had this effect, that it prevented foreign invasion and political earthquakes from remaining external facts for writers, artists, and humanist scholars. Direct consequences turned those facts into intimate experience. The troubled times became a time of trouble for those who selectively traced the contours of upper-class consciousness by means of their art and writings. One of the most aloof of thinkers, Guicciardini, striving for factual toughness and cold analysis in his monumental *History of Italy*, was writing, in effect, a chronicle of his own times conceived of as an age ravaged by Fortune. The substance of his message was a call to dignity among the defeated, his audience of educated bourgeois and aristocratic readers.

RELIGION AND LEADERSHIP

Despite the Renaissance papacy, the Italian people continued to see Rome as the center of Christendom. At the height of the Borgian pontificate, 1499–1500, no less a man than the cynical Ludovico Sforza declared, in his political testament, that he wanted his son and heir to the Milanese duchy "brought up . . . to give due reverence to the holy pontiff, the vicar of God."[8] It was a remarkable statement, coming from the mouth of an archetypal practitioner of power politics, from one who suspected that Alexander VI had bought the papal tiara and that his own brother, Cardinal

Ascanio Sforza, was one of the men bought. Ludovico was not, it should be stressed, distinguishing casuistically between man and office, Alexander Borgia and Pope Alexander. If nothing else, his statement warns us of the profundity of contradictions in the experience and consciousness of the age.

The religious dimension is given prominence here to underline the crisis in leadership and the fracture in conscience. For if the critical external contradictions in sixteenth-century Italy were in the polarities between poverty and concentrated wealth and between power and powerlessness, the most striking internal or psychological contradiction was in the antithesis between the practice and the ideal aims of religion, particularly as observed in the life of leading ecclesiastics and members of the regular clergy.

Religion gave the way to distinguish elementary right from wrong; it provided the only ready-to-hand measure of good and bad. Yet this seemed to be negated in the spectacle of everyday experience by the cynical attitudes and careerism of the upper clergy, by the examples of gross irregularity in conventual life, by the careless sale of pardons and indulgences, and by the incidence not only of absentee bishops but also of absentee parish rectors. In a word, leadership gave the appearance of having abdicated. And witnessing this in the close public space of fortified cities, populace and ruling elites were pitched into anxiety and other troubled states of conscience, or into mere cynicism. This is why Machiavelli could say that the Church had deprived Italy of religion.

But the need for religion remained, all the more so amid the terrors and wreckage of the Italian Wars. Mystical, prophetic, and apocalyptic preaching by friars and religious hermits increased noticeably in the late fifteenth and early sixteenth centuries. Popular piety sometimes took fire and burned brightly. Religious processions were common. In conditions of plague, large numbers of flagellants, children naked from the waist up, appeared in Rome in the summer of 1522, calling for mercy. Noted preachers attracted great throngs of people. On special occasions attendance at sermons was, in any case, high, even among Florentines, who "once sold cunning to all the world." The quotation, from the poet Cammelli, put such selling in the past tense so as to contrast it with the credulous religious frenzies of Savonarola's time, the 1490s; but Florentine events of the later 1520s also provoked a resurgence of religious fervor. At Milan, in the 1520s and 1530s, the laity was waiting and longing for religious guidance.

The governing class was deeply implicated in clerical abuse and the neglect of parishes because of its hold over the positions of authority within the Italian Church. And any major dignities for men of middle-class birth were likely to have been doled out by prelates born into the rich, noble, feudal, or princely families. This capture of the Church—not for the first time in its history—was fostered by the difficulties of the Renaissance economy, the slow spread of the disdain for active trade, and the illness of a social identity that knew not how to define itself save in terms of grandeur, ostentatious display, and the exaggerations of honor. Sons and nephews were thus pushed into the clergy. In the most successful cases, a man might finally hold two or even three bishoprics, in addition to a hoard of other benefices and preferments. Living as princes, prelates were often completely void of a religious calling, and the inevitable result in parish life was the decay of spiritual supervision.

In the 1460s, when Francesco Gonzaga was elevated to the cardinalate, his father, marquis of Mantua, wrote a letter of fatherly good counsel, urging him to avoid scandal, to study, to be humane, "and although you are a cardinal, be religious and observe your obligations."[9] The marquis had indignantly rejected the suggestion in 1460 that he buy the dignity for Francesco for 10,000 ducats of gold. By the beginning of the sixteenth century the price had gone up: a cardinal's hat then cost about 25,000 ducats. Popes Innocent, Alexander, Julius, Leo, and Clement handed out cardinalships as part of dowry and marriage arrangements for their close relatives, and they regularly used such appointments, as well as offers of episcopal titles, to procure advantages in political deals. Giovanni de' Medici, later Pope Leo X, became a cardinal at the age of thirteen. Others, such as Ercole Gonzaga and Catelano Trivulzio, became bishops at fifteen and sixteen. Some families had a virtual stranglehold on appointment to certain episcopacies. So it was entirely normal for Ludovico Sforza to press the candidacy of his natural son, Cesare, whose mother was the beautiful and clever Cecilia Gallerani, for the archiepiscopal dignity of Milan when the boy was not yet ten years old.

Historical scholarship has made much of a group of celebrated Catholic reformers, preeminent for their piety in the college of cardinals during the first half of the sixteenth century. Among these were the Italians Giacomo Sadoleto, Gasparo Contarini, Giovanni Morone, and Gian Pietro Carafa. For all their genuine fervor—and here again we touch the fracture in conscience —they were "pluralists," the beneficiaries of incomes from a plurality of church livings, and thus necessarily compelled to be nonresident clerics.[10] Yet the blame, if we can speak of blame, lay not with them. Conscience was here the victim of fiscal reality: if they were to live up to the rank and carry out their mission as cardinals, they had to draw on large pluralist incomes. This was imposed by ecclesiastical finance. Moreover, the few reformers in the cardinalate were greatly outweighed (and outclassed) by the number and variety of worldly prelates, not to mention the popes themselves: by men such as the author of a ribald comedy (*Calandria*), Cardinal Bibbiena— witty servitor of the Medici, elegant courtier, shrewd diplomat, and a great favorite with court ladies; Cardinal Ippolito d'Este, another ladies' man, whose father, Duke Ercole of Ferrara, once had to plead with him to re- frain, as cardinal, from putting on a dashing suit of white armor and taking up arms for Ludovico Sforza against Louis XII; or, later, the Venetian aristocrat and man of letters Cardinal Bembo, courtier and aesthete, as well as one-time lover, Platonic and otherwise; or other voluptuaries from the Medici, Farnese, Gonzaga, Della Rovere, Trivulzio, and families of like kind.

Studies of episcopal visitations confirm the essential picture drawn by the avalanche of anticlerical literature, regarding the neglect and laxity in parish and conventual life. At Lucca, during much of the sixteenth century, there was intense rivalry, occasionally erupting into open violence, among the cathedral canons, the Dominicans of San Romano, and the Lateran canons of San Frediano. The disputes concerned matters of property, ceremonial precedence (honor), appointments, and sexual abuse. In the diocese of Trent, in 1537, it was found that 20 percent of the priests kept concubines. Earlier, at Pavia, inquiries into twenty-six urban parishes turned up eighteen concubines. Again at Milan, in the 1520s and 1530s, citizens were seriously troubled by sexual irregularities among the members of religious orders, and the authorities often heard of sexual violence committed by monks, particularly in the country districts. But reform efforts there ran up against powerful family interests and were consistently blocked. When Milan's main public body, the senate, ordered the dissolution of a convent in 1538, owing to its reputation for sexual license, the abbess appealed to Cardinal Crescenzi in Rome and the proceedings were halted. Mariano da Genazzano, a fashionable Augustinian preacher, had refused to help reform a convent at Ferrara in 1491 because he foresaw trouble with certain influential families.

Confession and communion seem to have been general at Easter, but we shall never know what percentage of the population sometimes went without communion for years. The figure of 10 percent for Pavia cannot be taken as typical. There was, in any case, little enough direction and cure of souls in many a parish, if we judge by the findings of episcopal visitations at Piacenza and Pavia. In the former, between about 1510 and 1520, and "overwhelming" number of parish-church heads (rectors) were nonresident. Mass was said daily in only six of the nineteen parishes visited. And matters remained much the same under the next bishop, as shown by the visitation of 1554, in the time of Catelano Trivulzio, who resided in the diocese, all told, for only a few months, although he was bishop of Piacenza for thirty-four years (1525–1559).

The visitations at Pavia revealed that only four parish churches kept inventories of their real property and that there was general ignorance about the lands and buildings belonging to parish churches. The spiritual life of the laity can have been given no better care. The spoliation of Church property in Renaissance Italy is still rather an open question—not so the general identity of the beneficiaries. Alienated property tended to stick to the hands of princes and, even more so, of prepotent local families. Occasionally there was recourse to outright violence. The chief agents of such long-term theft ("usurpation") were the tonsured sons and relatives of the beneficiaries. They pilfered for their families, and very often, of course, records were destroyed in the process. In the economic and moral conditions of the age, the piracy of Church property became irresistible. The disease of nonresidence among rectors was also rooted in economics: a well-connected priest with a dozen benefices could not be in twelve different places at once, and so he hired substitutes, wretched vicars who had little training and a pittance in wages. Their lot was particularly grievous in country parishes.

In these circumstances, the lower clergy were too easily held in contempt, while the upper clergy were respected for their trappings and social rank. And stories did the rounds of court buffoons and dwarfs whose parodies of the Mass, in a macaronic Latin, were alleged to be more impressive than the real rite of many a poor priest.

In its bureaucracy and leadership, the Italian Church had gone aristocratic; it had lost vital touch with the populace. This is why it took the episcopate a generation to recognize that the spread of Protestant heresy in Italy was a major danger to itself. The arrogant hierarchy found it hard at first to credit the threat to its authority, yet it also feared and despised the broad support of the laity for any doctrinal novelty. The eleventh session of the Fifth Lateran Council (December 19, 1516) went so far as to forbid sermons on lax conditions within the Church, alleging that they made for scandal among the ignorant. Rome and the hierarchy believed that the common people were foolish and gullible, that doctrine was the business of the established authorities and of no one else. The paternalism of this viewpoint had ancillary support in the ideals of the ruling groups and oligarchies, as these became more exclusive, in-turned, and castelike.

Italian presses published Luther as early as 1519. Soldiers, merchants, and other travelers transmitted the new ideas; but the most effective agents of Protestant diffusion were the itinerant preachers. The control of heresy belonged to the office of bishops down to 1542, and conditions varied from diocese to diocese, so that if heretical preachers kept themselves on the move, they could count on a good deal of safety. By the 1540s, Lucca, Modena, Vicenza, and Como, with their small clandestine churches, were the main centers of Protestantism in Italy, but there were also important conventicles at Milan, Cremona, Piacenza, Bologna, Padua, and Naples. The core of Italian Protestantism was in the desire for a spiritual reawakening. Most converts came from the middle levels of society, ranging from modest artisans to rich merchants, minor noblemen, and even, here and there, a few patricians. Country folk produced few converts; so also, with notable exceptions, the powerful nobility and the very rich. Renée of France, the Protestant duchess of Ferrara, was progressively isolated by her husband and her contacts broken, until she returned to end her days in France. With the establishment of the Roman office of the Inquisition (July 1542), the dangers for religious dissenters increased a hundredfold, and soon diehard Protestants had either to suffer martyrdom or flee into exile. A generation of famous fugitives was born. In the 1550s the Protestant community of Lucca made a mass exodus to Geneva.

Calvin had denounced "Nicodemism," the belief of some Protestants in the value of keeping silence and worshipping in secrecy. This was a sign, said he, of weak faith. Silence was no instrument for the propagation of evangelism; and yet, so some believed, it allowed you to save your own soul. Especially widespread in Italy, the Nicodemist attitude underlined both the numerical weakness of Italian Protestantism and the strong element of elitism in society and consciousness. The attitude rejected the larger community and demoted civil society for the sake of the few who would have eternal salvation. The outstanding practitioners of Nicodemism, recruited almost entirely from among the nobility, were the followers (Valdesiani) of Juan de Valdes (d. 1541). They emphasized a deep inner spirituality and the saving power of a mystic faith. They also deemed the sacraments unnecessary but did not openly reject them; and if, after all, these gave some help, the believer might have recourse to them. Salvation, in any case, was only for a tiny minority. Valdesiani were thus moved by an aristocratic individualism and a strong sense of belonging to a highly select circle. There was no question of carrying such a message of salvation into the *piazza*. Salvation—like wealth and power—was for the fortunate few, the "six thousand" imagined by Valdes.

Neither princes nor oligarchies rallied to the cause of Protestantism, as often happened in Northern Europe; the peninsula's middle classes did not sufficiently respond; and reform-minded aristocrats either withdrew to the experience of an inner illumination or, like cardinals Morone and Carafa, longed for reform of the Church within the old structures. But the source of corruption was in the upper-class stranglehold on the Church's command positions. In short, there was no true challenge to the Church in Italy because none came from those with the power to effect change. Too many leading families had a material stake in the Church; too many looked upon it, in its antiquity, as the heir in some sense to the glory that was Rome (in their hour of defeat they were not going to give this too up to the barbarians); and too many had been rendered lukewarm or cynical by the corruption of the papacy and the wild venality of ecclesiastical office, though they themselves had connived in this. Ercole d'Este, duke of Ferrara (d. 1505), was a mixture of easy superstition and coldblooded political opportunism. He was much swayed by religious fads and the working of miracles. But his eminent daughter, Isabella, the worldly marquise of Mantua, did not share these interests, nor did her son, Federico, who in the 1520s kept around himself a buffoon named Crucifix. In November 1512, Isabella and her husband had one of their dwarfs, done up in bishop's attire, greet the duke of Milan. He "seemed the most beautiful thing in the world—and he came forward to meet the duke with great ceremony, which was no ordinary pleasure and made everyone laugh."[11] The lords of Mantua used to delight in watching their dwarf, Nanino, come out dressed as a priest to do a parody of the Mass by running through a litany of his supposed illustrious lineage. Nanino was deriding himself and the central mystery of the Church, to the hilarious delectation of the Gonzaga court.

Francesco Guicciardini concluded in the late 1530s (*Storia d'Italia*, IV, 12) that the papacy's unbridled love of power and lucre had worn away all reverence for the pontifical dignity in the hearts of the Italian people. This was not true. But certainly among the ruling groups, a Valdesian spiritualism and withdrawal, or Isabella d'Este's amused detachment, made more obvious sense than her father's credulous and capricious piety, particularly when upper-class belief is put into the context of the craze for violent pasquinades against popes and cardinals. This fashion issued in a richly defamatory literature, dished out in the form of witticisms, epitaphs, short poems, and well-wrought sonnets. The talent ranged from that of anonymous poetasters up to that of writers like Sannazaro, Berni, and Aretino. At the height of the craze (1500–1530), the most scurrilous lampoons and verses—often but not always posted on a statue in Rome—were passed greedily around from hand to hand and collected by diplomatic envoys to dispatch to their eager masters back home. No pope or cardinal escaped the parade of wit.

Of Paul II (d. 1471), for example, it was said that as he had a daughter, there must have been a mother; hence he should be called not "Holy Father" but "happy father." Sixtus IV (d. 1484), "triumphant in crimes," made Rome teem with usury, murder, robbery, and violence. "Rest be granted by the devil to Pope Sixtus, / Friend to Satan, enemy to Christ." Innocent VIII (d. 1492) had numerous bastards and died of overprocreation. Alexander VI (d. 1503) "sells the key, the altars, Christ. / Well he might, having bought them first." When Julius II died (1513), his poor soul could find a place neither in heaven nor hell, for "I brought God down so low, / He doesn't even know how to find lodgings for my soul." On the death of Leo X (1521), one wag wrote: "His last moments come, he couldn't even have the sacraments. By God, he'd sold them!" The pontificate of the Dutch pope, the "barbarian" Adrian VI (d. 1523), provoked an explosion of fury and hundreds of pages of lampoons against him and his electors, the college of cardinals. Accused of having betrayed the Church and Italy to foreigners and barbarians, the cardinals were called thieves, liars, traitors, forgers, scoundrels, criminals, and sodomites. The next pope, Clement VII (d. 1534), reportedly broke down and wept when he read Aretino's verses on his complicity in the Sack of Rome.[12]

POLITICAL THINKING: MAN AGAINST UNREASON

Machiavelli blazes forth in the political science of the sixteenth century because he dared to gaze at events in the name of action. Appalled by the Italian catastrophe and the puny stature of his native Florence, he yearned to change the course of events. In his zeal for action, he wrenched politics free from traditional morality, the better to chart its autonomous movements. And straightway he confronted the problem of relations between men and events, between will and Fortune (*fortuna*), between what is and what men desire and can accomplish. The posing of these unstable polarities, in part contradictory and in part complementary, represented the intellectual formulation of Italy's political ills.

The dynamic aspect in Machiavelli's vision of politics is in the shifting opposition and union between *virtù* and *fortuna* and in the conflict between the State and the antisocial beast in man. *Virtù* is talented will power in great political affairs, the stuff of leadership and success. It may belong to individuals as to collectivities. *Fortuna* is the sum of forces lying beyond *virtù*—forces hostile, neutral, or helpful, but always changing. In its changes, *fortuna* may include or at any moment exclude the antisocial vices, but *virtù* can never really include the beast in man, for when the prince elects to partake of the beast in order to accomplish a political end, the choice is a rational one, made to serve the ends of the state. If in *The Prince* Machiavelli emphasizes relations between *virtù* and *fortuna*, in *The Discourses*, looking to the political health of collectivities, he gives more emphasis to relations between *virtù* and political corruption (*virtù* gone decadent). In fact, these contrapuntal pairings were a formulation of the overwhelming question for Italian society: could the ruling classes rule? How much real control had they over political processes, over events, over the environment, over the peninsula's forthcoming destinies?

The obvious answer, as drawn in the preceding chapter, was alarming: for the concussion of foreign invasion had rudely exposed the inner weaknesses of the Italian states, particularly in their debilitating schisms and suspicions between rulers and ruled. Former differences had turned into disabling contradictions. Geared to action, Machiavelli caught the basic social contradiction (rulers-ruled) but posed it in the form of a challenge to leadership, a challenge viewed in terms of the conflict and concord between *virtù* and *fortuna* or of the difference between *virtù* and political corruption. The real test, however, shorn of its mystifications, was another: to govern unresponsive communities in a time of emergency.

Machiavelli's plunge towards action imposed the necessity to weigh the variety of forces that obstruct political achievement. The insistence upon action is what endows his vision with its disturbing and exciting unity: here realist and utopian are so closely entangled that it is almost impossible to pick them apart; and here too a grasp of contraries (e.g., *virtù-fortuna*, State-beast) bestows the vital tension. But Machiavelli was not alone in conceiving of politics in terms of contraries; he was alone only in achieving a unity of vision, thanks to his passionate dogmatism in 1513–1515 about the need for action.

Again and again, in sixteenth-century Italy, we come upon political thinkers who understand politics and states in terms of dualisms. They move in their reasoning processes between key, contrasting terms, in order to account for the sources of strife and to work out their *idealized* solutions. The main antitheses are these:

reason	—— passions
virtù	—— *fortuna*
man	—— beast
elites	—— multitudes
rich	—— poor
State	—— ambition (individual egotism)
civil society	—— anarchic nature
law	—— violence
order	—— disorder

There is much overlapping and terms are movable. Reason may be contrasted with beast or with *fortuna*; rich-poor may be another form of elites-multitudes; State may stand against nature; and order could be used to sum up all the terms on the left-hand side. In the title of this part of the chapter, the antithesis "man against unreason" has been used as shorthand for the list as a whole.

In his worldly maxims, the *Ricordi*, Francesco Guicciardini is repeatedly driven to pit experience and prudence against external forces: the constant opponents are the world and the honor-bound ego of the aristocrat. But he ended, in his *Storia d'Italia*, by making Fortune the chief winner in history and in contemporary politics. Another Florentine aristocrat, his friend Francesco Vettori, wrote a chronicle of his own times, *Summary of the History of Italy from 1511 to 1527*, which also concludes that Fortune is lord of the world and man the victim. Neither reason nor any assortment of virtues can prevail against it.

But apart from out-and-out moralists, political thinkers of the High Renaissance did not tend to remain stuck in the despairing pessimism of the two Florentines. From about 1530 on and to the late sixteenth century, there was an irresistible fashion for solving the problems of political instability by spinning forth ideal schemes: monarchies headed by good princes, or "mixed" constitutions (after the Venetian model) that found the perfect way to sublimate or to repress the irrational forces in society. Here, again, the elaboration of ideal schemes moved from destructive contraries to political tranquillities. Sebastiano Erizzo (1555) frankly invoked the much-admired Venetian constitution as the way to stop the wheel of Fortune and to establish a fixed polity. Time could have a stop.

Gasparo Contarini, Donato Giannotti, Giovan Maria Memmo, Bartolommeo Cavalcanti, Erizzo, and Paolo Paruta were among the best-known of a train of thinkers for whom the Venetian constitution was the supreme political construct. It was a wall against the forces of disorder, a way to honor for the nobility and to the good life for people of respectable and hardworking stamp. In the more articulated versions of this mythopoesis—Contarini, Giannotti—the Venetian state embodied the ideal mixture of monarchy, aristocracy, and democracy. The three classical polities were represented by the doge, the senate, and the great council, and in this form they made for a system of finely tuned checks and balances. But the true perfection of the system was that it satisfied all the "natural" civil desires of the worthy part of humanity—the middle and upper classes. It conceded grandeur to the few men who rightly aspired thus (monarchy: the doge and his powerful college of advisers); it granted major honors and the right of decision making to all the notable men of the community (aristocracy: the senate); and by according a basic participation in the political process to a large public body (democracy: the great council), it allowed for a substantial measure of political freedom, thus fulfilling the legitimate and natural desires of the whole collectivity of citizens. When frustrated by deficient political systems, the legitimate desires of the three social estates degenerated into dangerous passions, smashed forth in political tumult, and overturned states. The perfect constitution—utopia—had settled this problem for all times.

But the perfect solution oddly overlooked something: what did you do with the fourth estate, the large mass of people who did not qualify for citizenship? Intriguingly, they faded into the world of unreason. The process may be seen in Girolamo Garimberto's *De regimenti publici de la città* (Venice, 1544). Set among a changing party of lords, bishops, and other dignitaries, this dialogue draws a clean distinction between those who are born for rule and those born to be ruled. It is the difference between the few and the many. And nature, underlining this, has a physique for each. Generally, the servile are "brutish and robust of body" and hence "more fit for struggle," whereas "those of elegant and delicate form are more fit to have knowledge and to command." Old riches—nobility—provide the ideal social background to free the mind for virtue and leadership. Freedom from want makes for an unencumbered mind. This excludes the poor from the realm of virtue and knowledge because they are flogged around by need, so that "many of them incline toward vice and crime." There are two sorts of people among the multitude: one low and bestial, driven by the force of passion, the other honest and industrious, turned toward virtue and therefore fit for a voice in government. But the multitude of those denied citizenship includes the vast majority of people—the peasantry, hired labor, artisans, craftsmen, and even the class of merchants, for all these are motivated by a base preoccupation, namely, the desire for "earnings and profit [*guadagno*]."[13]

In coursing his way between contraries to the ideal city-state, Garimberto keeps to the exemplary image of Venice, where politics is the business of the nobility and a special grade of citizens (the virtuous fragment of the multitude). Even Sparta failed to attain Venice's superiority, for the Spartans excluded the subject population from their city, whereas the Venetians admit great throngs and exclude them only from government, thereby enhancing the city's riches. The decisive stroke in Venetian history, result- ing in a unique historical stability, was the decision to bar the plebeians from politics and government. Plebeians in Venice are such "a mixture of ignoble blood, sordid earnings, and different customs and peoples, that even if they had been given little authority, they would have been able constantly to shake up the quiet of the Venetian state, also because plebeians naturally hate the nobility." This statement nearly completes the range of Garim- berto's principal contraries: free–servile, virtue–vice, reason–passion, rich– poor, and nobility–plebs. The hints of a mind-body dualism are present throughout. The ideal republic has its ultimate justification in Aristotle's definition of happiness, which pits the intellect against the passions. Says Garimberto: "the supreme felicity . . . is in the speculative part of our soul. This is more worthy and more excellent than the active [practical] part, which is subject to the movement of the passions." The "contemplative" part of the soul aims "at that felicity desired by all men but attained by few." This is precisely why the perfect republic, aiming at the highest happiness for its people, puts all political authority into the hands of the few citizens, however large the body of subjects. They know better.[14]

The influence of Aristotle and Plato on sixteenth-century thought needs no commentary here. They were household names in educated circles; they were also the object of much secondhand knowledge and misinformation. Polite society used classical philosophy as it saw fit, drawing it deftly into its mental world of dualisms, its fractured consciousness. The fracture was reflected in "high" culture. Garimberto inadvertently points to it, in the art of the period, by his distinction between "free" and "servile" bodies. He all but identifies Mannerism's preoccupation with "elegant and delicate" forms. So far as this style depended on deliberate idealizations and distortions, on conscious departures from "nature," so far was there an active conflict between the given and the wished-for, what is and what ought to be, the real and the ideal. The tormented side of Mannerism has often been noted.

Garimberto's way of seeing is paradigmatic, owing to his array of dichotomies. His dialogue illustrates a typical operation in the thinking of the period: a winding between social-political contraries (nobility-plebs), a fade-in to their intellectualized equivalents (reason-passion, mind-body), and an arrival at ideal solutions.

A variation of this pattern moved from the contrast between *virtù* and *fortuna*, a reformulation of the supposed conflict between voluntaristic man and the resisting world. Garimberto, Giovan Francesco Lottini, Paolo Paruta, and other political thinkers of the middle and later part of the sixteenth century speak of the "external goods" of fortune, meaning riches, honors, and power. They set these off against the intellect and virtues, "the goods of the soul." This was an Aristotelian and medieval commonplace. But in the political and social thought of the High Renaissance, the pairing of opposites such as *virtù-fortuna*, or man-fortune, derived from a profoundly aristocratic vision and usually ended with a lurch into idealism. Guicciardini's historical universe is rife with such oppositions. All his personages in the *Storia d'Italia*, whether whipped or rewarded by fortune, are popes, kings, princes, aristocrats, generals, and oligarchs—quite naturally so. This is no setting for small men, who—being without *virtù*, ambition, or will—can only be mute and distant background shapes upon a stage meant for the great actors of the tragedy. Guicciardini observes in at least two of his *Ricordi* that the many usually stand in opposition to the few who make and execute high policy. In this alignment, the multitudes of men belong to the realm of fortune, to that part of fortune which may be subject to control by the few, though at any moment, in the form of "the people," it may also turn, in Guicciardini's words, into "a mad wild creature full of infinite errors and confusion, without judgment, loyalty or stability." Ludovico Sforza, in the noon of his success, called himself "the child of Fortune." Later, in his French dungeon, he would still be that.

The wheel of Fortune was a fitting cipher for the widespread feeling, among the upper classes, that men had lost control over their lives. The image summed up all the instabilities of the age. But more specifically, it was an ideological projection onto the events of history.[15] It was an effort—desperate, as we can now see—to make sense of the failure of the Italian ruling groups. It was *their* effort to explain the eruption and consequences of the Italian Wars. *Fortuna* was the world of unreason, looming just beyond the power of human control, although now and then, quite inexplicably, its motions coincided with the needs of states and rulers. And so it was variously described as a tempest, a fickle goddess, blind chance, an occult force, a providential mystery. When Fortune was linked to the punishment of sin and therefore to the hidden motions of God, it was still put beyond the ken of human reason. The question of relations between *virtù* (talented will) and Fortune had been discussed in the fifteenth century, but then *virtù* could be seen as the victor, especially in discussions set among the dominant social groups. After the outbreak of the Italian Wars, the *topos* invaded political reflection as well as literature and moral thought. In *The Prince* (Chap. 25) Machiavelli himself noted that in his time Italians had come to resign themselves increasingly to Fortune's sway over events, "because of the great upheavals in [our] affairs, beyond anything humanly imaginable, which we have seen and still see every day." And if, in the second half of the sixteenth century, certain writers tried occasionally to enlarge the scope within which man-will-virtue, seen as a unity, could be successful, the mere fact that the problem was so incessantly put, and so often answered in favor of Fortune, was testimony to the loss of faith in voluntaristic action. Rather, experience seemed to show that the scope of unreason had expanded and one of the stock responses was to plump for a species of stoicism.

In the obsession with categorical oppositions, the components of unreason (plebs, *fortuna*, passions, etc.) were habitually stacked on one side. This obsession was the measure of the Italian sense of being opposed by devastating odds—the politics and consequences of the Italian Wars. But the major shock in consciousness was taken by the class and groups in command; suddenly their identity was threatened; and the shock was inevitably registered in culture, in works of the imagination. The sense of being face to face with overwhelming odds led at once to an ardent search for solutions. From the time of Machiavelli and Guicciardini, to the late sixteenth century and the work of Paolo Paruta and Giovanni Botero, the great task for political science seemed to be that of breaking through appearances to get at putative essences. If inquiry could penetrate to the "real" nature of men and events, then an elite could point the way, offer some hope, or at least attain—so Guicciardini—the tragic dignity of knowledge. The enterprise seemed a daring search for political reality. Yet every breakthrough to an "essence"— to a law, a rule, a type, a pattern—bordered on a mystification or turned into a utopian sighting. The thinkers of the defeated overcame devastating odds by marching directly into them, so to speak, to grapple for essences and hence for ideal solutions. Paradoxically, the exercise ended in an evasion; reality collapsed into fantasy.

For Machiavelli, human salvation lay in politics and the state. His unity of vision derived from his unrelenting call to practical action. To this end he was brazenly ready to tailor facts and historical events into striking patterns, and these then became the guides to action. He envisaged a world renewed: realist and utopian were interlocked. Francesco Guicciardini, the great realist, leaned toward abstract rational solutions so long as he clung to his political hopes. In Book II of his *Dialogue on the Government of Florence* (1521–1525), seeking a solution to Florentine political instabilities, he sets out to outline a realistic constitution for Florence. Through his interlocutor, Bernardo del Nero, he warns against bookish political constructs and brainspun systems. He insists upon the application of experience and practicality, on the world as it is and not as men wish it to be. Yet by virtue of weighing all particulars, by taking a bit from here and a pinch from there, he ends by assembling a static political system, possible for states everywhere. Keeping in part to the Venetian model, Guicciardini's solution calls for a strong executive, a powerful senate, and a large legislative council. The lifetime executive office was to be held by a Medici lord, but the aristocratic senate would be the true pivot of power. Thus were the community's conflicting interests balanced and satisfied. One authority has concluded that the dialogue's second book "is nothing but a pure and abstract alchemy—a utopian political arithmetic."[16]

After Guicciardini came the mythologizing and ideal solutions of Contarini, Giannotti, Garimberto, L. P. Rosello, G. F. Lottini, Bartolommeo Cavalcanti, Sebastiano Erizzo, G. B. Pigna, Paruta, Botero, and others. The authors of "mixed" constitutions have been more studied than others because they were more inclined to deal with contrasting forces and real situations. But there was a line of monarchists (e.g., Rosello, Pigna, Lottini, and Botero) for whom the peace and justice of states was best realized by the government of wise, virtuous, God-fearing princes. Both schools, however, had an abstract rationalism in common. While seeing ignorance, the passions, and misguided ambition as the chief makers of discord and political weakness, both took reason and intellect to be the prime instruments of rule. All—aristocratic republicans as well as monarchists—tended to see the populace as a beast with many heads, a monster without a head, a continually changing sea, or an undistinguished mass: ignorant, vile, untrustworthy, gullible, and cowardly. Against these stood the few, the aristocrats and "true" princes, born free and born capable of intellect and virtue because of their social background. Stability and strength in government were achieved by keeping most people from its doors.[17]

The fracture in consciousness passed through political thinking. Foreign armies, resentful subjects, religious anxiety, and the pullulating signs of internal weakness apparently filled reality with dangers along a vast front. The world thus seemed to split into two realities, the realm of man and the realm of unreason. But "man" here signified the oligarch and the aristocrat. In the campaign to understand social earthquakes and failures in leadership, political intellectuals cast these problems in the form of a cleavage between reason (i.e., the self, man) and the opposition (unreason), and they then proceded to range most of humanity on the side of unreason. Seeing politics, with few exceptions, from the viewpoint of the ruling groups, and perceiving the danger to those in traditional command, they reproduced the fundamental social schism in their very thinking: they put the populace— throwing in too, for good measure, the "ignorant" part of the rich—among the forces of unreason and potential disorder. At this point, only one route remained open to them in the working out of their political ideas—the way of idealism and perfect constitutions. An old debate was suddenly brought back to life: which was "higher and more perfect," the life of action or the life of contemplation? In Venice, where the republic survived in company with the tenacious myth of a responsible and hardworking patriciate, the attempt was sometimes made, as in Paruta's *Della perfettione della vita politica* (1579), to balance the two ideals. But elsewhere, just as ideal constitutions won out, so also did the ideals of a "pure" intellect inclined toward reflection on the true, the good, and the divine. Idealism was an exit to a better, "higher" world. But it was grounded in the antinomies of a divided consciousness.

THE LANGUAGE QUESTION

One of the cardinal debates for Italian culture around 1500 concerned the question of a suitable literary language—*la questione della lingua*. Tellingly, in this debate, it was impossible to obfuscate the social core of the question. Italian culture entered the sixteenth century in crisis, and that crisis pressed men of letters for a candid decision on the question of whether a polished Latin or an Italian vernacular was the appropriate language for literature and imagination; and if a vernacular, which one? The answer came from the courts and oligarchies, not from the academy.

The humanists had preferred the Latin of the Augustan Age. A few produced works in Italian, but they sought to save their best labors for Latin, the only language worthy of true glory. They managed to impart this vision to a select part of the upper classes and received, in turn, social accreditation for their educational program. At the same time, however, and in the same circles, a strong interest persisted in vernacular literature. Dante, Boccaccio, and Petrarch were much read in the fifteenth century. Dante's *Divine Comedy* was almost the only work taken into exile by Ludovico Sforza. The outstanding vernacular poets of the Quattrocento—Lorenzo de' Medici, Poliziano, Sannazaro, and Boiardo—were formed in part by humanism. Lorenzo and his circle even entertained the idea of having classical Latin works translated into the vernacular, with a view to extending and promoting Florence's cultural primacy. Yet no debate had been held on "the language question" and no one could truly say when Boiardo died (1494) that imaginative literature was turning definitively toward vernacular usage.

Suddenly, right around 1500, amid the clangor of the Italian Wars, the debate broke forth. Two observations merit emphasis. First, the controversy originated in discussions held among courtiers at Urbino and Mantua, Rome and Milan.[18] Second, it drew immediately away from all provincialisms and looked to the whole peninsula, in pursuit of a literary language that would cut across dialects and give to Italy a unified tongue. In the 1460s, Lorenzo de' Medici had called attention to the riches and subtlety of the Tuscan vernacular and held that it was becoming ever more perfect: "daily it renders itself more elegant and noble [*gentile*]." However, his praise was really meant for the Florentine tongue. Later, after the debate had been launched, Machiavelli and other Florentine writers would repeatedly return to the Tuscan and Florentine character of the triumphing literary vernacular, but even they took for granted the concept of a single native literature for Italy.

The campaign for a unified literary vernacular started in the hour of Italy's gravest divisiveness, just when it had fallen prey to foreign invaders. Here was the first contradiction, though one which promised an apparent resolution in the debate's veiled attempt to heal *in culture* the peninsula's deep political and social wounds. For the concussion of invasion and foreign interference drew Italians together in a cultural sense, in no other sense. But the literary imagination could not perform the office that belonged to politics and social groups, and a new set of contradictions now sprang forth in linguistic and literary theory.

As late as the 1520s there were literati—Romolo Amaseo, for one—who defended Latin as the language of gentlemen and defined the vernacular as the speech of the lower classes. "A language of the plebs is a plebeian language," said the humanist, Francesco Bellafini, in 1530. Francesco Florido sustained in 1537 that Latin was more serious and dignified, "more noble, sweeter and more perfect than the vernacular." But these were minority views at cross-purposes with the mainstream. From the outset of the debate, the predominant judgment was that for imaginative literature—whatever about learned discourse—Italian was the equal of Latin and possibly superior. A fundamental question remained: there being so much regional variation, which of the Italian vernaculars was the best expressive vehicle for literature?

The sustained phase of the debate probably started with Calmeta (Vincenzo Colli, d. 1508), a literary courtier attached consecutively to the courts of Rome, Milan, Mantua, and Urbino, and for four or five years in the service of Cesare Borgia. His work on the subject, *Della volgar poesia*, written about 1503 and dedicated to the duchess of Urbino, was lost. But his thesis has been gleaned from contemporary sources. He held, it seems, that the ideal vernacular for poetry should combine the speech of courtiers and distinguished men at the court of Rome with the language of Dante and Petrarch. Converging on Rome from different parts of Italy, curialists, resident ambassadors, and others fell, reportedly, into favoring certain forms of speech, thereby fashioning a "courtly language" (*lingua cortigiana*)—the usage of the "best" men of Italy.

Although the stress on Roman curial usage passed, the idea of a courtly language, as the one best for literature, attracted strong advocates for the next two generations. Mario Equicola (d. 1525), another learned courtier and secretary to the marchesana of Mantua, argued that writers should draw upon the most cultivated Roman usage and considered the living Tuscan to be a plebeian language. "As in political life, so also in speaking," he noted, "we should distinguish ourselves in some fashion from the ignorant multitude." Baldasar Castiglione, the model for courtiers, urged in his *Il Cortegiano* (1528) the observance of the best usage—usage among the elite social groups—from all parts of Italy; and, like Equicola, he went so far as to accept the French and Spanish words that had already entered the current speech of the upper classes.

Three theses dominated the language debate: the one in favor of a cosmopolitan courtly language, as described above; the archaistic one advanced by Pietro Bembo, whose standard was the language of Petrarch and Boccaccio; and, finally, the thesis of the Tuscans, who favored the current Florentine or Tuscan.

Bembo's remarkably lucid *Prose della volgar lingua* (largely complete by 1512) was the most influential work to come out of the debate. This celebrated courtier had held discussions with Calmeta, Castiglione, and others at

Urbino and elsewhere. His criteria were both social and literary, as with the advocates of the curial and courtly line, but he gave particular care and emphasis to the literary and rhetorical ingredients of the debate. He transferred his theory of imitation from the ancients to the moderns. For him the great classical Roman writers were Cicero and Virgil; hence it was best for Latin composition to imitate them. Similarly, as the great masters of the vernacular were Boccaccio and Petrarch, they also should be imitated. Tuscan, he insisted, was to be preferred above all the other vernaculars, partly because it already boasted established masters, but also because of its rigorous grammatical rules. After all, what was a classicism without rules? But the elite vernacular had reached its summit in the fourteenth century, in the works of Petrarch and Boccaccio; therefore the vernacular for literature was their written language, not the changing (hence incorrect) speech of sixteenth-century Florence and the other Tuscan cities. Even Dante was sharply criticized for falling "too often into writing about the lowest and most base matters," and for using words "crude, filthy, ugly, and very harsh." Bembo concluded that "the language of literature . . . should not depend upon that of the populace." We are reminded of an English parallel, the Restoration's attack on Shakespeare: aristocratic taste censured him for seeming, in his imagery, to have been born the son of a wheelwright or rag vendor.

In the Tuscan-Florentine view, Tuscan was the peninsula's only recognized vernacular for literary endeavor and a direct line linked the language of the fourteenth-century masters to the speech of sixteenth-century urban Tuscany, Florence especially. Down to about 1560, this view gave importance to the vital relations between literature and the spoken language. Machiavelli, Ludovico Martelli, and others emphasized the Florentine character of the accepted literary vernacular. They maintained, like the Sienese Claudio Tolomei (d. 1566), that new words and forms could pass over into literature only by first being filtered through and incorporated into the spoken Tuscan. The Florentine Giambattista Gelli (d. 1563) ascribed so much value to the living speech and to its superior development in recent times that in his judgment, if the old masters had written in modern times, they would have been greater still, owing to the raised perfection of the Florentine-Tuscan vernacular.

A trichotomy—three theses, three points of view, but also the elements of a single consciousness: one thesis curial and courtly, in search of a peninsula-wide language for the educated, traveled men of the upper classes; another, Bembo's argument, more apparently literary, but also more elitist in its emphasis on the taste of the cultivated few, as in the courts and oligarchies, where much delight was taken from the careful reading or recitation of Petrarch and Boccaccio; and third, the more democratic thesis of the Tuscans, who, in their residual republican pride, praised the spoken language and displayed a pronounced streak of regional patriotism. But the single consciousness of the disputants was in their self-identity as Italians, in their quest for a common literary language, in their yearning for a cultural front to hold up to the pretensions of invading foreigners.

Nationalism remained an attitude in culture, and even there it lapsed into velleities. Once again the fracture in consciousness appeared: (1) in the aristocratic insistence on the linguistic cleavage between the ruling class and the lower orders, (2) in the assumption—whether realistic or not—that Italy could have one language only at the level of the dominant social groups and that the rest was a congeries of base dialects, (3) in the further assumption that if literature was subject to the effects of speech, it must be the speech of the ruling groups, and (4) in the notion—in the Bembian as in the courtly thesis—that the language of vernacular literature had to come in part or in whole from studying the great *trecentisti*, Petrarch and Boccaccio.

Seen in this light, the famous *questione della lingua* proposed resolutions that made for two cultural Italies: the Italy consisting of many dialects but possessing no true literature, and the Italy of the courtiers, oligarchies, and learned men, possessing one language and one great literature. In short, Italy's most disabling social division was perfectly reflected in the debate on language. On entering Italy, the armies of French, Spanish, Swiss, and Germans had found not only major regional differences but also profound social divisions that undermined the power of states and the coherence of governments.

Only the Tuscan-Florentine thesis appeared to provide an exit from the vision of the two Italies, and so it fell under sharp attack from the courtiers. Bembo observed that it was no advantage necessarily to be born a Florentine, especially because such writers slipped too easily into errors and into the use of words less "noble" and "pleasing" than those to be culled from the great *trecentisti*. The learned Vicentine nobleman Gian Giorgio Trissino, a leading exponent of the theory of a national courtly language, rejected the Tuscan-Florentine of his day because it was too regional, a dialect which had drifted too far from the language of the fourteenth-century masterpieces. The women of Lombardy, he claimed in his *Castellano* (1529), meaning the upper-class women, read Petrarch more easily than do the women of Tuscany because the particularity of the Florentine tongue is less evident in the poet than a more trans-regional Italian "parlance." Piero Valeriano, another courtly exponent, also denied that the Tuscan of the High Renaissance was the language of Petrarch; it had first to be purged of dialect. And yet another, Girolamo Muzio (d. 1576), assailed the reliance of Florentine writers on their daily, native usage, for the language of literature was learned best from writers, not, he asserted, "from wet nurses and the vulgar herd." More in Bembo's line of thought, Muzio's standard was a literary language shaped by the great vernacular writers of the Trecento.

But in due course even the Tuscan school drew in its "democratic" horns. Bruno Migliorini, the leading historian of the Italian language, has observed that after 1550 Florence had "an abundance of historians, scholars and grammarians, but no writers of the first rank." Intellectual conformism triumphed, and views on the language question fell largely into line with Bembo's thesis. Tuscan or Florentine came to mean the language primarily of the great fourteenth-century writers, not the spoken tongue. Benedetto Varchi's *Ercolano* (1564) is instructive. He distinguished four linguistic levels in Florence: that (1) of the learned, (2) the literate (*non idioti*), (3) the illiterate, and (4) "the lowest plebs and dregs of the base populace." The first were schooled in Latin and Greek; the second were merely literate but had the virtue of including the nobility and rich men. This was the cutoff point for vital links between literature and the spoken language. Varchi held that Florentine writers should know the work of modern grammarians and be guided by the masters of the Trecento, but he also wanted them to be familiar with the spoken language of the nobility and rich bourgeoisie.

The two Italies were never far from Bembo's view of literature. We see the marks of this social stamp in his conception of the literary lexicon: "and if it happens, every so often, that we cannot express our subject with fitting or decorous words, so that we must have recourse to words that are low or harsh or unpleasant . . . then it is better to be silent about that which cannot be suitably expressed than to express it and thereby sully the rest of the work."[19]

THE LURE OF UTOPIA

Love lyrics in the Petrarchan vein, Platonism, and a celebrated work of literature (Castiglione's *The Courtier*) all belonged to a powerful current in sixteenth-century Italy: the upper-class urge to create alternate worlds, imaginary and better than the real world around. The lure of utopia became so tempting as to seem self-validating. This leads us back to the experience of contradiction and to its moral or psychological resolution in the processes of idealization.

The sixteenth-century world was supremely demanding for the groups at the forefront of society because the challenge of the Italian Wars was to their identity and power, to their control over the affairs of Italy. Since power and place in society were the essential constituents of their identity, when peninsular independence broke down, the major tumult in consciousness was theirs. Unable to accept the changed and changing situation, yet unable to escape it, the old ruling groups and those who served to interpret the world for them developed a wavering, broken view of reality. The key experience, we have seen, was in sensitivity to the contradiction between reality and the demands of identity, between a reality that had lurched out of control and the need to fulfill the promise of a prestigious social identity. One of the inevitable solutions lay in idealization, in drawing back from the practical world to a buffer zone of ideal forms. Now the ensuing view of reality stretched along the wavering line where buffer zone and practical world met. And down to the 1560s and beyond, after the initial need had lost strength, Renaissance culture was marked by this protean struggle between idealism and the rude forms of the everyday world. In dramatic fashion, writers swung back and forth between modes of realism and fantasy. In his *Orlando Furioso* (composition: 1504–1532), Ariosto strikes an extraordinary balance between the two, but each, in its turn, often stands out. Raphael's achievement, classicism, also lay in this extraordinary balance, though in his last years (d. 1519) he was tilting the scales more towards fantasy and ideal forms. Agnolo Firenzuola (1493–1543) zigzagged between the realism of his stories and the idealism of his treatises and platonic discussions.

Lyric poetry—"the soul of an age"—is rarely taken seriously by historians because they do not know how to deal with it. The loss is history's and ours. For in its focusing and distillation of experience, lyric verse can seize aspects of consciousness from angles and in ways denied to all other expressive forms. By comparison, account books and diplomatic dispatches are paltry.

The entire first half of the sixteenth century saw a remarkable flowering of lyric poetry in Italy. In the 1490s, Ludovico Sforza's courtiers started a fashion for composing verses, and the taste spread quickly from Milan to Ferrara, Mantua, Urbino, and Rome. As intimate entertainment, this taste was not confined to courtly circles, but its high fortunes were there. The courts attracted, without exception, all the leading poets and some of the bad ones as well. Although subjects ranged from political events to anticlericalism and pagan myth, love was the favorite topic and the sonnet was the preferred form. The highest praise was reserved for love lyrics in the Petrarchan style: in form highly polished, in diction extremely selective, in imagery delicate or somewhat generalized, and elevated in thought and feeling. Typically, in a sequence of such lyrics, the poet first saw the lady, was at once struck by her unparalleled graces, began longing to be with her incessantly, fell victim to the ache of unreciprocated love, and for a long time passed continually back and forth between despair and luminous hope. Meanwhile, he gradually purged himself of all sensuality, until he finally transcended his residual earthly attachments in "higher" thoughts and in the newfound love of an eternal essence, God or pure beauty.

The fashion for the Petrarchizing love lyric reached its height in the first half of the sixteenth century, coinciding thus with Italy's epochal *crise de conscience* and with the adult life of the movement's finest practitioner, Pietro Bembo (d. 1547). After its eponym, Petrarch (d. 1374), but before Bembo, the form was badly and irregularly managed; after Bembo and poets such as Annibal Caro, Gian Giorgio Trissino, and Bernardo Tasso, the Petrarchizing lyric passed into stale convention and then went out of vogue.

But first, for about two generations, it ruled the art of poetry; and many courtiers and court ladies went around, clutching a *petrarchino*—Petrarch's lyric verse in small format—or composing and exchanging subtle sonnets in like vein. Italian presses issued numerous commentaries on Petrarch and at least 167 sixteenth-century editions of his love poems. Yet in line with the central thesis of this chapter, regarding the oscillations in consciousness between idealism and realism, it should be emphasized that Petrarchists came under the scoffing attack of Berni, Aretino, and other "comic realists," who regarded their sonnets as imitative preciosities, lies, and false idealism. But the "realists" or anti-Petrarchists seem to have been in the minority.[20]

If the Petrarchan taste had not been so widespread in the courts and upper-class enclaves, and if there were no parallel evidence from other aspects of Renaissance culture, there would be no way to situate the taste in the general Italian malaise; but it enters squarely into the expressive pattern of a consciousness haunted by menacing realities in politics, in religion, in economics, and in the inflationary—and compensatory—emphasis on prestigious place and honor.

The connections between social crisis and the Petrarchist taste are best traced by sustained textual and social analysis, but it must suffice here to summarize the arguments. Bembo's love lyrics provide the model.

1. *The courtly setting.* The genre relied heavily on the language of service and adulation. Obsessively the poet represents himself as servitor to his lady or to love, or both. Each of these is often made to equal a "kingdom," "rule," "sovereignty," or "power." We begin to see why the genre had its most appropriate ground in a courtly setting. The courtier had his distinctive identity in an ideal of service, as well as in the claims of power and place. His office was to keep the prince satisfied by whatever honorable means; adulation was one of his lots in life; and hence to flatter a lady, for whatever reason, was in the courtier's very makeup. The diction of service went back to the *stilnovisti* and beyond them to the medieval tradition of courtly love, but the tradition was revitalized by the crisis of the High Renaissance.

Tarts and street vendors aside, court or palace ladies had more social freedoms with men than the women of all other social groups; but the public lines of decorum were not brushed aside. Courtier and lady—she was usually married—observed an etiquette. The language of the love lyric was therefore dualistic, ambiguous: the poet knowledgeably threaded his way through an established glossary of sensual and spiritual terms. He could press toward a Christian Neoplatonism or turn suddenly around to a more sensuous diction. The more he did the latter, the further away he got from Petrarchism.

In the hands of a well-placed courtier such as Bembo, the refined love lyric was also a form of self-indulgence: a self-congratulatory exercise which made manifest the nobility of the suffering poet. But the style could not be authentic unless, as in Bembo's case, the poet wrote from an elevated social position. Otherwise, who could believe in the graces and light of his lady? The form itself was a social signature: until late in the cycle, its movements were playful and ardent by turns, ironic, artful, allusive, and illusive, and often combined flashes of flattery with learned self-promotion. The subtleties were too gentle and studied for any but a select social atmosphere.

2. *Utopia and salvation.* Sequences of lyric poems in the Petrarchan mode are mini-utopias. The poet idealizes his lady: he associates her with "celestial," "heavenly," and "divine" qualities, and with "graces" and "charms" never before seen on this earth. His love for her perfects *him*. Occasionally it sweeps him to the extremes of happiness, but even in tears his condition is more noble than that of the multitudes of mortals. There is a continual play of contrasts between forms of perfection and the earthly world of imperfections. As the poet goes through the cycle of love, gradually burning away his sensual attachments, he comes to reflect on death and on his soul. In the process he rises to a new knowledge of earthly vanity, as well as to a vision of personal salvation. But the traveled route is not only the way of Platonic love; it is also a way through poetry, the poetry which delineates the experience. As the poetic sequence unfolds, the poet watches and studies himself: he plots his own growth. There is a form of liturgy and prayer here; a discipline also. In the shade of a corrupt religious leadership and of neglected religious institutions, the austere art of the Petrarchan love lyric becomes a religious exercise. It is the negation of the moral madhouse around, of the suffocating jealousies and fears at court, and of the fierce scramble for favor. The poet is cleansed by the experience of unreciprocated love, but the task cannot be completed except by catching hold of the experience in poetry. Thus, the fervent study of Petrarch's *Canzoniere*, or the writing of a sequence of sonnets in this mode, turns into a quest for moral perfection; and at its best, the search seems to attain its goal. In reading such a sequence, we are witnesses to the building of a mini-utopia. Writing in an age of shattering instability and demoralization, the Petrarchist is able by his art to find moments of detachment and serenity. This experience was, in one sense, a mystification and a part of the general social crisis, but from the personal standpoint of the poet it was a mode of survival. Appropriately, sixteenth-century readers were also fully implicated: they exhibited an intense interest in Petrarch's personal life, in all the details of the history of his dedication to Laura, for in this love story there was a way of life and a way to salvation.

The taste for Petrarch led directly to Platonism, to the theme of Platonic love, and in the sixteenth century the two, Petrarchan love and Platonic love, were almost routinely part of one and the same discourse.

The work of Ficino, Poliziano, and Pico della Mirandola, late-fifteenth-century Neoplatonists, was not in vain. Their many contacts and the earnest work of popularizers, particularly in the dissemination of Ficino's views, helped to spread the gospel of Platonism to the academy and even more to upper-class circles with a bent for literature and intellectual entertainment. The taste, however, was for a dualist Platonism which accented the differences between perfect and imperfect forms, between mind and body (or intellect and senses), and between eternal and transitory values. Such a taste was an outgrowth of the evasive mood occasioned by the Italian Wars, rooted in the pointed threat to the identity of the ruling groups. Menaced, elite consciousness drew back fitfully from the intimidating practical world to erect idealized alternate worlds. This operation was most effectively performed by Platonism, with its opposition between the shadowy world of the senses and the *a priori* world of pure ideas, as occasionally given to the unclouded intellect. In the words of a leading expert, Eugenio Garin, Platonism became "the tone of a civilization." Men of letters, people at courts, bishops, statesmen, oligarchs, rich investors, big landowners, and a "classy" tart or two made up the modish audience for the varieties of Platonism and Christian Neoplatonism. The teaching and understanding even of Aristotle must have been dualistic, most likely in according excessive attention to the conflict and concordance between the Aristotelian categories of form and substance.

Three facts lock the fashionable interest in Platonism to the taste and outlook of groups at the head of society: (1) many "Platonists" got their ideas mainly from reading and discussing Petrarch and the Petrarchists; (2) the overwhelming majority of Platonist works were cast in dialogue form, and settings as well as interlocutors were upper-class, notably parties of aristocrats, learned men, bishops, ambassadors, courtiers, and rich folk gathered in courts, grand *palazzi*, or palatial villas; and (3) the favorite topics of Platonistic discussion were those most manageable in small gatherings—for instance, moral perfections of some kind, but above all the topics of love and beauty. These two prevailed over all others and were often, in any case, along with the subject of "honor," at the center of conversation in the courts. In 1570, at the Ferrara Academy, Tasso discussed and defended fifty points concerning love: present and masked at the third debate, held on the last Monday before Ash Wednesday, was the whole court of Ferrara.

The flood of sixteenth-century dialogues on Platonistic love and beauty highlights the penchant for ideal worlds: only the perfected lover or contemplator could enter the realms of true love or true beauty. Yet once more, accordingly, we see the lure of utopia and strong indirect evidence for our interpretation of Petrarchism. But the evidence was also direct: Bembo himself wrote the period's first dialogue on love in a Christian-Platonist vein, *Asolani* (1497–1498). More substantial philosophically were Ficino's seven orations (commentaries) on Plato's *Symposium* and Leone Ebreo's *Dialoghi d'amore* (ca. 1501–1502). Ficino's orations did the rounds in his own vernacular translation.

Love and beauty belonged to a single discourse in Platonism because they were linked in Plato's *Symposium* by the principle of reason. True love was not only love of the beautiful but also the desire to generate beauty *in* the beautiful, as when exceptional men beget immortal creations out of a vision of beauty and forms eternal. Hence true love was preceded by knowledge and ratiocination. Supreme beauty was an idea, and true love, therefore, was an act of pure intellect.

The concussed sixteenth century found these themes endlessly attractive. They offered a way of survival, an exit from defeat. There was first of all the saving preoccupation with love and beauty. But more significantly, in love and beauty, as in political theory, reason and unreason divided the world. "This" shadowy world of the senses stood in opposition to "that" luminous world of pure beauty and love. But then where was reality? Since "this" reality was tenebrous, unstable, base (*vile*), and hence inferior, the other had to be the one where things truly counted, where men could somehow perfect and fulfill themselves. So there were two realities; but whereas most people tumbled into the sensuous and unstable one (unreason), the few ascended to the other, which was the true reality and far more important. Variations of this Platonic conception had been set forth in the second half of the fifteenth century; they had taken, however, a much more positive view of the "lowly" world, for the peninsula's elite groups were then in charge of the affairs of Italy, in charge of their own destiny. But in the sixteenth century, the loss of leadership and the partial loss of control over pragmatic reality went to make for an evasive, withdrawing sensibility. With its vision of two realities, this crisis sensibility turned to stoicism, to imaginary heroics, to posturing, or to an attitude of mind that would seem to let the world go by for the sake of something higher. Thus Mannerism in art, with its heroic, escapist, anguished, or posturing idiom; and thus also Petrarchism, Neoplatonism, and abdication to the power of *fortuna*.

Plato's—the Diotiman—ladder of love was the ascent from love for a particular body up, through different grades, to love for and contemplation of the unchanging idea of beauty itself. Christianizing this, sixteenth-century discussions spoke of divine and bestial love. There was also a more varied terminology, linking the subject to the debate on language. Ficino, Castiglione, Giuseppe Betussi (1543), Benedetto Varchi (1560s), and others referred to "vulgar" love in opposition to Platonic or celestial love. Vulgar or "vernacular" love was the workaday love felt by most people: sensual, particular, fleshy, irrational. Varchi supplied more precise social referents. Between the two extremes of love divine and bestial, he put three other loves: (1) courtly, courteous, noble or honest love—*cortese, gentile, onesto* —which prefers the soul to the body and relies on only the two "spiritual senses," sight and hearing; (2) "civil or human" love, which loves both soul and body but the soul first—this love is tempered by "modesty" and "civility" and is the sort "required of a civil and moderate man"; and (3) the love of those who prefer the body: "these delight only in the earth, indeed in mud, just as pigs do, and this is called vulgar or plebeian love."[21] This interpretation of Christian Platonism found exact social analogues for its ladder of love: courtly-aristocratic, "civil" or bourgeois, and plebeian-bestial. Varchi was merely dotting the i's and crossing the t's of an ideology whose import we had already grasped: divine and aristocratic love should rule over the inferior loves, just as elites are meant to rule over multitudes and reason over unreason. Together with the Latin of the Augustan Age, Bembo's perfected literary vernacular—frozen, composed, idealized—constituted a linguistic utopia and was analogous to Platonic love of the highest sort.

One of the key works of European literature issues from the most troubled part of the sixteenth century, Baldasar Castiglione's *The Courtier* (1528), a study of manners published the year before his death. It is cast in dialogue form and ends with the interlocutor, Bembo again, in a state of Platonic love. He is entranced by a vision of abstract and divine beauty; Platonism and Christianity are fused. The vision is the logical conclusion to a work which sets out to draw an ideal picture of the supreme product of Italian Renaissance society, the courtier.

Castiglione's dialogue is a competitor, together with Machiavelli's *The Prince* and Guicciardini's *History of Italy*, for the claim to be the most remarkable prose work to come out of the Renaissance crisis: first, because it confronted the challenge to upper-class identity; second, because it established straightway its upper-class credentials; and, finally, because it suffers from a conceptual shyness that is a symptom of the crisis, while also managing, by its seductive mode of idealization, to transcend the Italian situation.[22] Fifty-seven editions of the work appeared in Italy before 1600, sometimes three in a single year. Facets of the dialogue reflect the imagination of the Italian aristocracy in crisis, yet owing to its transcendence of the Italian world, it had been translated into five languages by 1566 and swiftly became a social breviary for gentlemen outside Italy. Its art and idealism presented an enviable atmosphere and a cluster of near self-images that appealed to the socially ambitious men of Europe.

In modeling a perfect courtier, Castiglione imagines a courtly world tilted toward an ideal perfection. But he performs his task with so much art—e.g., by having different interlocutors complain about the dialogue's departures and distance from reality—that he is able to disguise his enterprise. For he is contemplating a courtly utopia: his imagined world is the perimeter of relations linking the model courtier to the model prince; and the result is as far removed from reality as anything imagined by Antonio Brucioli, Anton Francesco Doni, or Sir Thomas More.

The author of *The Courtier* was privately tutored in Latin and Greek and nourished on the syllabus of humanism. Related to the ruling family of

Mantua through his mother, Count Baldasar Castiglione (1478–1529) spent the years 1496–1499 at Milan, where he completed his studies and was well received at the Sforza court, which later he was to consider "once held the flower of the men of the world." In 1499 he succeeded to a large landed fortune and from this time on his career as courtier, administrator, soldier, and ambassador was tied successively to the courts of Mantua, Urbino, Mantua again, and then Rome. He took holy orders in 1521, became a bishop, was favored by the two Medici popes, and before his death in Spain he no doubt entertained the hope of becoming a cardinal.

The dialogue is set at the court of Urbino in 1506, among a company of lords and ladies from an assortment of noble houses—Gonzaga, Fregoso, Pallavicini, Pio, Canossa, Montefeltro, Medici, and others. Socially the low-liest contributors to the dialogue are the humanist courtier, Calmeta, and Bernardo Dovizzi da Bibbiena, servitor to the Medici and afterward a cardinal.

Casting around for an agreeable topic, the assembled company hit on "courtiership" and decide to discuss the qualities of "the perfect courtier." Their preoccupation will be, therefore, a social identity. In a series of four discussions—four books—they draw a picture of the ideal courtier and court lady.

The discussions wend their way toward the ideal recipe in a leisurely but controlled fashion. In sum, the model courtier is a nobleman born, educated in the classicism of the humanists, bred to the profession of arms, a lover of music and the arts, skilled in writing, gallant to ladies, a polished speaker in public, and in private an entertaining conversationalist. He is trained thoroughly in the school of grace—grace in every action and deed—and the setting for that school is the princely court. It is there the courtier learns the art that conceals art: the doing of all things to perfection, but doing them in such a way as always to keep a certain gentle aloofness (*sprezzatura*), be it in playing musical instruments, composing sonnets, taking up arms, or conversing with ladies and providing his prince with sound advice.

Although *The Courtier* was written largely between about 1513 and 1518, in the midst of the Italian debacle (and so betrays an undercurrent of melancholy), it faces the challenge to upper-class identity. To talk about courtiers and princes in those years was to talk about leading ailments in Italian society. But the dialogue does this with such charm, "naturalness," and the leavening of idealization, that the melancholy fact usually escapes notice. In setting his sights on the courtier, Castiglione was discussing nothing less than leadership in Italy: the qualities, real and desired, of the sort of men who governed states and rode the forefront of events. Even at Venice and the revived republic of Genoa, leading statesmen, much shaped by their ambassadorial experience, were likely to be the aristocrats acquainted with the princely courts and most at ease there.

Castiglione lays it firmly down that the courtier has his *raison d'être* in service to the prince. Everything else is secondary. But as he devotes himself mainly to "everything else" and gives very little space to direct relations between courtier and prince, this alerts us to the fact that there is some fumbling in the work's conceptualization, in the author's way of taking hold of his subject matter: it is a testament of the crisis. Every quality and virtue of the courtier—his education, military prowess, grace, goodness, and political wisdom—is aimed at putting him into the small circle of the prince's intimates, so that he can be in a position to counsel him. The conceptual heart of the work is here, in the salutary relations between prince and courtier. All other matters, including lessons of love and clever conversation, have their validation in the virtue at this core, but here, strangely enough, there appears a cluster of contradictions (Bk. II, 18–25).

The courtier ought "to love and almost adore" the prince he serves above everything else—for the prince's sake, not his own. He should seek favor at court, again for the prince's good, not his own. He should pretend to love the things loved by his prince, yet not be an adulator. His first devotion is to his prince, not to a higher good (e.g., community or state), yet he must ply the prince with sound political advice. His quintessential feature is a lordly nonchalance (*sprezzatura*), yet honesty is one of his prime virtues, particularly in relations with the prince, who is meant to trust him above all other men. The courtier should do everything commanded by the prince, but he must do nothing really evil or dishonorable. Faced with a thoroughly vicious prince, the courtier is advised to abandon his service. The dialogue quickly observes, however, that such princes are rare and that things which appear bad are often not so; hence the courtier will seldom find sufficient good reason to leave the service of his prince.

Castiglione's discomfort in this particular discussion is clear, and he soon changes the subject. When he finally returns to it in the last book (IV, 4–10, 29–48), he steps up the abstract and moralistic tone of the dialogue, turns somewhat bookish, and rises to a new level of idealization. It is the level at which the blameworthy reality of the princely courts can be made more easily acceptable, the level that will prepare us for Bembo's mystic vision.

Much of the work's appeal for the upper classes outside of Italy was in the picture of a relaxed and civilized nobility. The dialogue's swift shifting back and forth between the ideal and the reality made the ideal seem attainable. This is the key to the dialogue's seductiveness. In Italy, under the threat to their commanding identity, upper-class readers clutched the work to themselves because it rescued leadership in a mimesis the idealism of which was disguised as realism, and this was accomplished by means of the dialogue's steering back and forth between ideal forms and the real Italy of the princes. Castiglione won conviction through his literary style and tone. He fostered the illusion of reality by also continually raising the question of the work's unreality and then providing immediate disclaimers. Whereas outside of Italy the dialogue's shifts between ideal and reality seemed to put the ideal within reach, in Italy the same shifts made the ideal seem real. The recipe was, after all, Italian, and the harried ruling groups were driven by the need to believe in their own leadership and in the grace and beauty of their lives. Illusion became reality.

In the last book, the difficulties at the work's conceptual core flare forth again and the ascent (or fall) into undisguised idealism is inescapable. Here, once more, worldly reality provides the point of departure. The organizing image (IV, 6–10, 45–48) is a real image of the age: the prince standing at the center of a circle of unworthy courtiers, who have corrupted him by their falsehood and flattery for their own selfish ends. The perfect courtier, likened to a physician (IV, 46), stands outside the circle, striving to break in to rescue and heal the ailing prince. Each is sealed off in his solitude; around them avarice and poor leadership prevail. It is indeed the world of the courts, except that the perfect courtier does not exist, only the idea does. Whereupon Castiglione, in the most idealistic part of the work, boldly accepts the challenge and admits via his interlocutor, Ottaviano Fregoso, that the imagined courtier *is* a philosopher, inasmuch as he must teach virtue to the prince. Aristotle and Plato are brought forward as examples: the one counseled Alexander the Great; the other, Plato, was teacher to the kings of Sicily. The two were performing the office of the perfect courtier (IV, 47–48). Now the dialogue pitches into a discussion of the kind of love appropriate for an aging courtier. Bembo takes over and gradually leads the assembled party toward a vision of beauty both abstract and divine. Earth's shadows and tribulations fall away and the perfect courtier, in the guise of the rapt Bembo, momentarily realizes his spiritual identity in eternity. It is a flight from the world: the most fitting conclusion to a work which portrays Italy's dominant social identity in crisis. The terrifying vicissitudes in worldly reality compel the courtier to rise to the plains of heaven, for only there can he hold on to his leadership and untarnished identity.

CHAPTER XVI

THE END OF
THE RENAISSANCE

The Italian Renaissance came forth in two stages. The first extended from the eleventh century to about 1300, the second from the late thirteenth to the late sixteenth centuries. In the first stage, social energies—economics, politics, a vibrant demography—were primary and foremost; in the second, the lead went to cultural energies. There was inevitably some overlapping. The sustained study of Roman law, for example, was revived in the twelfth and thirteenth centuries, and this was an intellectual achievement of the first order. In the late fifteenth century and once more after about 1540, the Italian economy enjoyed an Indian summer. But in the period up to 1300, Italian urban life was governed overwhelmingly by economic, political, and demographic forces. These also coursed directly into the physical building of cities, with their many churches and fortified towers. After 1300, but especially in the fifteenth and first half of the sixteenth centuries, the innovative rush of developments belonged to "high" culture. Venetian painting and humanism around 1500 were more novel and daring than anything to be found in Venice's political or economic institutions.

In their respective strengths, the two stages were not afterward to be surpassed, whether in matters of invention (as in business technique), bold inquiry, or enduring addition to the history of Europe. Italians were of course deeply engaged in commercial enterprise throughout the sixteenth century, but they clung too often and harmfully to ancient commercial habits, apart from which, at any rate, the scope and volume of their transactions shrank before the explosive economic performances of the twelfth and thirteenth centuries. There were important Italian poets, painters, and thinkers in the late sixteenth and early seventeenth centuries, many of them really emerging in the final hours of the second Renaissance stage. These stand out, however, as individuals and even as eccentrics, rather than as participants in a collective surge of achievement. Often enough they were to prove themselves capable of impressive moral force, but, with a few striking exceptions, they would not bestow legacies like those of their cultural forebears. When they dared to show an audacious eye and mind, they were hounded, jailed, executed, attacked by assassins, poisoned, driven into flight, or moved to bouts of lunacy and criminality.[1]

The two stages of the Renaissance were joined inseparably: the first produced the shaping, long-term values from which the second took its rise. Quattrocento humanism would have been impossible without the civic ideals, however inchoate, that rose out of the thirteenth-century commune. A direct line linked Masaccio to Giotto and the school of Giottesque painters, whose style served the outlook and psychic needs of a triumphant *popolo.* Lorenzo de' Medici's verse (1460s) depended absolutely upon a literary vernacular which went back in its lineaments to the idealist and realist poets of the late thirteenth century; these, in turn, had gone to the language of the *popolo* and were trammeled by the crisis of values that resulted from the *popolo*'s victory. The grand architecture of the fifteenth century was called forth by the worldly patronage of princes, rich prelates, and oligarchs; but their processing of experience along more worldly lines ("secularization") had its validation in urban values whose obvious and deeper roots, again, were in the thirteenth-century commune. It required the upper-class psychology of the fifteenth century to convert those values into an optimistic and dominant ideology.

The cultural Renaissance had its direction in the needs and consciousness of the upper-class groups, though these could have no identity, and could undergo no changes, except in relation to all other social groups and to a function in the Italian economy. In this sense, the whole of Italian society was involved. Renaissance culture sprang, accordingly, from the independent life of the city-states, from ground native and local. So that when the Italian Wars and the hegemony of Spain tore away at Italy's autonomies, "high" culture bore all the marks of the wrenching and crisis. Now suddenly the climax of the Renaissance came into view. Sixteenth-century painters could draw upon the resources and achievement of the fifteenth-century schools. Poets and storytellers could look not only to the great *trecentisti* (Petrarch, Boccaccio) but also to the important vernacular writers of the later fifteenth century. And historians, even more than political thinkers, had the accumulated guidance of Quattrocento humanism, in addition to the convulsed atmosphere of the Italian Wars. In short, Italian writers and artists in crisis took a rich heritage and joined it to the sudden and wholly unexpected experience of a profound instability; the result was a brilliant flowering. Music and the most expensive of the arts, architecture, would go on flourishing—understandably so, in the fervid climate of the Catholic Counter Reformation and in response to the pressing demands of princely courts and opulent aristocracies. With a population of less than 100,000 people, sixteenth-century Rome was witness to the building of sixty major *palazzi* and villas. The rich and noble of seventeenth-century Venice had 332 grand villas erected on the Venetian mainland in that century alone, yet the city's population in 1633 barely exceeded 100,000 souls.

The culture of the High Renaissance was vitalized by the tensions of a divided consciousness, the tensions in a suggestive and fertile wavering between two conflicting views of reality. Amid the upheavals of the Italian Wars, the Quattrocento's dominant view of reality collapsed and the visible world ("quotidian reality") turned into the realm of instability and defeat for the upper classes. A vast menacing front appeared, with *fortuna* looming just behind. Writers and artists now turned to—or took refuge in—idealism, fantasy, flummery, or zigzag and contradictory commitments both to the external world and to extrapolated ideas of perfection. Quotidian and imagined realities competed. In the short run, this experience encouraged an extraordinary flaring of talent. But the urgency and fecundity of the experience could not last. In the long run, imagination required more vivifying relations with the external world, or it would end by feeding on phantoms—Mannerism at its worst—and go to shape the tormented lives of men such as Torquato Tasso, Giordano Bruno, and Tommaso Campanella. To make matters worse, the gathering force of the Counter Reformation also worked to inhibit intellectual and artistic activity. After 1542, the tracking down of heresy passed from the power of local authority (bishops) to Rome. The Inquisition, the Index of Forbidden Books, and the resulting funk blunted inquiry and induced conformity. The aging Michelangelo, Veronese, and Ammanati were rebuked for doing nudes or for profaning the majesty of their religious subject matter. Tasso, Patrizi, and others were nagged by the fear of having blundered into heresy. Still others passionately avowed their readiness to yield on any point found suspect by the Holy Office. Fear, cunning, compromise, and a preoccupation with fine points ("scholarship") made up a good part of the intellectual climate of the later sixteenth century. Even at Venice, where there was less fear, once its famous clash with the papacy had ended (1606–1607) and Paolo Sarpi was dead (1623), a closed ruling class would make it clear that this was not a place for intellectual nonconformity.

The sixteenth-century quest for perfect forms, for the Idea, could offer excitement, new solutions, and challenge so long as the contact with external reality was acknowledged to be important. But the rush of inventive talent —the High Renaissance—could not continue when the same quest was put into the context of a narrowing religious orthodoxy, frozen ruling classes, and an economy dipping yet once more toward prolonged stagnation. In this setting, the quest for the Idea—that is, the manner or mode of idealization— was pressed into established molds and perimeters; its give-and-take relations with the external everyday world declined; and it skidded toward closed systems, presupposed essences, orthodoxies, feverish but involuted imaginings, and overeasy categorizations.

Aristotle's *Poetics* was turned into a straitjacket for tragedy and even for other forms of poetry. Increasingly, from the second half of the sixteenth century, amazement and wonder (*la meraviglia*) came to be seen as the true end of poetry. In the late sixteenth century Bernardino Telesio (d. 1588), as well as Campanella and Galileo, denounced the reigning philosophy, Aristotelianism, because they saw that it had been turned into academic dogma, into a static system which brooked no true novelty. Platonism, for other reasons, fared no better in its literary posturings, its forms of mysticism and magical belief, and in its facile dualist platitudes. In the course of the sixteenth century, it lapsed into "banality" by all but "spending itself in the fashion and rhetoric of love," notes a leading historian, Eugenio Garin.

After the conclusion of the Council of Trent (1563), Italy was enmeshed in the tightening web of religious and political orthodoxy. Rome, Spain, and local princes demanded obedience, and the old ruling castes knuckled under. The age of the Index of Forbidden Books had started. Issued between 1554 and 1596, six separate but overlapping lists of proscribed books and authors banned the publication of the following:[2] Dante's *On Monarchy*, Marisilius of Padua, Boccaccio's *Decameron* (unless expurgated), four of Petrarch's sonnets, four of Lorenzo Valla's major works, Poggio's *Jocular Stories*, Piovano Arlotto's *Jokes and Tales*, Giannozzo Manetti's *On the Dignity and Excellence of Man*, Luigi Pulci's *Morgante*, Machiavelli's works, the Latin edition of Guicciardini's *History of Italy* (until expurgated), Castiglione's *The Courtier* (unless expurgated), Ariosto's *Satires*, Bandello's *Stories* (unless expurgated), Folengo's macaronic works (unless expurgated), Pietro Aretino's *Opera omnia*, the poetry of Luigi Tansillo and Veronica Franco, and works by Telesio, Patrizi, Cardano, and many others, including even, in the Parma Index of 1580, the verse of Pietro Bembo.

Any and all criticism of the clergy was considered an affront to the Roman Church; anticlericalism became tantamount to heresy. Free political discussion had rarely if ever been tolerated in Renaissance Italy. Yet the Florentine republic had lived through years of intense controversy and debate (1494–1512, 1527–1530). Siena, Lucca, Genoa, Venice—the oligarchical republics—had offered examples of an alternative polity. The Italian Wars had elicited searching political and historical reflection. And criticism of the Church hierarchy, as well as derisive attacks on clerical vices, had been common enough down to the 1520s. But all this had vanished by 1560. Church and state in Catholic Italy, as in Protestant Germany and Switzerland, had lurched into religious fanaticism. The main lines of Italy's political fortunes had been fixed, remaining so until the early eighteenth century—and then only the bosses changed. With the collaboration of native local councils, Spain ruled the Italian north and south via its viceroys and agents. Siena had been swallowed by monarchy, the Medicean grand duchy of Tuscany. The tiny republic of Lucca, now an anomaly, remained. Republican Venice and Genoa endured in their sealed oligarchies, the former still poised enough to tease aristocractic political imaginations for another century.

The keen interest in history persisted in the late sixteenth century and beyond. Educated Italians continued to believe that there was something terribly important to be learned from it. But good intentions were no substitute for a probing, questioning eye; they were no instrument for piercing through the conformities laid down by Tridentine Catholicism, Spanish viceroys, and the stepped-up surveillance of princes. In their call for the study of history, Francesco Patrizi da Cherso (1560), Lorenzo Ducci (1600), and Traiano Boccalini (1611) emphasize politics, method, and the search for truth. It was not enough. Their call could have no mobilizing effect where the framework of politics excluded the very possibility of alternatives. And this reality—the actual disposition of power in an environment of ruling castes—could not be absent from historical thinking intended for the upper classes. It followed, accordingly, that Machiavelli, who had been moved by an intense faith in the possibility of change, was abused and rejected, even apart from his supposed impiety. Moreover, argument based upon the ends of the state in itself—"reason of State"—could have no place in the consciousness of the Counter Reformation. Ethico-Christian ends were put back into the heart of political discourse. The mythicizing of the Venetian republic aside, Italian political thought turned eminently monarchist; it put the life of politics into the hands of "good, wise, and pious" princes. This was no world for political history of a critical, exploratory sort.

Appropriately, the triumphant current in historical thinking ranged the study of history under rhetoric and ethics. Historical writing came to be seen as an exercise in literary form or as a type of oratory.[3] It was also seen as edification, a teaching of virtue by means of concrete example.[4] "Tacitism," the fashionable study of the Roman imperial historian Tacitus, was meant to give an understanding of princes and monarchs, of the secrets of their counsels and motives. This, at least, was the aim of the more acute readers. But very often, instead, Tacitism led to a preoccupation with purely moral questions. And many leading students ended by dismissing Tacitus into infamy because he seemed too overly concerned, like Machiavelli, with public vices, tyrants, and power politics. The demystifying of matters pertaining to power and privilege was an impossible labor in this stubbornly shibbolethic age. Even when the writing of history was guided by an ideal of rigor and truth, as in the case of Scipione Ammirato's *Histories of Florence* (written ca. 1575–1600), it boomeranged into antiquarianism: into a vast storehouse, chronologically stacked, of countless facts and events, leavened now and again by trivial reflections on the awfulness of the mob and the necessity of princely rule. Only Venice offered a temporary setting for resonant historical thinking, in a line that peaked and passed quickly away with Boccalini (d. 1613) and Sarpi (d. 1623).

The successes of the Italian economy in the sixteenth century should not be divorced from questions of power and social structure. Genoese and Florentine bankers piled up enormous fortunes. Italian merchants remained heavily involved in the spice trade. Textiles, above all luxury textiles, were still a mainstay of the urban economy. But luxury silks could never have a large market and they promoted aggravated class snobberies, as well as old modes of production. By contrast, cloth production in Northern Europe was diversified so as to reach more humble folk and broader popular markets. Italian pertinacity in the spice trade also meant the perpetuation of deeply traditional business habits, in a world in which, in any case, the new sea lanes were revolutionizing the transportation and flow of spices. And profits from banking, however large, derived not from production as such but from intermediate operations, such as the transport of bullion, the buying up of tax gabelles, and money exchange, but most especially from mammoth lending to debt-ridden princes and states, where the inevitable result was more crushing taxations.

Nor did the profits from Italian trade and banking go to help revitalize politics and the economy. For the new rich—and the century produced many—were not drawn into government on a scale large enough to give rise to new political voices in the state, let alone to menace local ruling castes, whether at Venice and Genoa or in the princely states. Much wealth, perhaps far too much, flowed into architectural grandeur, from which no further material issue was possible. In the agrarian economy, finally, as Ruggiero Romano has argued, even the age's remarkable improvements were more the result of heavier labor impositions, of the sly appropriation of ecclesiastical land, and of government intervention and subsidy, as in the Veneto, than of the outright large-scale investment of monies.

In the last quarter of the sixteenth century, in tandem with the splendors of the new music and the rising villas and *palazzi* of upper Italy, waves of criminal anarchy and mass brigandage gripped the Abruzzi, Calabria, and large parts of the Papal State. A pulverizing fisc drove men to desperation. Everywhere the renewed surge in population fell off, and many localities, the cities especially, lost hearths as well as heads. The agrarian economy returned to an era of distress and shortages. The magnificence of the life in villas bled the peasantry and countryside; this was so even in the regions where a more productive reorganization of agriculture had been taken furthest, as in the Veneto, Lombardy, and parts of Tuscany. From about 1580 or 1590, the Italian urban economy—wool, silk, and shipping above all—slipped at first gradually, then precipitously after 1620, into the general European contraction and crisis of the seventeenth century.

NOTES

CHAPTER I

1. A. Visconti, "Note per la storia della società milanese nei secoli X e XI," in *Archivio storico lombardo*, 3 (1934), 289–329.

2. C. Campiche, *Die Communalverfassung von Como in 12. und 13. Jahrhundert* (Zurich, 1929), pp. 31–32, in Vol. 15, 2 of *Schweizer Studien zur Geschichtswissenschaft*. A privilege from Henry III of 1055 confirmed the bishop's possessions, specifying monasteries, churches, baptismal churches, courts, fields, the public meeting grounds, the city walls, river and banks, the Como marketplace, and other items. But whether or not the totality of these entailed general comitial powers, once belonging to a marquis, remains in question.

3. As noted apropos of Milan by H. Keller, "Die soziale und politische Verfassung Mailands in den Anfängen des kommunalen Lebens," in *Historische Zeitschrift*, Vol. 211 (1970), pp. 54–55.

CHAPTER II

1. *Nobiltà e popolo nel comune di Pisa dalle origini del podestariato alla signoría Donoratica* (Naples, 1962). See also H. Keller, "Die soziale und politische Verfassung Mailands in den Anfängen des kommunalen Lebens," in *Historische Zeitschrift*, Vol. 211 (1970), pp. 39–51, for a discussion of the problem in eleventh-century Milan.

CHAPTER III

1. See his *De vulgari eloquentia*, Chap. 2, differences between "the Bolognese of the Borgo di San Felice and the Bolognese of the Strada Maggiore."

CHAPTER IV

1. G. de Vergottini, "Il 'Popolo' di Vicenza nella cronica ezzeliniana di Gerardo Maurisio," in *Studi Senesi*, 48 (1948), cit., p. 364.

2. P. Santini, "Studi sull' antica costituzione del Comune di Firenze," in *Archivio storico italiano*, 32 (1932), cit., p. 35.

CHAPTER V

1. *Libellus de descriptione papie* (1339), in F. Gianani, *Opicino de Canistris* (Pavia, 1927), p. 103.

2. K. Vossler, *Die philosophischen Grundlagen zum "süssen neuen Stil"* (Heidelberg, 1904), pp. 24–41.

3. *Cronica*, I, 20, 27.
4. "Viva chi vince, ch' io so' di sua parte!" in A. F. Massèra, *Sonetti burleschi e realistici dei primi due secoli* (Bari, 1940), p. 146.
5. *Rime*, ed. E. Pasquini (Bologna, 1965), p. 61, begins: "Novella monarchia, iusto signore."

CHAPTER VI

1. L. Martines, *The Social World of the Florentine Humanists*, p. 20.
2. E. Salzer, *Über die Anfänge der Signorie in Oberitalien* (Berlin, 1900), pp. 88–90.
3. Sonnet begins, "Il mondo vile è oggi," in *Poeti minori del Trecento*, ed. N. Sapegno (Milan, 1952), p. 324.
4. In *Rimatori del Trecento*, ed. G. Corsi (Turin, 1969), pp. 689–690.
5. Anonimo Genovese, *Poesie*, ed. Luciana Cocito (Rome, 1970).
6. *Note:* All citations of the Anonimo's verse will be from L. Cocito's critical edition (Rome, 1970).

CHAPTER VII

1. Printed in N. Valeri, "L'insegnamento di Giangaleazzo Visconti e i consigli al principe di Carlo Malatesta," *Bollettino storico-bibliografico subalpino*, XXXVI (1934), 452–487.

CHAPTER VIII

1. In the sonnet "S'i' veggio in Lucca bella mio ritorno," *Poeti minori del Trecento*, ed. N. Sapegno (Milan and Naples, 1952), p. 316.
2. From the *canzone* "Gente noiosa e villana," *Poeti del Duecento*, ed. G. Contini, 2 vols. (Milan and Naples, 1960), I, 200.
3. Contini, ed., *ibid.*, I, 627–637.
4. *Poesie*, ed. L. Cocito (Rome, 1970), pp. 399, 416.
5. *Li Livres dou Tresor*, ed. F. J. Carmody (Berkeley and Los Angeles, 1948), Bk. III, 1, pp. 318–319. All other *Tresor* citations will be from this edition.
6. *Tresor*, Bk. III, lxxv, 1.
7. *Ibid.*, lxxv, 3.
8. *Ibid.*, lxxv, 14–15.
9. *Ibid.*, lxxxxvii, 3.
10. *Ibid.*, lxxxiv, 2–3.
11. *Ibid.*, lxxxvii, 4–6.
12. *Ibid.*, lxxxii, 7.
13. *Ibid.*, lxxxii, 9.
14. *Ibid.*, lxxxxviii, 4–5.
15. *Ibid.*, cii.
16. *Ibid.*, lxxxxix, 2.
17. Fava selections from appendices in A. Gaudenzi, *I suoni, le forme e le parole dell' odierno dialetto della città di Bologna* (Turin, 1889), pp. 144, 146, 156, 160.
18. *Trattato sopra l 'uffizo del podestà*, ed. P. Ferrato (Padua, 1865), p. 9.
19. *Poesie*, ed. Cocito, pp. 380–382.
20. A. P. d'Entrèves, *Dante as a Political Thinker* (Oxford, 1952), p. 11.
21. References and citations above are in the following: C. T. Davis, "An Early Florentine Political Theorist: Fra Remigio de' Girolami," *Proceedings of the American Philosophical Society*, Vol. 104, 6 (Dec. 1960), 662–676; and R. Egenter, "Gemeinnutz vor Eigennutz: Die soziale Leitidee im Tractatus de bono communi des Fr. Remigius von Florenz," *Scholastik*, 9 (1934), 79–92.
22. *Purgatorio*, VI, 143–151.

Notes

CHAPTER IX

1. G. Brucker, "The Ciompi Revolution," in *Florentine Studies*, ed. N. Rubinstein (London, 1968), pp. 314–356.

2. W. M. Bowsky, "The *Buon Governo* of Siena (1287–1355): A Medieval Italian Oligarchy," *Speculum*, 37, III (1962), p. 371.

3. See especially N. Rubinstein, *The Government of Florence Under the Medici, 1434 to 1494* (Oxford, 1966); and G. Brucker, *The Civic World of Early Renaissance Florence* (Princeton, 1977), pp. 92–93, 248–257, 354–355.

4. Cit. M. Berengo, *Nobili e mercanti nella Lucca del Cinquecento* (Turin, 1965), p. 34.

5. As revealed by the unpublished diaries (1490s) of Piero Parenti, National Library of Florence, *Manoscritti*, II, II, 130–134; II, IV, 169–171.

CHAPTER X

1. On the observations in this paragraph see also the last two sections of Chap. XIII.

2. P. J. Jones in *The Cambridge Economic History of Europe*, Vol. 1 (Cambridge, 1966), p. 416.

3. E. Fiumi, *Demografia, movimento urbanistico e classi sociali in Prato dall' età comunale ai tempi moderni* (Florence, 1968), p. 140.

4. In *Storia economica di Venezia dell' xi al xvi secolo* (Venice, 1961), pp. 172–173.

5. There was some scaling of the salt gabelle, or of the quantities of obligatory purchase, relative to the consumer's supposed income or assets.

6. *The Finance of the Commune of Siena, 1287–1355* (Oxford, 1970), p. 276.

7. L. Martines, *Lawyers and Statecraft in Renaissance Florence* (Princeton, 1968), p. 380.

8. Palmieri, *Della vita civile*, ed. F. Battaglia (Bologna, 1944), p. 157.

9. In *Il Pensiero pedagogico del rinascimento*, ed. F. Battaglia (Florence, 1960), p. 161.

10. G. Cherubini, *Signori, Contadini, Borghesi: richerche sulla società italiana del basso medioevo* (Florence, 1974), pp. 435ff.

CHAPTER XI

1. A view developed, in his capacity as ambassador, in an oration held at the University of Paris in February 1461. See P. H. Labalme, *Bernardo Giustiniani, A Venetian of the Quattrocento* (Rome, 1969), pp. 169ff.

2. D. J. Wilcox, *The Development of Florentine Humanist Historiography in the Fifteenth Century* (Cambridge, Mass., 1969), p. 34.

3. V. Branca, "Ermolao Barbaro and Late Quattrocento Venetian Humanism," in J. R. Hale, ed., *Renaissance Venice* (London, 1973), p. 228.

4. Hence the acute anxiety to be found in so many fourteenth- and fifteenth-century Florentine memoirs, family chronicles, and letters. This paragraph broaches Georg Lukács' neo-Hegelian distinction between psychological and ascribed consciousness.

5. Reflecting his own and others' practice, Poliziano explicitly posited the first two of these rules in his unfinished *Miscellaneorum centuria secunda* (1489–1494).

6. F. Tateo, *Tradizione e realtà nell' umanesimo italiano* (Bari, 1967), Chap. 8.

7. In Buonaccorso da Montemagno's *De nobilitate*, the two are done as ancient Romans and consciously cast as foils.

8. See his *Coniurationis commentarium*, ed. A. Perosa (Padua, 1958).

9. "Fatum et Fortuna," in G. Ponte, ed., *Il Quattrocento* (Bologna, 1966), p. 268.

10. Passages in C. Trinkaus, *In Our Image and Likeness: Humanity and Divinity in Italian Humanist Thought*, 2 vols. (Chicago, 1970), I, 261–262.

11. Cit., *ibid.*, II, 484.
12. Cit., *ibid.*, I, 192.

CHAPTER XII

1. B. Castiglione, *Lettere inedite e rare*, ed. G. Gorni (Milan, 1969).
2. P. J. Jones, *The Malatesta of Rimini and the Papal State* (Cambridge, 1974), p. 248, of Roberto Malatesta (d. 1482).
3. Testament published in P. D. Pasolini, *Caterina Sforza*, 3 vols. (Rome, 1893), III, 416, drafted in late 1499 or early 1500.
4. L. Mazzoldi and M. Bendiscioli, eds., *Mantova: La Storia*, 3 vols. (Mantua, 1958–1963), II, 443.
5. F. Calvi, *Bianca Maria Sforza-Visconti* (Rome, 1888), doc., p. 148.
6. J. Dennistoun, *Memoirs of the Dukes of Urbino*, 3 vols. (London, 1909), I, 159–161.
7. Mazzoldi, *Mantua*, II, 312, 396–397.
8. For what follows, F. Malaguzzi Valeri, *La corte di Ludovico il Moro*, 4 vols. (Milan, 1913–1923), I, 301ff.
9. A Frizzi, *Memorie per la storia di Ferrara*, 5 vols. (Ferrara, 1847–1850), IV, 73.
10. Malaguzzi Valeri, I, 421.
11. Letter in J. Cartwright, *Isabella d'Este Marchioness of Mantua*, 2 vols. (London, 1903), I, 89.
12. *Ibid.*, II, 329–330.
13. Verses cit., V. Cian, *La Satira*, 2 vols. (Milan, 2nd ed., n.d.), I, 391.
14. A. Luzio and R. Renier, "La coltura e le relazioni letterarie di Isabella d'Este Gonzaga," *Giornale storico della letteratura italiana*, xxxiv (1899), 15.
15. Malaguzzi Valeri, III, 271.
16. Cit., Cartwright, *Isabella*, I, 32.
17. *Lettere inedite*, p. 68.
18. See also pp. 256–258.
19. Cit., Malaguzzi Valeri, I, 383.
20. Letter in A. Luzio and R. Renier, "Il lusso di Isabella d'Este marchesa di Mantova," *Nuova Antologia*, vols. 63–65 (1896), vol. 65, 682.
21. Letter in Malaguzzi Valeri, I, 733, italics mine. On hunting details see D. Gnoli, "Le cacce di Leon X," *Nuova Antologia*, 43 (1893), 433–458, 617–648.
22. Illegal in the sense that they had, as yet, no imperial titles and were open to challenge.

CHAPTER XIII

1. C. Bozzo Dufour *et al.*, eds., *La Pittura a Genova e in Liguria* (Genoa, 1970), p. 78.
2. Frederick Hartt, "Art and Freedom in Quattrocento Florence," in L. F. Sandler, ed., *Essays in Memory of Karl Lehmann* (New York, 1964), pp. 114–131, for the quotations and argument in this and the following paragraph.
3. See Peter Herde, "Politische Verhaltensweisen der florentiner Oligarchie, 1382–1402," in *Geschichte und Verfassungsgefüge: Frankfurter Festgabe für Walter Schlesinger*, Frankfurter historische Abhandlungen, V (Wiesbaden, 1973), pp. 156–249.
4. See pp. 186–190, 214 ff., 229 ff.
5. In the *comento* on his own verse, *Opere*, ed. A. Simioni, 2 vols. (Bari, 1939), I, 68.
6. As touched on repeatedly in Chaps. IX–XII.
7. See Chap. XV for the protean forms of this retreat.
8. Francesco di Giorgio, *Trattato di architettura civile e militare* (Turin, 1841), Bk. V, pp. 122–124; Alberti, *op. cit.*, Bk. IV, 1.

Notes

9. In *Science and Civic Life in the Italian Renaissance*, tr. Peter Munz (New York, 1969), p. 37.

10. M. J. Friedländer, *On Art and Connoisseurship* (Oxford, 1946), p. 117.

11. *The Renaissance Discovery of Linear Perspective* (New York, 1975), pp. 24, 31, 56.

CHAPTER XIV

1. P. J. Jones, *The Malatesta of Rimini and the Papal State* (Cambridge, 1974), p. 321.

2. B. M. Hallman, *Italian Cardinals, Reform, and the Church as Property: 1492–1563* (doctoral dissertation, University of California, Los Angeles, California, 1974), pp. 23–24, 192–193; P. Partner, *Renaissance Rome: 1500–1599* (Berkeley and Los Angeles, 1976), p. 135.

3. In the Einaudi *Storia d'Italia*, eds. R. Romano and C. Vivanti, vol. 2, ii (Turin, 1974), p. 2134.

CHAPTER XV

1. See Chaps. XI–XIII.

2. E.g., Machiavelli, Guicciardini, Berni, Aretino, the early Titian.

3. E.g., Bembo as lyric poet, Castiglione, Ariosto, Giorgione, and the whole school of Mannerists.

4. In *Saggi sul Rinascimento* (Florence, 1969), p. 189.

5. "Chierici e laici," in his *Geografia e storia della letteratura italiana* (Turin, 1967), pp. 47–73.

6. *Lettere inedite e rare*, ed. G. Gorni (Milan, 1969), p. 32.

7. About 1,500 gold ducats per year in 1499, rising to 2,000 by 1506.

8. P. D. Pasolini, *Caterina Sforza*, 3 vols. (Rome, 1893), doc. in III, 414.

9. P. Torelli and A. Luzio, eds., *L'Archivio Gonzaga di Mantova*, 2 vols. (Ostiglia and Verona, 1920–22), II, 49, n. 3.

10. B. M. Hallman, *Italian Cardinals, Reform, and the Church as Property* (doctoral dissertation, University of California, Los Angeles, 1974).

11. Cit. in A. Luzio and R. Renier, "Buffoni, nani e schiavi dei Gonzaga ai tempi d'Isabella d'Este," *Nuova Antologia*, vols. 34–35 (1891), 618–650, 112–146.

12. For this paragraph and further references, Mario dell' Arco, *Pasquino e le pasquinate* (Milan, 1957).

13. Garimberto, *De regimenti*, pp. 5, 17, 28, 55.

14. *Ibid.*, pp. 29, 60.

15. G. Procacci, "La 'Fortuna' nella realtà politica e sociale del primo Cinquecento," in *Belfagor*, VI (1951), 407–421.

16. V. de Caprariis, *Francesco Guicciardini: della politica alla storia* (Bari, 1950), pp. 81–82.

17. P. Paruta, *Della perfettione della vita politica* (Venice, 1579), distinguishes between free-born men and those born for servility. The servile are not meant "by nature" for freedom, wit, nobility, or virtue. They (*servi*) are "animated instruments" for urban and domestic labor, "just as tools are a sort of inanimate *servi*," pp. 289–292. Even G. Botero, *Ragion di stato* (1589), who held the most positive view of the populace, noted occasionally that "they are for the most part of a sensual sort" (Bk. V, 3).

18. C. Dionisotti, *Gli umanisti e il volgare fra quattro e cinquecento* (Florence, 1968).

19. *Prose della volgar lingua*, II, 5, in *Prose e Rime*, ed. C. Dionisotti (Turin, 1960), pp. 137–138.

20. L. Baldacci, *Il petrarchismo italiano nel cinquecento* (Milan, 1957), p. 39.

21. *Cinque lezzioni d'amore*, in *La seconda parte delle lezzioni* (Florence, 1561), pp. 11–13. A Varchi concordance would show that he associated *civile, civiltà, modestia*, and *moderato* with the rich and responsible bourgeoisie.

22. Cf. my "The Gentleman in Renaissance Italy," in R. S. Kinsman, ed., *The Darker Vision of the Renaissance* (Berkeley, Los Angeles, and London, 1974), pp. 77–93.

CHAPTER XVI

1. Hounded: Francesco Patrizi da Cherso, Galileo, Cesare Cremonini. Jailed: Tommaso Campanella. Executed: Niccolò Franco, Giordano Bruno, G. C. Vanoni (in France). Assaulted: Paolo Sarpi. Poisoned: Traiano Boccalini. Fled: Alberico Gentili, G. F. Biondi. Lunatic: Torquato Tasso, Campanella. Criminal: Caravaggio.

2. All in Fr. H. Reusch, ed., *Die Indices Librorum Prohibitorum des Sechszehnten Jahrhunderts* (Tübingen, 1886).

3. E.g., by G. B. Adriani, S. Speroni, and F. Robortello.

4. As in the views of Robortello again, D. Atanagi, G. A. Viperiano, F. Strada, and others.

BIBLIOGRAPHY

This bibliography is for interested readers more than for specialists. I list the names of many of the historians whose scholarship has been central in my research.

Abbreviations:

Brescia = *Storia di Brescia*, directed by G. Treccani degli Alfieri, 4 vols. (Brescia, 1963–1964).

Einaudi = *Storia d'Italia*, ed. R. Romano and C. Vivanti, issued by the Einaudi publishing house, 6 vols. (Turin, 1972–1977).

Italia = *Storia d'Italia*, ed. N. Valeri, 5 vols. (Turin, 1959–1960).

Mantova = *Mantova: La storia*, ed. G. Coniglio and L. Mazzoldi, 3 vols. (Mantua, 1958–1963).

Milano = *Storia de Milano*, issued by the Fondazione Treccani degli Alfieri, 16 vols. (Milan, 1953–1963).

Piemonte = *Storia del Piemonte*, ed. D. Gribaudi and others, 2 vols. (Turin, 1960).

Verona = *Verona e il suo territorio*, issued by the Istituto per gli studi storici veronesi, 3 vols. (Verona, 1960–1964).

Chapters I–V. The ascent of communes, the nobility, early communal institutions, relations with the empire, the popolo.

Recent work in English appends useful bibliographies: J. K. Hyde, *Society and Politics in Medieval Italy* (London, 1973), and *Padua in the Age of Dante* (Manchester, 1966); D. Waley, *The Italian City-Republics* (London, 1969); D. Herlihy, *Medieval and Renaissance Pistoia* (New Haven, 1967), and *Pisa in the Early Renaissance* (New Haven, 1958). W. F. Butler's *The Lombard Communes* (London, 1906) and C. W. Previté-Orton's "The Italian Cities till c. 1200," *Cambridge Medieval History*, V (Cambridge, 1929), remain worthy of study. See also the notes in R. Brentano, *Rome Before Avignon* (London, 1974), and the telescopic treatment by Y. Renouard, *Les villes d'Italie*, 2 vols. (Paris, 1969).

The standard Italian work is L. Salvatorelli, *L'Italia comunale dal secolo XI alla metà del secolo XIV* (Milan, 1940). But there are also brilliant syntheses by G. de Vergottini in *Storia Universale*, ed. E. Pontieri (Milan, 1961–1962), IV, ii; by C. Violante, *Italia*, I; and by G. Tabacco, *Einaudi*, I, i.

The agrarian economy has received major attention from P. J. Jones, in *Cambridge Economic History of Europe*, ed. M. M. Postan (Cambridge, 1966), and in *Einaudi*, II, ii. His bibliography in the former and references in the latter are numerous, pointed, and suggestive. V. Fumagalli, *Terra e società nell' Italia padana* (Turin, 1976), presents a summary up-to-date picture of agrarian social change on the Northern Plain. Basic in his bibliography (pp. 185–202) are the items by G. P. Bognetti, R. Caggese, G. Cherubini, E. Dupré-Theseider, G. Fasoli, P. S. Leicht, G. Luzzatto, G. Miccoli, C. Mor, F. Niccolai, P. Torelli, and C. Violante. Much of this work combines institutional and social history with a legal-juridical line of inquiry, a genre in which Italians and Germans have excelled. Fasoli is one of the primary workers in this field; her *Scritti di storia medievale* (Bologna, 1974) collects many of her major articles on different aspects of the early commune. An old classic work in the legal-institutional vein is A. Solmi, *Il comune nella storia del diritto* (Milan, 1922).

Scores of general and particular works deal with the origins of communes. Most of the pertinent references are in L. Chiappelli, "La formazione storica del comune cittadino in Italia," *Archivio storico italiano*, in five installments (1926–1930); in G. Fasoli, *Dalla civitas al comune nell' Italia settentrionale* (Bologna, 1969); and *Italia*, I, 230–232. Two noteworthy German works are W. Goetz, *Die Entstehung der italienischen Kommunen im frühen Mittelalter* (Munich, 1944), and G. Dilcher, *Die Entstehung der lombardischen Stadtkommune: Ein rechtsgeschichtliche Untersuchung* (Aalen, 1967). But Goetz errs, strangely in my view, in situating the emergence of communes in a peaceful context. Cf. E. Sestan's *Italia medievale* (Naples, 1968), pp. 76–120. A fundamental review-discussion of Dilcher's book is H. Keller, in *Historische Zeitschrift*, 211 (1970), 34–64. Excellent specialized inquiries, as on Milan, Verona, Genoa, Padua, Florence, Treviso, Pavia, and Bergamo, have been done by C. Manaresi, G. Zanetti, L. Simeoni, F. Niccolai, I. Peri, A. Bonardi, A. Lizier, B. Dragoni, and A. Mazzi. See bibliographies in Dilcher (pp. ix-xvii); in P. Brezzi, *I comuni medioevali nella storia d'Italia* (Turin, 1959), pp. 44, 53, 70; and in A. Simioni, *Storia di Padova* (Padua, 1968), pp. 271–278. Always exciting on communal origins and institutions is G. Volpe, *Medioevo italiano* (Florence, 1951) and *Studi sulle istituzioni comunali a Pisa* (Pisa, 1902).

Early communal institutions command a formidable body of work, done as well by legal as by social and institutional historians. Most of the general work is by legal historians—F. Schupfer, A. Solmi, E. Besta, A. Pertile, G. Salvioli, C. Calisse, and P. del Giudice—and appears in their histories of Italian public law. But the critical work is monographic: e.g., R. Davidsohn on Florence, G. Volpe on Pisa, C. Manaresi and G. Zanetti on Milan, L. Simeoni on Verona, R. Cessi on Venice, V. Vitale on Genoa, A. Hessel on Bologna, C. Campiche on Como, A. Solmi on Piacenza, E. Zorzi on Padua, and A. Bosisio on Brescia, in *Brescia*, I, part xii.

A thoroughly conventional problem—relations between communes and empire—has attracted an enormous amount of inquiry, especially by German scholars. A succinct bibliography is appended to the piece by P. Brezzi, "I comuni cittadini italiani e l'impero medioevale," *Nuove questioni di storia medioevale* (Milan, 1969), pp. 177–207. The essential works are those of J. Ficker, E. Mayer, H. Meyer, R. Morghen, G. von Below, and a series of articles, as listed by Brezzi. But he omits a fine synthesis by E. Jordan, *L'Allemagne et l'Italie aux XIIe et XIIIe siècles* (Paris, 1939). •

Communal society. Basic for this topic among the books already cited are Davidsohn on Florence, Hessel on Bologna, and Volpe on Pisa. See also G. Salvemini, *Magnati e popolani* (Florence, 1899); N. Ottokar, *Il comune de Firenze alla fine del dugento* (Florence, 1926); G. L. Barni and G. Franceschini, *Milano*, III–IV; G. Cracco, *Società e stato nel medioevo veneziano* (Florence, 1967); E. Cristiani, *Nobiltà e popolo nel comune di Pisa* (Naples, 1962); E. Fiumi, *Storia economica e sociale di San Gimignano* (Florence, 1961); and for the pre-communal period, C. Violante, *La società milanese nell' età pre-comunale* (Bari, 1953).

The nobility, guilds, and the question of neighborhood contexts. G. Gozzadini, *Delle torri gentilizie di Bologna* (Bologna and Modena, 1875); A. Mazzi, *Le vicinie di Bergamo* (Bergamo, 1884); A. Gaudenzi and G. Fasoli on guilds and armed societies at Bologna; P. Santini on tower societies in Florence; F. Niccolai on sworn associations of noblemen;

Bibliography

A. Doren, P. S. Leicht, G. M. Monti, M. Roberti, P. Valsecchi, and G. de Vergottini, all on guilds. The references are in Hyde (1973); Waley; *Nuove questioni*, p. 175; G. de Vergottini, *Arti e popolo nella prima metà del secolo XIII* (Milan, 1943); and in Vergottini's synthesis (ed. E. Pontieri). There are important recent studies on Genoa by D. Owen Hughes; see her "Kinsmen and Neighbors in Medieval Genoa," in *The Medieval City*, eds. H. Miskimin and others (New Haven and London, 1977), pp. 95–111. An excellent recent volume on urban growth and real-estate speculation is F. Sznura, *L'Espansione urbana di Firenze nel dugento* (Florence, 1975).

The *popolo* has been best treated by G. de Vergottini, not only in the two works cited above but also in pioneering inquiries on Modena and Vicenza. I. Ghiron, U. Gualazzini, U. G. Mondolfo, and W. Montorsi have done basic pieces on the *popolo* at Milan, Cremona, Siena, and Bologna. The references are in Hyde (1973, p. 210) and Waley (p. 249). They omit G. Luzzatto, "Gli statuti delle società del popolo di Matelica (1340)," in his *Dai servi della gleba agli albori del capitalismo* (Bari, 1966). A searching and as yet unpublished study is J. C. Koenig, *The Popolo of Northern Italy (1196–1274): A Political Analysis* (doctoral dissertation, University of California, Los Angeles, 1977).

Chapters VI, VIII. Urban values and political feeling.

Values. A good start is G. Fasoli, "La vita quotidiana nel medioevo italiano," and her bibliography in *Nuove questioni*, pp. 497 500. We must add H. C. Peyer, *Stadt und Stadtpatron in mittelalterlichen Italien* (Zurich, 1955); G. Martini, "Lo spirito cittadino . . ." in *Nuova rivista storica* LIV (1971), I, 1–22; and major collections of verse, such as *Poeti del Duecento*, ed. G. Contini (Milan, 1960); *Poeti minori del Trecento*, ed. G. Corsi (Turin, 1969); and of course the Anonimo Genovese. Heresy has had the attention of some of the best scholars in the field: G. Volpe, C. Violante, R. Manselli, E. Dupré-Theseider, and A. Frugoni. Violante's collection *Studi sulla cristianità medioevale*, ed. P. Zerbi (Milan, 1972), provides full references.

Political feeling. Verse again, as noted above; Brunetto Latini, the Anonimo, and Remigio, as textually cited. Cf. also the references and views in N. Rubinstein, "Marsilius of Padua and Italian Political Thought in His Time," in *Europe in the Late Middle Ages*, ed. J. R. Hale and others (London, 1965); G. Arnaldi, *Studi sui cronisti della Marca Trevigiana nell' età di Ezzelino da Romano* (Rome, 1963); and the rhetorical-podestaral literature cited in Hyde (1973, p. 215), notably by L. Rockinger, C. Sutter, G. Vecchi, F. Hertter, and A. Sorbelli. J. H. Mundy, *Europe in the High Middle Ages: 1150–1390* (New York, 1973), pp. 442–459, offers one of the best discussions in English.

Chapter VII. Despotism: Signories.

Despotism has made for the most discussed of all problems. The chief surveys are by C. Cipolla, E. Salzer, L. Simeoni, and N. Valeri; the essential analytical essays are those of A. Anzilotti, F. Ercole, G. B. Picotti, F. Chabod, G. Masi, and E. Sestan; and the fundamental local studies are the work of Simeoni, Picotti, G. Sandri, F. Cognasso, N. Rodolico (on Bologna), G. Franceschini, P. Torelli, and W. Hagemann. Consult the bibliographies in B. Pullan, *A History of Early Renaissance Italy* (London, 1973); Simioni, *Storia di Padova*, p. 525; M. Fuiano, "Signori e principati," *Nuove questioni*, pp. 350–355; and Sestan, *Italia medievale*, pp. 193–223. The outstanding English studies are P. J. Jones, *The Malatesta of Rimini and the Papal State* (Cambridge, 1974); J. Larner, *The Lords of Romagna: Romagnol Society and the Origins of the Signorie* (London and New York, 1965); J. K. Hyde (1966); and D. Waley, *Mediaeval Orvieto* (Cambridge, 1952). Writing for collaborative regional histories, teams of Italian historians have produced excellent monographic work, some of it on the problem of despotism: see *Milano*, IV–V; *Mantova*, I; *Piemonte*, I; *Brescia*, I–II. *Verona*, III, 1, 763–802, has very comprehensive bibliographies, taking in the entire communal period and ranging generally over northern Italy.

Bibliography

Chapter IX. Oligarchy: Renaissance Republics.

Scholarship on the republics is rich in quantity as in diversity. Following are the names of the historians whose work should be pursued. Their books are easily found and their learned pieces as easily traced. On Venice: F. C. Lane, *Venice: A Maritime Republic* (Baltimore and London, 1973); the essays by different hands in *Renaissance Venice*, ed. J. R. Hale (London, 1973); and the pertinent books of H. Kretschmayr, R. Cessi, G. Luzzatto, G. Maranini, G. Cracco, A. Ventura, G. Cozzi, B. Pullan, and J. C. Davis. On Florence: G. Brucker, *The Civic World of Early Renaissance Florence* (Princeton, 1977), and two other books by the same scholar; N. Rubinstein, *The Government of Florence Under the Medici, 1434 to 1494* (Oxford, 1966) and his edited volume *Florentine Studies* (London, 1968); particular attention should be drawn to the work of E. Conti, C. M. de la Roncière, and D. Herlihy; see also books and studies by A. Tenenti, P. Herde (three papers on Florence), A. Molho, R. Trexler, J. Kirshner, F. W. Kent, R. Witt, M. B. Becker, and R. A. Goldthwaite. On Genoa: V. Vitale, *Il comune del podestà a Genova* (Milan and Naples, 1951); T. O. De Negri, *Storia di Genova* (Milan, 1968); and the papers on Genoa by R. S. Lopez. On Siena: W. M. Bowsky, *The Finance of the Commune of Siena, 1287–1355* (Oxford, 1970), and his papers on Siena. On Lucca: M. Berengo, *Nobili e mercanti nella Lucca del Cinquecento* (Turin, 1965); and D. J. Osheim, *An Italian Lordship: The Bishopric of Lucca in the Late Middle Ages* (Berkeley and Los Angeles, 1977). Bologna and Perugia have had no serious modern works of synthesis, but there is V. J. Ruttenburg, *Popolo e movimenti popolari nell' Italia del '300 e '400* (Bologna, 1971) for workers' revolts at Florence, Perugia, Siena, and elsewhere; also *Einaudi*, V, i. L. Simeoni, *Le Signorie*, 2 vols. (Milan, 1950), I, 256, lists the substantial studies on Bologna by V. Vitale, N. Rodolico, A. Sorbelli, and L. Sighinolfi. The Ambrosian republic: F. Cognasso, *Milano*, VI, 387–448.

Chapter X. Economic Trends and Attitudes.

The main lines of inquiry and interpretation in this field have been set down in recent times by A. Doren, H. Sieveking, B. Barbadoro, G. Luzzatto, R. S. Lopez, and C. M. Cipolla. In business history and the history of banking, the names to reckon with are A. Sapori, R. de Roover, F. Melis, Y. Renouard, and again Lopez. More recently, brilliant and ground-breaking work has been done in agrarian history, demography, public finance, village life, wages, and economic change. Consult in this connection the books of E. Conti, C. M. de la Roncière, E. Sereni, D. Herlihy, W. M. Bowsky, E. Fiumi, J. Heers, R. Romano, C. Klapisch-Zuber, V. Ruttenburg, G. Cherubini, and C. Rotelli. Some of the basic references are in Hyde (1973) and Pullan; all and many more are in the notes to Jones and Romano, *Einaudi*, II, ii, 1469–1931. Use also the author index in Cherubini, *Signori, Contadini, Borghesi: ricerche sulla società italiana del basso medioevo* (Florence, 1974). The Banchi material is from F. E. de Roover, "Andrea Banchi . . ." *Studies in Medieval and Renaissance History*, ed. W. M. Bowsky, III (1966), 221–285.

The major work on Italian demography is K. J. Beloch, *Bevölkerungsgeschichte Italiens*, 3 vols. (Berlin, 1937–1941). But many of his figures are being revised by specialized local inquiry—the work of G. Aleati, E. Carpantier, B. Casini, E. Fiumi, D. Herlihy, A. Tagliaferri, C. Traselli, and others. Consult C. Klapisch-Zuber and A. Belletini in *Einaudi*, V, i.

Chapter XI. Humanism: A Program for Ruling Classes.

This is another much-studied field with a mammoth bibliography. Some of the key texts are in E. Garin, ed., *Prosatori latini del Quattrocento* (Milan and Naples, 1952), and in G. Ponte, ed., *Il Quattrocento* (Bologna, 1966), the latter in the series "Classici italiani" directed by W. Bini. Rich bibliographies are appended to F. Tateo's syntheses, *Tradizione e realtà nell' umanesimo italiano* (Bari, 1967) and *I centri culturali dell' umanesimo* (Bari, 1971), now both in Vol. III of C. Muscetta, ed., *La letteratura* (see below). V. Branca's essay in *Renaissance Venice* (ed. J. R. Hale) provides a valuable bibliography on Venetian humanism. Specific mention should be made of C. Trinkaus, *In Our Image and Likeness: Humanity and Divinity in Italian Humanist Thought*, 2 vols. (Chicago, 1970); E. Garin, *Milano*, VII, 541–597; F. Gaeta, *Lorenzo Valla* (Naples, 1955); C. Vasoli, *La dialettica e la retorica dell' umanesimo* (Milan, 1968) and *Umanesimo e Rinascimento* (Palermo, 1969). The work of masters in the field, such as H. Baron and P. O. Kristeller, comes swiftly forth in the bibliographies.

Chapter XII. The Princely Courts.

Readers here may begin with the material textually cited: B. Castiglione (his letters), A. Frizzi on Ferrara, P. D. Pasolini on Caterina Sforza (with a rich appendix of documents), J. Dennistoun on Urbino, F. Malaguzzi Valeri on the court of Ludovico Sforza, A. Luzio and R. Renier on Isabella d'Este, J. Cartwright and P. J. Jones on the Malatesta; also G. Coniglio, *I Gonzaga* (Varese, 1967); *Mantova*, I–II; *Piemonte*, II; and various sections in *Einaudi*, V, i. The court of Ferrara in particular has attracted much study. V. Cian, *La satira*, has intriguing sidelights on the courts and cites the poets worthy of study. There is additional material in *Milano*, VI–VIII; W. L. Gundersheimer, *Ferrara: The Style of a Renaissance Despotism* (Princeton, 1973); M. Mallett, *The Borgias* (London, 1969); and P. Partner, *Renaissance Rome: 1500–1559* (Berkeley and Los Angeles 1976).

Chapter XIII. Art: An Alliance with Power.

Readers could spend a good part of their lives trying to master the bibliography posted in F. Hartt, *A History of Italian Renaissance Art* (New York, 1969). I add only a handful of background items: M. Wackernagel, *Der Lebensraum des Kunstlers in der florentinischen Renaissance* (Leipzig, 1938); J. Larner, *Culture and Society in Italy, 1290–1420* (London, 1971); P. Burke, *Culture and Society in Renaissance Italy, 1420–1540* (London, 1972); S. Y. Edgerton, *The Renaissance Discovery of Linear Perspective* (New York, 1975); and E. Castelnuovo's essay in *Einaudi*, V, ii. The field cries out for a study of sixteenth-century patronage, rather along the lines of F. Haskell's work on the baroque in Italy, *Patrons and Painters* (London, 1963). The pertinent studies of the late P. Francastel are often illuminating: *La réalité figurative, Éléments structurels de sociologie de l'art* (Paris, 1965) and *La figure e le lieu, L'ordre visuel du Quattrocento* (Paris, 1967). Two recent studies on the architecture and layout of Renaissance cities are: L. Benevolo, *La città italiana nel rinascimento* (Verona, 1969); G. Simoncini, *Città e società nel Rinascimento*, 2 vols. (Turin, 1974). The building boom in *palazzi* and villas, a key to Renaissance consciousness, has scarcely been studied. See *Milano*, VIII, 361–362; A Wirobisz, "L'attività edilizia a Venezia nel XIV e XV secolo," in *Studi veneziani*, VII (1965), 307–343; G. Cuppini and A. A. Matteucci, *Ville del Bolognese* (Bologna, 1967); L. Ginori Lisci, *I Palazzi di Firenze*, 2 vols. (Florence, 1972); and R. A. Goldthwaite, "The Building of the Strozzi Palace: The Construction Industry in Renaissance Florence," *Studies in Medieval and Renaissance History*, 10 (1973).

Chapter XIV. Invasion: City-States in Lightning and Twilight.

The obvious point of departure is Guicciardini's *Storia d'Italia*. Then directly we enter a sea of books, articles, and interpretations. A recent discussion of bibliography is F. Catalano, *Nuove questioni* (above), pp. 386–398. The basic overviews are E. Fueter, *Geschichte des europäischen Staatensystems von 1492–1559* (Munich, 1919) and P. Pieri,

Il rinascimento e la crisi militare italiana, 2nd ed. (Turin, 1952). The following general accounts are recommendable: L. Simeoni, *Le signorie*, II; N. Valeri, *L'Italia nell' età dei principati, dal 1343 al 1516* (Verona, 1949); A. Visconti, *L'Italia nell' epoca della controriforma dal 1516 al 1713* (Verona, 1958); F. Catalano and G. Sasso, *Italia*, II; C. Vivanti, *Einaudi*, I, i. More particular studies are L. von Pastor, *History of the Popes*, vi–xiv; *Mantova*, II; *Piemonte*, I; and the excellent analyses by F. Catalano, N. Valeri, G. P. Bognetti, G. Franceschini, and F. Chabod, all in *Milano*, VII–IX. Sixteenth-century Florence is in need of a new general history.

Chapter XV. The High Renaissance: A Divided Consciousness.

Bibliographies for this and the preceding chapter are closely intertwined. But the religious crisis may be given priority. This means the pertinent work of D. Cantimori, F. Chabod, C. Cantù, F. Ruffini, E. Cattaneo, G. Miccoli, A. Cistellini, O. Ortolani, A. Rotondò, and others, in addition to studies of episcopal visitations. Consult the footnotes in Miccoli, *Einaudi*, II, i, 875–1079; *Brescia*, II, part ii; and especially the apposite bibliographies in *La letteratura italiana storia e testi*, under the general editorship of C. Muscetta, 9 vols. (Rome and Bari, 1970–   ), IV–V, done by a team of literary scholars.

Political thought. The jumping-off points here are the political works of Machiavelli, Guicciardini, Contarini, Giannotti, and a company of lesser theorists, both monarchists and exponents of republican oligarchy. The guides for Florence are: F. Gilbert, *Machiavelli and Guicciardini* (Princeton, 1965) and R. von Albertini, *Das florentinische Staatsbewusstsein im Übergang von der Republik zum Prinzipat* (Bern, 1955). The guides for Venice are G. Cozzi and W. J. Bouwsma; see the latter's *Venice and the Defense of Republican Liberty* (Berkeley, 1968). A more general orientation is offered by the following: G. Ferrari, C. Curcio, T. Bozza, L. Firpo, F. Battaglia, and R. de Mattei. See the bibliographies in A. A. Rosa, *Il Seicento*, in *La letteratura*, ed. C. Muscetta (above), V, i, 45–46, 107–110; and S. Bertelli, in *Il Seicento*, in *Storia della letteratura italiana*, eds. E. Cecchi and N. Sapegno, 9 vols. (Milan, 1965–1969), V, 404ff.

On the question of patronage there are C. Dionisotti, "Chierici e laici," in *Geografia e storia della letteratura italiana* (Turin, 1967) and P. Grendler, *Critics of the Italian World: 1530–1560* (Madison, 1969).

The language question, Petrarchism, Neoplatonism, Castiglione. There is an excellent assortment of treatises in G. Zonta, *Trattati d'amore del Cinquecento* (Bari, 1912). Apart from the literary texts themselves, I have made use of general as well as highly specialized studies. The reader should begin with the well-known histories of Italian literature, F. de Sanctis and F. Flora, and go on to the multi-volume enterprises by teams of scholars, more particularly the volumes on the fifteenth and sixteenth centuries by V. Rossi and G. Toffanin. The two best such undertakings now are those issued by the publishers Garzanti and Laterza. Garzanti's *Storia* is edited by Cecchi and Sapegno (as above), Laterza's *La letteratura* by C. Muscetta (as above). The latter is remarkably rich in up-to-date bibliographies. I have profited from individual studies and volumes by the following: G. Petronio, G. Getto, R. Ramat, C. Dionisotti, B. Migliorini, M. Vitale, L. Baldacci, E. Bonora, N. Borsellino and M. Aurigemma. Certain poets—among them Ariosto, Bembo, Berni, and Folengo—seem to me basic to an understanding of the century's *crise de conscience*. Castiglione is quintessential.

Chapter XVI. The End of the Renaissance.

This topic leads us slyly into the problem of the Renaissance itself: what was it? Study here therefore begins with J. Burckhardt and G. Voigt, the leading formulators of the problem. The argument, really dating as from the fifteenth century, may be followed in W. Ferguson's classic account, *The Renaissance in Historical Thought*

Bibliography

(Cambridge, Mass., 1948). Among searching essays on the subject, some of the most important are by F. Chabod, E. Panofsky, and E. Garin: see the bibliography in D. Hay, *The Italian Renaissance in Its Historical Background* (Cambridge, 1961). More detailed material on the sixteenth and seventeenth centuries may be found in E. Garin, *Storia della filosofia italiana*, 3 vols. (Turin, 1966); G. de Ruggiero, *Storia della filosofia*, I, iii (Bari, 1930); R. Romano, *Tra due crisi: l'Italia del Rinascimento* (Turin, 1971) and in *Einaudi*, II, ii, 1813–1931; G. Quazza, *La decadenza italiana nella storia europea. Saggi sul Sei-Settecento* (Turin, 1971); E. Battisti, *Rinascimento e Barocco* (Milan, 1962) and *L'antirinascimento* (Milan, 1962); E. Cochrane, ed., *The Late Italian Renaissance, 1525–1630* (London, 1970) and his *Florence in the Forgotten Centuries, 1527–1800* (Chicago, 1973); and finally the outstanding work and bibliographies in two histories already cited above: Cecchi and Sapegno, eds., *Storia della letteratura italiana*, IV–V; and C. Muscetta, ed., *La letteratura italiana storia e testi*, IV–V.

ACKNOWLEDGMENTS

To Gene Brucker, of the University of California, Berkeley, for reading this book in manuscript and persuading me that it is not mad.

To Samuel Y. Edgerton, of the Fine Arts Department of Boston University, for his critical reading of Chapter XIII.

To students present and past, in the University of California at Los Angeles, who suffered the themes of this book.

To the National Endowment for the Humanities, for a senior fellowship (and freedom) in 1971.

And finally to the University of California, for research grants across a decade.

To these all, my sincere thanks and gratitude.

L. M.

INDEX

Lauro Martines was born in Chicago, Illinois, in 1927. He received his B.A. in English literature from Drake University and his Ph.D. in history from Harvard. He has taught at Reed College and was for several years a Fellow of the Harvard University Center for Italian Renaissance Studies in Florence. Since 1966, he has been Professor of History at UCLA. Mr. Martines has been the recipient of fellowships from the American Council of Learned Societies, the Guggenheim Foundation, and the National Endowment for the Humanities. His previous books include *The Social World of the Florentine Humanists* (1963), *Lawyers and Statecraft in Renaissance Florence* (1968), *Violence and Civil Disorder in Italian Cities, 1200–1500* (1972), and, in collaboration with his wife, Julia O'Faolain, *Not in God's Image: Women in History from the Greeks to the Victorians* (1973). He is now engaged in a study of English poetry and society in the seventeenth century.

A NOTE ON THE TYPE

This book was set on the Linotype in Janson, a recutting made direct from type cast from matrices long thought to have been made by the Dutchman Anton Janson, who was a practicing type founder in Leipzig during the years 1668–87. However, it has been conclusively demonstrated that these types are actually the work of Nicholas Kis (1650–1702), a Hungarian, who most probably learned his trade from the master Dutch type founder Dirk Voskens. The type is an excellent example of the influential and sturdy Dutch types that prevailed in England up to the time William Caslon developed his own incomparable designs from them.

Composed by Maryland Linotype
Baltimore, Maryland
Printed and bound by
The Haddon Craftsmen, Inc., Scranton, Pennsylvania

DESIGNED BY GWEN TOWNSEND